h86

# Governance as Conflict Management

## Publications of the Brookings Institution's Conflict Resolution in Africa Project

*Conflict Resolution in Africa*, edited by Francis M. Deng
and I. William Zartman (1991)

*South Africa: The Struggle for a New Order*,
Marina Ottaway (1994)

*The New Is Not Yet Born: Conflict Resolution in
Southern Africa*, Thomas Ohlson and
Stephen John Stedman with Robert Davies (1994)

*Somalia: State Collapse, Multilateral Intervention, and Strategies for
Political Reconstruction*, Terrence Lyons and Ahmed I. Samatar (1995)

*War of Visions: Conflict of Identities in the Sudan*,
Francis M. Deng (1995)

*Sovereignty as Responsibility: Conflict Management in Africa*,
Francis M. Deng, Sadikiel Kimaro, Terrence Lyons,
Donald Rothchild, and I. William Zartman (1996)

*Governance as Conflict Management: Politics and Violence
in West Africa*, edited by I. William Zartman (1997)

# Governance as Conflict Management

Politics and Violence in West Africa

I. WILLIAM ZARTMAN, ed.

Brookings Institution Press
*Washington, D.C.*

B J L 9011 - 9/ /1

ight © 1997 by

BROOKINGS INSTITUTION
Massachusetts Ave., N.W., Washington, D.C. 20036

of Congress Cataloging-in-Publication data
nance as conflict management : politics and violence in
t Africa / I. William Zartman, ed.
     p.     cm.
cludes bibliographical references and index.
   BN 0-8157-9706-0 (cl : alk. paper). —
   BN 0-8157-9705-2 (pa : alk. paper)
   1. Africa, West—Politics and government—1960–     2. Conflict management—
Africa, West.   3. Legitimacy of governments—Africa, West.
4. Political stability—Africa, West.   I. Zartman, I. William.
JQ2998.A91G68   1997
320.466—dc20                                                                    96-18821
                                                                                  CIP

9 8 7 6 5 4 3 2 1

The paper used in this publication meets the minimum requirements of the American
National Standard for Information Sciences—Permanence of Paper for Printed Library
Materials, ANSI Z39.48-1984.

Set in Palatino

Composition by Blue Heron, Inc.
Lawrence, Kansas

Printed by R. R. Donnelley & Sons, Co.
Harrisonburg, Virginia

*To Jimmy Carter*

# Foreword

Governance, according to the authors of this volume, is about managing conflict. In contrast to prevailing images of Africa as a continent defined by violent chaos, West Africa presents a record of relatively successful conflict management. This book examines the efforts of Côte d'Ivoire, Ghana, and Nigeria and evaluates their prospects for the future. The cases depict how leaders and parties of the three key West African states have conducted governance and managed conflicts—sometimes badly, sometimes well—among various groups in their respective societies.

The volume's conclusions could not be more clear. Unmanaged, conflicts can escalate into violence; managed, they give governments choice, direction, and energy to carry out their programs. To handle conflicts well, states need a consensus on norms relating to how conflict should be managed, legitimate institutions, and resources. Even with these, regimes will face substantial challenges as they attempt to manage conflict. If the regime fails to meet this challenge, the ability to quickly establish alternative institutions and principles that enjoy legitimacy is critical if violence and state collapse are to be avoided.

This volume is part of a series of publications in the Brookings Institution's Conflict Resolution in Africa Project. Previous volumes were devoted to South and Southern Africa, Somalia, and the Sudan. The concluding volume of the series focuses on the notion of sovereignty as responsibility. Now, with this work on West Africa, we hope we have made an important contribution to understanding what has happened in Africa and to generating a body of ideas that, if implemented, has the potential to promote stability and discourage violence throughout that continent.

I. William Zartman, editor, is Jacob Blaustein professor of conflict resolution and international organization and director of the African

Studies Program at the Paul H. Nitze School of Advanced International Studies at the Johns Hopkins University. Tessy D. Bakary is professor of political science at Laval University. A. Adu Boahen was professor of history at the University of Ghana, Legon. Alex Gboyega is professor of political science at the University of Ibadan. Donald Rothchild is professor of political science at the University of California, Davis.

The editor thanks Robert Lloyd, Anandi Rajakumaran, and Anne Russell for research assistance. At Brookings, Theresa Walker copyedited the final manuscript, and Gary Gordon, Christina Larson, and Andrew Solomon verified it. Julia Petrakis prepared the index.

The Conflict Resolution Project was made possible by a grant from the Carnegie Corporation of New York. Other activities supporting the project were funded by the Rockefeller Brothers Fund and the Rockefeller Foundation. Brookings gratefully acknowledges this support.

The views expressed in this book are those of the authors and should not be ascribed to the individuals or organizations whose assistance and support have been gratefully acknowledged or to the trustees, officers, and staff of the Brookings Institution.

MICHAEL H. ARMACOST
*President*

December 1996
Washington, D.C.

# Contents

1. Introduction                                                          1
   *I. William Zartman*

2. Governance as Conflict Management in West Africa                      9
   *I. William Zartman*
   The Nationalist Movement and the Suppression of Conflict             17
   Independence and the Social Contract                                 18
   The Military and the Repression of Conflict                          24
   Ethnoregional and Socioeconomic Demand Groups                        31
   The Rise of Procedural Demands                                       36
   The Future of Substantive Demands                                    43

3. Political Polarization over Governance in Côte d'Ivoire              49
   *Tessy D. Bakary*
   Social Ranking and Ethnic Classification:
      Culture and Social Legitimacy                                     51
   The Plantation: Economics and Social Legitimacy                      53
   From Conflict to Consensus: 1945–65                                  57
   From Consensus to Conflict: 1965–90                                  69
   Succession as a Political Opportunity Structure                      85

4. Ghana: Conflict Reoriented                                           95
   *A. Adu Boahen*
   The Nkrumah Regime                                                   99
   The National Liberation Council Regime, 1966–69                     105
   The Busia Regime, 1969–72                                           107
   The Era of the Men on Horseback, 1972–79                            111
   The Limann Regime, 1979–81                                          118
   Rawlings and His PNDC Regime, since 1981                            124
   The Return to Democracy and Political Pluralism,
      1988 and after                                                   136
   The Nature of Conflict and Conflict Resolution in Ghana            144

5.  Nigeria: Conflict Unresolved                                      149
    *Alex Gboyega*
        Roots of Conflict in Colonial Rule                            151
        Political Conflict in the First Republic                      158
        Management by Violence and the Military Regime                164
        Conflicts under the Second Republic                           168
        Conflict Management under the Military after 1984             172

6.  Conclusion: Management of Conflict in West Africa                 197
    *Donald Rothchild*
        The Tenuous Balance between Group Demands and
            State Responses                                           200
        The Structuring of Cooperation                               216
        Implications for Conflict Management                          237

    Tables
        2-1. Nationalist and Military Single-Party Regimes            25
        2-2. National Conferences, Elections, and Their Outcomes      41
        5-1. Recurrent Revenue, Federal and Regional Government,
            1953–60                                                   160

    Figures
        2-1. Terms of Trade for Selected Countries in West Africa,
            1973–92                                                   28
        2-2. Gross National Product per Capita for Selected Countries
            in West Africa, 1967–93                                   30
        6-1. Regime Options for Managing Societal Demands             200

    Notes                                                             243

    Contributors                                                      279

    Index                                                             281

# Chapter 1

# Introduction

*I. William Zartman*

A FRICA IS KNOWN AS a continent of conflict. As other books in the Africa Project of the Brookings Institution's Foreign Policy Studies program have described, entire regions of the continent have been caught up in violent conflict, sometimes so destructive that states themselves have collapsed.[1] Yet West Africa, where the independence movement in Black Africa began and had its first success in the 1950s, has had comparatively little interstate conflict. Although it has known two major civil wars, in Nigeria (Biafra) 1966–70 and Liberia (1990–96), its sixteen states have generally managed their conflicts with stability. If the additional six continental states of Equatorial or Central Africa north of the Congo River are also included,[2] western Africa contains nearly half the states of the continent in a region where conflict has been contained and often rechanneled in productive directions.

Governance is conflict management. Governing a state is not only the prevention of violent conflict from destroying the country; it is the continual effort to handle the ordinary conflicts among groups and their demands which arise as society plays its role in the conduct of normal politics. As organized interests or groups bring their demands to government, they necessarily conflict with others: either the demands themselves meet opposition from competing groups and demands, or, even if they do not, the measures required to satisfy the demands conflict with competing resource allocations or programmatic orientations. Managing these conflicts is government's job.[3] Resolution of these conflicts is often out of the question, since they are normally ongoing, recurrent, and inherent. But unmanaged, they threaten to escalate, leading to a variety of debilitating outcomes: blockage of the governing process, a widening split between state and society, outbreaks of violence, and collapse of the state.

1

Despite their poverty and problems of underdevelopment, western African states have been somewhat effective in managing their conflicts. Given human nature and the difficult conditions under which their governments are operating, it would be absurd to expect perfection. Given those same conditions, something less than perfection can still be considered exemplary. Whether the glass is viewed as half full or half empty, it contains lessons. Instances of reduction of conflict, pursuit of normal politics, promotion of cooperation, and effectiveness in governance produce insights into the way governing can be accomplished. Times of breakdown in state-society relations, government deadlock or instability, and ineffective conflict management can provide lessons in reverse. By suggesting explanations for such successes and failures, a study of western Africa can make its best contribution to an understanding of governance and conflict management.

In contrast to other regions of the continent, western Africa has largely been free of interstate conflicts because of its better-developed sense of the state and because its states are preoccupied with the management of their own internal conflicts. Although historic causes are hard to prove, part of the explanation may lie in the existence of a more developed state system in West African history. Another part may be found in the interlocking colonies of different metropoles—largely French and British—which add a modernizing and colonial dimension to national identities.

But much more has to do with three lessons of this book, which explain the presence of effective conflict management, where it exists, and its absence, where it does not. Effective governance depends on the establishment of a national consensus on norms, the reinforcement of those norms and values as a legitimizing regime, and the establishment of new institutions and principles as a replacement regime if the former values and institutions prove inadequate.

The first element in a national consensus on values is the development of national traditions growing out of critical junctures in individual countries. At salient moments in individual states' history, when social and political patterns were inchoate and in the process of formation, major directions were established through a significant conjuncture of social forces; these directions were thereafter maintained.[4] In some cases, these critical junctures produced consensus or at least a strong current that pushed contrary values aside. In other cases, the imprint was ambiguous or clearly contradictory, and the basis for a political regime was unstable. Because the contradictory values were impressed on the polity at a critical moment, significant energies and much time are needed to work out contradictions or replace them with a new consensus.

In some cases, this critical juncture occurred under colonial rule as early as the turn of the century, as, for example, in Nigeria, where the tripartite unity of the country was established. Diverse parts of the country with different value systems were locked into unstable confrontation. In Nigeria, the colonial ruler worked to maintain structures of unity; when independence came, pressures for separateness remained to test the unity of the federated state, but diverse parts also fought among themselves for dominance in internal politics. That conflict structured Nigerian politics for the rest of its life, to date. Elsewhere, the critical juncture could occur coincidentally with independence, when the new political status and the need for new independent institutions create a conjuncture propitious to long-term structuring of energies and efforts within the polity. Thus, in Ghana, with independence came a split nationalist movement, setting up political tensions that were not erased by the momentary victory of the more radical tendency under Kwame Nkrumah. As one side or the other took over the state in the first quarter century of independence, the vertical split was converted into a generalized conflict between the state and society that has gradually come to dominate Ghanaian politics. Or the critical juncture can come some time in between, in the middle of colonial rule, as it did in Côte d'Ivoire, when, much as analyzed in other countries by Barrington Moore, the introduction of commercial agriculture and its adoption by specific parts of Ivorian society created the conditions for social ranking, political consensus, and a coopting oligarchy that has provided stability and an inward-looking focus to politics.[5] Whether structured on conflict or on its management, the results of the critical junctures in these and other cases have reinforced western African states and oriented political energy within their boundaries (and even those boundaries have not been a major source of contestation).

The second lesson of this book is that when West African states have had a central normative code about the way conflicts should be managed, coherent strategies other than simple repression, a legitimizing institutional structure, and resources for allocation, they have been more successful at managing their internal conflicts than when they have lacked these attributes. To the extent any of these elements is missing, conflict management is more difficult. If all are absent, conflict is likely to be turned against the government itself, an evolution that will be difficult to reverse no matter what the form of government, including that of a democratically elected regime. Even when resources become scarce, the other elements can make up for the loss or, more precisely, can help overcome the loss and maintain effectiveness in governance. Although states may have only partial control over the availability of resources (given, for example, the state of the world market for oil or cocoa), elements of governance such as value codes, institutionalized regimes, and conflict management strategies are human creations, the product of state-society interaction.

Normative value codes legitimize patterns of behavior and help them become accepted as the legitimate formula for the exercise of power.[6] Such domestic regimes reinforce themselves when they are successful in managing conflicts among groups and demands placed on them by society. Success produces longevity, and longevity produces stability; the cycle is beneficial, strengthening the ability of the regime to deal with conflict and hence its legitimacy. When the regime lacks a normative base, or fails in its ability to handle conflicts, it is further weakened in a downward spiral that can ultimately produce state collapse.[7]

The West African record is diverse and illustrative. Starting with its normative consensus that rooted sociopolitical hierarchy in the system of economic development and established material allocation as a legitimate basis for conflict management, Côte d'Ivoire built a centralized, cooptive, single-party state that captured loyalties and managed conflicts. Although this regime was most effective when the fortunes of the state were high, even under the world recession of the 1980s it provided a legitimate framework for politics, allowing the opening of the institutional structure at the end of the decade to multiparty competition and presidential succession within a well-socialized political class.

Other examples in the region are less successful and so less stable. The split normative heritage of Ghana found institutional expression in a succession of military and political attempts to establish a consensual regime, after a decade of radical party-state rule had only depleted state resources, exacerbated conflict, and produced institutional incoherence. But the later 1960s and the 1970s in turn only continued that conflict and incoherence, leading the state to the edge of collapse at the turn of the decade. As a result, normative as well as interest conflict grew to overcome the institutions designed to manage it. Similarly, in Nigeria, the conflicting normative heritage of the colonial period, institutionalized as the basis of government, also produced rather than reduced conflict and destroyed government's ability to manage it. Decisive military regimes kept the state from collapse until the mid-1990s but have not removed that possibility for the rest of the decade. Nonetheless, they were able to manage conflicts for short periods through a fistful of strategies—military repression, reconciliation, resource allocation, and institutional engineering, among others. Yet normative consensus, strategic consistency, and institutional stability have been absent, so that even the boom times of plentiful resources did not produce a durable regime.

The third lesson of this study is that regime failure or government inability to manage conflicts on a sustained basis leads to obdurate repression or to reinstitutionalization and regime restructuring.[8] Changing a regime is not a neat and rapid process. It takes long periods of preparation, longer the more profound the regime failure, and it can be orderly and peaceful or violent and destructive. It is always incremental, the difference being only in the form the increments take. Even apparently sudden changes, such as sovereign national conferences or revolutions, have long preludes and aftermaths.

Like any matter of normative or institutional regimes, challenge and change are similar and related. Challenges to the regime are frequent during its life, although they may vary in nature, interval, and intensity; their successful management only strengthens the regime. When they start coming with greater frequency, greater intensity, and greater resistance to successful management, they begin to constitute pressure for change. "The only solution is for a new arrangement of institutions to be brought forth out of the interactions of the various social forces at play in the system."[9]

Such moments of institutional or regime change are hard to determine up close, and indeed "moment" may have far too narrow connotations in time to be appropriate. All three of the West African states portrayed here are going through tests, accentuated by the broader seachanges worldwide in regimes moving toward liberal and competitive economic and political systems. Sociopolitical patterns remain until no longer functional and are then replaced, suddenly or gradually, by new patterns and institutions. Major changes and challenges are present in the 1990s that could introduce institutional restructuring. Fissiparous conflict in Nigeria leads the state closer to collapse, an authoritarian reform regime in Ghana tends to restructure the political sides, successions to the national paramount chief in Côte d'Ivoire shake the national consensus. Yet none of the events of the 1990s unambiguously promises a reorientation of the countries' institutional structures, and nothing indicates any change in the level of regional interstate conflict. Pressures operating from within and without West African countries for privatization and competition in economics and politics are not certain to bear fruit, but to the extent they do, they actually strengthen the internal focus of national activities, whether they are successful in the end or not in providing either a market economy or a democratic polity.

For successful regimes, such as Côte d'Ivoire, these events may only be challenges, whose management reaffirms the reigning system. After decades—indeed, half a century—of institutional centralism, much depends on whether institutional pluralism reforms or is subsumed by the allocation mechanisms, materialist ethos, and cohesive ruling class which are the basic ingredients of the country's conflict management system. This study suggests that the system will absorb its conflicts and continue to produce regime stability.

It is much more evident that Ghana and Nigeria are struggling with regime change. The rule of Flight Lieutenant Jerry Rawlings, currently a decade and a half and almost guaranteed to last through the second decade, has created its own support group, ethos, and institutions (and institutional changes), both coopting and displacing the two previously conflicting value systems and groups. By restoring a firm hand to government as no previous military regime was able to do, Rawlings has created a third tradition between the two others and thus opened the way for alliances with each of them and the absorption of their values and members. Conflict between the new system and the groups and values of the old still remains dominant. Large groups and vocal spokesmen still sputter outside of his regime, which remains too personalized to stand the test of institutionalized durability. But fifteen—or twenty—years in power is long enough to change the political scene. He has restored the state; he may well institute a new regime.

The moment of change is less clear in Nigeria, and it may take state collapse, bloodier and more protracted than in Ghana, to clean out the old and open the way to a new regime, with new values and institutions for conflict management. For out of the conflicted value system and destroyed institutions has emerged a further conflict between two different ways of reacting to the challenge. One way is a reconstitutive response, shown in the presidential election of June 12, 1993, and the consensus behind the duly elected candidate, Chief Moshood K. O. Abiola, who received crossethnic and crossregional support throughout the country. To many, "Nigerians . . . declared themselves a nation" in that event, showing support for institutional legitimacy rather than regional claims.[10] The other response was the pursuit of the downward spiral by the military takeover of General Sani Abacha, a predatory coup, not a restorative attempt as tried by his predecessors. Maintenance of Abacha postpones the moment of change and hardens the challenge; restoration of democracy would open possibilities of a regime transformation.

The purpose of this book is to analyze how governments have handled different types of demand-bearing groups and managed their demands in these three major western African states since independence, and to show the effects of this process on the institutions and legitimacy of regimes. What types of groups and demands have arisen? How has government handled them and with what effects on the construction of viable institutionalized entities or regimes? The search for appropriate institutionalized forms—the procedural question—has marked politics in all three states since independence. This search does not take place in the abstract but responds to the changing types of groups and demands that are thrown at government.

Similarly, the relation between institutionalization and group demands is reflected in two aspects of government's attitudes—its strategies of power toward groups and its own attitudes toward its position in power. Although institutional policies refer to the projects for long-term state structure, strategies of governance refer to the way government addresses groups in general, usually by denying or destroying their existence or by recognizing or using their existence. Government may seek to ignore group identity, divide groups, or repress them. It may also seek to make them compete with one another, institutionalize them, transform them into other (party, corporate) structures, and so on. Either strategy requires resources and so is determined by their availability as well as by government's attitudes toward demand-bearing groups. Attitudes toward power can include monopolistic views, notions of alternance and succession, or simply "time at the trough." These attitudes too are related to the availability of resources. Thus both strategies and attitudes are likely to reflect times of growth and times of penury, times to which they also contribute.

This book explains why different regimes—illustrated by the three leading states of the region, Ghana, Nigeria, and Côte d'Ivoire—have different histories of managing their evolving conflicts and how these histories affect the current process of establishing new democratic regimes. One conclusion of the analysis of conflict management in the region points out the difficulties facing democratization. The experience during more than three decades of independence has moved conflict from an intergroup phenomenon managed by a neutral government to a phenomenon characterized by societal groups' pitting themselves against government. This development places heavy burdens on a new government, even ones democratically legitimized.

Chapters 3, 4, and 5 in this book, discussing Côte d'Ivoire, Ghana, and Nigeria, address these questions in a dynamic succession of phases over three decades of independence. The phases identify periods when a given combination of elements—groups, demands, institutions, strategies, attitudes, power, and legitimacy—were present. The aspects of each phase that led to its transformation into the next are discussed. The chapters focus at greater length on the nature of the current phase experienced by the country and on its prospects for the future in terms of its potential for creating appropriate institutions and managing conflict. In the conclusion, the experiences of the three countries are compared in order to provide a better understanding of alternative regimes as a basis for appropriate policy.

Chapter 2

# Governance as Conflict Management in West Africa

*I. William Zartman*

GOVERNING IS CONFLICT MANAGEMENT. In the long-established systemic understanding of governing, demands emerge from the body politic and are brought to the attention of the governors, who then handle them as best they can and will.[1] But these demands are never harmonious and are often downright contradictory, so that interest aggregation and policy choice become the crucial exercise of governing. Often unanswered demands inspire their makers to move from substantive to procedural impositions on the governing process. Ultimately, the demanders may seek to overthrow and take over the government. Whether dealing with conflicts among demands or among demanders, conflict management is the nature of governance.

In internal governance, even more clearly than in international politics, the management rather than the resolution of conflict is the maximum attainable goal. Conflicts among domestic demands and demanders are rarely eliminated; they are only reduced, satisfied, downgraded, contained, at best, until the demanders get new ammunition, new evidence, new pressure, new followers, or until new issues and demands break up their ranks and overshadow their earlier appeals. Issue realignment then causes new demands and demanders to enter into new conflicts for the governors' attention, but that does not prevent old demands from remaining or reemerging. Management of conflict means reacting responsively to reduce demands in a manner consistent with human dignity so that the conflict does not escalate into violence.

West African states were born as sovereign units—for the most part, in 1960—through the management of a major conflict between nationalist elites and colonial rulers over independence. That conflict was only managed, settled in principle by the granting of sovereign status.

Implications and details were left to be worked out over time once the danger of violence had been removed. Issues such as the degree of independence a country enjoys, relations between internal and external demands, relations between state and regional sovereignty, and others, remain. For nearly four decades of independence the sixteen states of West Africa have avoided wars among themselves with very few exceptions, but they have been subject to many different internal conflicts—social, factional, civil-military, ethnic, religious, and others. A few of these conflicts have nearly torn apart their countries and have been managed primarily through military means. Most other conflicts provide the grist for the managing business of governance, often handled in a postponing and aggravating way, but sometimes in a way that leads to resolution or to ongoing care. Despite (or because of) their newness and poverty, the states of West Africa have lessons to convey about the way conflict management is practiced and its pitfalls navigated.

Although governance has been analyzed from many different angles—as institutionalization, legitimization, lawmaking, problem solving, nation building, integration and allocation, to name a few—all of these can be related to the process of handling conflicting demands in a way that retains the allegiance and participation of the demanders in the national political system. Thus conceived, state building becomes a matter of establishing the institutions for this task; legitimization becomes a matter of building reliable support for those who carry out the task; lawmaking becomes the formulation and implementation of rules for managing conflicting demands; problem solving becomes a matter of creating the power and procedures for providing appropriate answers to the groups' demands; nation building means transferring a sense of belonging from the group to the managing state unit; integration and allocation means bringing such groups into a national interaction in such a way as to provide and distribute returns to them; and so on.

The basic element of this approach to governance as conflict management is the demand-bearing group, the sociopolitical collectivity that supports and articulates the demands that make up politics. Three elements distinguish this type of collectivity from other aggregations of individuals. One is the groupness, the sense of cohesion and action on the part of some members of society. They distinguish themselves from others. Groups can come together and stay together for varying amounts of time and for various reasons. Groups range from the spontaneous street mob whose cohesion is short-lived and volatile to the institutionalized professional or ethnic identity association that continues to exist even when not in action. There are many levels and many bases for such a sense of cohesion, several often coexisting in the same group. Like the demands that the group expresses, these sources of cohesion can be categorized as ethnoregional, socioeconomic, age, and ideological.[2] These categories are only theoretical and potential; whether they are present in any particular case is an empirical question. Categories can be plentiful, but until they cohere and act, they are not political groups. Demand-bearing groups are groups that identify themselves and stand up to be recognized. Thus this approach lies between Marxist class analysis, which assumes the existence of groups along a particular dimension, whether they exist or not, and Bentleyan group analysis, which focuses on groups inductively without any dimensional categorization.

The second basic element is the demand itself, including its subject, intensity, and goal. The demand distinguishes relevant groups from mere identity or anomic groups, that is, categories or crowds; only when the group turns its identification or its momentary existence into a purposive demand-oriented action does it become relevant to the governance process. The demand may be substantive, relating to a particular grievance, or procedural, relating to means of handling grievances (including constitutional questions, regional autonomy and secession, changes in government, and so on). Again, there are no assumptions about the nature of demands, other than the notion that substance precedes procedure. People try to get their grievances handled within existing channels before they turn to demanding changes in the channels themselves. It is probably a mistake to try to categorize demands, since specific or general issues may override general or specific issues according to the intensity and breadth of concern and the conditions of the moment. The same categorization as mentioned above, that is, ethno-, socio-, ideo-, and evipolitical [age], may be used but is probably too restrictive for present purposes. Nor is the calculus of demands worked out specifically yet; inattention on the part of the governors can either discourage or intensify demands, attention can either encourage or satisfy (or satisfice) demands, and multiple demands can either reinforce or neutralize one another, whether coincident or crosscutting or not. But other effects and intervening variables need to be worked out.

The third element, between cohesion and demands, is supports, an elusive but important element that has been little recognized in the previous group literature from Karl Marx to Jeremy Bentham and beyond. Groups do something for their members (cohesion), but they also have a potential contribution to make to the larger politicoeconomic society in which they exist. As a corporate entity or as an aggregate of members, they may sell real estate or enforce the law or fight wars or pump oil or contribute to the cultural tissue of the country. These contributions may be large or small by nature, and they may be well or fully accomplished or not. The point is that demands have a corollary: "what your country can do for you" also carries with it "what you can do for your country."[3] Even where the group is constituted about a demand that stems from an inherent right of citizenship—for human rights or defense against attack or consumer goods—these demands have corresponding citizenship supports, such as loyalty, allegiance, compliance with the law, and so on. In an era where the demands of the citizenry and the responsibilities of government are highly emphasized, it is important to remember that every card has two sides.

Conflicts can be managed in a myriad of ways, and categorized along different dimensions, but there are only a few helpful beginnings of typologies for the present analytical purposes.[4] The following sixfold typology begins with procedural attempts at dealing with the conflicting groups, progresses to substantive attempts at dealing with the conflicting demands, and returns to procedures again: reconciling, allocating, institutionalizing, submerging, adjudicating, repressing (RAISAR). Reconciling means managing conflict by bringing the parties together to overcome their own differences. Allocating is a direct government decision to resolve the conflict; the government decrees the shares of the disputed goods and services that the conflicting parties will have or adds new goods and services as payoffs. Institutionalization refers to the establishment of procedures that would allow society to deal with the conflicts through a decision on either the issues or the groups. The institution is most commonly electoral, although a judicial decision might also be included if the judiciary is seen to be independent of government. Submerging refers to a government initiative that overcomes the conflict by putting forth new programs, higher goals, overarching concerns, or reframed perceptions.[5] Adjudication is a more specific extension of submerging; the government decrees the rights and wrongs in the conflict among groups in other than merely allocative terms. Finally, repression can be used to eliminate the conflicting group. Repression is the least effective as a tool of conflict management (although it may be necessary in extremis), but the others all have their place. The first three, however, involve the conflicting groups in the management of the conflict under government guidance, whereas the latter three treat groups as petitioners to and subjects of government.

Earlier predecessors of the institutional and systems analysts were the social contract theorists of the eighteenth century, whose roots went back to the *Politics* of Aristotle.[6] The social contract established the system for managing society's conflicts. Despite the extraordinary insights of social contract analysis, the theory is weakened by its highly philosophical or ahistorical nature. Finding the moment when the social contract was drawn up is generally quite difficult. The closest event to drawing up the social contract in the life of an ongoing polity is the constituent assembly or the sovereign national conference (CNS) frequently used in West Africa. These constituent assemblies, however, vary in the success of representativity, and they take place within an already determined contractual context. The CNSs have sometimes proven less decisive than the social contract would imply.[7] In new states, however, an even better approximation of the social contract is found in a combination of the independence bargain and the constitutional determinations carried out by the nationalist movement. The nationalist movement is a rare moment in a nation's history when a single demand overrides all (or most) others, an ascriptive identity subsumes all (or most) others, and other conflicts are managed by being submerged. This moment, as the "funnel phase" of national political action, thus represents an appropriate as well as convenient moment to begin the analysis of governance as conflict management.

The independence bargain is flawed, however, as a social contract in one way. It is not merely a contract among the constituent demand-bearing groups of the polity, but between them and the decolonizing power.[8] To be sure, the domestic constituents must come together in some way to present their demands to the foreign state, but tactical considerations and the nature of the opponent also impinge on the process. Consequently, conflict is indeed only managed, the social contract of the moment rarely sticks, and the history of new nations is marked by an ongoing dispute over who should govern and who should benefit from government and a periodic return to the encounter to redo the contract with new players.

Whether negotiated once or many times, the social contract is not merely a resolution of momentary conflicts over the division of rights and obligations. It also provides, whether explicitly or not, for mechanisms of further conflict resolutions and management, in the form of institutions of governance. This dual nature of the contract, as an act of governance and an act creating the rules for further governance, makes it a doubly key moment in the evolution of the polity. The institutions thus created frame the exercise of governance until the next revision, again explicitly or implicitly.

Government of course is not the only conflict management mechanism, only the highest one. Society can mange its own conflicts, and in a well-balanced state-society relationship, many of the conflicts originating within society stay there. Society can manage its conflicts in three ways, either by unilateral restraint and accommodation on the part of one party to a conflict, by bilateral negotiation and accommodation between the two (or more) conflicting groups, or by third-party mediation on the part of another group in society external to the conflict (including those specifically constituted for the purpose). When conflicts cannot be handled by society itself, when a court of appeals is needed, or when conflicts are so broad as to be national in scope, the state is needed as conflict manager. If all conflicts are taken to the state, political inflation takes place, and the state is overburdened and probably prevented from carrying out its functions properly. If no conflicts are taken to the state, the state is useless and not performing its proper functions. It is reduced to a symbolic representation to the outside world.

This approach contains a specific, even American, interpretation. It assumes that, appropriately, government is (or should be) a conflict management mechanism independent of and over and above conflicting groups but not an element in the conflict. When groups accede to supreme authority, they take on the roles and interests of government, losing in part or at least overshadowing their original group interests and demands.[9] Hence, "is" is used here to identify the appropriate function of government, not the way it really works in all cases. "Normal politics" is thus considered an exercise in which social groups place their demands before government, which is then held accountable by the groups of society for the ways in which it handles their demands. An African assumption could be quite different, that conflict is essentially between groups and government and that in governance, government is managing its own conflicts with society. "Normal politics" has broken down; the real nature of politics is a war between society and government, which continues even when a new group of society becomes government and takes its turn at the trough.

African governments grew out of the second notion, of politics as a conflict between society and government—between the *pays réel* and the *pays légal*—in the late colonial period of rising nationalism. Upon independence, newly sovereign states tried to return to the first interpretation of the state as manager of conflicts, but many of them more or less rapidly slipped back into the second view. That shift is important for two reasons. First, it makes conflict management more difficult, by turning it from a third-party exercise into a direct exercise between the conflicting parties. The basic wisdom on conflict management indicates that a third party is helpful to the resolution of bilateral conflicts, implying that these are the most difficult to handle since in bilateral conflicts the parties are too absorbed in the conflict to be able to think creatively of its management.[10] Thus an indicated role for government is lost when government becomes party to conflict. Second, by extension, this situation weakens and even delegitimizes government, since government is seen by large parts of society as part of the problem, not part of the solution. Such an image is self-perpetuating, creating a situation that becomes hard to escape.

This book seeks to describe the evolution of governance as conflict management in West and Equatorial Africa from Mauritania to Congo and to explain the origin and outcome of conflicts and governance patterns over the three decades of independence. Succinctly, colonialism created differentiation and repressed its expression; nationalism created a management mechanism and squandered it; single-party and military regimes created pluralism and repressed it; democratization suffers as a result. Colonialism effected the essential cleavage in society, providing the source of both conflict and its management as the modernized sectors of society made common cause with their own people to oust the modernizing colonizer and set up government for their own benefit. Pluralism provided the motor for that government's overthrow through the democratization movement based on increasing pluralization of interests. But that movement has become the victim of the failure of its predecessors to manage conflict.

West Africa has arguably the best developed sense of regional identity on the continent, not only because of its geography, which leaves only its eastern boundary imprecise, but also because of its cultural unity. That eastern boundary imprecision and the similar colonial experience of Equatorial Africa argue for its inclusion as well. West Africa was for centuries before colonization an area of interdependent heterogeneity among proto-states. That characteristic continued even as the two major systems of colonial order, the British and the French, as well as the German, penetrated the area. After Ghana inaugurated Black Africa's wave of successful nationalism in 1957, fourteen of the extended region's twenty-one territories received their independence in 1960, on dates throughout the year that were closely related to one another. All turned their nationalist movements into single parties (one for each region in Nigeria), and Senegal and Côte d'Ivoire have retained their original parties the longest. West Africa began the continent's series of military coups with Togo in 1963 and then Ghana followed on Nigeria in 1966. Ghana (and Sierra Leone) in 1969 were succeeded by Nigeria (and Upper Volta) in 1979 in returning to civilian rule, and then in reverting to corrective military rule. All have come under the spell of democratization and responded in their individual fashions. In this ragged course, the twenty-one countries of the region have provided precedents—positive and negative—for one another. Indeed, largely because of the French connection, the West African countries have served as precedents for the six countries of the neighboring region of Equatorial Africa in the northern Congo basin, which can also be included as an annex to the region.

The other remarkable shared characteristic is that West Africa has not been torn by the interstate conflict that ties other areas of Africa— the Horn, southern, North Africa—together into conflict systems.[11] Conflict in West Africa is internal to the states, and they have dealt with it in many different ways. Of the twenty-one states in the region, Nigeria, Ghana, and Côte d'Ivoire are the largest in population and economy. Nigeria has had its war in 1966-70 over a secessionist region, Biafra, and has combined allocation, institutionalization, and repression as the means of managing persistent social and geoethnic conflicts. Ghana's conflicts have been social and ideological, and their most extreme form, the military coup, has been merely one expression among others of institutionalization and repression to manage what reconciliation and allocation could not. Côte d'Ivoire has known remarkable stability through a system that manages its social and geoethnic conflicts by allocation, reconciliation, and institutionalization. Although these are not the only mixtures of the means of management, they are typical of the continent. Other cases could be added (for a thicker book) and comparisons could be made with smaller or poorer countries. In short, West Africa has a message: that governance can be understood and practiced as conflict management.

## The Nationalist Movement and the Suppression of Conflict

Typically, the struggle for independence in West Africa went through the characteristic stages of nationalist protest—acquiescence, imitation, reform group, and nationalist movement.[12] After the initial submission to colonial conquest, some elements of the population began to see the path to dignity and participation in an imitation of the ways of the colonizer, designed to bring the colonial individual into the modernized ruling community. The necessary rejection of these individual efforts, poignantly documented in such works as Cary's *Mister Johnson*, Chinua Achebe's *Things Fall Apart*, and Margaret Laurence's *This Side Jordan*,[13] turned individuals to collective action, and they banded together as reform groups. At this, the first group stage of protest, the demand-bearing group still recognized the legitimacy of the colonial order and still identified with the colonizer as the modernized segment of the population. The first stage sought equal treatment—wages, social benefits, participation in councils—along with the rest of the modernized. The colonizer's rejection of these collective efforts led to a reexamination of identity and legitimacy as well as politics. Reformers—some with great difficulty—rejected their modernized identification and their self-alienation from the rest of the population. They sought a new identity as nationals, forced on them by the colonizer's rejection. They in turn rejected the legitimacy of colonial rule and found redress of their demands possible only through their own control of power. They therefore sought to seize the state.

The achievement-based identification between the modernized or *évolué* population and the colonizer, which underlay the reform group stage, was overcome in a new ascriptive identification as nationals or colonized. Substantive demands for equality within the modern system in the previous stage were replaced by procedural demands for control and replacement of the illegitimate colonial state, with national leaders "making articulate a general dissatisfaction with colonial rule."[14] The many different groups covered by the national identity gathered together into a Great Coalition behind the demand for independence. In the process, particular demands were used as campaign material, but the general appeal was to nationality and self-determination.[15]

Whatever the marginal differences among various groups, the nature of colonial rule in nationalist terms was such that very few saw benefit in the status quo. The major conflict in the nationalist movement phase was over tactics and leadership, not over substantive demands. Cooperation versus opposition to the colonial administration as the way to independence and confidence in one leader's versus another's abilities (including ethnic-based sources of such confidence) were the principal sources of division among competing parties, and therefore conflict was subsumed under the competing organizations. "These coalitions were large, . . . while many of their opponents almost by default stressed specific affiliations."[16]

The effect of the nationalist movement's success, however, was to raise demands, both general and particular. Independence was the effect and the cause of the much-mentioned revolution of rising expectations, by which the mobilized African populations expected to benefit as much from self-rule as they suspected the colonial populations had benefited from colonial rule. In fact the African populations expected even greater benefits because greater development was expected to follow as a consequence of independence. But specific demands also increased with independence to strain the nationalist movement, as the rising expectations spurred the emergence of narrower groups that felt they had a special claim on the benefits of independence. The result was what Aristide Zolberg referred to as "two contrary trends: . . . the bandwagon effect [and] . . . the threat of fragmentation."[17] All sorts of groups—professional, students, workers, ethnoculturals, farmers, traditionals, and so on—had made common cause in the nationalist Great Coalition. Yet each expected to receive complete satisfaction for its demands despite the obvious conflict they posed to the demands of other groups.

### Independence and the Social Contract

Independence brought the leaders of the nationalist movement to power, giving them the authority to write the social contract but removing the unifying goal of independence that made a contract possible.[18] As a complication, the contract was twofold: an agreement with the departing colonial power to take over as a successor state and maintain the existing institutional regime and some degree of economic privilege, and an agreement among the nationalist winners to set the rules and share the spoils of independence.[19] Unlike the classical notions of a social contract, the domestic portion of the African agreement was not drawn up among the ruled or even between the ruled and the rulers but among the new rulers in the name of the ruled. The disparities of development accentuated the normally elite nature of politics, making personal charisma one major source of legitimacy,[20] but the nature of nationalism meant that the language of legitimacy had to be couched in terms of the single, united nation, providing institutionalized revolution as the other source. A contract made with oneself rather than between two contracting parties is only as valid as the sanctions that underwrite the good faith of its intentions. But there were no sanctions in the hands of the ruled.

The new contract put power into the hands of the nationalist elite, organized into a single party that incarnated the single nation. It foresaw a plebiscitary, consensual system of the General Will, with no provision for competition, opposition, losers, or civil and human rights. It considered pluralism, division, and conflict an ever-present danger carrying a threat of colonial return, never successfully banished by the unitarian nature of the contract and therefore needing to be kept under careful control. Born of the struggle for independence, it was a contract for the protection of power, shielding the new state from attacks similar to those that its owners had used to take it over, not a contract guiding or limiting the exercise of power. The new powerholders were not specifically identified in the nationalist agreement, but they were implied in its political evolution, along the diverse elite dimensions. It included an ethnic dominance—Baule in Côte d'Ivoire, Hausa-Fulani in federal Nigeria and Igbo and Yoruba in its eastern and western provinces, Soussou-Malinke in Guinea, Americo-Liberian in Liberia, Bambara in Mali, Sara in Chad, Creole and then Mende in Sierra Leone, Zerma-Songhai in Niger, Ewe in Togo, Akan in Ghana—which did not always correspond to the proportion of the population, with other ethnic groups merely being represented. The new contract also included a socioeconomic bias in favor of the urban population, and specifically of the capital city, with proconsular relations with the provinces and exploitative relations with the rural areas.

The implications for government, only partially analyzed,[21] were the need to turn a Great Coalition into a Ruling Coalition and to develop coherent and realizable programs. New institutions for decisionmaking and implementation had to be set up and broken in, at the same time as decisions were being made. Stagnation, clogged decision apparatus, and political criteria for decisions on allocation threatened the process.

The allocation strategy rested on an equally great array of resource-generating means involving aid, investment, exports, and nationalizations. For parts of the first decade, governments could run on the legitimacy of their nationalist heritage and on the fat of the colonial goose that laid the golden egg before their inability to respond to demands or to shrink them became apparent.

The implications for politics, often analyzed,[22] were that political competition was admissible only within the party-state-nation and that those outside were treasonous, disloyal to all three elements. Groups were coopted into the single party or pushed back on their specific, sectarian, or ethnic base. Cooption was selected on the basis of contribution of the group to national unity and political stability, not always for the purpose of meeting urgent demands. Since the nationalist movement was a Great Coalition, it encompassed all the demands it needed, and indeed the raised expectations amid the characteristic underdevelopment meant that demands were in overabundance. Demand groups that were not part of the original contract, either left out in the beginning or newly arisen thereafter, continued to be excluded from the benefits of independence; these included late-developing ethnic regions such as the Bete and northern groups in Côte d'Ivoire, Kabye of Togo, and the Ashanti and Gurma of Ghana, and the new generations of students.[23] Demand groups included in the Great Coalition were brought to heel to limit their demands. A gradual process began of crowding out others for whom there was no longer any room at the fixed or shrinking trough. Late losers included Yorubas in Nigeria, among others.

In this situation, the major mechanism of conflict management was the single party. By serving as a mechanism of cooption and ostracism, it managed the demand-bearing groups rather than the demands themselves, a strategy that was natural if not appropriate during the initial years of power consolidation of the new regime, since demands were basically procedural. Probably the most prominent source of demands involved the revival and final settlement of personal rivalries left over from the independence struggle. The affairs of Mamadou Dia in Senegal, Jean-Baptiste Mockey in Côte d'Ivoire, Chief Obafemi Awolowo in Nigeria, Reuben Um Nyobo in Cameroon, Jean-Hilaire Aubame in Gabon, and J. B. Danquah and Kofi Busia in Ghana, all had their origins in tactical and clientele differences before independence that were revived and settled once again after independence.[24] Occasionally, personal and tactical opposition was reinforced by generational differences as well.

The second source of demands was ethnic, where groups already left out in the nationalist movement protested by reinforcing their exclusion. Some were organized, some were not. Ewes and Ashantis in Ghana, Toubou in Chad, Betes and Sanwis in Côte d'Ivoire, Tuareg in Mali and Niger, indigenes in Liberia, Temne in Sierra Leone, Casamançais in Senegal, Hausas in Niger, Mossi in Burkina Faso, Igbos in Nigeria[25] were all exceptions to the Great Coalition who took to politics and frequently resorted to violence to attack the system for excluding them from its expected benefits.[26] Other ethnic oppositions based on narrower demands also arose as the new elite consolidated its position and narrowed its own base, downgrading groups that were formerly part of the national coalition, such as original inhabitants of capital cities displaced by new immigrants or earlier beneficiaries of colonization bypassed by new urban centers.[27]

Other, socioeconomic, groups grew only slowly with their separate demands, partly because it took time for them to reach individual corporate existence and partly because they were the targets of a mixed strategy of gratification and control during the early years of independence. The most striking cases are the labor, youth, and women's organizations, which, despite whatever autonomy they may have had before independence, became tightly controlled party auxiliaries. Faced with the standard confrontation between demands of the workers and demands on the workers, labor unions became instruments of national unity and development rather than demand-bearing groups acting on government.[28] Such efforts at control were not necessarily conclusive or uncontested, but they marked the general trend beginning soon after independence and lasting for decades.

Unity was decreed, organized, monopolized, enacted, and enforced by the party-government as the primary strategy of conflict management. Conflicts among demands and demand-bearing groups were exorcised, denied, and suppressed. Like the party auxiliaries, the representatives in the national assemblies were nationalized, removed from their constituents by being elected on a single-party national list; they thus became accountable only upward, to the national leadership, and not downward to their voters and their diverse interests. The standard political mechanisms—formal or informal—for bringing demands to the attention of government, for enforcing accountability for meeting them, and—importantly—for negotiating effective and enforceable compromises were largely eliminated. The account of two decades of

Sierra Leone politics is a slow-motion microcosm of the phenomenon: "The government of Sir Albert Margai began to utilize the power of the state to stifle criticism and coerce its opponents into silence," spreading in the mid-1960s "the idea of solving their political difficulties through the institutions of the one-party state. . . . Thus, by 1978, legal opposition to the APC was ended. The power of the state was highly personalized and centralized, all major institutions of the state and many nongovernment institutions were either under government control or had lost the ability, the means, and sometimes the will to act independently. This remained the case in 1984."[29]

With the elimination of political channels of representation and accountability, and the executive takeover of most of the functions of government, there remained only one channel for handling demands and managing conflict—the administrative structure provided by both the state and the party, often in uncertain relation to each other. Local groups brought their needs to the attention of their governors or prefects and party federations. Where the system worked, the uncertain relations between party and administration and the divergent pulls of ethnic homelands provided the constructive basis for competition among provinces and districts for available resources. Regular party congresses and periodic *conférences des cadres* confirmed the orientation of the party-government at frequent and crucial intervals. After a decade, a prime minister was introduced as a minister of governmental affairs to organize allocation and to preserve the national leader's position as chief of the nation.

The first test of the single-party system of governance came as early as the mid-1960s, when the allocation strategy collapsed and the system of conflict management underwent serious strains as a result. Market failure for single crop economies, combined with shortfalls in foreign aid and investment, suddenly reduced available resources and heightened the pressure of expectations. At the same time, demands gradually rose for better social services, accentuating the allocation conflict. Although there were small country variances in this timetable, all states in West and Central (and even North) Africa who had gained independence around 1960 were on the same schedule.

Their response, however, varied. In some, the single party proved flexible and resilient, combining strategies of response with strategies of control. Market and product diversification, special aid appeals, and external currency support combined to produce resources to take the edge off conflicting demands from the capital, provincial centers, and rural populations. What could not be satisfied was dampened, as the single party turned to demobilization and handed over its allocation functions to the state administration. The party offices, formerly acting as a ministry of mobilization, reduced their personnel and their hours, managing competing demands by restricting the channels—and hence the expectations—for their expression.

Such retrenchment strategies provided a breathing space and a chance for a new orientation. The social base of the ruling coalition was reduced and refocused on the urban population, narrowing and concentrating the scope of demands and the groups that expressed them. New economic policies were undertaken, involving an increased state role in the organization of production through parastatals, increased public investments particularly in the boom years of the mid-1970s, increase in urban construction and urban services, and increased food imports—programs that responded to the ongoing demands of the regime's social base. Increased nationalization of foreign holdings, export diversification, import substitution and transformation industry, infant industry protection, and foreign borrowing were the strategies used to increase available resources. Armed with these efforts to meet a restricted list of demands and dampen the rest, some single-party regimes were able to combine measures of supply and control to hang on. Such was the case in Côte d'Ivoire, Guinea, Sierra Leone, Gambia, Senegal, Cameroon, Gabon, and Liberia.

But in all cases the political organization persisted only by reducing and denaturing its own activities. Nowhere did it continue to operate as an organ of interest articulation and aggregation, conveying and combining the demands of critical groups in the population to the governors. On one hand, the demands of allegiance and development were so obvious that an elaborate articulation mechanism was unnecessary. But on the other hand, demands being so numerous and overwhelming, government had to make choices, even for the narrowed referent group. The party's functions were overtaken and taken over by the needs of control and of downward dissemination of information, replacing upward flows of demands.

In other cases, however, the inability of the single-party system to contain increasing and conflicting demands clearly showed the nationalist generation to be more skilled in taking power than in exercising it. The party itself became a burden on government, significant demands made their way to the top outside the party channels, and the executive found itself unable to reduce or to satisfy the demands piled on it. Sometimes demands culminated in riots, strikes, demonstrations, and other evidence that the nationalist leaders were no longer in control even of public order. Labor strikes in Ghana in 1961, election riots in Nigeria in 1964, 1965, and 1966, veterans' protests in Togo in 1963, a general strike in Upper Volta in 1963, the outbreak of the rebellion in northern Chad in 1965—all were major breakdowns in civil order preceding a change in regime.[30] Occasionally but less frequently, these groups were ethnic rather than socioeconomic, and their demands were for a greater share in the shrinking pie and an elimination of discrimination.

In other (and also in overlapping) cases, the pinch of the late 1960s, before the boom of the next decade, hurt specific groups, notably the military, who had the ability of doing more than just disturbing civil order. When political and economic mistreatment turned the military from a support group to a demand group of the regime, it had the means to do something about it and to resolve the government's problems of ineptitude and overextension at the same time. The army took over government. The coup became the standard method of elite succession since the normal election process was used to restrict competition and conflict and to keep the nationalist leaders in power. Coups were admirably suited to the purpose, since they brought in representatives of new demands groups and also performed some of the restrictive functions that the party system was unable to fulfill (table 2-1).

## The Military and the Repression of Conflict

Military takeover of government was not a frivolous or incidental event in African history but a characteristic response to the inability of party government to manage the conflicting demands at the time. The military took some initial steps to deal with the situation: it restored civil order and banned politics, resolving by gun and fiat the debilitating dilemmas of its predecessor. Over the longer run, it took measures to manage conflicting demands by raising resources, employing the same strategies that civilian regimes had used to tap foreign and domestic sources, and by installing measures, such as a single party and a guiding ideology, to increase its support and control and keep demands down. The military's first job was to clamp down on demands and shrink the political arena, so that government would not be called on to

**TABLE 2-1.** *Nationalist and Military Single-Party Regimes*

*Military in italics*

| Nation | Date | Party[a] |
|---|---|---|
| Liberia | 1860–1979 | True Whig Party |
| Côte d'Ivoire | 1957–90 | Democratic Party of the Ivory Coast (PDCI) |
| Guinea | 1958–84 | Democratic Party of Guinea (PDG) |
| Mali | 1959–67 | Sudanese Union (US-RDA) |
| | 1977–92 | *Democratic Union of the Malian People (UDPM)* |
| Niger | 1960–74 | Nigerien Progressive Party (PPN) |
| | 1988–91 | *National Movement for Society and Development (MNSD)* |
| Upper Volta (Burkina Faso) | 1960–66 | Voltaic Democratic Union (UDV) |
| Ghana | 1960–66 | Convention People's Party (CPP) |
| Mauritania | 1961–78 | Mauritanian People's Party (PPM) |
| Central African Republic | 1966–79 | Movement for Social Evolution of Black Africa (MESAN) |
| | 1979–81 | *Central African Democratic Union (UDC)* |
| | 1986– | *Central African Democratic Rally (RDC)* |
| Chad | 1962–75 | Chadean Progressive Party (PPT), then National Movement for the Cultural and Social Revolution (MNRCS) |
| | 1980–90 | *National Union for Independence and Revolution (UNIR)* |
| Congo | 1964–69 | *National Movement of the Revolution (MNR)* |
| | 1969–92 | *Congolese Workers Party (PCT)* |
| Senegal | 1966–74 | Senegalese Progressive Union (UPS) |
| Cameroon | 1966–91 | Cameroonian National Union (UNC) |
| Gabon | 1968–90 | Democratic Party of Gabon (PDG) |
| Zaire | 1966–90 | *Popular Movement of the Revolution (MPR)* |
| Benin | 1967–70 | *Union for the Renewal of Dahomey (URD)* |
| | 1975–90 | *Popular Revolution Party of Benin (PRPB)* |
| Togo | 1969–91 | *Togolese People's Rally (RPT)* |
| Equatorial Guinea | 1970–79 | *United Single National Workers Party (PUNT)* |
| Guinea-Bissau | 1974–91 | African Independence Party of Guinea and Cape Verde (PAIGC) |
| Sierra Leone | 1977–92 | All-People's Congress (APC) |

Source: *Africa South of the Sahara 1996*, 25th ed. (London: Europa Publications Limited, 1995).

a. Parties may continue to exist after given dates but no longer as single parties.

manage the conflicts stemming from competing pressures for shrinking resources. Parties were banned, constitutions abrogated, supreme military councils created, and a new order decreed. Typically, power was to be returned to civilians once the stables were cleaned. Government became an affair of technicians, with the technicians of control—the military—associating the technicians of supply—the technocrats—in governing, free of the encumbering demands of diverse and conflicting groups. For a while military regimes succeeded in these tasks although often at the expense of the nation's growth and development. However, the nature of a military regime also raised problems. Demand-bearing groups arose, which troubled and sometimes ended the regime's life, from the one source military regimes could not control and to which they themselves were prey, notably, ethnic groups. Demands also came from socioeconomic or generational groups that a coup and its ideology invited, notably, students and youth. Finally demands arose from factions within the military regime.

Thus demand-bearing groups were not to be abolished by the military. Indeed the military itself was one, or perhaps several. Often the military was torn between some factions who saw themselves as the spokesmen for the cause of good, clean government, and others who insisted on making corporate demands on the budget. Corporate needs competed with domestic development and demands for services, gradually exacerbating the economic difficulties of the countries. In some cases, new coup attempts were corrective measures, the junior officer's replay of the senior leader's efforts to weed out internal deviation and consolidate power.[31]

In other cases, the military was riven by subgroups, competing military factions who sought to use the available means of succession for their own accelerated benefit. New, usually younger, military groups struck for their time in power, introducing a "turn at the trough" ethos of political office as short-term elite occupation, carrying no responsibility to the governed and their needs.[32] Finally, the military was also divided by and representative of ethnic groups and demands. With all other group demands on hold, ethnic demands rose to the fore, ethnic groups suddenly had direct access to power, and intramilitary differences suddenly dropped to conflicts of primordial identities. Thus the first Nigerian military government immediately split along tribal lines, and attempted coups in 1968 and 1977 in Congo and 1975 in Ghana were born of ethnoregional dissatisfaction in the ruling military, among other things. By eliminating troublesome demands from the outside, the military merely enhanced the demands that surfaced within. However, the nature of the military government and the measures it took to consolidate its power also raised its vulnerability to new demands from the outside. These groups seized on the military's self-proclaimed progressive image, identifying with it and using it against the governors themselves. Moreover, the new demand-bearing groups were by their nature aggregative, not specific, and so had a broader claim on government's attention. They were youth, with generational demands, and intellectuals, with ideological demands—the two often combining their forces and identities. The radical turn of government and its consolidation in power in Benin in 1972 and in Congo in 1979, labor pressures on Thomas Sankara in Burkina Faso after 1983, and the return of Rawlings in 1981 are examples. In other places such as Liberia, Mali, and Equatorial Guinea, student and labor groups were not successful in influencing the military regime and so turned against it with their demands, preparing for its later overthrow.[33] These demands were invited by the very measures the military took to overcome its own vulnerability.

In taking power, the military traded in a vulnerability to crowds of specific demands for a more generic vulnerability—its own illegitimacy. Military regimes benefit from a passing moment of revolutionary legitimacy (and sometimes a bit of charisma) but must soon make plans for seating themselves regularly and institutionally in office.[34] They must build institutionalized support for themselves, especially if their program is one of dampening demands and conducting development on their schedule. The two instruments available to the military government are ideology and, ironically, the single party. Both promote control and mobilization, designed to channel and limit upward demands and make them compatible with the predetermined directions of the ruler. As a consequence, however, both instruments magnify the upward pressures that do get through the controls and force government to resolve conflicts by steering programs in the demanded direction. Ideology was centralizing, consumptionist, and socialist, reinforcing the hold of the urban sector on government programs.

The new single party was a creation from the top—the Movement for Social Evolution in Black Africa (MESAN) as a single party in the Central African Republic in 1962, the Chadian Progressive Party (PPT) in Chad in 1963, which became the National Movement for the Cultural

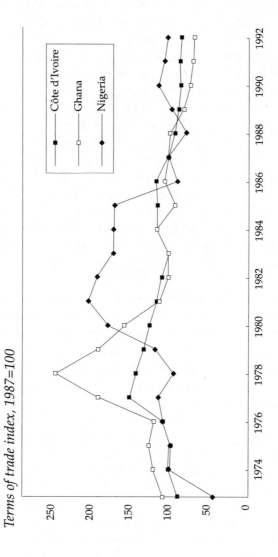

FIGURE 2-1. *Terms of Trade for Selected Countries in West Africa, 1973–92*

*Terms of trade index, 1987=100*

Source: *World Tables, 1993* (Johns Hopkins University Press, 1993); and *World Tables, 1994* (Johns Hopkins University Press, 1994).

and Social Revolution (MNRCS) in 1973, the National Cameroonian Union (UNC) in 1966, the Democratic Party of Gabon (PDG) in 1968, the Togolese People's Rally (RPT) in 1969, the Congolese Labor Party (PCT) in 1969, the Democratic Union of the Malian People (UDPM) in 1974, the Party of the People's Revolution of Benin (PRPB) in 1975, the All-Peoples' Congress in Sierra Leone in 1978, and the National Movement for Society and Development (MNSD) in Niger in 1988.[35] But otherwise the new single party shared many of the characteristics of the fossilized single parties in civilian-ruled states—a downward transmission of instructions and a method of local organization and control paralleling that of the ministry of the interior, which was effective at best in mobilizing a narrow support group for, and watchdog over, the governors.

Like their civilian contemporaries, the military regimes benefited from the boom years of the mid-1970s, when the terms of trade for tropical products as well as oil peaked (figure 2-1). The military also used the same strategies as the civilians for developing resources—expansion of parastatals, increased borrowing, greater public investment, further nationalizations—and spent them for similar purposes (plus military expenses)—providing food, housing, and services for the urban base to their regime.

But the terms-of-trade peaks of the mid-1970s (early 1980s for Nigeria and the other oil states) occurred against a background of other rising indicators for consumers. Food prices tripled in the early 1970s, energy prices quadrupled in 1974 and then doubled again in 1978, and droughts occurred throughout the period and again after 1982. Finally foreign aid collapsed after 1982 as a result of the developing countries' recession. As a result, except for oil-producing countries (Nigeria, Gabon, Cameroon, and Congo), the turn of the decade brought a resource failure that exceeded that of the previous decade (figure 2-2). This failure brought on a new series of coups in the region, each with its peculiar national forms of the common cause: Mauritania in 1978, 1979, and 1980, Equatorial Guinea in 1979, Guinea-Bissau and Liberia in 1980, Upper Volta in 1980 and 1983, Guinea and Niger in 1985, Ghana in 1979 and 1981, Nigeria in 1983 and 1985.

In the end, the military regime had only two possible futures. It enjoyed its time at the trough, found it impossible to leave, and clung to power for unconscionably long times (three decades in Zaire and Togo, twenty-two years in Mali, twenty in Benin) unless overthrown by a clone, outrunning any new ideas, legitimacy, or ability to govern that it

**FIGURE 2-2.** *Gross National Product per Capita for Selected Countries in West Africa, 1967–93*

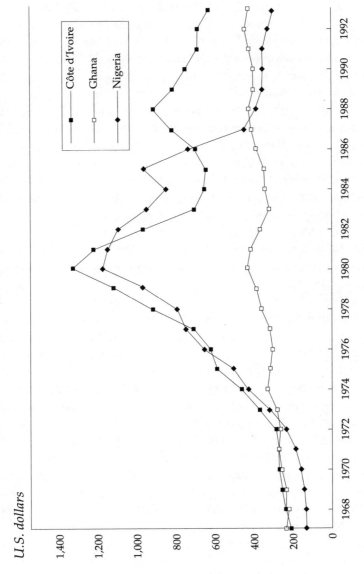

Source: *World Tables, 1993, 1994.* Per capita figures calculated according to World Bank Atlas method. The conversion factor for any year is the average exchange rate for that year and the two preceding years, adjusted for differences in rates of inflation between the country and the United States.

might have had at the beginning. Or it realized that its contribution to government was limited to helping the members of the independence generation to retire and to clean the stables after them, but that (contrary to the academic as well as the public myths of the time) the military had no special skills for governing. In that case the military prepared for civilian return and an opening of the system to the free competition of groups and demands. Attractive as the latter sounds, it has not been easy. Resources are as limited, demands as conflicting, and politicians as venal as ever. As many a corrective military ruler throughout the world has learned, the stables are not easy to clean thoroughly, and the horses when let back in keep their old habits. Military rulers returned their polities to civilian rulers in competitive elections in Sierra Leone (1968), Upper Volta (1978), Ghana (1969, 1979), and Nigeria (1979), only to find that the old crowd of independence politicians and their followers were the only ones with the skill and taste to take up politics.[36] The military could only come back again and clean the stables more thoroughly, barring more stringently the return of those with political experience, as it did in all four countries in 1978, 1980, 1972 and 1981, and 1983, respectively.

## Ethnoregional and Socioeconomic Demand Groups

Development means social differentiation, and the 1970s and 1980s were years of enough socioeconomic change to produce horizontal income, status, and professional differences in society, to awaken generational antagonisms, and to accentuate vertical distinctions and loyalties. The nature of the regime—civilian or military—mattered relatively little in its effects. Both sought to handle mounting and conflicting demands by squeezing politics out of society and monopolizing what was left of politics as a bureaucratic exercise. Both tried to maximize fluctuating resources to provide benefits for their urban power base, keeping the rural areas under control. Both were perceived as favoring one region or ethnic group over another. Under the pressures of growth, constraint, and favoritism, society heaved and crumbled into component pieces.

As cities grew at an extraordinary rate—6 percent a year on the average in the 1970s and in the 1980s in West Africa, more than in any other subregion and roughly double the population growth rate—strata and occupations grew and gave rise to groups with conflicting socioeconomic demands.[37] Two large and strategic urban groups have been particularly important: students and labor. In Nigeria between 1971 and 1987, five out of every fourteen public protests were conducted by students and four by labor, compared with only two by peasants.[38] Another significant group was market women.

Students are a predesignated group whether they are formally organized or not; their very existence brings them together, gives them demands, confirms them in an intergenerational conflict, locks them into an expectational shortfall, and provides them with a locus and a proto-organization.[39] As a segment of the population trained to replace its elders, African students are still under the independence ethos, expecting a subsidized existence in school and an important job on their graduation. The timing of examinations gives convenient deadlines for interruption; the most prominent sanction is to close the universities (conscription not being readily available) so that the students are only somewhat dispersed and free to carry out their protests more effectively. Party regimes sought to control their students through official unions, which gave them an organization to protest through or against, as in Côte d'Ivoire in mid-1991. Typically, student protests have been directed against fees and cafeteria conditions, issues symptomatic of the expectations of the students and the shortfalls from the tightening economic conditions. But students also protested larger policy issues, such as American policy in Angola or government deprivation of human rights in Côte d'Ivoire in the mid-1970s.[40]

If student groups and demands are an indicator of generational conflict, labor groups and demands are an important aspect of socioeconomic conflict. Labor, including civil service, is the social base of African regimes; even if its programs are often targeted on the middle class, the mass component of their urban base that must be satisfied is labor, and the category of government employees with common interests toward their employer often blurs the standard class distinction. Paradoxically, even though African exports are generally agricultural and hence of rural origin, labor has a major hold on the resources of the country, since manufacturing is primarily urban. Labor's position at the crossroads of resource supply and allocation demands give it a crucial role in the governance process. Unions have traditionally been strong in services and in industry, with teachers' and government employees' unions as well as railroad and small manufacturing trade unions playing an active role since the time of the nationalist movement. Labor demands have focused directly on living conditions and specifically on government pricing policies, continually recalling to government the terms of the social contract providing cheap food in exchange for support and productivity.

Although labor's existence does not provide the same automatic organization as that of students, the reigning ethos requires unionization, posing the classical labor dilemma of organization for national solidarity versus organization for labor demands.[41] Universally, nationalist labor unions have been tamed by the single party or military regime, setting up a target for rank-and-file rebellion as demands grow. Either these official unions have been taken over by the membership, or they have been circumvented by breakaway unions who carry membership demands to the government (the largest employer). Even in populist regimes as in Ghana and Burkina Faso, the conflict in the 1980s between established trade unions on one hand, and the workers' defense councils and committees for the defense of the revolution, on the other, weakens effective spokesmen and exacerbates conflict over social demands.[42] In the process, the breakup of labor unity frees smaller professional organizations to pursue their own demands. Of these, teachers' unions are the most active, and they reinforce their weight by providing a bridge to the demands of student organizations. Some of these groups were beneficiaries of government programs and had their demands taken care of to some degree, at the expense of others who were left out.

Inevitably, over the two generations of independence, as in any polity, demands change and issues realign. However, it is more difficult in Africa to make any certain statements since the data are unavailable. Polls and surveys, election campaigns and votes, even content analyses of press and public debate—the normal measures of issue evolution—are generally not to be found.[43] Moreover, the general nature of African problems of development and related demands have been constant since independence. The baseline of demands remains the same. However, new conflicts arising from reorientations in demands have been less frequent than a simple resurfacing of the same old demands. People want clean government, better living conditions, and greater liberty, and they oppose corruption, austerity, and repression with a new vigor born of a growing awareness of pluralistic interests and a changed international climate in favor of pluralism and civil liberties.

But West African governments in the 1980s were also under pressure from ethnic demand-bearing groups. They used an array of strategies to handle ethnic conflict, including assimilation, cooptation, competition, autonomy, and conquest, and ethnic groups responded with their own strategies, from petition to secession to overthrow. In Senegal, for example, a new nation was gradually being created through assimilation, built about a central core or "nationalizing zone" on the basis of the French and Wolof languages but ignoring ethnic distinctions; the negative side of the consolidation and expansion of the core implied a neglect of the peripheries, notably in the South (Casamance) and the East. In Mali, a similar assimilation was practiced through the use of Malinke and French; in Sierra Leone, conscious government policy sought to mix Creoles and up-country people in positions of power.[44] In Gabon, where politics has been controlled by a tight coalition of small ethnic groups held together by a common interest in fending off potential dominance by the one largest tribe (the Fang, with 40 percent of the population), both the minorities and the majority have been kept under control by cooptation of their representatives into ruling circles and remunerative positions, supported by the country's export-fed resources. In Chad, Benin, and Togo, the periphery simply took over the center as an army of occupation, allowing the populations of the capitals to benefit from being there but using the central power to benefit parts of the hinterland.

In Côte d'Ivoire, the government encouraged competition among the various regions and their ethnic components for benefits from the center; prefects and party leaders were rewarded, and through them their regions, for efforts to keep people away from the center through development projects. In Nigeria, a rare case, a policy of autonomy has created a proliferation of centers in an ever-increasing number of federal states, each with its own resources and payoffs.

By their nature, all these strategies implied the denial or neglect of some regions and groups of the population and led to their coalescence around demands as groups being discriminated against. Many of these groups came from outlying rural areas that were only just receiving the disruptive effects of administration from the capital without any corresponding benefits.[45] In effect, a late-blooming nationalism took hold against administrative "colonization" from the center, similar to the nationalist movement's reaction to colonial rule from the metropole. Conceptually, the demands moved from protest toward the center, to secession from the center, to overthrow of the center, with examples of all three phases. Ironically, the forerunner of this type of ethnic protest in all three phases occurred in Chad after 1965, when the northern region went into dissidence, eventually to conquer the capital a decade and a half later.

The same dissidence was repeated in the Casamançais of Senegal after 1982, the Targui regions of the Sahara in Mali, Algeria, Niger, and Libya after 1964, and the northern region of Cameroon (particularly after the northern president retired in 1985). It also showed up in reverse in discrimination against the Halpulars in Mauritania in the valley of the Senegal River and the Moors in Senegal. In the above cases, the effects of the Sahelian drought of the 1970s and 1980s on the national economies reduced resources and exacerbated the allocation problem. A similar dynamic took a sharper form in Liberia in the 1980s, where the *comprador* behavior of the Americo-Liberians drove the hinterland not into secession but into takeover: the Krahns, let into the capital as soldiers, took over the power they had been hired to defend. When, under Samuel Doe, they turned around and hired the Americo-Liberians for the technical skills they needed to govern, the Mandingos, Geos, and Manos revolted under Charles Taylor to oust them, in turn, at the end of the decade.

These ethnic demands evoked strong responses from their governments. Although a minority of the states in the region have been affected by such sharp ethnic and regional protests, where they did occur they were violent and were met with violence. In the extreme cases of Chad in the early 1980s and Liberia in the early 1990s, they brought about the collapse of the state itself, pulling down the pillars of government on their own heads.[46] The other cases have been peripheral enough not to disturb the functioning of government, but the social fabric of the country has sometimes been torn—as in Senegal in 1989, Cameroon in 1992, and Congo in 1993—ripping into the heart of the capital itself. Unlike earlier cases, the result has not been the militarization of government but a weakening of its authority and integrity, as in Senegal and Mali. That eventually contributed to the government's overthrow from the base, and not from above, as happened in Mali, Benin, Togo, Niger, and Congo.

Consequently, by the end of the 1980s, pressure and conflict from ethnic and socioeconomic groups were increasing, stemming from the reduction of resources because of drought and recession and from proliferation of demands because of centralization and pluralization. For an area where the state has been characterized as both weak and soft,

West African states have done remarkably well in keeping their integrity while facing such increased demands. But the particular governments that operated the state have done less well. The rise of demands has also raised questions about the forms of government and the social contracts underlying them and carried demands from substantive matters to procedural ones.

## The Rise of Procedural Demands

The capping of substantive demands for specific benefits by procedural demands for participation in the conflict management process has occurred for simple, straightforward, and proper reasons: dissatisfaction with centralized, monistic governance coupled with a desire and willingness to open demands and participation to the political marketplace. The change came at the beginning of the 1990s rather than before for reasons of both demand and supply: although the gradual effects of development had produced pluralization and new groups with demands for pieces of the national pie, the world economic recession meant that the pie was shrinking and monistic governments were called to account for their stewardship. The world context reinforced the second part of the equation in three ways—by withdrawing economic resources, by imposing requirements for adjustment, and by providing numerous examples of the illegitimacy of centralized political and economic control throughout the communist world. Although the wave broke at an identifiable moment, at the end of the 1980s, like other such social movements it was foreshadowed much earlier by premature and preparatory moves.

One preparatory strain was the insecurity of the military in English-speaking countries over its legitimacy as ruler. English-speaking West Africa (except for the special case of Gambia) provides most of the instances where the African military voluntarily returned power to the civilians in the 1960s and 1970s. That occurred not just once, as in Sierra Leone (in 1968) and Nigeria (in 1979), but twice in Ghana (in 1969 and 1979), before the returns planned to take place in all three states in the 1990s. Only Upper Volta among the French-speaking states returned to civilian rule, in 1978, as an interlude between a first-generation and a second-generation military ruler. Although all of these civilian returns were reversed soon afterward by a second- or third-generation military officer, they indicate a basic uneasiness in the military about its own legitimacy in power.

A second forerunner was the sporadic appearance of opposition to single parties. Ever since a group of colleagues announced to Sekou Touré their intentions of forming an opposition party in 1960—whereupon he promptly arrested them—politicians have sought to challenge the single path of party regimes and to provide alternatives. Many of these parties were ideological, without a social basis other than among intellectuals, and some were ethnic, but a few emerged from other sources of demands and even the supposedly ethnic parties often had a reform element independent of their tribal source of members. Among the first category were the African Independence Party (PAI) in Senegal and the Communist Party of Dahomey (PCD).[47] Among the second were the Fang-based National Reform Movement (MORENA) founded in 1981 in Gabon. Among the rarer cases of the third were the Progressive People's Party (PPP) and the Movement for Justice in Africa (MOJA) in Liberia. The most successful precursor has been Senegal, which even during the nationalist movement had a history of pluralism and which became a three-party state by decree in 1974. Although few states emulated the Senegalese experience, either in its early multipartyism or in its smooth presidential transition, it remained an eloquent example of the potentialities and only limited dangers of pluralism.

The third precursor of competitive political pluralism was the human rights movement, which set up Leagues (Ligues des Droits de l'Homme) and Amnesty International chapters throughout the region. These organizations were not just clubs organized about an idea but an institutional expression of the concerns of groups and individuals with a social basis and a supportive set of their own substantive demands. They included lawyers with an interest in cases and causes, professors concerned about open debate, and business executives looking for discussions on alternative economic systems. Human rights concerns entered African countries through Amnesty International in London and the Ligue des Droits de l'Homme in Paris, but gradually chapters and local leagues were set up in the African countries themselves. As international concern increased, it became unseemly for repressive regimes to continue to oppose the creation of a local human rights organization, even though regimes continued to block the efforts of such groups. As time passed and pressure built up, it even became unseemly for regimes to block the the groups' efforts too. The best that regimes could do was to create their own competing leagues and human rights organizations, weakening the original group but at the same time reinforcing its message.

Leagues were set up in Cameroon in 1984, in Mauritania in 1986, in Burkina Faso, Côte d'Ivoire, and Nigeria in 1987, in Senegal and Mali in 1988, in Togo, Benin, and Guinea, in Niger in 1990, and in Liberia and Guinea Bissau and Gambia in 1991. Amnesty chapters sprang up in Côte d'Ivoire in 1979, Ghana and Senegal in 1980, and Nigeria and Sierra Leone in 1989; human rights commissions formed in Togo in 1988 and Benin in 1989, and regional human rights organizations established themselves in Gabon in 1978 and 1980, Gambia in 1986 and 1987, Ghana in 1989, Nigeria in 1986, Côte d'Ivoire and Benin in 1990, and Senegal in 1979 and 1983. Furthermore, an impressive number of professional and issue-oriented associations were established throughout the region with human rights and political development among their goals—notably bar associations in Senegal in 1976, in Ghana, Gambia, Sierra Leone in 1979, in Nigeria in 1983, and Gabon.[48]

A fourth antecedent of political pluralization was the evolution of social organizations around the issue of employment. Student fortunes took a peculiar twist after the mid-1980s that turned them from restive targets of party-government organization to the avant garde of the pluralist opposition. As the economic fortunes of African states declined in the mid-1980s, the guarantee of employment given to students faded away, and urban streets became filled with unemployed graduates. They were trained to know more than government incumbents but were blocked by the same incumbents from putting their knowledge to work. The effect of lessened demand was in turn to reduce the supply of graduates but not of unemployed. Youth dropped out of school and college since their efforts gave them no jobs. They took up the petty trades of the unemployed—windshield washers, parking attendants, sunglass salesmen, and so on. They thus became available for political employment as demonstrators, while their brothers and sisters who stayed in school became a demand-bearing group for change.

Similarly, those who did achieve government employment for their efforts then constituted the other already mobilized group—the labor unions. They also shifted their position toward the end of the 1980s to become a force for pluralism and political change.[49] Formerly organized, however restively, under party government control as a source of support for the monistic system, labor unions became the immediate target of government reform programs when structural adjustment programs were adopted under the pressure of the international financial institutions, the United States, and eventually even the European

Community. Up to this point, labor had been held in control by rising salaries and bloated bureaucracies. When these means of cooptation were no longer available, unions turned to bite the hand that no longer fed them. They called for accountability from the governors. Underlying the unions' complaint against the austerity of structural adjustment was the deeper complaint that change had been decided without their participation.[50]

All these antecedents created momentum for demands for a new social contract and a direct, open, pluralistic participation of the governed in their governance. The underlying grievance was that monolithic governments, whether civilian or military, were not able to resolve conflicts in demands from the increasingly pluralistic and disappointed population. Thus another contributor was the sudden disrepute of socialist and single-party regimes, beginning with the Soviet Union. However, this development so closely paralleled the evolution of attitudes in Africa that establishing a cause and effect is difficult. Similarly, although the growing procedural demands echoed the pressures of the international financial institutions—World Bank, International Monetary Fund—and the private sector for economic openness, accountability and competition, those pressures were generally so unpopular in Africa, even or especially when finally adopted by the governments, that they might have been predicted to undermine the development of political openness and competition.[51] That they did not is testimony to the strength of grass-roots demands for debate and participation. Instead, austerity measures required by the IMF often triggered popular uprisings against the corrupt authoritarian regimes that enacted them, creating a particularly difficult dilemma for the resulting democratic regimes.[52] In sum, conflicts increasingly gravitated from group versus group to groups versus government.

What did give pause to the movement was the failure of the democratic experiments, most often in those countries where the military had once withdrawn at the end of the 1970s. They all showed that, however unsuited the military might be for governance, it had cause for removing the civilian politicians of the independence generation who were just as unsuited to rule. Return to civilian rule in Ghana, Nigeria, and the Central African Republic in 1979 meant a return to the independence generation and demand politics and to a time-at-the-trough ethos that was at least as pervasive among the civilians as among the military. Military and civilian officials in turn treated incumbency as a fast-feeding frenzy, as they awaited replacement by a new group of military taking its turn. Yet to disbar all people who had any contact with the previous regime—as General Ibrahim Babangida did in Nigeria in 1987—would be to eliminate anyone with any experience in politics and probably to open politics to those who had devoted their time exclusively to the trough in business and finance.

It has not been because these problems have been solved that procedural demands have won the day on occasion but because the pressures for participatory conflict management have been so strong. Indeed, West Africa to date has confirmed Winston Churchill's famous judgment that "democracy is the worst form of government except all those other forms that have been tried from time to time."[53] Military regimes in many West African countries—Ghana, Benin, Togo, Mali, Guinea, Niger, Chad, Congo, Sierra Leone, the Central African Republic, and Mauritania—have been forced by the irresistible pressure from below to edge toward the restoration of civilian rule, in a form that allows demand-bearing groups to compete for scarce resources. Others, however, have drawn back from the edge of change at the moment of decision. Some military regimes, or originally military regimes, that did not give in on their own were simply overthrown by varying means to make way for a new social contract. In Mali, mounting pressure from student, civil servant, professional, and civil rights groups opened the way for the army to remove the tyrant and prepare for democracy; and in Benin the same groups forced the tyrant to face his people in a national town meeting or national conference in 1990 and conform to the regulations of a new social contract, by which he was ultimately retired (for six years). Other military rulers, all ruling over smaller or less developed societies, were gradually pressured to follow suit, in Niger, Congo, Central Africa, Sierra Leone, Guinea, and Guinea Bissau. In Liberia, a grass-roots revolt destroyed civil order and murdered the tyrant in 1990 but then turned on itself and murdered society. In Togo and Zaire the tyrant, able to defeat the pressures for accountability, has become a prisoner of his own army; and in Nigeria, the leaders of the regional military intervention that was to bring democracy and conflict management to Liberia could not bring themselves to recognize the results of their own elections in 1993 and clung to power instead.

The regimes already civilianized have been much more difficult to pluralize.[54] Single-party regimes democratize with difficulty, since they have monopolized political experience and are operating within a party skilled in winning elections. Unless it is totally discredited, the single

TABLE 2-2. *National Conferences, Elections, and Their Outcomes*

| Nation | Date | Duration | Election[a] | Outcome[b] |
|---|---|---|---|---|
| Benin | Feb. 1990 | 1 wk. | F&f, Feb. 1991, Mar. 1996 | Alternance (Soglo; Kerekou) |
| Gabon | Mar. 1990 | 3 wks. | Dec. 1993 | *Bongo reelected* |
| Congo | Mar. 1991 | 3 mos. | F&f, Aug. 1992 | Alternance (Lissouba) |
| Mali | July 1991 | 15 days | F&f, Apr. 1992 | Alternance (Konare) |
| Niger | July 1991 | 40 days | F&f, Feb. 1993 | Alternance (Mahamane) |
| Burkina Faso | Aug. 1991 | 2 mos. | Dec. 1991 | *Campaore reelected* |
| Ghana | Aug. 1991 | 7 mos. | F&f, Nov.– Dec. 1992 | *Rawlings reelected* |
| Togo | Aug. 1991 | 1 mo. | Aug. 1993 | *Eyadema reelected* |
| Zaire | Aug. 1991 | 1 yr. | 1997 or 1998 | . . . |
| Central African Republic | Oct. 1991 | 2 mos. | F&f, Aug. 1993 | Alternance (Patassé) |
| Chad | Jan. 1993 | 3 mos. | June 1996 | *Deby reelected* |

Source: *Africa South of the Sahara 1996.*
a. F&f means free and fair.
b. If the status quo was maintained, the election outcome is in italics.

party remains a powerful player during the transition. The earliest and most successful record of evolutionary pluralization was Senegal, which has had competing parties since the mid-1970s, even though then, as twenty years later, the opposition had little chance of making major electoral inroads. As in other countries of the region, Côte d'Ivoire faced a year of political upheaval in 1990 from students, faculty, labor, and civil servants in response to major attempts at reductions in civil service salaries and benefits and increases in taxes, in the continuing context of a controlled political system. Elsewhere, as already noted and as analyzed below, such unrest led to an overthrow of the system. Yet Côte d'Ivoire opened its 1990 elections to competition without the slightest threat to Félix Houphouët-Boigny or his Democratic Party (PDCI). In the other two major French-speaking states, Paul Biya and Omar Bongo have been able to use the Cameroonian Peoples' Democratic Rally (RDPC) and the Democratic Party of Gabon (PDG), respectively, to coopt and hold off pressure for pluralization for a while. Yet the pressures of pluralism can no longer be contained by a single party, as they were in the past (table 2-2).

The sovereign national conference, invented by professor Robert

Doussou of Benin in 1989 but grown out of a long experience in *conférences des cadres* in Benin, Côte d'Ivoire, and elsewhere, became the meeting grounds for the new demand-bearing groups of society and the venue for the elaboration of a new social contract.[55] The conference was an innovative political move—a political revolution—that took sovereignty into the hands of a self-constituted body of civil society and wrote a new social contract creating a new political system. The combined action of civil servants, teachers, students, labor, lawyers, and sometimes military groups, supported by a suddenly blossoming press, testified to the pluralism that had grown up under the wraps of the authoritarian regimes. In Benin the demands came from two of the groups most favored by the regime of Mathieu Kerekou, the public sector employees, and the students, who launched a strike in January 1989 against austerity measures imposed by the IMF without their being involved in the decision (the third favored group, the army, did not participate and remained an independent guardian of the transition). After the national conference of February 1990, Kerekou was allowed to preside over the transition and then run in the presidential elections a year later, which he lost; six years later, he was returned, "reformed."

Explicitly or implicitly, the national conference declared itself sovereign and wrote a new social contract for its country. The terms were all similar: debate and expression on public issues would be free and open, and critical or deviant opinions would not be punished; minorities would not be considered a danger to state security nor would their security be in jeopardy; free and fair elections would register the strength of groups and issues behind candidates at periodic intervals; and political and economic pluralism and competition would be the basis of a continuing search for the best future for the country and its citizens.

Of the twenty-four states in western Africa, nine (Benin, Gabon, Congo, Togo, Central African Republic, Niger, Burkina Faso, Mali, and Chad) plus Zaire had national conferences, three more (Ghana, Guinea, Mauritania) had constitutional revisions that converted their military regime to an elected multiparty system, and three others (Cape Verde, Senegal, Côte d'Ivoire) opened their single-party system to electoral competition, bringing alternance in the first, contested continuity in the second, and continuity in the third. In some of these states, pluralism was a safety valve, an occasion for free speech and expression of grievances without any serious challenge to the authoritarian regime, which had turned merely from a power monopoly to a power oligopoly. But in half the cases, by one mechanism or another, a profound change was introduced, turning the management of conflict from an authoritarian, top-down exercise into a participatory, bottom-up process. Details often blurred the sharp distinction between the two types, and the larger question remains whether the second will revert back to its authoritarian precedent or hold its own.

There is clearly a fork in the road and an open contest over which of the two paths will dominate the evolution of each country and provide the decisive demonstration effect for its neighbors. In the early 1990s, the democratic path seemed to be the high road, overshadowing the countries that still clung to their authoritarian regimes. Togo and Zaire seemed bent on being pariahs. But the hypocrisy of General Babangida and the Nigerian junta in 1993, in invalidating the electoral victory of their own handpicked candidates, added sudden weight to the authoritarian option and added support to the recalcitrance of other laggards such as Paul Biya in Cameroon, Gnassinbe Eyadema in Togo, and Lieutenant Colonel Ibrahim Bare Maïnassara in Niger. History continues in West Africa, as the region enters into a conflict between two different ways—authoritarian and participatory—of managing conflict.

## The Future of Substantive Demands

The culminating question is whether West Africa and other regions at the fork in the road face a systemic crisis and a major shift in demands, as they did around 1960, or whether the demand-bearing groups that surface today are merely the long-repressed emanations of a system frozen at the moment of independence. Have demands and groups changed in the interval since independence? If so, have the patterns of governance—of managing intergroup conflicts—been able to keep pace with those changes?

The West African focus on procedural demands for greater participation in governance in the early 1990s is an exceptional phase expected to last only as long as the governance issue is not settled. But that phase could be a long time, particularly if the various national attempts to settle the issue are not reasonably well synchronized. In the early and mid-1990s, expectations outside and inside Africa put pressure on Nigeria, Cameroon, and Ghana but also on Sierra Leone, Niger, Guinea, and the Central African Republic to open up and civilianize military regimes. A successful consolidation of power by the Democratic Party regime in Nigeria elected in June 1993 would have passed that pressure down the line. External donors withheld aid and castigated authoritarian rulers in Nigeria and Cameroon in 1993, in Niger in 1996, and in Zaire after 1992. Events in the states of the national conferences put pressure on the holdouts—Togo, Zaire, Cameroon, Gabon, Central African Republic—to place governance in the hands of pluralistic participation.

But the successful efforts of the holdouts to coopt the new prime ministers, divide the democracy movements, and control the elections for their succession, as in Zaire and Togo, also created their own pressures on the movements of pluralism, just as a failure of the transition in Nigeria in 1993 added to the success of Jerry Rawlings in Ghana. He was elected as his own successor in 1992, part of the trend to contain procedural demands. Senegal's elections in 1993 were not as free and fair as in previous years, yet Abdou Diouf and his Socialist party won, as in previous years. Niger's reform regime, hopelessly deadlocked in its new institutions, was overthrown by the military in 1995 and then swept out of office by the same military, who won elections, not so freely and fairly. Even in Benin, the deposed dictator was returned to office in the elections of 1996, freely and fairly. To that is added the temptation for newly elected regimes to curb the pressures from below against structural adjustment by reasserting state authority against demand-bearing groups of society. As a result, in many countries, efforts to put governance in the hands of society, rather than in the hands of an authoritarian regime, may well become stuck at an intermediate level. There pluralistic forces exist as safety valves for pressing demands but are not realistic contenders for governance—la démocratie à la Sénégalaise (although Senegal itself is under pressure to move on to the next step of alternation in power).

On this intermediate level, tactical questions become crucial. Is a dominant party system with a safety-valve opposition sufficient to satisfy societal demands? How does one break the voters' habit of voting for the incumbents because they have power, and the governors' habit of treating the opposition as a nuisance of which it has no fear? Should opposition leaders be given some experience to make them more responsible, for example, an opportunity to govern as a minister (often without portfolio) in an essentially dominant-party government? Or should he be locked out of power until his time comes, with that time being delayed because of his lack of experience? Should new opposition parties be given official subsidies so they can get started, even if it means that they are on the tether of the state (the "dominant party"), or should they be left to raise their own independent funding, even though few if any business executives would invest against the government? The success of procedural demands depends on such tactical and technical dilemmas.

Procedural demands may also be kept alive for ideological reasons quite distinct from a distributive or substantive base. Pressure for a communist or African socialist system has little prospect for rising in the rest of the decade (although such ideas could easily return thereafter, as the insufficiencies of competitive democracy become apparent). Pressures for Islamic government are quite likely across the sahel, even if they are not necessarily decisive. Such pressures, it should be emphasized, owe their support to the insufficiencies of current modes of governance. Their appeal comes not from a belief that Islamic (or any other) governance is better for Muslims (or for socialists or anyone else), but from the idea that the Koran provides the right way to govern and to eliminate conflict within society.

Substantive demands, however, continue to evolve, and they remain the basis of domestic political conflict and governance as the management of that conflict. In Africa's developing states, as elsewhere, material and distributive concerns remain the basis of politics. In some times and areas, these are reduced to demands for basic needs, but usually they concern relative shares of a shrinking pie and conditions of welfare. They are the same demands as expressed at the time of independence. Indeed they are the demands that underlay the nationalist movement itself, which protested discrimination against Africans in the distribution of the benefits of colonial development. Like the 1980s, the irresponsibility of government in the 1950s turned African demands from substantive to procedural as Africans felt that only by taking allocation into their hands could they assure themselves a proper distribution. As in the pre-independence period, the conflict to be managed is between beleaguered government and demand-bearing groups in Nigeria and Ghana and is in danger of becoming so in Côte d'Ivoire. The 1990s are a return to the 1960s in a more complete form.

But if demands remain the same, the nature of the demand-bearing groups has changed. Urban society is well entrenched, less precarious, and more differentiated. Privatization and restrictions on the public sector mean more competition and so more conflict among groups to be regulated and mediated by government. Cooperation between urban groups that may have previously formed the social basis of government, such as labor and business, is undergoing increasing strains, and they are turning to competition and conflict.

Rural society is diminishing, exploited, and relatively undifferentiated (except by geography and ethnicity). It is held in place by intermediaries—Mourides in Senegal, planters in Côte d'Ivoire, commercial farmers (Big Men) in Nigeria. In all these characteristics, the situation is typical of world history. But there are no unambiguous signs of classical historical evolutions into a Green Revolution or to commercial agriculture.[56] The world collapse of agricultural terms of trade has seen to that. Peasant votes are not enough to outweigh a loss of the urban voters, and rural alliances with parts of urban society provide an unstable base. Land tenure is not enough of a distributive issue in West Africa to provide a galvanizing issue for the peasant.

In this situation, ethnic groups continue to be functional, providing crosscutting bases for urban-rural and intraurban alliances. Some of the new regimes (Congo, Benin, Niger, Cameroon) represent ethnic or geographic shifts from the old regime (fear of which also occasioned the annulment of democracy in Nigeria in 1993), and as ethnicity writ large, geography provides the pooling of resources and the aggregation of demands that can foster responsive politics. Yet there is also potential for conflict, not only among ethnic groups and regions but between ethnic and socioeconomic bases of groups. When a labor union becomes a specific ethnic preserve or a business or other professional group is ethnically dominated, neither its corporate interest nor its productive basis of demands is enhanced.

There is an additional new demand-bearing group with its own needs and interests that was not present in the 1950s, called the incumbents. Enjoyment of the perquisites of office (time at the trough) and fear of retaliation for mismanagement (as Rawlings and Doe did to their predecessors), as well as the normal politician's belief that he or she alone has the answers and needs just a bit more time to make them stick, lower the interest of incumbents in Nigeria, Ghana, Senegal, Cameroon, Gabon, Togo, and elsewhere (not to mention Zaire) in following the rules of democratic alternance. A major obstacle to a shift to a different mode of conflict management, using institutionalization rather than decree or repression, is the absence of democratic rules of the game, a typical vicious circle. Incumbents and challengers alike have not yet learned or have no grounds to believe that losing an election is not permanent and fatal; indeed, in some places, they have learned the contrary lesson. Incumbents and challengers alike have learned to operate on the assumption that winning an election *is* permanent or at least beneficial enough to last a lifetime.[57] Breaking that vicious circle is necessary to breaking the revitalized anticolonial notion that government is the enemy of society rather than the manager of conflicts.

Besides being a crisis of institutionalization, the current crisis is also one of allocation, brought on by incompetence at governing but also by the world recession. Countries such as Côte d'Ivoire, Cameroon, and Gabon owe their stability to a long record of economic growth that made allocation possible as a strategy of conflict management. The economic context of the 1990s is not propitious for such strategies, and the argument that times of austerity require democratic consensus is more comforting to theoreticians than to practitioners. The lesson is straightforward, however: austerity can be made palatable if its necessity is conveyed convincingly and if resulting reduced allocations are made to meet a sense of fairness.[58]

Governance as conflict management is an internal affair; social contracts, self-government, and conflict management are beyond any external meddling. External powers, like any third-party mediators, can communicate a better understanding of the situation, help formulate responses, and provide incentives and cushions for appropriate responses, but they cannot impose or provide national policies.[59] Even if others provide the means for the better management of conflicts, those external sources cannot do the actual managing without delegitimizing the process, and in the process delegitimizing the government that should be the agent of management. But this process does operate in an international context with policy implications for the outside world.

Two strategies of conflict management evoke important, if indirect, foreign roles. Allocation has been seen to hold a dominant position in effective governance, and yet it is hampered by the world markets' treatment of African production. If African governments are to be able to correct the mismanagement of their predecessors, often practiced with foreign connivance, they will need fair and reliable terms of trade for their production. The world has a responsibility to help square their economic position of dependent price-takers with their political position of sovereign policymakers. As in regard to domestic conflict management, if the substantive grievances of African societies concerning unfair economic treatment are not managed effectively, African polities will turn to procedural demands, recalling either the southern revolt in the period of the New International Economic Order of the 1970s or the ideological revolt of the nationalist and communist movements against the systems of world order in the 1950s and 1960s. Whether that proceduralist reaction has any chance of success or not is a matter quite separate from the higher chances of its disruptive impact on orderly and constructive world relations.

Institutionalization is the other salient mode of conflict management. Normal politics, executive allocation, national assembly as a buffer, judiciary as manager, structural adjustment and management by the market, and transnational compensation in regional cooperation provide a formula for ongoing conflict management with periodic corrections. Again, African states need external encouragement and assistance during democratization. Western democracies have done a poor job of explaining the goals, procedures, and values of democracy and of relating it to African needs and practices. A better inspirational exercise is required, and a better sense of helpful but nonintrusive ways of promoting democracy.[60] Western democracies have been more effective in using diplomatic pressure or worse, including manipulation of foreign aid, to help keep African states on various economic courses than they have been in using the same means to promote responsible conflict management as governance. Condemnation of Nigeria's and Niger's arrested democratization in 1993 and in 1996 and suspension of aid to keep Cameroon (and Zambia and Kenya) on track to political pluralization in 1992 are examples with mixed results. Working democracies cannot make others democratic, but they can help others make themselves democratic. Only then can state and society together manage their own conflicts.

Chapter 3

# Political Polarization over Governance in Côte d'Ivoire

*Tessy D. Bakary*

DESPITE ETHNIC, CULTURAL, and linguistic fragmentation, Côte d'Ivoire was able to achieve consensus, even before independence, on governance as the management of conflict. The country stressed the economics of development and the "politics of distribution," first giving priority to economic growth and "colonial improvement" and then to "development" and "the well-being of the Ivorian man."[1] Success, evidenced by the high growth rates of the 1950s, 1960s, and 1970s, was transforming the political landscape, eroding ideological outcroppings, shifting commitments, and reducing or removing conflicts.

By the end of the 1970s, however, this state of affairs had changed drastically. Domestic and above all international contexts long favorable to growth started to contract. Uneven development among regions and material inequalities among groups and individuals became more and more obvious, and the increasing scarcity of economic resources owing to competition for them among an increasing elite population brought new constraints on affluence and payoffs.[2] The policy consensus slowly deteriorated and, as early as 1978, repoliticization, ideological contentiousness, and social discord over the "politics of distribution" and thus over governance began to rise. The social and political conflicts that broke out abruptly but not so surprisingly during the decade following the student and faculty strikes of 1982–83 showed that the political reforms of 1980 were barely adequate to manage the new and growing political, social, and economic demands. Instead, pressure rose throughout the decade for increased social benefits and political participation.

Severe riots, civil strife, strikes, and diverse disturbances from 1989 to 1992 marked the crises of combined social and political demands expressed by many groups and led to the restoration of multipartyism and basic political liberties merely by the effective application of article 7 of the 1960 constitution.[3] Nevertheless, for many Ivorians, the explosion of substantive or social demands and then procedural or political demands in the 1990s constituted the most important crisis the country had experienced since it became independent.

The conservative politics of a country that was at the forefront of the anticolonial movement in the 1940s and 1950s and its political stability in the midst of prophecies of economic collapse and social turmoil are distinctively Ivorian paradoxes.[4] So is the problem of how consensus over governance, expressed through the domination of the same ruling group since the 1940s, has been achieved and maintained for half a century despite all ethnic, regional, cultural, and linguistic cleavages. Ethnic groups are said to be at the core of the state and politics,[5] but Ivorian ethnic group relations do not have the bitterness and the violence found in next-door Liberia or even in Nigeria, or in Kenya, a country with a similar level of socioeconomic development.

The argument is that despite the apparent monolithism of the political system and the consensus over governance epitomized by the "eternal presence" of Félix Houphouët-Boigny as head of the state until his death in 1993, political demands and political conflicts since the beginning of autonomous political life in 1945 have remained constant. This is true even though they have taken various forms over the years as new demand-bearing groups moved into the social and political arena. But equally striking and intriguing is how little the structure of cleavages has changed and how stable the management of political conflicts has remained over the years. The main hypothesis is that the social alignments were frozen at a critical juncture in the 1950s, resulting in the construction of the ruling social legitimacy. Since then, the behavior of demand-bearing groups has been predictable, allowing for continuity in the management of conflicts.[6]

Ivorian politics are divided into two periods. One is "the taking over of power in the most noble and democratic meaning of the word," and the other is "the preservation and management of the power."[7] The first, 1945–65, is characterized by the shift from conflict to consensus, while the second, 1965–90, shows the erosion of that consensus leading ostensibly to a new political order. Each period ended with a time of intense conflict or crisis, in 1959–64 and in 1989–94. I analyze these shifts from conflict to consensus and then to dissensus over governance and its underlying conflicts in terms of the actors or demand-bearing groups involved (the social basis), the issues (demands) at stake, the values and the modes of action (strategies, political action repertoires), and the outcomes.[8]

## Social Ranking and Ethnic Classification: Culture and Social Legitimacy

Of the many factors that shaped the character of politics in Côte d'Ivoire, three are especially important. The first is the nature of the precolonial status systems as described by the ethnographic work of the colonial state.[9] "Self-fulfilling prophecy," how the ranking and roles, attributes, and value system ascribed to the different social groupings became reality and were internalized by ethnic groups, is most important.[10] The second is the way in which Ivorian ethnic groups reacted to the new economic setting, the commercialization of agriculture through the plantation economy.[11] That led to a pattern of ethnic dominance called the Akanization/Baulization (from Akan/Baule, Houphouët-Boigny's ethnic group) of national politics.[12] Third, and closely linked to the preceding factor, is how the colonial authorities reacted to the demands of Ivorians for the right to participate first in the plantation economy and then in politics.[13] The development of a plantation economy thus led to a consensus on economic policy, which is the main source of conservative politics in Côte d'Ivoire.

The survey, identification, and classification of the Ivorian population have been above all the work of the colonial governor, Maurice Delafosse. As the title of his book, noted earlier, indicates, he started with an inventory of languages and dialects to produce an ethnographic science, which was supplemented but never challenged in its main findings. Governor Delafosse identified more than sixty languages and dialects; he did not identify ethnic groups as such. Official speeches and academic writings of many disciplines perpetuate the idea of sixty tribes in a Côte d'Ivoire labeled a "human puzzle"[14] or "racial dustbin."[15] The existence of numerous ethnic groups is a blessing in disguise: since none of them can rule the country alone, the Ivorians are condemned to political cooperation and stability. Aristide Zolberg quoted Houphouët-Boigny as saying, "If unity had not been in our heart, we should have discovered it in our head."[16] Ethnicity is the con-

tent of the essential building blocks of political stability, which are social and cultural rather than economic. Economic changes have occurred through social motivations.[17]

In implementing its project, the colonial state relied on practical
learning made of stereotypes, representations, and values ascribed to
some and denied to others. It established a scale based on a group's
ability to be colonized following the differentiated ways in which the
social groupings encountered reacted and fit into the state's project. At
the top of the list were the leading subgroup of the Akan, the Agni (initially merely associated with the Baule; note its low profile and lack of
saliency), because of its early encounters with the Europeans and ability to accept and propagate the "civilizing mission." Next came the
Dioula and the Senufo from the northern part of the country, mainly because most of them are Muslim, and France had experience with Islamic people in North Africa. At the bottom of the classification were
the Bété, a generic ethnonym for the social groupings in the western
part of the country. Because of the late colonization and the very difficult military pacification of this part of the territory, negative traits were
ascribed to its inhabitants.[18]

As the first region to be colonized by the French, where the first
school was opened, and where the new economic activities (cash crop
agriculture) developed and the new social elite promoted, the Agni-
dominated Southeast until the 1930s was the center of the country. Because of its "advanced" social structure and its high rank in the French
ethnic classification, the Agni exercised a form of leadership over the
rest of the African population. At the end of the 1930s, as the plantation
economy spread to the entire forest region in the central and western regions, the Southeast started to lose its leadership, and, just as the independence struggle and the formative moment of politics came to the
fore, the Baule replaced the Agni to advance the Akan leadership of
Côte d'Ivoire.

The construction of "ethnic reality" is an integral and important part
of the process of the invention of Côte d'Ivoire. Once its territorial
boundaries were drawn, the bipartition of the country resulted in the
opposition of the East to the West, contrary to the North/South antagonism usually observed in many neighboring states. But more important was the Ivorians' adoption and internalization of the values and
roles ascribed to them, legitimating the colonial representations and references. The colonial state made self-fulfilling prophecies, but it did not

create tribes senselessly as has been said.[19] Nor did it invent the values and roles attributed to different ethnic groups. Indeed, if the Ivorians fit so well into the social attire more or less designed for them by the colonizer, it is because they themselves provided the fabric.

## The Plantation: Economics and Social Legitimacy

The development of cash crop agriculture under colonization was a historic watershed that established both political cleavages and consensus in Côte d'Ivoire in the same sense as the different patterns of the commercialization of agriculture determined the political development of Europe.[20] More than colonization in its entirety, the development of a plantation economy was a critical juncture, a period of fundamental change that led to different reactions and roles for different ethnic groups and set the different regions of the country and their inhabitants on different paths to the "modern world."

A quick look at the literature on the plantation economy in Côte d'Ivoire[21] reveals the presence of all the elements in the definition of a critical juncture provided above.[22] First, if colonization in general brought fundamental social and economic change with the formation of new social groups expressing new demands, needs, and aspirations,[23] the system of the plantation economy generated specific demands for equal participation and benefits by the colonized. The resistance of the Europeans forged the bearers of those demands into a broadly based reform coalition.[24] Second, the change took place in distinct ways in different parts of the country because of ecological or natural factors (in the northern savanna region) on the one hand and cultural reasons (in the Southeast, Center, and West) on the other. The differential reactions of ethnic groups illustrate successful or unsuccessful accommodation to social change. But the reactions of the ethnic groups are distinct from those of the majority of the population in its infatuation with growing cashing crops. The former are part of the explanation of social asymmetry and unequal regional development, while the latter lay the basis for consensus on economic policy. Third, the consequences of the plantation economy can be observed not only in the economic backwardness of certain regions of the country but also in the politicization of "primordial ties" and in the freezing of the structure of political cleavages.

Standard analyses of the plantation economy in Côte d'Ivoire, following a path set by Samir Amin,[25] present it as a dependent, extroverted, enclave economy, a legacy of colonization. It is shown as a success story in the policy of "colonial improvement,"[26] the ancestor of today's "development." Recent studies, most of the time through a meticulous factual reconstitution, challenge many aspects of this picture.[27]

Approaches to the plantation economy highlighting the contradictions between the decisionmakers, the development makers, and the developed are far more fruitful than the picture popularized by Amin in his analysis of the development of capitalism in Côte d'Ivoire.[28] The recognition of multiple logics of the peasants, of individual or collective social strategies, and of the many levels where they are expressed helps one understand the gap between the colonial project of improvement and its final outcome.[29] First, the plantation economy was instrumental in creating social asymmetry and uneven regional development. It was also the main setting for the successful socialization of ethnic groups and the building of consensus on economic policy across the lines of ethnic cleavages.

Mainly because of the abilities of the Agni to accept economic innovations and their "advanced" social structure, which was oriented toward the accumulation of wealth, the Southeast became the first economic center of the territory.[30] The first important investments therefore were concentrated in this region, which benefited from better treatment in the implementation of the colonial constraints, mainly measures of exemption of forced labor.

The West, however, remained resistant to commercial agriculture because its inhabitants, pacified and colonized belatedly and with great difficulty, were considered "savages" or "barbarians."[31] Thus the colonial hardships (repression, forced labor) were here more draconian and led to the emigration of the inhabitants to the Southeast. In fact, the first indigenous cocoa and coffee plantations appeared in the extreme Southwest of the colony in Tabou's region by 1880. According to Jean-Pierre Chauveau, the plantation economy developed without administrative or foreign intervention in the so-called segmentary societies that had no centralized political power or organization and were reputed to be less advanced.[32] Colonial conquest, administrative intervention, and discrimination between the Southeast and Southwest then led to the marginalization and stagnation of the plantation economy in this area.

The North, while remaining at the periphery of the development of the plantation economy in the rain forest areas of the South, did participate in its own way because of the traditions of commerce and migration of its inhabitants. Tradesmen for the most part, they were hired by the planters and involved in cash crop agriculture. It was they, after the French and along with the Baule, who colonized the western part of the country.

This first phase of the development of the plantation economy, from 1910 to 1930, installed the Southeast in its dominant role. It set up the process of uneven development among the regions and established social asymmetry through the enrichment of many planters in the southeastern region.[33] Then, in the words of Jean-Pierre Dozon,"Ethnic significance became really operational, overloaded with the sense of that unequal structuring of Ivorian society. Manipulated by the colonial state, they [the planters] become the central figures in the Ivorian society in the process, mediating the entire global relationships (regional and social) in terms of ethnicity."[34]

At the end of the 1930s, the plantation economy started to spread to the entire forest region, and with the introduction of coffee, the Southeast slowly lost its leadership role. The rise of new economic centers in the Baule region (Center) and in the West polarized the country and increased the regional disparities and the social inequalities of the previous period. The North, still the reservoir of manpower, kept on disgorging its inhabitants into the other regions. In the West, the native populations, whose farming activities were smaller, became a dependent part of the plantation economy and were obliged to get along with the "alien" presence of the French.[35]

This second period was characterized by the rise in power and social visibility of a new ethnic actor, who not only altered the previous identifications and classifications but also shifted the course of Ivorian society. Although they were one-fifth of the entire population by 1900, the Baule were mentioned only as a subgroup of the Agni by Governor Delafosse. Their various reactions to the colonial situation did not allow them to be assigned roles and judgments like other ethnic groups. "In fact it is precisely this diversity of responses emanating from the Baule world, this polymorphism translatable with great difficulty in terms of the ethnic stereotype that was making itself apparent at the end of the 30's . . . that constituted from that moment on, the main moving force in the accelerated formation of an Ivorian civil society."[36] The diversity of Baule activities (trade, craftsmanship, agriculture, civil service) and social practices (migration and female exogamy), contributing to a strong demographic progression in the 1930s,[37] explain among other factors the peculiar contribution of the inhabitants of the center. In so doing, the Baule have long had an eminently national vocation, the more so since they have without a doubt and more than any other Ivorian ethnic groups, "symbolized the fast process of formation of an Ivorian civil society against the colonial state."[38]

The broad trends that appeared under colonization, the "original" inequalities between ethnic groups and regions, remain evident in the historical lead of some groups or the lag of others reinforced by independence. The other dimension in the legacy of the development of plantation economy that remained unchallenged over the years was the consensus on economic policy.

The differential reactions, behaviors, and social fate of distinct ethnic groups developed alongside the infatuation of the majority of the population with the growing of cash crops, another unexpected outcome. A measure of the rapid and thorough adaptation of a great number of Ivorians to the new economic roles can be seen through the increasing numbers of African planters—about 40,000 in 1944, 120,000 in 1956, and around 200,000 in 1959—and through their share in the production of coffee and cocoa. In 1942 the European planters were producing about 55 percent of coffee and 8 percent of cocoa; ten years later, only 6 percent and 4 percent. "Since 1947 Africans produced 90 percent or more of the coffee and cocoa exported."[39] Thus the plantation economy was not the privileged pasture of a minority. Members of both the traditional and educated elites were involved in the same farming activities, and the alliance of these two social groups helped determine the history of the country. The widespread acceptance of the new economic activities was based on the previous importance of agriculture in this natural setting but also on social and cultural factors.[40] With the development of cash crop agriculture, economic matters and material improvement quickly took precedence over the other preoccupations, so much so that many emerging conflicts have been mediated by economic exchanges. This trend was abetted by the economic boom of the 1950s, following the rise in commodity prices and the priority given to economic achievement over political reform. The "enrich yourselves" policy of Houphouët-Boigny—"If you don't want to vegetate in bamboo huts, concentrate your efforts on growing good cocoa and good coffee. They will fetch a good price, and you will become rich"—can be compared with the words of the first president of Ghana, Kwame

Nkrumah, "Seek ye first the political kingdom and all things else shall be added unto you."[41] The development of plantation economy thus led to a consensus on economic policy that is one of the sources of conservative politics in Côte d'Ivoire.

Most studies of the period from 1945 to 1980 and, more striking, analyses of the pluralist and competitive presidential, legislative, and municipal elections of 1990 miss this crucial characteristic of Ivorian polity and society.[42] In so doing they are missing the most interesting phenomenon of half a century of politics in many African countries, including Côte d'Ivoire, Algeria, Benin, Burkina Faso, Cameroon, Congo, Mali,[43] Ghana, Kenya, Niger, Nigeria, Togo, and Zaïre: the same freezing of the political cleavages with the "resurrection" of pre-independence political parties, as if political actors are resuming a competition stopped some thirty years ago.

### From Conflict to Consensus: 1945–65

In the words of French colonial administrator Governor Gabriel Louis Angoulvant, the first "pacification" took the form of military conquest completed by 1917. That led to social and political conflicts and unrest within the colonial territory and then in the independent state.[44] Because of the way demands were handled, conflict gave way to consensus between 1945 and 1965 in a "second pacification," where, unlike the first, the weapons were social, political, and economic. This consensus, which has lasted half a century, rested on the management of two different conflicts. One was between the colonial state and the population led by the planters over the demand for the recognition of the indigenous economy and polity (independence). The other, lasting and pervasive, was related to internal divisions and demands within the Ivorian society. As Chauveau rightly puts it, "In some ways, the victory of the RDA led by Houphouët-Boigny sanctioned the autonomy of the plantation economy from the colonizing action and its projects of development. From 1953 on, it was as much the colonial polity which chose to collaborate with the representative leaders of the indigenous plantation economy as the opposite."[45] As in Ghana and contrary to Cameroon, for example,[46] independence was "awarded" to the very political party that fought the most vigorously against the colonial administration, thus legitimizing the exercise of political power by the PDCI (Democratic Party of the Ivory Coast)–RDA (African Democratic

Rally). Both conflicts were of the same nature, political conflicts over incumbency rather than class conflicts. Their common nature also determined the general mode of conflict management in Côte d'Ivoire, through consensus built across ethnic and political cleavages around economic policy and a charismatic leader.

## Political Conflicts over Incumbency

The nature of the new Ivorian social and political community and the electoral opportunities provided to it by the French colonial system determined both the groups and their demands.[47] The groups involved the members of the modernizing elite enrolled in newly created social (cultural associations), professional (unions), and political (parties) organizations, and their demands focused on competition for administrative and political positions available in the territorial institutions, that is, the competition for the control of the structures of allocation of resources and rewards. The allocation of resources, or what has been called the "politics of distribution," has been the key to the management of conflict among groups and their demands in Côte d'Ivoire; it was the backbone of governance because it was the most important way "to retain their allegiance and participation in the national political system."[48] Administrative and political careers became attractive and lucrative and, after education, represented the first sources of social mobility. Political position constituted the main access to economic resources.[49]

After World War II, the social elite[50] produced by the socioeconomic transformations induced by the French colonial system had three components: the traditional elites—old chieftaincies or new creations of the French administration; economic elites—planters, traders, and so on; and educated elites—"evolués" or "lettrés." The three groups vied for power in pre-independence electoral competition through the Progressive and Democratic political parties.

The conflict between Democrats and Progressives, however, was not grounded on varying social bases of the political organizations. Contrary to some catchall explanations, there was no "planters bourgeoisie" opposed to a stratum of intellectuals.

Indeed, the party most closely linked to the agrarian or landed bourgeoisie because of its origins in the African Agricultural Syndicate (SAA) was also made of "lettrés," some of them being at the same time planters. And the traditional elite, notably in the Southeast, provided a strong support for the Progressive Party (PPCI), whereas the African Socialist Movement (MSA) found its support in the West. This double membership of the leaders of the PDCI, usually absent in many analyses, must be stressed, because their belonging to the educated elite (very often before becoming planters) had more influence than is suggested by the emphasis on the planters.[51] Moreover, despite the social profile drawn from the leadership, members of the parties were recruited without great distinction in the different social strata, all the more so since the social bases of the parties combined with other factors such as ethnic origins.

The cleavage between Democrats and Progressives from 1946 to 1950 is not reducible to an opposition between planters and intellectuals, such as the conflict at the same time in the neighboring Gold Coast between the "verandah boys" and the "lounge boys."[52] The first symbolized the rather pejorative way in which members of the educated elite, personalized by political leaders J. B. Danquah and K. A. Busia, named the less educated or illiterate followers of Kwame Nkrumah. The latter and his constituency used "verandah boys" as a title of glory, opposing it to the "lounge boys" or "been-tos" in three-piece suits whose behaviors have been well described in works such as Ayi Kwei Armah's *The Beautiful Ones Are Not Yet Born* and Bernard Dadié's *Monsieur Thogô-Gnini*.[53] In Ghana, this distinction was "class" based and has structured the Ghanaian political life ever since, with the alternation in power of the two political currents analyzed in chapter 4.[54] Contrary to the Ghanaian situation, in Côte d'Ivoire the conflict over demands from Democrats and Progressives lacked sociological foundation and resulted in political cleavage and paradoxical positions. On the basis of their programs, action, and relationships with the colonial administration, the political parties were divided into two antagonistic groups. The PDCI was against the colonial administration, and the other political parties worked with it. Political life was structured into two currents, nationalist-reformist and conservative-assimilationist. The positions are quite the opposite of those suggested by the apparent logic of the distinction between planters and intellectuals.

The reasons for this anomaly can be found in the short-term concerns and the long-term goals of the two groups. Because it originated in a trade union, the African Agricultural Syndicate (SAA), the PDCI had a program of demands based on the defense of the interests of its

most numerous members, the planters, interests upon which the institution of forced labor infringed significantly. Hence the Democrats were
involved in an overt conflict with the colonial administration for two
main reasons. First, their actions were aimed at stopping the inequalities and discrimination between European and African planters regarding their access to manpower. On the basis of their corporatist or trade
unionist claims, Democrats asked for reforms to improve the material
conditions of the major part of the population, the peasants who were
more and more committed to export agriculture. Second, the relationships with the colonial administration worsened after 1948 because of
the PDCI alliance with the French Communist Party (PCF) when the
latter was no longer a member of the French government. The Democrats in fact did not call into question the colonial system; they only
called for a reorientation on certain points, hence their reformism.

The reformism of the PDCI was rooted in its members' acculturation,
in a larger sense, and their quick assimilation of the new economic and
social norms, largely determined by the fact that its leaders were members of the educated elite. But more important was the absorption of
the new economic and social deal by the majority of the population, the
cultural reasons of which are yet to be described and understood. The
achievement of the Democrats' program of reforms, symbolized in 1946
by the abolition of forced labor, was the starting point for their tremendous popularity and that of their president, Houphouët-Boigny. However, it was also a clear indication of a major tactical change—the end of
conflictual political action, the need to have better relationships with
the colonial administration, and inevitably, the reexamination of the
political alliance with the PCF. By then the positions of the Democrats
began to appear closer to, if not undifferentiated from, those of their
adversaries.

The political parties opposed to the PDCI between 1946 and 1950
were characterized by their deep affection for France, their deep-rooted
anticommunism, and their defense of the colonial status quo. They had
an elitist conception of political action, evidenced by the niceties of their
electoral discourse, which was the language of a tiny elite and was very
far from the concerns of the large majority of the population.[55] This elitism also had links with the social features of the region of the country
that was the first to be colonized.[56] But the intellectual structure of the
Democrats was not very different from that of the Progressives. Moreover, pro-French elitism does not mean a lack of concern for the condi-

tion of the masses; were it not for the long lead of the SAA in 1944 through its cooperation with the PDCI, the creation of the Syndicate of African Planters and Herders of Côte d'Ivoire in 1946 by the Progressives could have resulted in corporatist demands made by the planters and herders as interest groups.

Similarities between the political parties were more important and outnumbered their differences. On one hand, the leaders belonged to the same segments of the social elite and their members were recruited in the same social groups. As a matter of fact, some parties were created by renegades of the PDCI. On the other hand, none of these parties really called into question the colonial system in its general framework. The PDCI's closer collaboration with the colonial administration meant in turn the end of colonial support for its opponents. Furthermore, the overall coalition strategy first used by the PDCI in the municipal elections of August 1945 in Abidjan with the creation of the "African bloc" was capped by the promise of political offices. These two factors exhausted the most implacable opponents who faced the alternative of collaborating or retiring from politics.

Within the core ethnic group of the social elite, however, conflict did develop at the same time over the question of which of the two main branches of the Akan group, Agni or Baule, should have the political leadership. This issue was settled in favor of the Baule through the electoral opportunities provided by the colonial system and the creation of political parties in the mid-1940s. Houphouët-Boigny's victory in 1945 and again in 1946 was the political translation of the social hegemony of an ethnic group. Thereafter, conflict rose to the territorial (national) level where it took another dimension because of what was at stake, the leadership of the would-be independent state. It turned from an intraelite into an anticolonial struggle, resulting in the delegitimization of the colonial state.

## Consensus across Lines of Cleavage

In a colony and would-be independent state with artificial boundaries, an ethnically heterogeneous population, and varying effects of the European presence and action, it was inevitable that the bedrock of politics would be the ability to build coalitions among various demand-bearing groups.

The first generations of political leaders, led by Houphouët-Boigny, were convinced of the necessity of this approach to politics, even though rapid changes in the colonial society, sharp differences in conceptions of leadership, and personal and communal rivalries in the new social elite and in the society at large made coalition difficult. The process of coalition building began rather early, prior to 1945 through voluntary associations,[57] and then, after 1945 to 1959, through political parties.[58] Thus, at an early stage of political life, alliances and conflicts of groups and personalties took form during critical elections, which brought about the freezing of the political alignments.

Voluntary associations were the first expression of alliances across ethnic lines. By their names (Association for the Defense of the Native Interests of Côte d'Ivoire, ADIACI; Fraternal Union of the Natives of Côte d'Ivoire, UFOCI; Bété Mutuality; Union of the Natives of the Six Circles of the West, UOCOCI), by the places where they have been created (Southeast, Center, and West), and by the ethnic background of their members (Agni, Baule, and Bété), the voluntary associations were the institutional translation of social processes and economic dominance. Each expressed social and regional inequalities, the history of colonization, the nascent national and regional consciousness, and varying involvement in the making of the new Ivorian space.

The creation of the SAA indicated a new and essential step in this process since it marked the recognition of the indigenous plantation economy by the colonial state. The SAA, by its name, vocation and objectives, and membership and leaders, was a microcosm of Côte d'Ivoire's composite histories. First it was an illustration of uneven regional development, confirming the bipartition of the country into East and West, roughly a region of small farming interests and one of larger ones, and of social and income inequalities. It crystalized ethnic and regional identities and expressed the shift of the dominant economic and social center to the heartland of the country and the "Baulization" of Ivorian society, following the cleavage within the Akan group. Under the leadership of the Akan in the Center and Southeast, the SAA stood for particular interests in the name of the general interest, demanding the abolition of forced labor and the system of "indigénat," and independence. If pushed to the extreme, one could say that a movement, which embodied the "general" interest and fought for the emancipation of the entire population, explains to a large extent the strategy of the one-party system. Thus the voluntary associations have been at the origins of political organizations in Côte d'Ivoire.[59]

Analysts of social change in different parts of the world have studied the impact of the initial incorporation of the masses into national political life.[60] The seminal work of Ruth Berins Collier has rightly stressed the importance of the rate and sequence of the introduction of mass electoral participation in Africa and assessed the extent to which it was supportive or destabilizing of existing political, economic, and social relations.[61] The sudden incorporation of the politically active part of the population into the territorial political life between 1945 and 1960 contributed to the freezing of the political cleavages and the institutionalization of existing demand-bearing groups.[62]

Right from the beginning, party and electoral politics constituted strategic political resources that the members of the social elite successfully exploited to their own advantage. Competition for scarce political positions led to divisions within the Ivorian society. It also, in spite of the colonial situation, provided the opportunity for the political expression of the dominant social legitimacy that had developed within the plantation economy. Thus social position and political power were linked. The August 26, 1945, municipal elections in Abidjan won by the anticolonial front, the "African bloc," were a significant example of coalition building among groups by Houphouët-Boigny in the pre-independence period.[63] Weiskel has rightfully summed up the lessons to be learned from this experience for an understanding of the political development of Côte d'Ivoire since 1945:

From this very first campaign, a pattern of electoral politics developed in the Ivory Coast that was to characterize in its essentials all the subsequent elections in the territory to the present day. The overwhelming feature of political activity was that it proceeded structurally from the top downward, that is, from the elite toward the dissatisfied masses and from Abidjan toward the hinterland. It is important to emphasize that the first territorial election was fought prior to the creation of a political party. Indeed, the creation of an organized political movement to represent popularly based sentiment was not foremost in the minds of the politically active African elite. The essential goal was to win the legislative seat. The means to that goal was one of mobilizing groups that already existed in the urban and small town constituencies to vote as a united bloc in favor of a selected candidate. Questions of ideological consistency or class interests were not uppermost in anyone's mind. What mattered most was mustering a strategic set of alliances that would last until the vote was counted.[64]

The most important dimension of this experience is the nonideological, pragmatic, flexible, incremental, and all-inclusive approach to politics, a feature that partly explains the post–1945 political development and the survival of the so-called parties of the left into the new political era. "The building up of a heterogeneous coalition in which components retain their distinctive identity" made the would-be political entrepreneurs and the leader of the SAA aware of the necessity of coalition building.[65] Again and again they tried to replay the strategy of the African bloc in the creation of political parties in the following elections.[66] This strategy has consequently helped determine consensus across party lines. The lack of a basis for association and of preexisting networks of groups to be mobilized accounts for the weakness of political parties other than the PDCI and the PPCI before independence. It also explains the weakness of those created since 1990.

The number of candidates (fourteen) in the first round of the elections for a representative of the territory to the first constituent assembly on October 21, 1945, indicated the great competitiveness of the race and illustrated a pervasive infatuation with politics. The leader of the SAA appeared to be in the best position to win the elections, but he had to stand again at a second ballot to do so, as he did again in the elections to the second constituent assembly in 1946. Houphouët-Boigny's victory, to which the UOCOCI contributed, also meant the loss of the Southeast's hold on the leadership of the colony and its shift within the Akan group from the Agni to the Baule.

The parties' strong regional roots (PPCI in the Southeast, PDCI–RDA in the center, and MSA in the West) were the political expression of the internal socioeconomic divisions of the Ivorian population. In most cases ethnicity was the most salient source of conflict and voting "behavior of the mass of rank-and-file citizens."[67] However, several studies of the Ivorian political enterprises, particularly the PDCI–RDA, have shown ethnicity, though it mattered a great deal, was not the only influence on political activity.[68] Ideology, the anticommunism of the PPCI, socioeconomic asymmetry, and uneven regional development (in the case of the MSA) were also important.[69]

Along with the 1945 municipal elections in Abidjan, six out of the ten territorial elections from 1945 to 1959 were decisive for the party alignments in Côte d'Ivoire for the next half century. They included the 1945 and 1946 elections to the French constituent assemblies; the November 10, 1946, election for the first indigenous representatives to the French national assembly; and the December 1946 election to the General Council of Côte d'Ivoire. Other decisive events were an alliance of demand-bearing groups, such as the alliance with UOCOCI in the constituent assembly elections; the electoral alliance of the PDCI with the PCF during the June 17, 1951, elections to the French national assembly, or the Union for the Economic Development of Côte d'Ivoire (UDECI), sponsored by the PDCI for the March 30, 1952, election to the territorial assembly; and the 1954 municipal elections. These alliances caused some leaders and voters to leave their previous political homes and form new attachments, sometimes with such emotional force as to weaken the cohesion of the resulting coalitions, mainly in the territorial assembly, where the PDCI lost the majority between 1947 and 1949.[70] The same circumstances also highlighted the growing success of coalition building between 1952 and 1957.[71]

The outcome of the 1951 elections to the French national assembly and the 1952 elections to the territorial assembly were important measures of the voters' realignments on the PDCI. At that time eight of the prominent and most outspoken leaders of the PDCI were in prison, following their arrest after demonstrations in Abidjan on February 6, 1949.[72] The first renewal of the territorial assembly in March 1952 was critical for two main reasons. First, the electoral campaign was the perfect illustration of the high-level mastery of the strategy of coalition building through the UDECI in a rather difficult context.[73] Second, the outcome—twenty-eight seats out of thirty-two for the UDECI coalition with 72 percent of the valid votes cast, and leading opponents defeated in their home constituencies—revealed the strength of voters' allegiance. This phenomenon was confirmed by the outcomes of the January 2, 1956, elections to the French national assembly and the March 30, 1957, elections to the territorial assembly. These were the first territorial elections on the basis of universal suffrage, and the PDCI won fifty-eight out of sixty seats.[74]

The reasons for freezing party alignments, the persistence of political cleavages, and the success of coalition building are complex. First, the process of party formation is rather nonideological. Political enterprises, when officially authorized in 1946, were the mere political expression of the structures of social domination. The overlapping social bases of the parties, as already noted, restricted the parties' ability to pursue radical policies consistent with their dominant ideologies. The "disalliance" from the PCF played an important role in the building of consensus across party lines because it meant the end of ideology and a subsequent depoliticization after 1950 in Côte d'Ivoire.[75] But paradoxically, electioneering also encouraged the formation of the one-party system because leaders of the parties learned (because of what was at stake) that the most important thing is winning, not participating. Since the end justifies the means, it is good to receive 99.99 percent of the valid votes or even to run without any opponents in order to become the unique "valid interlocutor." This dimension in the creation of one-party systems has seldom been taken into account, although, generally speaking, how political cleavages were affected by the changes in the legal and administrative framework for political activity has been well documented by the literature.[76] The freezing of the structure of political cleavages also benefited from a consensus, an "agreement on fundamentals," which has lasted for more than half a century. The first fundamental concerned economic policy and the politics of distribution, in other words, the infatuation with cash crop economy to provide tangible benefits to key components of the social elite, made possible by economic growth. The second fundamental was the legitimacy of the charismatic leader, based on his skills, his "personal equation" (to quote Général de Gaulle), and his historical role as founder of the RDA enhanced by the same politics of distribution.

The strategy of coalition building has important implications for governance because it constitutes the key to balance between demands and allocations. The resulting consensus across ethnic and political lines provided solid foundations for the control and the participation of demand-bearing groups by retaining their allegiance to, and participation in, the national political system.

But consensus and coalition are not unanimity. Despite its success, the Ivorian system of conflict management still faced crises. Because of the nature of the demand structure (actors, issues, modes of action), the monolith built through coalitions was naturally heterogeneous. Because the main foundation of the allocation mechanism was economic growth, shortfalls between conflictive demands and allocations could take place. Crisis can originate in the demand or the allocation structure or both. The crises in Côte d'Ivoire have their roots in its particular system of governance, but their occurrence did not invalidate the techniques of coalition building.

The first crisis occurred in the midst of the ongoing process of depoliticization and demobilization brought about by successful coalition and election when the youngest members of the educated elite tried to voice their demands and assert their claims to leadership. Caught between and within the Democrats and the Progressives, a new breed of political leaders who emerged at the end of the 1950s attempted to challenge the old political generation. Despite their efforts, the youth did not succeed in building up a third distinct current; the new social generation of the moment did not bring about a new political generation, a failure frequently repeated in Ivorian politics.

At the end of the 1950s, the transformation of a social category into a movement vying for power, in Côte d'Ivoire as in many other African countries, was quite predictable, as was its failure to overthrow the first generation of leaders. Young adults then and now constitute a very large part of the total population, and the improvement and lengthening of the academic curriculum and the availability of scholarships for study in French high schools and universities after World War II led to the birth of a new generation of intellectuals.[77] At the end of the conflictual period of the PDCI in the early 1950s, the first university graduates began to enter the job market in numbers, expecting to replace their elders. They based their claim to govern on their higher level of education and accused their elders of treason for collaborating with the French. The elders expected them to cooperate under the established leadership and without ideological dispute. The high point of the crisis was the election of Jean-Baptiste Mockey as secretary general at the third PDCI congress in March 1959 and his forced resignation in September. The new leaders' integration into the political elite quickly turned into a generational conflict, which did not end until the brutal crisis of 1963–64 during which many young leaders were arrested, tried, and imprisoned.[78]

The collective behavior of the intellectuals of the second-generation youth was quixotic. Their attempt to replace the elders failed at the political and the ideological level: they did not have the numbers, their ideological and political postures were running against the dominant trends in society, and they lacked the necessary social backing for their demands. Technical competence does not mean social support to rule. The elders, although less educated, were better entrenched socially, politically, and economically and were in a position to maintain their leadership and to determine the course of the political life.

The 1959 civil servants' strike,[79] the attempts at secession by the

Sanwi in the Southeast,[80] and the contrived "plots" that constituted the 1963–64 crises[81] illustrate further conflicts challenging the newly established coalition and consensus, conflicts that straddled the independence date (1960) and marked the end of the first political period. Conflict with the trade unionists and the youth, the university students, on the issue of independence was a new development. The "disalliance" with the PCF meant colonial collaboration and the end of anti-French activity and was the cause of a new circumstantial cleavage. Later that developed into a conflict over immediate versus delayed independence, the advocates of "no" versus those of "yes" in the referendum of September 1958. The choice made by the PDCI in 1958 was postponement, not rejection, of independence. The outcome of the 1963–64 crisis was the result of the interaction of foreign events (because of the cycle of instability opened up in 1963 by the coup d'état and assassination of Sylvanus Olympio in Togo) and of legitimate ambitions and personal rivalries among potential successors to the president. Its main outcome, the imprisonment and even death of those who were called "the brightest and best of Côte d'Ivoire," was the clarification of the relations of force within the political leadership. After 1965, more strongly than in the previous two decades, Houphouët-Boigny became the sole kingmaker, the only crocodile in the swamp (following the folk saying that "there are not two crocodiles in a swamp"), thus modifying fundamentally the structures and process of conflict management. The "ideological mortgage" hanging over from the alliance with the French communists was lifted (an ideological cleansing), and independence from France put an end to polarization over the issue, even if the way in which independence was granted ("halfheartedly") did not provide ideological satisfaction to the left of the social elite. It meant the total political and ideological victory of the conservatives and the failure of the radicals.

    The 1963–64 conflict was a systemic crisis, one that threatened the constitution of the polity and its established rules of the game for allocating authority and rewards. It destroyed the position of the second generation of political leaders, all members of the incumbent coalition. The outcome of the crisis was a structural change, "a fundamental change in regime that alters the institutional power balance among the contenders."[82] The fourth congress of the PDCI-RDA, the first after independence, had been postponed many times, but it was convened in 1965, shortly after the crisis, a sign of the birth of a new regime and power balance.

Exile, detention, intimidation, death, diverse forms of violence, repression, and political prophylaxis (such as the modification of the electoral code to make competition impossible or very costly for competitors) characterized the crisis.[83] Presidential pardon and reconciliation and the granting of high political or administrative positions were also taking place.[84] This "use of coercion during the periods of crisis and movement in a more liberal direction when the regime has regained confidence illustrate the shift from power to force observable in many African countries in the early 1960s."[85] Rulers, however, did not "abandon completely their reliance on the techniques of machine politics to maintain themselves in office."[86]

The 1959 and 1963–64 crises in Côte d'Ivoire exemplified the handling of crises perpetrated by demand-bearing groups. The results contributed to the consensus on governance by shifting attention from the strategies of allocation to the structures of accountability and authority. The old techniques of coalition building were shown to be adequate and effective. But the momentary shift from power to violence as a way of managing these conflicts simply suppressed them, relieving or subduing their symptoms. The two issues of allocation and authority remained and structured the post–1965 Ivorian polity and society.

## From Consensus to Conflict: 1965–90

Besides continuing the modernization of the society, the rulers during this second period primarily wanted to extend and enhance their control over all aspects of the social and political life of the country.[87] They succeeded. The modernization of the society, by African standards, has been effective, thanks to the rates of sustained economic growth, as shown in chapter 2, from the 1950s through the 1970s. The control over all aspects of life in the country and the monopoly of the political activities were a reality until 1990 in spite of many social and political conflicts. The return to multipartyism in 1990 put an end to the "consensus" reached by Ivorians on the ways they wanted to be governed. Why and how did this significant political change occur? Was 1990 another systemic crisis, and why and how did it come about? Was it resolved by a return to the previous equilibrium, as occurred after the crisis of 1963–64? Can the origins of the crisis be traced to long-term and short-term changes in the domestic and international environment?

In any political system, important environmental changes (domestic and international) bring about changes in the structure and composition of political demands. Although the international environment played an important role in the genesis of the crisis because of the economic and cultural extraversion of the country, domestic factors have been most influential. Yet the roots of the crisis at the end of the period were in the system of governance itself. As the number of demand-bearing groups increased and resources became scarce, the resulting mismatch between demands and allocations led to the crisis of 1990.

## The Primacy of Politics: Power and Wealth

Houphouët-Boigny's "eternal presence" in politics at the highest level since 1945 was the guarantor and symbol of continuity in the political system. The second period (1965–90) was characterized by continuities in the way resources and rewards were allocated and conflicts managed. Houphouët-Boigny was also the living symbol of the freezing of the demand structure, of continuities in the nature of the demand-bearing groups despite their increasing size, resulting in the petrification of the winning coalition. He epitomized the "investor politician." His wealth, whatever the origins of his fortune, and his notorious generosity, an important aspect of the politics of distribution and a constitutive dimension of African traditional rulership, typify the coincidence of political and economic power.[88] They explain why social actors during this second period were still competing for the same resources (political or administrative positions in order to get access to material resources). Conflicts remained conflicts over incumbency.

Houphouët-Boigny was moreover the principal architect of the two major processes that have generated the Ivorian stability through the management of conflict. On one hand, the self-aggrandizement of the heterogeneous monolith dictated by the desire of the rulers to retain power has been sustained by successful enculturation—the population's internalization of the values promulgated by the rulers—and by the politics of distribution, which benefited from the high rates of economic growth. Paradoxically, on the other hand, this process of social regeneration and enlargement contributed to the permanence of the demand-bearing groups begun under the French colonization and to the freezing and the reproduction of the structure and composition of their political demands.

State intervention in the economy in Côte d'Ivoire as in many African countries was dictated by the lack of domestic capital and investors. In spite of its liberal and capitalist option and the existence of a private sector, the Ivorian state became a major economic actor through the development of a more dynamic and important public sector of the economy than in officially socialist countries. As the state represented a resource in itself, its control was equivalent to the control of the economy. Political competition became competition for economic resources, just as economic allocation was used to manage political corruption. The modest origins of the leaders made conflicts over the control of political position the only door to economic resources, in Côte d'Ivoire as in Ghana next door, in Nigeria further away, and across West (and Central) Africa.

Unequal access to power and the politics of distribution are reflected not only in social inequalities but also in uneven regional development, increasing ethnoregional demands, growing sophistication of ethnic arithmetic, and interest representation, which have characterized the post–1965 period.[89] The construction of the sugar complexes in the northern part of the country exemplifies the politics of distribution to meet ethnoregional demands, reduce the gap among regions, and at the same time retain the allegiance and the participation of the region in the national political system even if the project has been an economic failure.[90]

But the best example of the conflicts over incumbency during this second period of the political life has been political succession, not only at the national but also at the regional level. The question "After Houphouët-Boigny, who?" dates back to the day he was elected to the first French constituent assembly in 1946. It remained a hidden issue during the 1959 crisis with the resignation of Mockey and during the "plots" of 1963–64.[91] The issue was publicly raised for the first time by the president himself in 1965 during the first congress of the PDCI after independence. From that time on, it gained prominence and became a dominant political issue.

Houphouët-Boigny's personality and long political career, his charisma, and the role he played in the history of his own country and of West Africa explain the importance of the issue. The strategies of political survival he used, the successive episodes of the problem, the ups and downs of potential heirs, and the possible scenarios since 1965 are fully documented and need not be recalled in detail.[92] What needs to be stressed is how, within the framework of a personally ruled, depoliticized, one-party state, individual rivalries and competition became the basis for temporary political cleavages. Indeed, the long story of the po-litical succession in Côte d'Ivoire is that of natural and legitimate per-sonal ambitions and rivalries. It is also the story of social cleavages and coalition building, political alignments, disalignments, and realign-ments that occurred with the rise and fall of successive potential heirs or "*présidentiables*."[93]

In the 1950s, rivalries among the three main lieutenants of the presi-dent—Jean-Baptiste Mockey, Auguste Denise, and Philippe Grégoire Yacé—were notorious, until Mockey emerged as heir apparent. A "hero and martyr of the RDA," Mockey by 1959 was vice prime minister and minister of interior, assuming interim power as president when the president was out of the country and becoming political secretary of the PDCI. Mockey, perceived as "radical" by the French, was very close to, if not the leader of, the young intellectuals who challenged the leader-ship of the founding fathers at the end of the 1950s and who supported him in his election as the secretary general against the will of the presi-dent. This dimension has been part of the explanation of Mockey's elimination from the race in 1959, when he resigned from all his politi-cal functions.[94]

After 1965, when Yacé, president of the national assembly since 1959, deputy secretary general of the PDCI in 1959 and acting secretary gen-eral after Mockey's resignation, was confirmed in this position by the congress of the party, he became the heir apparent. In 1966 a challenger emerged in the person of a young minister of economy and finances, Henri Konan Bédié. In the early 1970s the coalitions supporting each of the two pretenders were engaged in feuds behind the scenes and an ideological tone was added to mark the cleavage: Yacé was said to be pro-French and nationalist, while Bédié was perceived as pro-American, mainly because he was ambassador to the United States in the early 1960s.

The next steps were marked by disalignments and realignments from one coalition to another. Two episodes occurred to the benefit of Yacé when he became the constitutional heir in 1975, following an amendment to article 11 of the constitution, and again in 1977, when Bédié was fired from the government. A major reshuffling of political alignments occurred around the political reforms introduced in 1980. New semicompetitive elections, elimination of the position of secretary general, and an amendment to article 11 of the constitution, resulted in the elimination of Yacé from the presidential race. However, Bédié's election to the presidency of the national assembly in 1980 put him for the first time in the position of heir apparent. His reelection in 1985 and 1990 and the new amendments (1985, 1986, 1990) to article 11 improved his position. But lacking the political might that the position of secretary general of the PDCI conferred on Yacé, his hold was not ensured and he had to face many challengers, among whom were the former mayor of Abidjan, Emmanuel Dioulo, and the prime minister, Alassane Ouattara. From 1980 to 1990, the system of realignments developed into a liberal-conservative cleavage within the PDCI. The liberals rallied behind Bédié and were open to a further democratization of the political system, while the conservative group surrounding leading figures like former ministers Camille Alliali and Jean Konan Banny were perceived as less favorable to this process.

The return to political pluralism in 1990 opened a new cycle of disalignments and realignments on the basis of political and ideological postures illustrated by the existence of forty political parties in 1992. These new cleavages brought important changes in the issue of the political sucession; for instance, the choice of a successor to Houphouët-Boigny moved from the national agenda to that of each political party. In fact, the bipolarization of the presidential election between Houphouët-Boigny and Laurent Gbagbo in October 1990 was fortuitous, and the electoral campaign indicated the high degree of the personalization of the race and the continuing importance of conflicts over incumbency. The outcome—nearly 20 percent of the votes going to Gbagbo of the Ivorian Popular Front (FPI)—revealed the permanence of cleavages dating back to the pre-independence competitive elections.

## The Self-Aggrandizement of the Heterogeneous Monolith

To retain power, the elite needed to garner more support in a process of self-aggrandizement, a key to the understanding of political stability and social peace in Côte d'Ivoire and also of the 1990 crisis and the ensuing political change. The self-aggrandizement of the winning coalition was based on a general system of cooptation of representatives of various demand-bearing groups, whether ethnic or socioprofessional, into the political and administrative elite. Leaders of key and potentially challenging groups were recruited and turned into "president's men." Great care had been taken since the early 1960s to meet the claims of different ethnic groups to representation in the political elite, but at the same time to make their representatives accountable only to the president, not to their natural constituency. The usual strategy was to select someone not really representative of his group, for example a person of inferior traditional social status, or a young, educated unknown. Then the new leader, aware of his low representativeness, could not claim a strong social basis of his own to retain or challenge power, but neither could the ethnic group object that it was not represented in the elite.

The incorporation of new members into the political and administrative elite has been timely and gradual, for example, following an effective threat (the military after 1973), anticipating a potential one (the third generation of intellectuals, born after World War II, in 1980) or filling an obvious lacuna with a neglected group (women in 1976). Violent measures of exclusion (exile, imprisonment, suicide) were sometimes used between 1958 and 1964, but after 1965 the renewal and the enlargement of the political elite were made by the replacement of leaders who died, by the slow Ivorization of positions occupied by expatriates, by the creation of new political and administrative positions, or by the nomination of new candidates for elections after 1980.[95]

If measured only by the number of the members of the main political institutions (government, national assembly, Economic and Social Council, the two ruling institutions of the PDCI), the rate of cooptation was rather slow between 1957 (the creation of the first local executive body) and 1965 (the first PDCI congress after independence). It gained full speed in 1965–66 and reached its maximum height ten years later, in 1975–76. Indeed by this time, with 36 ministers (14 in 1961 and 18 in 1966), 120 members of Parliament (70 in 1960, 85 in 1965), 70 members in the Economic and Social Council (20 in 1961, 36 in 1965), 71 members in the Political Bureau (15 in 1959, 26 in 1965), and 201 members in the Steering Committee (28 in 1959, 60 in 1965), the Ivorian political class was equivalent to the country's entire social register. Almost all ethnic and socioprofessional groups of importance had representatives in the political elite. Moreover, the uniformity of the levels and modes of recruitment for many years by the same kingmaker, the modest social background of the members of the political elite, their values and beliefs, intermarriages, and many other social interactions resulted in a homogeneity that explains why the ruling group did not split, as was the case in Ghana, Nigeria, and many other African countries, at the moment of democratization.

This process of self-aggrandizement benefited from sustained rates of economic growth from the 1950s through the 1970s (see chapter 2).[96] The continuous expansion of the economic pie during this period was crucial for the precedence of social and material achievement over political concerns, the consensus on economic policy, the increasing number of political entrepreneurs, and the consolidation of webs of patron–client relations to garner support to retain power. The translation of the important economic resources at the disposal of the rulers into political resources brought political stability and for the moment contributed again to economic growth. But in the longer run, political stability and the distributional coalition were part of the cause of economic inefficiency.

The politics of distribution to build coalitions and manage conflicts used two simultaneous and complementary channels, an expanded civil service and growing welfare services, leading to the relative autonomy of the state.[97] The first and major concern of the incumbents upon independence was to create an adequate apparatus and then to expand it as an allocative resource, measurable in the successive fragmentation of the ministries. The Ministry of Education was divided into four ministries, the Ministry of Agriculture into three, and so on. Consequently, offices and public services multiplied, and an important and dynamic public sector developed in the economy. To provide access to economic resources, as many positions as possible were created not only in the political institutions (500 in the mid-1970s) but also in the civil service (92,000 in 1980) and in the public sector of the economy. State-owned enterprises grew to 266 in 1979, employing 43,000 people.[98] As in any other African country, the control of public enterprises became an important part of the power structure, although contrary to many African economic experiences, the state was not in charge of the entire economy.[99] Rent-seeking positions were created in the private sector (agriculture and commerce, for example).

The politics of distribution then underlay the expansion of public expenditures for health, education, and welfare, a "welfare shift" by African standards, and an important ingredient in the crisis of the authoritarian state in 1990. Health care and welfare provided to the civil servants and their families through the "civil servants' insurance" and to the employees of the parastatals and the private sector and their families through the National Fund for Social Benefits have been sources of many abuses, leading in part to the crisis of the health care system in the 1980s.

An important part of conflict management through redistribution of income has been the proliferation of special statuses, according to the General Status of the Civil Service, which means higher salaries for specific categories of civil servants such as university and secondary school professors, magistrates, police, doctors, and others. Education as the "priority of priorities," with 40 percent of the total budget, has been another example of the allocative function of the state.[100] Students were totally spoiled by university scholarships for almost all secondary school graduates, room and board at extremely low prices, free busing, a high rate of scholarships for African students in France, and so on.[101] Furthermore, the teaching profession at primary, secondary, and university levels has been one of the most attractive in the country. Teachers receive higher salaries than civil servants with the same degree, and university professors receive free housing in the affluent suburb of Cocody. These material advantages have attracted hundreds of teachers and professors from throughout French-speaking West Africa.[102] The discontinuance of some of the material advantages provided to professors, such as free housing, the reduction of scholarships to students and suspension of free busing, and salary reductions for new recruits led to the university professors' strikes between 1980 and 1983 and to the long crisis and social unrest at the University of Abidjan between 1989 and 1993.[103]

## Freezing the Demand Structure

The second political period in Côte d'Ivoire (1965–90) was punctuated by social and political crises of demands from four crucial groups: students and youth in general (almost every year from 1968 to 1989), the military (1973), civil servants (1969, 1982–83, 1989–93), and women (1976). Fairly abundant scholarly literature centered on the state[104] has accounted for these social and political crises occurring between 1965 and 1990, as well as for the transformation of the Ivorian economy, social formations, and politics,[105] the changes in the nature of the demands, and conflicts ranging from "ethnic politics" to "interest politics."[106]

But how new were these categories of individuals in their preferences and resources, how challenging were they for the political order, and how systemic were the post–1965 crises? In other words, did "modernization," the chief goal and motto of the rulers, and the continuous process of urbanization, industrialization, literacy, education, and communication since the 1950s, create new social groupings available for political mobilization? Did it make changes in the distribution of political resources, leading to a shake-up of the resource pattern on which the rulers were based? A close look at these demand-bearing groups, within and outside the political system, their resources and preferences, their values and beliefs, shows that they are not new but merely the delayed effect and reproduction of the social formations produced by the colonial system.[107] The evolution of social formation has been nothing more than the expansion of the social statuses generated by the French colonial system.[108] Continuities rather than changes in the social formation are also documented by the debates about the state-society relationship and about the characterization of the dominant class interests (bureaucracy's or planters' bourgeois): who governs Côte d'Ivoire and to the benefit of whom?[109] Thus the postcolonial modernization of the society did not fundamentally transform the structure of society in Côte d'Ivoire.

However, industrialization, urbanization, communication, literacy, education, and economic growth induced and stimulated new forms of social mobilization and social behavior within the same structures. The burgeoning of religious sects (Celestial Christianity, Assembly of God, Jehovah's Witnesses, and so on), prayer groups, and fraternal or esoteric societies like the Rosicrucians was an important social factor of this period. Another was the blossoming of exclusive elitist clubs for women and men (Lions, Rotary, Rotaract, Soroptimist, Kiwanis, Young Chamber of Commerce, and so on) and investment clubs (The Financier). This busy association activity is related to the "show-off" way of life or "nouveaux riches" life-style of the elite. The Ivorian equivalent of the "yuppies," "golden boys," and "career women" (locally called "dynamic young cadres") pull down six-figure salaries. They live in the wealthiest areas of Abidjan (Cocody, Deux-Plateaux, Marcory résidentiel, and the Riviera) and drive Mercedes, BMWs, and Renault 25s. More recently, Japanese four-wheel-drive cars (Pajero, Patrol) are among their preferred social accessories.

Could these new forms of social mobilization be conducive to new forms of political mobilization? The modernization of the society did not generate really new preferences and resources to change the substance of the political issues in the first three decades of independence. In their fundamental principles, the overall structure and composition of political demands remained the same. The only major changes were the growing size of the demand-bearing groups and, by 1980, the cooptation or the election into the political elite of the heirs of the political leaders of the first generation.[110]

The natural increase in demands for political participation did not represent a qualitatively different demand; the new forms of social mobilization reinforced the existing distribution of preferences, and new resources were redistributed in the same way as before. The religious sects did not have a specific and collective political project and because of their atomistic nature could not be mobilized politically. As evidenced by their social behaviors and political attitudes, the youngest social generations could hardly be politically distinct from their predecessors because they were trained to share the predecessors' values and beliefs.[111]

This ideological homogenization, performed through the politics of distribution and through representation of the expanding heterogeneous monolith, has greatly benefited from the process of enculturation. The values promulgated by the leaders—liberal economic policy, prevalence of economic concerns, the search for "the well-being of the Ivorian man"—have been internalized by the population. Since the end of political activism in 1950 and the ensuing depoliticization, the recasting of the social value system to develop a new Ivorian has been a success. Schools, official press and documents, and social discourse, helped by the extraordinary cultural extroversion of the country, a logical corollary of its economic dependence on France and the West in general, have contributed decisively to the process of Westernization/Francization of the elite and the masses.[112]

The Ivorian value pattern finely analyzed by the sociologist Abdou Touré asserted the cultural dimension of political change. Traditions of subservience to authority existing in many precolonial societies have been enhanced by colonial rule and by "the culture of complaint." Ivorian value patterns can be defined as authoritarian, passive, differential, and traditional. Despite the lack of data from polls on public value systems similar to those used by Ronald Inglehart, it is apparent that Côte d'Ivoire did not experience dramatic changes in sociopolitical value orientations throughout the second period of its political life.[113] Nothing indicates that Ivorians have become less preoccupied with the materialist *"Attiéké poisson,"*[114] "the well-being of the Ivorian man," and the "bread and butter" issues of the old politics. Nor have Ivorians become more concerned with the postmaterialist "new politics" demands of democracy, participation, social equality, and environmental protection, among others. The old political values of law and order, economic growth, distribution, and ethnic rewards have prevailed over new political values of individual freedom, social equality, a nonmaterialist quality of life, and so on.

The success of the process of value formation is evidenced in the nature of conflicts and the social behaviors during this second phase of political life. The development of a "parallel polis" or counterculture was thus unlikely. Nonetheless, a gap exists between the dynamism of a society fueled by total openness to foreign culture and influences and the immobilism of the political microcosm, a gap very similar to that which existed under colonization before and shortly after World War II. It was an important dimension of the anticolonial struggle. The entire process of self-aggrandizement, the politics of distribution, and value formation resulted in the petrification of the political elite. A rather high level of elite homogeneity by African standards occurred with a powerful impact at the time of reform in 1990. The leaders succeeded in buying social and political peace for about three decades, but the main outcome of the increasing size of the demand-bearing groups was the incongruence between the demands and the allocation of resources and rewards, which led to the outburst of the 1990 economic protests.

## The Crisis of the Authoritarian Welfare State and the Return to Democracy

Although the rulers continued to rely on the same system of conflict management through allocation, the incongruence between the system's demand and allocation structures led predictably to the crisis of 1990. The genesis of the crisis can be traced to the mistakes in the management of the economy, the slowing of the rates of economic growth, and the worsening of the world economic crisis, which could no longer support the distributional and expansionist logic of coalition building.[115] The quick passage from economic protest to political demands around the themes of multipartyism and democracy marks an intensification of conflict and its conversion from "issues having to do with the legitimacy of the allocation of rewards into the general issue of the legitimacy of the authority structure itself."[116]

The international environment since the mid-1970s induced and stimulated domestic social and political mobilization by becoming less favorable to economic growth and at the same time more favorable to procedural protests and democratization. To a country that is a cultural extrovert, the major changes in the marketplace of ideological values brought on by the collapse of communist regimes increased the intensity of political demands, generated new preferences and resources (social movements and mobilization of friends, financial means, and public opinion and allies abroad) and so expanded political opportunities for groups with new demands and conflicts.[117] For a moment a new demand structure seemed to emerge spontaneously, leading to polarization over governance.

The deterioration of the economic situation in Côte d'Ivoire has its index in the growing number of jobless school leavers and young intellectuals, compared with the previous full employment that was assured for many years for graduates. The informal sector of the economy has grown through the blossoming of the "little jobs," such as public parking keepers, windshield cleaners, fresh water sellers, and the more unusual footwashers during the rainy season.[118] Economic decline, following a long period of improvement, has been the main cause of the social unrest and political change in Côte d'Ivoire.[119] Indeed people took to the streets in the winter of 1990 at the official announcement of salary reductions by the president.

The worsening of the economic crisis reached the core of the Ivorian system of governance, the politics of allocation. The rapidly expanding economic pie that was used to meet citizens' demands from the 1950s to the 1970s started to shrink at the end of the 1970s. The political compromise worked out at the time of independence was less and less bearable, and opposition and conflict mounted to unprecedented levels to reach a political boiling point.

There may be several explanations for the conversion of the economic crisis into political change. De Toqueville points to the importance of frustration produced by previous periods of economic growth. Present economic gains cannot meet expectations generated previously, which are exacerbated by new hopes resulting from the example of political liberalization in eastern Europe. A revolution of rising expectations is defined by George Blanksten as "the process by which people on a lower standard of living become acquainted with the benefits of a higher standard, and in consequence of this demonstration effect come to desire or demand the goods of the higher level."[120]

From the mid-1970s to the end of the 1980s in Côte d'Ivoire the "heightening of the incongruence between demand and allocation structure [was] accompanied by the polarization of the demand struc-ture."[121] "Relative deprivation conflicts" and "mass conflicts," as ana-lyzed by Michael Cohen, and a zero-sum pattern of distribution with all the rewards going to some at the expense of others, resulted from this polarization and the failure of allocation policies.[122] A change in the sys-tem of governance was needed to handle the polarization and increas-ing conflict of demands and antagonistic preferences.[123]

But interpreting the 1990 protests in Côte d'Ivoire primarily as a function of structural economic crisis is only half the truth. The roots of the crisis are not really in the structures of a developing and externally constrained economy but in the economic dynamics of authoritarian governance. In a "rent-seeking society," the organizations for collective action are distributional coalitions because they are overwhelmingly oriented to conflicts over the allocation of income and wealth rather than focused on the production of additional output.[124] Dependence on the state for education, health care, school tuition, jobs, and other pri-mary needs, and the management of consequent demands necessitates the development of clientelist networks and systems of patronage for the expansion of resources and their distribution.[125]

The costs of political stability in this context are much higher than in developed countries because economic inefficiency will result from the attempt to match the politics of distribution with the requirements of "ethnic arithmetic" in the heterogeneous monolith while at the same time avoiding divisive tendencies.[126] The "welfare authoritarianism" in Côte d'Ivoire (or the welfare state of the poor) was self-destructive, for here the limits of growth, in Hirsh's argument, are not only social—the unhappiness of those supposed to benefit from the expansion of state expenditures—but also technical or structural.[127] Given the structures of the economies and their dependence on foreign capital and markets, it is difficult to increase social spending as well as develop prebendal and rent-seeking activities beyond a certain point. By the end of the 1970s the political formula reached its extreme limits and the money deposits were exhausted.[128] The "miracle" was not the rates of growth but why and how the system lasted so long and did not collapse much earlier. Côte d'Ivoire and nearby Benin are indicative of the high eco-nomic costs of political stability in nondemocratic systems.

With an overloaded government, the exhaustion of its economic ba-sis, and its inabilty to meet rising frustrations, the passage to the politi-cal was rapid and inevitable for three main reasons. First, as already discussed, politics was made primary through the overvaluation of political power by social actors. Second, political demands can be met easily and speedily. Officials, for example, can sign a decree for the creation of political parties rather than implement social and economic reforms.[129] Finally, demands must be depolarized and recontained in order for the conflict management system to be able to respond, by repression, allocation, or institutionalization.

In Côte d'Ivoire, the need for liberalization and democratization of the political structure appeared rather quickly as an obvious solution intended to harmonize the demand and allocation structures. Indeed, the authoritarian system was technically and politically obsolete. Because of the proliferation of elites with the same characteristics since the 1950s, the shrinking economic pie, and the uncertainty of the political elite, the only way to ease the frustrations of the political entrepreneurs was to change the prevailing general system of cooptation for a system of competition. Thus the institutionalization of conflict among the political contenders operated as a system of conflict management. The return to political pluralism was made in two steps.

First, as early as 1978 municipal elections were canceled, three years after the system of cooptation had reached an unprecedented level in recruitment to political offices. The candidates were selected as usual by the secretary general of the party. Yacé, president of the national assembly and constitutional successor, was at the apex of his power. Most of the candidates selected were already members of the political elite (ministers, members of Parliament, and others). Those left outside of it in 1975 protested against this zero-sum game and presented their claims to the president, who decided to cancel the elections. The introduction of semicompetitive elections (municipal and legislative) in 1980 was the first attempt to liberalize the system. Subsequent municipal and legislative elections were characterized by high levels of competition. Six hundred and fifty candidates vied for 125 legislative seats in 1980 and 577 for 175 seats in 1985. Elections were also marked by the high social status of the candidates, low turnouts by the voters, and "friends and neighbors" electoral behavior.[130] This experience of semicompetitive elections has received little or negative attention from Ivorian and non-Ivorian scholars, contrary to the attention given to the situation in Tanzania or Kenya.[131] Yet this short experience of semicompetitive elections, compared with Tanzania's since 1965, had more impact than recognized. The elections were a strategy of democratization from above, and they contributed to a gradual and smooth transition to full-blown democracy.[132]

Although it could be difficult to assert that the Ivorian president was against multipartyism and democracy, he had his own conception of democracy and the way to bring it about. He conceived his own strategy of incremental democratization from above, one he would be able to control, a sort of "tutelary democracy." He never revealed an agenda, although in early 1989 rumors abounded of a move toward a limited multipartyism (one or two other political parties) for the 1990 legislative and municipal elections. In the fall of 1989, during the Dialogue Days, he said, "For the moment, multi-partyism is merely a mental image."

In fact a parallel can be made between the handling of independence and of democracy in Côte d'Ivoire. Houphouët-Boigny dealt with democracy in the same way that he did with the isssue of independence. The choice he made for the "yes" response in the 1958 constitutional referendum meant postponement but not the rejection of independence. The refusal of multipartyism in the fall of 1989 also meant postponement, not rejection, of democracy.

The choice in 1990 was simply for full implementation of article 7 of the constitution, which since 1960 has allowed multipartyism. That the decision was taken by a regular meeting of the executive bureau of the PDCI and that no constitutional amendment was necessary made the event commonplace and reduced the drama of the situation.

However, when people took the 1990 crisis to the streets, their first goals were not multipartyism and democracy but the bread and butter of previous social crises. The conversion from "bread and butter" to "bread and ballot" was the result of corporatist protest by students, soldiers, policemen, and other civil servants, and the overload and breakdown of accepted conflict management mechanisms. The new political enterprises that blossomed as flowers in the spring of 1990 were not agents of different or opposite visions of Côte d'Ivoire's social destiny but rather products of an overdeveloped society in relation to the state, the deep contradiction between the dynamism of society and the obsolescence of the "political microcosm." Thus the 1990 crisis was a quick and violent way by which society and state were brought to the same stage, similar to what had happened at the end of colonization. The crisis also illustrated the shifting concerns of the Ivorians, which had moved in the last decade from the private focus on "the well-being of the Ivorian man" to public action for economic and political reforms. Arguments in favor of the private life, of disengagement from politics to take advantage of the economic miracle, reinforced a cycle of demobilization and depoliticization and political immobilism that had lasted until the end of the 1970s. The return to public action begun in the 1980s received a violent acceleration in 1990.

What is the real meaning of the social protest led by civil servants, university and secondary professors, and students?[133] Was the protest and its political conversion a systemic crisis? Can the return to democracy, and a new consensus on the ways in which Ivorians want to be ruled, fundamentally alter the previous conflict management structures of allocations and rewards? Did a structural change take place?

These questions are important because what is really at stake with the processes of liberalization and democratization goes far beyond a change in the rules of the political game or the mere adoption of a new principle of political legitimacy. Liberalization and democratization could dramatically call into question the previous structures of patronage and rewards, the allocation of resources, and the relations between politicians and their constituencies.

According to the definition of systemic crisis, democracy is formally a threat to the established rules of the game for allocating authority and rewards in an authoritarian polity, a threat to the position of contenders included in the incumbent coalition.[134] "Democracy is a contingent outcome of conflicts."[135] As such, theoretically, it implies a structural change, a fundamental change in regime that alters the institutional power balance among the contenders.

But in Côte d'Ivoire, the 1990 crisis was not a systemic crisis. In Côte d'Ivoire, the regime has changed within the same ruling elite. With the competitive elections, the structures and processes of recruitment have changed. But no fundamental change in the regime to alter the institutional power balance among the contenders has occurred. The extent to which a new system of recruitment could fundamentally alter the established structures of allocation and reward depends on how the "nomenklatura question" will be solved in Côte d'Ivoire. How can the political and administrative elite associated with the PDCI succeed in transforming wealth and influence into political power as some former nomenklaturists are doing in Russia and eastern Europe?

There may be at least two explanations for the absence of a systemic crisis in Côte d'Ivoire. The first is that nothing at all has changed, democratization is just a joke, and the regime is still authoritarian. This judgment could be excessive because one cannot expect the regime to become a full-blown democracy in just four or five years. The second explanation recalls that elements of personal and authoritarian rule and one-party culture are still present in the formally new democratic regime, as preparations for the 1995 elections have shown. Then, in a reassessment of the general hypothesis of this study, it is suggested that the current situation can be understood as the legacy of the freezing structures of cleavages installed at a critical juncture, a period of crucial transition that made all the difference and still governs the Ivorian way of doing politics.

## Succession as a Political Opportunity Structure

Since the mid-1970s, the fear of what might happen after the president's death developed not only in Côte d'Ivoire among aliens and Ivorians but all over West Africa. Specters of chaos, interethnic warfare and killing, and the collapse of the entire social and economic system were partially sustained by the radical approach to the Ivorian political economy popularized by Samir Amin.[136] Apprehension has increased in recent years with the worsening of the economic crisis, the consequent social unrest of the early 1980s, and the social and political turmoil of the 1990s. This fear is commonplace whenever the succession or the passing of a charismatic African leader is faced. But as a survey of eighteen various experiences of transfer of power has acknowledged, political succession in sub-Saharan Africa has been more peaceful and orderly than thought.[137]

Indeed, more than any social or political event of the past thirty-three years, Houphouët-Boigny's succession is a major test for the entire system of governance. It will indicate how successful Houphouët-Boigny was in transmitting to the institutions he had so profoundly personalized the respect and legitimacy devoted to him by Ivorians. Houphouët-Boigny's "personal equation" and strong hold on Ivorian politics were obvious to the end, even after 1990 and the return to political pluralism. His "eternal presence" has been perceived by many political and social actors as an inhibiting factor, not only in Côte d'Ivoire but also throughout West Africa.[138]

As a political opportunity, his succession could speed up some social, political, and economic processes, thaw many frozen cleavages, and thus affect the demand structure at two levels. One, different ethnic groups could claim greater access to economic resources, challenging the socioethnic basis of the demand structure. Two, opening the door to the broadly based, demand-bearing groups, with new social, economic, and political agendas, allows them to take full advantage of the new democratic framework.

## Political Succession and Socioethnic Reshuffling

The emergence of new demand-bearing groups as a result of socio-economic change has not been very obvious in the past experiences of succession in Africa (Angola, Cameroon, Equatorial Guinea, Guinea, Guinea-Bissau, Kenya, Mozambique, Sierra Leone, Senegal, Tanzania, to name a few). The most common phenomena have been a reshuffling of socioeconomic groups, a spoils system based on ethnic lines, and a change in the access of some ethnic groups to power and economic resources. When the new president comes from a different ethnic group than that of his predecessor, members of that group and of other culturally or geographically related groups will take advantage of the new political context to acquire more access to power and thus to economic resources. In Côte d'Ivoire, the heir, Henri Konan Bédié, is from the same ethnic group (and religion) as his predecessor, producing a rather different socioethnic reshuffling, but the main contender, Alassane Ouattara, is from the North (and Muslim).

The political, social, and economic new prominence of the Kalendjin, the Soussou, and the Beti, for instance, has been determined by the access to power of Daniel arap Moi in Kenya, General Lansana Conté in Guinea, and Paul Biya in Cameroon. As illustrated by ethnic killings in the Rift Valley in Kenya, this spoils system based on ethnic lines is conducive to a greater ethnicization of politics, as in Paul Biya's Cameroon as well. But the best example is found in Lansana Conté's Guinea, where tribalism and regionalism, avoided by Sekou Touré despite his authoritarian rule, have reached levels unknown since the 1984 coup.

From the early years of independence to the end of the 1970s, the four ethnocultural areas (the Akan South and Center, the Manding Northeast, the Voltaïc Northwest, the Kru Center-West and Southwest) of the country have been characterized by different patterns of regional leadership. The Akan core was united under Houphouët-Boigny's leadership with subregional and national leaders such as Philippe Yacé and

Mathieu Ekra. So was the Great North (the Manding and the Voltaïc sides) under the banner of Mamadou Coulibaly (one-time minister and former president of the Social and Economic Council). On the contrary, the Kru region was characterized by competing poles (Gagnoa, Daloa, and more recently, Issia) and leaders (Sery Gnoleba, Bra Kanon) vying for regional leadership.

After the passing of national and prominent figures like Marcel Laubhouet,[139] Alexis Thierry Lebbé, and Mamadou Coulibaly at the end of the 1970s, the situation of the regional political leadership evolved. The Akan area remained apparently united with the still-indisputable leadership of the president. The Great North, orphaned after the passing of its emblematic leader, was still in search of another father, a role that Lazéni Coulibaly (former leading figure of the PDCI, ambassador, minister of justice, and president of the Supreme Court) has tried in vain to fill,[140] until Ouattara arose as a candidate. One reason for Coulibaly's failure is found in the fact that the northern part of the country is pulled apart between its Senufo (Korhogo, Sinémantiali) and Manding (Odienné) poles as shown by the division of Lancine Gon Coulibaly's family. The Kru area did not succeed in uniting under one regional leader and may not be likely to do so in the near future because of cultural factors, multipartyism, and the fact that even before the return to political pluralism, new competing poles (Issia, Oura-gahio, Sahioua, Soubré) and leaders (Djédjé Mady, Laurent Gbagbo) emerged.

Political succession is not only a national concern. The changing of the guard is also an important regional issue for it could influence the political bargaining within the democratic framework in general, and, more important, within the power-sharing deals associated with the succession. A major test is in the Akan area: will it continue to support the heir as it did the founding father, or will it split into many potential competing poles (Aboisso, Abengourou, Bouaké, Dimbokro, Yamous-soukro, and others)? Despite rumors of some leading Baule figures opposed to a smooth succession, it is more likely that the core and body of the Akan group, the Baule, will remain united under Konan Bédié's leadership. The socioethnic reshuffling after the succession may also take the form of new ethnopolitical alliances. The basic and lasting alliance since colonial times was between the Akan and the Manding-Voltaïc. The Akan-Baule political domination is something very recent,[141] a social construct within the framework of the plantation economy and not just the result of Houphouët-Boigny's coming to power in 1945, even if his long and uninterrupted tenure increased and strengthened the phenomenon.[142] Remember that the stability of the legacy of the critical juncture rests on mechanisms of reproduction (social and cultural practices) that have been perpetuated through institutional and political processes since colonial times. Thus political succession at this level will not be the end of the legacy.

However, the impact of the succession on the demand structure could go beyond ethnic reshuffling. Given the current political and socioeconomic context, more broadly based, new demand-bearing groups could emerge.

## Consolidating Democracy

Political liberalization and semipluralism were used in Africa in the 1980s to provide societal support and legitimacy to a new president designated by the incumbent. In Senegal after Leopold Sedar Senghor's resignation in 1981, his successor, Abdou Diouf, moved the political system from a limited number of political parties to a fully fledged multipartyism. Paul Biya of Cameroon did likewise when he replaced Ahmandou Ahidjo by setting up (and controlling) a semicompetitive electoral system. General Lansana Conté of Guinea made the promise of establishing a democratic political system in 1984 even though it took him a decade to keep his words. General Joseph Saidu Momoh of Sierra Leone, Teodoro Obiang of Equatorial Guinea, General André Kolingba of Central African Republic, Ali Hassan Mwinyi of Tanzania, Daniel arap Moi of Kenya, to name but a few cases of succession, made no such promise of political liberalization (some of them have done otherwise by becoming more authoritarian than their predecessor) until forced to start a process of democratization (with the exception of Joseph Momoh, who was overthrown by a coup d'état for not doing so).

It is more likely that besides personal commitment to democratic values and human rights, President Konan Bédié, lacking his predecessor's charisma, authority, and economic resources, will have to expand and consolidate the new democratic system (of which certain dimensions and actors were inhibited by the late President Houphouët-Boigny's personality). He will have to do so as a strategy of political survival, not only to legitimize his power but also to manage the pressure of two types of new demand-bearing groups with new political, social, and economic agendas. The first is associated with the new political framework (political parties, unions, civic organizations), and the second is generated by the current socioeconomic context (various socioprofessional groups oriented toward economic development).

After April 1990, forty to sixty political parties were legalized. Opposition parties attempted unsuccessfully to get access to political power during the 1990 presidential and legislative elections. Then, through rallies and other types of demonstrations, through their press, and through the 1994–95 electoral campaign opposition parties pushed for further democratization of the political system: rule of law, respect for human rights, equal access to public mass media, better governance and transparency in the exercise of power, and so on. The resignation of the president of the Supreme Court after the coverage of a financial scandal by opposition press has been one important success in this domain. Taking advantage of the political context, unions in various professions have proliferated as well, most of them closely linked to the political parties. Some of them have been very active since 1990, as illustrated by the strong action of the unions of students, secondary schools, and university professors in favor of democracy, the protection of the rights and interests of their members, and the defense of human rights.

The new political context has also favored the creation of new civic organizations more oriented toward the promotion of democracy, social and economic development, and the defense of human rights than the elitist "service clubs" (Rotary, Lions, Young Chamber of Commerce, Soroptimist, Kiwanis, and others) of the 1970s and 1980s. The Ivorian Movement of Democratic Women (MIFED), the Group for the Study and Research on Democracy and Economic and Social Development (GERDDES-Côte d'Ivoire), the Ivorian League of Human Rights (LIDHO), and the Association of Women Jurists (AFJ) are among the new groups. Rallies, seminars, conferences, press releases, civic education programs, and periodic public statements on national and international issues related to the development of democracy and election monitoring have been, and some still are, prevalent, but they are also controversial. Indeed, allegations of partisanship have been made against the MIFED, AFJ, and most of all LIDHO because of their close links with opposition parties. But still, the social and economic demands and agendas of the opposition parties were vague even into the 1995 campaign, as were those of unions associated with them.

Within the framework of the implementation of the Structural Ad-

justment Program, Ivorians took to the streets the issue of salary reduction contemplated by the government in 1990, a social turmoil that developed into political claims for democracy and led to the return to multipartyism. After the promise made by Prime Minister Ouattara to leave
the salaries at their current levels, unions almost completely lost initiative
on the social and economic front, mainly because of the lack of economic alternatives to the SAP. The SAP was ostensibly a prime issue in
the electoral campaign but without precise, realistic alternatives.

The return to political pluralism and democracy in general helps enable economic development. In Côte d'Ivoire, the persistence of the economic crisis, the disengagement of the state from many economic activities, and the political succession favors the development of a "class"
of entrepreneurs, operating at different levels (local and regional) in the
country and in West Africa. This class or group of entrepreneurs is
made of grass-roots entrepreneurs already operating in the informal
sector in the country and in the neighboring states. Jobless secondary
school and university graduates, eager to create their own enterprises
and make money as the state can no longer fulfill their needs and
dreams, are among them. The entrepreneurs also include former
nomenklaturists of the PDCI and many others who became rich under
the one-party system and have invested abroad with assets that under
certain conditions could be brought back. This group will strive for the
creation of an environment enabling freedom of enterprise and real
regional economic integration. It wants less bureaucracy and time-
consuming restraints on small businesses and fiscal incentives for new
entrepreneurs.

Regional economic integration could become a crucial political issue
in the near future. The inefficiency of national solutions to economic recovery, an elitist and bureaucratic approach to problem solving (the creation of a West African Parliament) instead of a grass-roots and pragmatic strategy built on concrete and existing informal experiences, and
interested social groups in Côte d'Ivoire and outside of its borders high-
light the importance of regionalism.

Despite his commitment to liberal economics, Houphouët-Boigny always opposed the creation of a class of capitalists in Côte d'Ivoire. Thus
the development of the role of the state in the economy and the strong
dependence of the potential class of entrepreneurs on the state help explain some aspects of the current privatization process. Initially, Konan
Bédié did not appear to have a different policy, but he may be obliged

to devise one. The "class" of entrepreneurs is potentially one of the most powerful demand-bearing groups expected to coalesce in the years to come. Democracy and political succession will offer this group the historical and unique opportunity for the political and administrative elite to sever its umbilical cord with the state and to convert its various resources into more economic power as former nomenklaturists are doing in eastern Europe. The shift from strong reliance on state action to private initiatives is of dramatic importance for the Ivorian system of governance in the post–Houphouët-Boigny era and central to the establishment and consolidation of democracy.

The setback or the halt of the democratization process observed by many since 1992, when Houphouët-Boigny repressed popular demonstrations, and into the 1995 campaign clearly reveals the double deficit plaguing the entire process. Intellectual deficit, the lack of new ideas and efficient strategies to lead the movement, exists mainly because of the absence of intellectual and ideological preparation for democracy. A social deficit also prevails, that is, an absence of autonomous social actors illustrated by the inability of the new political parties, unions, and civic organizations to integrate social movements. Economic recovery and its link to further democratization in Côte d'Ivoire raise the question of which actors carry the hopes for future action for democracy and good governance: political parties, unions, or civic organizations, that is, the civil society or the state?

The new political parties, because of their number, strong regional basis, and ideological postures, have split the intellectual elite into small political elements. Currently they are weak, lack efficient strategies, and have polarized political life along ideological partisan and ethnic lines, which seems to suggest that partisanship might not be the appropriate way to build a stable, durable democracy. The FPI of Gbagbo, the PDCI-breakaway Republican Rally (RDR) of Djeny Kobina (stalking horse for Ouattara) and the Union of Democratic Forces (UFD) of Bamba Morifere united in a Republican front to attempt a structural change in Ivorian politics but still remain within the established consensual elite. Political development from above prevails, a permanent feature of Ivorian politics evidenced by the creation of a one-party system in the 1950s and 1960s, the initiation of democracy from above by the president in the 1980s, and the execution of the democratic idea in the 1990s.

Of course, the new president will have to take initiatives for the consolidation of democracy, but it is likely that his action will be preceded by many demands. To be successful, his action must be supported and relieved by civic organizations. Despite its current weakness, Ivorian civil society organized along powerful, multiethnic, and nonpartisan civic organizations, as exemplified by GERDDES-Côte d'Ivoire, appears to be where the future lies for the democratization process, and thus for governance, after Houphouët-Boigny.

New demand-bearing groups will emerge, following an eventual socioethnic reshuffling, but strong civic organizations in the new political framework will not really challenge the system of allocation. It will, however, change how the system works. Moreover, maybe paradoxically, democracy will help the new president a great deal for it will enhance the capacity of the system to handle the conflicts among various groups.

In fact in Côte d'Ivoire the real threat to the conflict management system is the scarcity of economic resources. In this matter Houphouët-Boigny, whatever his personal beliefs, values, and preferences, was a shrewd and visionary politician. In 1945 during the electoral campaign, he talked and focused on the betterment of the life of average "côtivoirien," while other leading candidates were arguing about the subtleties of the constitution to be adopted. He succeeded by making "the well-being of the Ivorian man" the Ivorians' creed, and this emphasis could be one of the most important aspects of his legacy. Thus the nature of the demand, the politics of distribution, will remain the same in spite of eventual or real change in the demand structure.

However, the nature of the conflict is under change. There is less and less conflict over incumbency but more and more "class conflict." The shift in the economic system, owing to the implementation of the SAP, and the renewal of the relationships between political or administrative positions and economic resources contribute to the switch. Consequently, democracy and a market economy are very useful for the new president. They provide the opportunity for the political and administrative elite to sever the umbilical cord with the state and to legitimize their domination. The incremental democratization initiated in 1980 with the semicompetitive elections was aimed at what Pierre Bourdieu calls the process of "naturalization" of the ruling group's domination. A formally full-fledged democracy is still compatible with the goal if the process is controlled from above as the president has tried to do since April 30, 1990, when multipartyism was reestablished. When the power elite succeeds in converting its position into more economic power, the system will be less and less likely to require a president or the state to arbitrate conflicts among the various groups. Instead electors and the market will fulfill this function.

Conflict management in Côte d'Ivoire means the stability of the legacy of the critical juncture. That stability prevails to the extent that Côte d'Ivoire's mechanisms of reproduction (social and cultural practices) have been perpetuated through institutional and political processes: the colonial system, the one-party regime, semicompetitive elections, and now, multipartyism and democracy. History also suggests the stability of the "basic attributes produced as an outcome of the critical juncture,"[143] for example, the different reactions to the plantation economy and colonization. Whatever internal and external changes have occurred since then, Côte d'Ivoire has been and will long continue to be governed in its ways of managing conflict by coherent values and a normative set of codes, as well as by a self-reproducing and cohesive ruling class.

# Chapter 4
# Ghana: Conflict Reoriented

*A. Adu Boahen*

THE PATTERN OF CONFLICT MANAGEMENT in Ghana was established in the critical juncture of the late 1950s by the way in which the nationalist movement divided and its militant wing took over and exercised power in the first decade of independence. Moderate nationalists were repressed and conflict exacerbated, and the heritage of a split ideology was created. The conflict was one between two political tendencies that could be managed at regular intervals by elections, despite the groundwork laid for such a situation in the early years. But it also became a conflict between state and society, in which the demand-bearing groups of society were encouraged to regard the state as a milch cow, more appropriate as a target for demands than for supports, and the state was trained to regard the groups of society as a hostile and noncontributing nuisance. Yet at the same time, the sides of the conflict are now stronger and more competent in their own right than ever before.

Ghana's is the story of a partially vigorous state's and society's difficulties in playing their respective roles in consonance, responsibility, and mutual respect. It shows that when the state does not fill its role of managing conflicts with and among the groups of society, it will be felled by them, no matter how it seeks to repress them. This was the experience of the first three republics, which gradually turned most groups of society against them until the one best suited for the purpose—the army—overthrew them. The first overthrow, in 1966, was an exceptional corrective, short-lived, and destined to restore republican rule rapidly. The second republic, under Kofi A. Busia, was ended in 1972 by the National Redemption Council (NRC), followed by the Supreme Military Council. The third overthrow, in two acts in 1979 and again in 1981, gave an even shorter shrift to the republic it installed; finding it flabby, unsupported, and without a conflict management strategy, the military acted to remove it. In all three instances, a civilian-led state alienated the increasingly pluralist society by its economic program—one overexpansionist, the other two reformist—and was unable to manage the conflicts it engendered.

But Ghana's experience also shows that when the groups of society pile their demands on the state without concern for the need for equally strong supports for it, through alliegiance, participation, and productivity, they will create a state that alternately ignores, represses, or panders to them. The firm or lasting relationship needed to manage conflicts by other than ad hoc methods will not be developed. Nkrumah's republic of 1960 taught the groups it generated and suppressed to oppose government but to pile demands on the state. When he was removed, in 1966, the next republic was led by the repressed liberal opposition and could have been expected to benefit from the support of the groups that had opposed its predecessor. Instead, a mixture of government ineptitude and negative socialization by the previous republic led some groups of society to oppose the second republic as they had the first. By the third republic, in 1979–81, that habit had become ingrained, and corruption and mismanagement had become unacceptable. The fourth republic, which is the military regime legitimized by civilian elections, has gone the same way.

As a predicament of the moment, this confrontation—between state and society among liberals, radicals (Nkrumaists), and Rawlings—is grave. But as a situation that becomes a habit and a heritage, it is a debilitating trap for all sides from which they cannot easily escape. The political consensus in Ghana has changed from enthusiasm to partisanship to anticivicism. "Ghana today," wrote Naomi Chazan in 1983, "lacks a coherent value model about which consensus can be achieved. Although many political values are at work, no central normative set of codes has been constructed."[1] But worse yet, by 1995, behind the normative vacuum are political habits of endemic distrust between state and society. "To achieve self-sustaining development," wrote Donald Rothchild, just before the civilianizing elections of 1992, "the state as a political manager must complement and reinforce the state as an economic manager."[2] "The central, overarching feature of this phase was one of recession: of economic impoverishment and of reduction in political capabilities," wrote Chazan on the period between the second and third republics (1969–82).[3] Low productivity and support by society and little capacity for conflict management on the part of the state are continuing signs of recession as a heritage of governance in Ghana.

This chapter on the ways in which the different types of demand-bearing groups and their demands have been managed in Ghana is divided into sections dealing with the six regimes that the country has had since independence in March 1957. Kwame Nkrumah's Convention People's Party (CPP) ruled the first ten years of independence until 1966. The first republic was ended by the National Liberation Council (NLC) regime of Generals Joseph A. Ankrah and Akwasi A. Afrifa, which in turn handed over power to the winner of the 1969 elections, the Progress Party (PP) regime of Kofi A. Busia. The second republic under Busia only lasted three years, and it was ended in 1972 by the National Redemption Council (NRC) followed by the Supreme Military Councils (SMC) I and II of Colonels I. K. Acheampong and Frederick W. K. Akuffo, which were removed in 1979 by the Armed Forces Revolutionary Council (AFRC) of Flight Lieutenant Jerry J. Rawlings. The AFRC handed over power to the winner of the 1979 elections, the People's National Party (PNP) of Hilla Limann. The third republic under Limann lasted fewer than two years and was ended by the return of Rawlings with the Provisional National Defense Council (PNDC) on December 31, 1981. After a decade, the PNDC converted to a multiparty regime but rather than handing over power to a different party, Rawlings ran for office as a civilian and remained in power with the National Democratic Congress (NDC) as the winner of the 1992 elections, inaugurating the fourth republic. The growth of pluralism and diversity in society and the succeeding phases of government's handling of demands and management of conflicts, without eliciting full support from these groups, are the themes of this evolution.

Ghana was the first country in West Africa to gain independence from the colonial power, in March 1957, under the leadership of Kwame Nkrumah and his CPP. At the time of independence, several demand-bearing groups had emerged. These were the main political groups consisting of the United Gold Coast Convention (UGCC) and its allies of the National Liberation Movement (NLM), the Northern People's Party (NPP), the Togoland Congress (TC), the Anlo Youth Organization (AYO), the Moslem Association Party (MAP), and the Convention Peoples' Party (CPP). With the exception of the CPP, the leadership of all these groups consisted of the commercial, intelligentsia, upper and middle class, and the traditional rulers.

The CPP leadership consisted mainly of the lower middle class, trade unionists, and farmers' representatives. The principal socioeconomic or pressure groups were the Trade Union Congress (TUC), the Ex-Servicemen's Union, the United Ghana Farmer's Council (UGFC), the Cooperative Alliance, and the Ghana Cooperative Marketing Association. Although the first three socioeconomic groups had all become integral wings of the CPP, the last two were still nonpartisan. The third cluster of groups was ethnic, regional, or subnational in character. Principal among these were the Ewe groups of the Volta Region, the Asante of the Asante Region, and the Mole-Dagbani, Guan, and Gurma groups of the Northern Region of the country. Their political equivalents were the TC, AYO, NLM, and the NPP, all of which formed part of the opposition coalition.

Until the formation of the CPP in 1949, political conflict in the country was a direct one between all the nationalists spearheaded by the UGCC and the colonial government, and it centered on the issue of self-government. With the rise of the CPP, the conflict now became three cornered. Though both parties agreed on the issue of self-government, they now disagreed about strategies to be adopted and which group should replace the colonial government in an independent Ghana. Although the UGCC advocated the strategy of "self-government step by step" and claimed to be the natural successors to the British, the CPP advocated "self-government now" and insisted that as the populist party, it should inherit the independent kingdom. Since the leadership of these two parties had bifurcated along class lines—a bourgeois, merchant, intelligentsia, professional, traditional elite class, and a lower-middle commoner class. This conflict also assumed the nature of a class conflict.

The formation of the TC by the Ewe in 1951 introduced a new and fourth factor, the ethnic or subnationalist factor. This factor assumed crucial and disturbing proportions in 1954 with the formation of the NLM by the Asante and the NPP mainly by the Mole-Dagbani groups of the North. Though all these groups remained united on the central issue of self-government, they disagreed on the ethnic and subnationalist demands and on the timing. Although the Ewe demanded their separation from the Gold Coast and unification with their kith and kin in French Togo, the Asante called for a federal system of government while the peoples of the North wanted a guarantee of their peculiar interests. Most of these issues were temporarily resolved as a result of a series of elections in 1951, 1954, and 1956, the plebiscite of May 1956 on the irredentist issue, and the adoption of a semifederal independence constitution. The populist CPP emerged as the undisputed leader at the time of independence; however, the opposition groups and, in particular, the Ewe and the Asante remained unimpressed, casting a rather foreboding shadow on the legitimacy of the new government.[4]

## The Nkrumah Regime

The first three years of independence were a period of bitter conflict between the newly independent regime of Kwame Nkrumah and the opposition groups.[5] The NLM and its allies insisted on their demand for a federal system of government and boycotted the elections held in October 1958 for the regional assemblies worked out as a compromise solution by the British government. In the Volta region, the Togoland Congress remained uncompromising in its demands, boycotted the independence celebrations, and broke into open rebellion in the Kpandu area. A new ethnic-regional movement also emerged in the capital of the country, the Ga Shifimo Kpee (the Ga Standfast Association), to protect the interests of the Ga-Adangbe ethnic group and to drive away strangers who had occupied their lands, especially in Accra. All the opposition parties and the Ga Shifimo Kpee came together to form the United Party (UP), which was inaugurated in November 1957 under the leadership of Kofi A. Busia. All these activities on the part of the opposition and its new ally, the Ga Shifimo Kpee, constituted a serious challenge to the legitimacy of the new CPP government and the integrity of the new state.

The government's answer to these challenges was to repress them and to assert and sustain CPP and government power.[6] Repressive measures included the Deportation Act, which was quickly applied to two of the leading members of the opposition in Kumasi and to a number of anti-CPP Syrians and Lebanese in the country, and the Avoidance of Discrimination Act, which was passed to ban parties, organizations, and societies organized on a regional, religious, or ethnic basis. The most notorious of these measures was, however, the Preventive Detention Act (PDA) rushed through Parliament in July 1958. This act gave Nkrumah powers to detain people without trial and was used to detain some thirty-nine leading members of the Ga Shifimo Kpee and the UP in November 1958, twelve people in 1959, of whom nine were prominent UP members in the Asante Region, and sixteen people by July 1960, all of whom were members of the UP in the Volta Region.

The final measure of the CPP government was the conversion of the new state of Ghana from a commonwealth under a governor general appointed by the queen of England into a republic under an executive president elected by the people after a plebiscite held in April 1960. Ghana became a republic in July 1960 with Nkrumah as its first executive president.

These measures stifled opposition to the CPP both in and outside Parliament by 1960 and suppressed ethnic-regionalist sentiments in favor of the holistic nationalism of the CPP. Starting in 1960 Nkrumah began to advocate and implement Marxist socialism in a modified form, which he first termed African socialism, then scientific socialism, then Nkrumaism, and finally consciencism.[7] Politically, this meant in practice making the party supreme and synonymous with the state, converting the country into a one-party state in 1964 after a referendum marked by massive intimidation and fraud, and finally strengthening his diplomatic and economic ties with the communist countries.

Economically, the socialist approach meant changeover from the laissez-faire policies of the first three years of independence to new policies that emphasized state-owned import substitution, industrialization, and mechanization in agriculture and industry. For the domination of the mining, diamond, construction, and marketing sectors, state corporations were established.

However, import substitution had to rely mostly on imported raw materials and inputs; it was financed by short-term and medium-term borrowing at usurious rates of interest; mismanagement and corruption became widespread while a catastrophic drop in the world cocoa price from $603 a ton in 1958 to $241 in 1965 occurred.[8] For all these reasons most of these projects were a disastrous failure. The country therefore found itself with depleted foreign exchange holdings, huge debts, and acute shortages of basic needs and very high food prices. Indeed by 1966 the country was on the verge of bankruptcy and economic collapse.

Just as Nkrumah's policies and strategies changed, so did the groups and their demands. Politically, the Togoland Congress and the UP remained the only active groups and were joined by the antisocialist or capitalist wing of the CPP. The TC continued to press for the reversal of the results of the UN plebiscite of 1956 and for the unification of the two former Togos. The new independent state of Togo under the leadership of Sylvanus Olympio and the Comité de l'Unité Togolaise (CUT) actively supported the congress from 1960 onward. The overthrow of

Olympio's government and his assassination in the coup d'etat of 1963 did not end the irredentist demands of the congress.[9]

The UP, however, abandoned its sectarian and subnationalist demands, such as federalism, and concentrated on achieving the rule of law, the liberty of the individual and other fundamental human rights, and above all, the overthrow of Nkrumah and his regime through fair or foul means. For this objective, the UP was joined in the 1960s by the capitalist or antisocialist wing of the CPP. Among the strategies adopted by the opposition forces were legal actions to challenge the validity of the deportation order and the PDA, antisocialist motions in Parliament, demands for commissions of enquiry into allegations of bribery and corruption, various critical motions and subversion, violence and assassination attempts. Thus an unsuccessful attempt was made to assassinate Nkrumah at Kulungugu in northern Ghana in August 1962 by the UP forces, and a policeman narrowly missed him in another attempt at Flagstaff House in Accra in January 1964. The Kulungugu attempt was followed by the throwing of bombs at crowds in busy urban centers.

Nkrumah's reaction to the activities and demands of these political groups was ruthless repression through preventive detention and trials. Thus the number of people detained rose from 174 between June and December 1960 to 311 in 1961, dropped to 254 in 1962, and rose again to 586 in 1963. Among those detained in 1961 were UP leaders including J. B. Danquah, CPP members of Parliament, and CPP antisocialist members. Fear of detention also drove people like Komla A. Gbedemah, Nkrumah's first minister of finance, and K. A. Busia and Kow Richardson, both of the UP, into exile. He also sent three people wrongly accused of the Kulungugu incident, Tawia Adamafio, Coffie Crabbe, and Ako Adjei, to court to be tried for treason.

Conflict during the period was not confined to political groups and the CPP government but involved two other forces, namely, state organs and new socioeconomic groups. The former consisted of the Civil Service, the Police Service, the army, and the judiciary, while the latter came from "education, traditional authority, public enterprise, cooperatives, private enterprise (both indigenous and foreign), the professions, labor and the manufacturer's association and religious and student bodies."[10] The most prominent of these groups were the universities and their students, the TUC, the bar association, and the Christian Council and Catholic Secretariat, both of which became independent of their mother European churches during the period under review.

During this period Ghana saw the greatest development of higher education. The number of universities increased from one to three. These were the University College of the Gold Coast founded in 1948 and turned into the University of Ghana at Legon in 1961, the University of Science and Technology founded at Kumasi in 1961, and the University of Cape Coast opened in 1962. The total number of students at the three universities had risen to 4,286 by the academic year 1965–66,[11] when the National Union of Ghana Students (NUGS) was formed.

Initially both the academic staff of the universities and the students showed little involvement in politics.[12] It was not until 1964 that the students openly confronted the government by passing a resolution condemning the president for dismissing the chief justice. A month later, students protested against the deportation of six Legon university lecturers. Apart from these two episodes, the students kept aloof from national politics. In February 1965, however, three Legon students were arrested for calling for two minutes of silence in honor of J. B. Danquah, the great nationalist and scholar, who had then died in detention.

In keeping with Nkrumah's mobilization program and his determination to bring all institutions and associations under its control, the CPP government assumed the offensive against the universities, particularly the University of Ghana. To enhance his control of the university, Nkrumah made himself the chancellor of the universities in 1961 while he terminated the appointment of six expatriates whom he accused of fostering antigovernment feelings on the campus. A branch of the party was also opened at Legon.

In reaction to the protest against the dismissal of the chief justice in 1963, the government deported six senior faculty members and closed all the universities for seventeen days. After the reopening of the universities, the government intensified its attacks on the universities. A massive demonstration was staged on the Legon campus by the party. This was followed by the formation of the Ghana National Students Organization (GNSO) as a rival student organization to NUGS, and the arrest and detention of five NUGS leaders and a professor. Reading rooms for party literature were established in all educational institutions and a committee was established to remove all antisocialist and antiparty books from libraries and bookshelves in Ghana. The arrest of three students following the death of Danquah in 1965 was the final move to bring the universities of Ghana into line. Though all these measures succeeded in preventing the universities and students from embarking on any militant political action, they failed to convert them into supporters of Nkrumah and his party. It was not surprising then that their overthrow evoked such spontaneous and open jubilation on the campuses.

It was not the universities alone which failed to embark on confrontational activities against the government. So did the TUC, the Ghana Bar Association, and the churches. The TUC certainly cooperated with Nkrumah and the CPP in their struggle for independence. By using the Industrial Relations Act of December 1958 and by ensuring that the head of the TUC was always a government nominee, the CPP government managed to turn the TUC into an integral part of the party after independence.

It was, in the end, not the conflict between the CPP government and the ethnic and socioeconomic parties and associations that brought nemesis upon Nkrumah and his party but that between the state government and its organs. The judiciary and the police were certainly the objects of attack by the party. Although the chief justice was sacked in 1963, following the attack on Nkrumah in January 1964, two heads of the police were detained and all regional police heads were dismissed. By that time, the only institution that had not been effectively cowed into submission was the army.

Like the universities, the army witnessed unprecedented growth and expansion during the Nkrumah period, from 4,000 troops in 1957, to 6,000 to 7,000 in 1960–61, and to a record 14,600 by February 1966. An air force and a navy were added immediately after independence and by 1966 were 650 and 970 strong, respectively. This increase was accompanied by a rapid Africanization of the officer corps, completed by September 1960 with 200 Ghanaian officers; by 1966, between 550 and 650 officers were serving in the three armed forces.[13] This phenomenal expansion of the armed forces was undertaken by Nkrumah, as is generally agreed, to enable him to realize his dreams of the total liberation of the African continent from colonialism and apartheid, the political union of all African states under his presidency, and Pan-Africanism.

Relations between the military and the government were quite cordial until Nkrumah dispatched army units to the Congo in 1960 under UN command. The total mishandling of this adventure by Nkrumah and the Ghanaian politicians, which resulted in the death of some

Ghanaian soldiers, provided the first source of conflict between the two institutions.[14] The armed forces did not escape the politicization of all structures and institutions of the state from 1960 onward. The British Chief of Defense staff Brigadier H. T. Alexander protested against this state of affairs and reminded Nkrumah of the well-known British doctrine to "keep the army out of politics and politics out of the army." Partly for this reason Nkrumah terminated Alexander's appointment and accelerated the Africanization process.

Following the attempt on his life in 1962, Nkrumah established an armed forces bureau and a military counterintelligence unit to mount surveillance on the military, which aroused strong resentment among officers. But what increased the growing tension between the army and the government was the establishment and development after 1962 of a presidential detail department for his own security made up of small civilian security units and of the President's Own Guard Regiment (POGR) trained by Russian officers. Although the regular army troops were going about in tattered uniforms and were badly equipped, the POGR forces were well equipped with modern weapons and well dressed. They had control over secret military camps in different parts of the country and especially around Accra. The dismissal of Chief of Defense Staff S. J. A. Otu and Army Chief Joseph A. Ankrah toward the end of 1965 and the alerting of the army for offensive operations in Rhodesia following that country's unilateral declaration of independence, together with the deteriorating economic and social conditions, precipitated the coup of February 24, 1966, which overthrew Nkrumah and his CPP government. The dictatorial and oppressive regime of Nkrumah, whose principal mode of conflict management was repression, was replaced by the National Liberation Council led first by Ankrah and later by General A. Afrifa. In its zeal to become the leading country of a newly independent Africa, Nkrumah's regime alienated an increasing number of groups in Accra by turning their demands into conflict and causes for repression. Even his erstwhile supporters, such as the labor unions, were not spared, and the party government moved whenever possible to take over the groups and repress their demands. Since his economic policies of nationalization and industrialization created more demand-bearing groups, by the same token, they also created more opposition and conflict. Economic reserves were used to buy off some of these demands, but for the most part, demanding groups were treated as subversive, causing them in turn to confirm the treatment and escalate their demands. The pattern of governments acting as the main party to, rather than the main manager of, conflict had been established.

## The National Liberation Council Regime, 1966–69

The National Liberation Council (NLC) was composed of four army and four police officers. In terms of governance and conflict management, the NLC was easily the most successful regime that the country has ever had. Indeed, with few exceptions, such conflicts as emerged during the period were not between the demand-bearing or pressure groups and the government, or between the government and the state, or between the military and the civilians. They were rather conflicts within the army and among the civilians, especially the political groups themselves, signified by the countercoup of April 1967 and the Otu affair of November 1968 on the one hand and interparty struggle for power on the other. The government proved to be an effective manager of these conflicts by maintaining domestic security and by providing free and fair elections as an arbitrating mechanism.

There was a tremendous increase in the number and tempo of activities of demand-bearing groups in society during the NLC regime. The decree (NLCD. 299 of November 5, 1968) establishing the constitutent assembly lists thirty-eight organizations that were to be represented on the assembly. Pinkney also lists about thirty other bodies as a sample of "a random list of bodies reported in the press to have made demands on the Government."[15] Another important pressure group that emerged immediately after the coup was the Legon Society on National Affairs (LSNA), formed by some concerned lecturers of the University of Ghana with its mouthpiece, the fortnightly journal, *Legon Observer*.

However, apart from the TUC and the LSNA, there was hardly any serious conflict between these groups and the NLC, and the conflicts between the demands of the various groups did not have the time to develop. The relationship between the TUC and the NLC steadily deteriorated, as is evident from the fact that the number of strikes mainly over daily wages increased from thirteen in 1965 to twenty-nine in 1966, twenty-four in 1967, and fifty-nine in 1969. It was only the return to civilian rule in October 1969 that averted a complete collapse of NLC-union relations.

In the universities, both the academic staff and the students readily

and heartily welcomed the coup. The students showed a certain interest in the activities of the NLC. The NUGS sent one or two memos, including one containing constitutional proposals in December 1966 and
also criticized the NLC decrees on rumor-mongering and detention
without trial as "extremely dangerous and capable of being abused."
However, the students on the whole continued their precoup attitude of
nonparticipation in politics. By the end of the NLC regime no student
activism had developed nor had any new militant political groups
emerged.[16] It was only the LSNA that clashed with the NLC.

Like the students and other members of the academic community
and the professional class in general, the founders and members of
LSNA readily welcomed the coup and did everything they could to ensure the success of the NLC. Their support for the NLC was, however,
not unconditional, and they did not hesitate to criticize the measures
and policies of NLC in the editorials and in a section of the *Legon Observer* (LO) called "Notes and Queries." Such critical articles and editorials provoked the anger of the NLC, which culminated in its dragging
the LSNA to court in January for contempt for its comments on a case
pending before an Accra high court.[17] The chief justice readily accepted
the society's plea of guilty and merely cautioned and discharged its
members. This was the only major clash between the NLC and the intelligentsia.

Other instances of conflict during the period were within two of the
components of these groups, namely, the army and the political elite.
Evidence of a split in the army was provided by the countercoup
launched on April 17, 1967, by two young lieutenants, S. B. Arthur and
Moses Yeboah, because of lack of promotion.[18] Though the move failed,
it resulted in the capture and murder of General E. K. Kotoka, the principal architect of the 1966 coup.

The second was the conflict that broke out among the politicians following the lifting of the ban on party political activities on May 1, 1969.
Though more than twenty parties mushroomed after the ban was lifted
at the time of the election on August 29, 1969, five parties had survived
the campaign. They were the Progress Party (PP) led by K. A. Busia,
the National Alliance of Liberals (NAL) led by Komla A. Gbedemah,
the All People's Representative Party (APRP) led by P. K. K. Quaidoo,
the People's Action Party (PAP) led by Imoru Ayarna, and the United
Nationalist Party (UNP) led by H. S. Bannerman. As shown by both the
leadership and the election results, the conflict among these parties was
not only class based but also ethnic and regionalist.

The leadership of the PP was solidly professional-merchant upper-middle class, identical with that of the former UGCC/UP party. The NAL leadership was professional and middle class at the national level but very lower-middle class at the local level. A majority including its leaders were members of the right wing of the former CPP, hence the identification of NAL with the CPP. The APRP ended up as an amalgamation of a number of parties and interests founded by some trade unionists and led by the ex-CPP businessman P. K. K. Quaidoo.

In the elections, the PP gained a landslide victory, winning 105 of the 140 seats, followed by NAL with 29 seats, UNP and PAP with 2 seats each, APRP with 1 seat, and one independent candidate. Though the PP won seats in all the regions of the country, it won all the seats in Asante, Brong Ahafo, Central, 18 out of the 22 in Eastern, and 10 of the 13 in the Western Region[19]—all regions occupied by the Akan. The NAL won 14 of the 16 seats in the Volta Region, the predominantly Ewe region, while the PP won only 2 seats there. The UNP, which was generally seen as the Ga Party, won both its two seats in the Accra Region, which is predominantly Ga, while PAP won its 2 seats among the Nzema of the Western Region of the country. It is quite evident from these figures that in the southern parts of the country, the elections were perceived and contested in purely ethnic terms and essentially between the Akan and the Ewe. By the end of the NLC regime, the ethnic factor in Ghanaian politics had become crucial, and the country had become more polarized ethnically than before. By conceiving their identity in ethnic terms, the parties lost their ability to manage interethnic conflict and rivalry, and elections became suppression.

Conflict was reduced to a minimum during the NLC regime, confined as it was, essentially between the TUC and part of the intelligentsia over allocative demands on the one hand, and within the army and the political elite on the other over claims to rule. Relations between the government and the other numerous pressure or demand-bearing groups remained smooth and peaceful, and the former enjoyed the full support and active cooperation of the latter. It is not surprising therefore that the NLC peacefully handed over power to the new civilian regime of Busia and his Progress Party in October 1969.

## The Busia Regime, 1969–72

Like its predecessor, the Busia regime started its administration, as borne out by the election results, with an unquestioned legitimacy. It enjoyed the support of practically all except the Ewe and the NAL and a few of the numerically small opposition groups. However, unlike the NLC, the regime had within the even shorter period of only twenty-seven months lost the support of practically all the demand-bearing groups of society except one, its rural constituency, which, though numerically the largest, lacks political clout, salience, or muscle.

Busia and his PP government first took on the enormous socioeconomic problems facing the country—shortage of essential goods such as drugs, food items, and spare parts, rising inflation, the inconvertibility of the cedi with its thriving black market trade, high unemployment, the rural-urban contrast, huge international debts, and above all the high and unfulfilled expectations of the electorate. Unfortunately, in the process of handling each of these serious problems, Busia and his government managed to come into conflict with practically every important demand group or center of electoral power after the first year or so of honeymoon between them.

The first group to be alienated was the armed forces. Having voted overwhelmingly for Busia—as 65 percent were estimated to have done—they were expecting ample rewards. On the contrary, instead of seeing their conditions of service improve, the reverse took place. In both the first and especially the second budgets, even the few privileges that they were enjoying were abolished or reduced—free rent, free water, free electricity, and especially car maintenance allowance—while the 1971 budget also reduced the vote for the armed forces. It was also in protest against the drastic cut of the army vote that the Chief of Defense Staff Air Vice Marshal M. A. Otu resigned and retired. This event eventually led to the appointment of Lieutenant Colonel I. K. Acheampong as the commander of the First Infantry Brigade, who was to overthrow Busia's regime shortly after.[20]

The second demand group that Busia took on was the civil service. In the 1970 budget, Busia took the courageous and overdue if in retrospect foolhardy step of abolishing or reducing perquisites introduced by the colonial regime for its civil servants. Thus, while the car maintenance and table allowances, among others, were abolished, the mileage allowance was reduced, and rent for housing was increased from the nominal 10 percent to 20 percent of the tenant's salary. The impact of this draconic measure on the morale and pockets of civil servants was obvious and so also was their reaction.

Busia and the Progress Party government also alienated the business community with several measures, such as the abolition of the import license system, which many, especially the Lebanese and Indian businessmen, had exploited, and the sharp devaluation of the cedi by as much as 44 percent. That led to the closing down of several businesses and industries and an increase in the cost of living and inflation. Though the government introduced measures that benefited this constituency, such as the Small Business Loan Schemes, the Ghanaian Business Bill, which restricted a number of businesses to Ghanaians, and the Aliens Compliance Order, it never won back the full support of the business community. The incredible devaluation of December 1971 was the final straw.

Another prop of the government that Busia lost was the university students. To raise more funds for development especially of the primary and secondary sectors, and to extend the austerity measures and sacrifices being imposed on the society at large, the government abolished free university education and substituted for it an interest-free loan scheme. The university students, who had actively campaigned for the PP during the elections, became increasingly disillusioned.[21] The students' loan scheme sharpened the conflict between the two even further, and they reacted with insulting behavior to Busia when he went to the Legon campus.

Even the judiciary did not escape the PP government's aggressive moves. This became obvious over an episode that became known as Apollo 568. Taking advantage of the necessary provisions of the constitution, Busia's government dismissed 568 members of the public service for unstated reasons. When one of these people, E. K. Sallah, contested his dismissal in the Supreme Court and won, Busia in a highly emotional public radio and television speech attacked the judgment of the Supreme Court, boasting that no court could enforce any decision that sought to compel the government to employ or reemploy anyone. This speech not only shocked the bench, it also disappointed all those who had read Busia on democracy in Africa, the rule of law, and the theory of the separation of powers.

But with no other interest group did Busia and his government get into such violent conflict as they did with the TUC. The PP regime aroused the suspicions of the TUC at the third TUC Biennial Congress in June 1970 when it tried to remove B. A. Bentum, the incumbent secretary general, by backing K. A. Mensah of the General Transport and Petroleum Workers Union. Bentum had already soundly defeated him in a vote of 194 to 17. The regime also began to support unions that wanted to break away from the TUC.[22] But what worsened relations were clashes over wages, wage arrears, dismissals, and collective agreements. To forestall a possible general strike and to break the TUC's campaign against the development levy of 1 percent introduced in July 1971, the PP government in September rushed through Parliament a new Industrial Relations Act. Under this act, the TUC created in 1958 by Nkrumah was abolished, and individual unions were requested to reregister and hold new elections. New unions were allowed to be formed, check-off dues were ended, union funds were frozen, and strikes were made illegal.[23] It is therefore not surprising that the TUC indeed welcomed Colonel Acheampong as a redeemer. This abolition of the TUC by Busia and his government made up of professionals and intellectuals of the day sowed a seed of distrust and suspicion between workers and the professional-intellectual class, which influenced the course of history during the Acheampong regime.

The final group that the PP government alienated was the opposition. The mainline CPP politicians were not allowed to participate in the 1969 elections when their own party, the Peoples' Popular Party, led by William Lutterodt and Imoru Egala, was banned. They therefore looked anxiously for a return to the fray, and they and some of the NAL instigated Acheampong's coup of January 1972.[24]

It should be evident from the above that within the incredibly short period of twenty-seven months (October 1969 to January 1972) Busia and his PP government were entangled in serious conflict with practically every important group in the country. As the object of conflict with various groups in society, the government was unable to manage society's conflicts. Its early overthrow in the bloodless coup of January 1972 was not entirely a bolt from the blue. Yet it was only naiveté and lack of political skill that brought the government to this pass. Its program was sound and necessary after Nkrumah's extravagant decade and the fall of producer prices on the world market. Busia applied a comprehensive reform program that trimmed the excess benefits of most of the sectors of modern urban society—its own supporters. But the government had a decade of populism and a mountain of expectations to overcome, and it applied its measures in an authoritarian fashion without explanation or negotiation with affected groups. These groups demanded the maintenance of an untenable status quo, and instead of bringing out the conflicts between their demands and mediating them, the government took them on one by one and became their enemy.

## The Era of the Men on Horseback, 1972–79

The era of the "men on horseback" was the most turbulent, violent, and conflict-ridden period in the history of the country. Ghana's move from conflict among groups to conflict between groups in society and the government led increasingly to the government's resorting to repression when other means failed. During this short period of less than eight years, there were as many as three regimes: the National Redemption Council (NRC), which was changed to the Supreme Military Council (SMC)I in 1975; SMC II in 1978; and the Armed Forces Revolutionary Council (AFRC) in 1979. And there were three heads of state: Colonel I. K. Acheampong, Lieutenant General F. W. K. Akuffo, and Flight Lieutenant Jerry J. Rawlings.

The NRC regime of January 13, 1972, consisted of Colonel Acheampong (promoted to general in March 1976), ten other senior military officers, the inspector general of police, and a lawyer appointed as commissioner for justice and attorney general. Moreover, all the commissioners appointed to take charge of the various ministries as well as those placed in charge of some corporations were soldiers.[25] Though almost all the major demand-bearing groups in society had been alienated or annoyed by the Busia regime, none but the TUC and the students really welcomed Acheampong's coup. Nor did the general populace accept it, since people were unanimous that never again should the military intervene in political affairs. The NRC therefore faced a crisis of legitimacy unlike its two predecessors.

Among the steps that Acheampong took immediately after the coup to achieve legitimacy and survival were the abolition of some of the harsh economic measures introduced by Busia, revaluating the cedi, abolishing the development levy, and restoring fringe benefits for the military and civil servants. However, what captivated and won the support of large sectors of the society, especially students and the radical elements, was the "Yentua (We Won't Pay) Speech" of February 5, 1972, in which he unilaterally repudiated $94.4 million of the nation's debts from contracts that were said to be tainted with "fraud, corruption or other illegality" and seized 55 percent of equity shares in foreign mining companies. Finally, to buttress the support of labor, he repealed Busia's Industrial Relations Act of 1971 to reestablish the TUC. He also paid a great deal of attention to agriculture under the Operation Feed Yourself campaign to make the nation self-sufficient in food. As a result of all these measures, the NRC by 1974 had achieved legitimacy, and

Acheampong had become the most popular and successful ruler that the country had ever seen. He had bought himself out of illegitimacy through populist payments to the most critical groups—students, labor, business, civil servants, military—out of the public purse of reform.

However, the period of the SMC I rule (1975–78) was one of general economic decline characterized by falling agricultural and industrial productivity, galloping inflation (which rose from 3 percent in 1970 to 10.1 percent in 1972), acute shortage of essential inputs and spare parts, and an incredible rise in the cost of living. The government then sought to submerge the ensuing conflicts in 1976 by imposing a nonpartisan system of Union Government (UNIGOV), composed of the army, the police, and civilians, through a referendum on March 30, 1978.

In the execution of its plans, the NRC clashed with a number of demand-bearing groups. Among the most important were the workers though not the TUC, some ethnic groups, the students, professional groups, political groups, the churches, and finally even the armed forces. Relations between the NRC and the reestablished TUC became very close and friendly throughout the NRC regime. Between 1972 and 1974, the NRC made clear its opposition to strikes and industrial protests and went out of its way to meet the demands of the workers. As a result of this stick and carrot approach, strikes dropped sharply from a record of seventy-eight in 1971 to only fourteen in 1972 and fourteen in 1973. From 1974, however, the workers resumed their strikes mainly over wages, the number rising from fourteen in 1973 to forty-three in 1974. Though the number stabilized at thirty-three in 1975 and forty-five in 1976, relations between the workers and the NRC became strained because of the failure of the NRC to contain inflation.[26]

Like the TUC and the workers, the students of the universities became the regime's most ardent supporters. However, also like the workers, the students became disillusioned with the NRC's economic and security policies from 1974 onward, and the conflict escalated thereafter. The breach came into the open when NUGS organized a demonstration in February 1974 on all the three campuses in protest against military and police brutalities against civilians. The NRC's response was to close down all three universities on the same day and not reopen them for a month.

The students then became more critical of the NRC, calling its revolution a caricature and a myth,[27] and in January 1975 they again demonstrated against the government. Throughout 1977 the students continued their opposition to the government, which led to the closure of the universities in May and June until September 1977.[28] On January 13, 1978, on the occasion of the sixth anniversary of Acheampong's coup, students demonstrated on all three campuses and fought bloodily with the police. After the referendum of March 1978, many student leaders were arrested and detained, and the universities were once again closed from May until mid-July.

The political groups with which the NRC clashed were the former CPP, which had divided into the Justice Party and the People's Popular Party, (the ex-PP group), the Ghana Peace and Solidarity Council, and the Movement for the Liberation of Western Togoland, revived in 1973 with Togolese support to reunite the former two Togos and banned in March 1976.[29] New anti-NRC groups that emerged included the People's Movement for Freedom and Justice (PMFJ), the Third Force, and the Front for the Prevention of Dictatorship (FPD). These three groups were formed in late 1977 and early 1978 primarily to campaign for the restoration of civilian rule, especially for a no vote in the referendum on UNIGOV.[30] They were assisted by the Christian Council, the Catholic Secretariat, the NUGS, the Bar Association, and the Association of Recognized Professional Bodies (ARPB), all vehemently opposed to UNIGOV. The methods used by these groups included countercoups, subversion, newspaper campaigns, political campaigns, demonstrations, rallies, and petitions to outside bodies, among others. In July 1972 and in June and October 1973, some of the political groups attempted to overthrow the NRC through a countercoup. They failed and all the leaders were arrested, tried, and sentenced to twenty-five years' imprisonment.[31] In March 1975, the former leader of the People's Popular Front and four others were arrested for allegedly organizing people for subversion through the Ghana Peace and Solidarity Council. In November 1975, the minister of finance of the Busia regime, Busia's private secretary, and a former PP member of Parliament were arrested and tried for sedition and convicted. In August 1977, a former commissioner in Acheampong's government, a PP activist, and two army captains were also detained for suspected subversion.

In opposition to these movements, Acheampong formed and financed a host of clubs and societies. These included the Ghana Peace and Solidarity Council, the African Youth Command, the Ghana Cooperative Council, the Association of Market Women, Fishermen, and Bakers, the Constitution Study Group, the Friends, the Kumasi Youngsters Club, the Ghana National Reconstruction Corps, the Volta Youth and Development Association, and the Organizers' Council.[32] Most of these bodies did not enjoy any support. Some traditional rulers, some of the Pentecostal and sectarian churches, and the Muslims also supported UNIGOV.[33] It was mainly the mobilization and education of the people in clandestine political campaigns by the anti-UNIGOV forces that led to the rejection of UNIGOV.

However, the groups that posed the greatest challenge to the NRC-SMC regime were the professional groups. These included the Legon Society on National Affairs (LSNA), the Ghana Bar Association, and the ARPB with its own magazine, *News Bulletin*, established in 1977.[34] The main issues between the professionals and the government were the rule of law and the return of the country to democratic civilian constitutional rule based on a multiparty system, considered the best way to have demands aired and conflicts resolved. The LSNA, through its mouthpiece, the *Legon Observer*, continued its criticisms as the NRC blundered along. These criticisms became more and more acid until it was compelled to stop publication in July 1974. It did not resume publication until after the palace coup of July 1978.

The next professional body to join the fray was the Ghana Bar Association. At the Conference of Faculty, Bench, and Bar at the State House in June 1974, the president of the association criticized the Armed Forces Special Powers Decree of 1973, which empowered the arrest and indefinite detention of anybody in military custody. The Bar Association followed this up later with a petition to the government to abolish military tribunals and to guarantee the liberty of the individual.[35] The government turned down all these requests.

In reaction to the declaration of the UNIGOV concept in October 1976, the Bar Association asked the SMC I for the first time in December 1976 to return the country to civilian rule no later than 1978. In February 1977 the Bar Association called on Ghanaians to reject the idea of UNIGOV as inimical to the interest of the people and called for the dissolution of the fourteen-member ad hoc committee established in January 1977 to collate proposals on a union government. It also repeated a call for return to civilian rule by the end of 1978. In reply to Acheampong's contention that there should be economic recovery before the restoration of civilian rule, the Bar Association argued that "the inherent right of the people to representative government cannot depend on the economic situation of the country at any particular time."[36]

In June 1977 the Bar Association was joined in its opposition to UNIGOV and its call for return to civilian rule by the powerful ARPB. Incensed by Acheampong's intransigence, the closure of all universities, and the dismissal of some senior public servants, including the governor of the Bank of Ghana, the chief justice, and two professors of the Ghana Medical School, the ARPB passed a resolution on June 23, 1977. The statement accused the government of "incompetence and corruption" and issued an ultimatum that if the SMC had not resigned by July 1, 1977, it would withdraw its services. Instead of resigning, Acheampong tried to placate the ARPB by announcing a timetable for the restoration of civilian rule on July 1, 1979.

The timetable, however, did not satisfy the Bar Association or the ARPB. They therefore went on strike or, as they said, "withdrew their services" on July 6, 1977. Made up of engineers, doctors, university lecturers, nurses, and lawyers, the ARPB brought the whole country to a halt with all hospitals, universities, and the courts closed while Accra was plunged into total darkness without light, water, or petrol. Had the TUC joined the strike or the ARPB held out a little longer, the SMC would have resigned. But the TUC flatly refused to join because of its experience under Busia. However, through the intervention of a former Supreme Court judge, senior citizens, and church dignitaries, negotiations between the government and the ARPB on July 12–14 ended with an agreement on return to civilian rule in 1978; members of ARPB were not to be victimized or molested and there was to be freedom of the press.[37] On the basis of this agreement, the strike was called off on July 18. Six days later, however, Acheampong went back on his word and decided to stick to his original timetable.

The UNIGOV referendum took place, as was planned, on March 30, 1978. It is generally believed that the elections were rigged, but even according to the results published by the government only 56.6 percent of those who voted were in favor of UNIGOV. Acheampong's moves immediately after the referendum confirmed that he was not satisfied with its outcome. He banned the PMFJ, the Third Force, and the FPD, and on April 4 he detained all their leading members who had not been able to slip out of the country.[38] This quixotic reaction, the results of his own referendum, contributed to his fall four months later.

The last important demand-bearing group to come into conflict with Acheampong was the army. This conflict assumed two forms, ethnic and professional, and ended in the overthrow of Acheampong through a palace coup in July 1978. Until March 1974, the NRC operated smoothly without any splits, and the original architects of the coup, the two Akan officers and the two Ewe officers played the leading roles. From then on, however, reports of conflicts in the NRC and favoritism toward the Akan and against the Ewe by Acheampong himself resulted in replacing the NRC with the SMC in October 1975. The composition of the SMC drastically reduced the Ewe representation. In protest the two Ewe officers and one Akan officer who were among the original architects of the coup, resigned on October 15, 1975, and were immediately retired from the army. This step was followed by the promotion of more Akan officers at the expense of Ewes, completely destroying the Akan-Ewe solidarity in the armed forces.

It was undoubtedly to restore a Ewe leadership role in the army that a coup was attempted by young Ewe officers on December 4, 1975. The brain behind the attempt was said to be a retired Ewe brigadier, and the leaders were four young Ewe officers, a retired Ewe captain, and an Ewe lecturer at Cape Coast University.[39] They failed and were tried and convicted. These events further heightened the tension between the Ewe and the Akan in the armed forces, whose repercussions are still being felt two decades later.

The other conflict within the army was purely professional. The rank and file were in conflict with the NRC-SMC and the top officer corps. Unlike the NLC, the Acheampong's SMC government and the commissioners were made up exclusively of officers. Most of the soldiers appointed to head some boards and corporations were also officers. Unfortunately, few of them could resist the temptation of using their offices to amass wealth and property through fair or foul means and living ostentatious and flamboyant lives with their wives, concubines, and girlfriends. By 1974 reports were circulating of a growing rift between the other ranks and the officers mainly because of the cancerous growth of corruption at the highest level.

To heal this conflict Acheampong set up the Armed Forces Advisory Council to act as a liaison between the government and soldiers in July 1974 under the chairmanship of the air force commander. The replacement of the NRC by the SMC in October did not end but rather intensified bribery and corruption and property acquisition by the top officer corps and even by some of the rank and file. It was partly to save the country from economic collapse, to end the arbitrary detention of civilian leaders and professionals, to end the dictatorship and corruption of

Acheampong, and finally to rehabilitate the tarnished image of the armed forces that Acheampong was removed in a palace coup on July 5, 1978. This was led by Brigadier Neville A. Odartey-Wellington and Lieutenant General F. W. K. Akuffo and resulted in the establishment of SMC II headed by Akuffo.

Had the new regime taken effective measures to rehabilitate the image of the armed forces by punishing Acheampong and all the other officers noted for their corruption and immoral living, it would probably have survived. But it failed to take these necessary measures mainly because all the members of the new SMC were part and parcel of the corruption, moral degeneration, and social injustice of the previous regime. It was not surprising therefore that the junior officers and other ranks under the leadership of Flight Lieutenant Rawlings successfully staged a countercoup, after the failure of their May 15 attempt, on June 4, 1979.[40] This led to the overthrow of SMC II and its replacement by the Armed Forces Revolutionary Council (AFRC). This council was composed of Rawlings as chairman, two majors, a captain, a warrant officer, and seven other ranks. Notably, not a single officer beyond the rank of major served on the council. Equally significant, as in the first NRC government, there was an ethnically broad-based council with the Akan and Ewe once more in dominant positions.

It was evident from the first broadcast of Rawlings to the nation on June 17, 1979, that the main motives of the AFRC were to rehabilitate the image of the armed forces and embark on a housecleaning exercise. The revolutionary council remained true to its word. It confirmed the timetable drawn up by the SMC II for the return to civilian rule and exposed and punished with death by firing squad or very long terms of imprisonment "after some sort of trial" by ad hoc tribunals all those accused or suspected of corruption, tax evasion, and other forms of social injustice not only in the armed forces but also among the civilian population. The council executed by firing squad the leading members of both SMC I and II, including General Acheampong and General Akuffo, mostly on charges of corruption and abuse of office. Most unfairly and regrettably, General Akwasi A. Afrifa of the NLC, who had already been cleared by a commission of inquiry of all these charges, was also executed.

On June 18, 1979, the general election took place. It was contested by six parties, including the People's National Party (PNP) led by Hilla Limann, which descended from Nkrumah's CPP, the Popular Front

Party (PFP) under Victor Owusu, and the United National Convention (UNC) under William Ofori Atta. Owusu and Atta identified themselves with Busia's PP. The elections were narrowly won by the PNP with 71 of the 140 seats, followed by the PFP with 42 seats, and the UNC with 13 seats.[41] On September 21, a week earlier than stipulated, the AFRC handed power over to the PNP government under Hilla Limann, and the third republic was born.

The military regimes of the 1970s won popularity by "reforming" the reforms of the previous regime and thereby exacerbating the worsened economic conditions of the world market by overspending and lowered productivity at home. The negative effects reversed Acheampong's popularity and fueled the greatest activity of demand-bearing groups in civil society since Ghana's beginnings. The perpetuation of the regime under UNIGOV was effectively defeated. The SMC regimes also introduced a new political ethos, the idea of time at the trough, of rapid enrichment from public office. Rumors, populism, predator incumbency, and fiscal irresponsibility activated the groups of civil society but focused them against government rather than in favor of substantive reforms. Thus they were poorly trained for constructive support of the civilian government that they had demanded.

### The Limann Regime, 1979–81

Limann started his administration with the goodwill of virtually the entire civilian population and the unquestionable legitimacy won by free and fair elections. However, contrary to all expectations, a series of conflicts limited the regime to only twenty-seven months. Before the end of its first year in office, it become obvious that Limann and his government could not cope with the serious socioeconomic situation they had inherited. On the contrary, the situation steadily grew worse. Inflation continued and increased from 50 percent in 1980 to 116.5 percent in 1981. This growth was caused mainly by budget deficits, which rose from 2.94 billion cedis in 1980 to 5.49 billion cedis in 1982.[42] Acute shortages of all basic commodities, spare parts, and raw materials led to rising prices and corruption while food scarcities hit all classes in general and workers in particular. The workers responded with a series of strikes that compelled the government to increase the minimum and all other wages threefold in November 1980. These increases, however, did not solve the conflicts over production and allocation and were quickly thrown out of gear by the high inflation. The strikes by workers resumed, culminating in a general strike by the TUC in the spring of 1981.[43]

Even more hostile was the attitude of students toward the PNP regime. They staged strikes and demonstrations in protest against the deteriorating economic conditions. These were suppressed with brutality by the police, resulting in the killing of one student and the closure of the universities in April 1980.

The main professional groups that came into conflict with the Limann administration again were the Ghana Bar Association and the ARPB. The principal bones of contention between the Bar Association and the government were the administration of justice and the economy. Limann accused the bench of "not having recovered from its deep slumber of the past," of delaying the administration of justice and together with the bar of "using legal technicalities which becloud common sense and smother plain truth." The Bar Association denied the use of legal technicalities but admitted the delay of justice, which it attributed to "the failure of the Executive to provide the necessary facilities and support for the judiciary." It also pointed to the intolerably poor conditions of service, which together with the above lapses "have introduced a deep sense of frustration and low morale in the judicial service."[44]

The Bar Association and the professionals also clashed with the government over the economy. At its annual conference in November 1980 and its emergency general meeting held in April 1981, the Bar Association criticized the "general deteriorating conditions of the national economy and the deplorable health services" and suggested measures to be taken to deal with the situation. In October 1981, the Bar Association condemned the huge sums committed to the celebration of twenty-five years of independence, the Silver Jubilee, on the grounds that the funds should "be used in a manner that shall be beneficial to the suffering people of this country and to alleviate the day to day problems of the ordinary man in the street."[45] Since "nothing appeared to have been done by the President" on all these issues raised by the Bar Association by December 1981, it was not surprising that it very reluctantly though instantly welcomed the coup at the end of the month.

Besides the workers, students, and the professionals, the Limann regime came into conflict with some political groups. Some of them were traditional, but others were entirely new and populist and ideological in orientation. These newly emergent groups were to have a revolutionary impact on the politics of the country.

The old parties that constituted the opposition in Parliament were the PFP, UNC, ACP, and SDF. Unfortunately, instead of cooperating with the PNP to solve the serious socioeconomic problems of the day, they went out of their way to make things as difficult as possible. For instance, they teamed up to reject the PNP's 1981–82 budget proposals, the first time that happened in the parliamentary history of Ghana. It is also generally believed that some of them, especially the leaders of the PFP, in their eagerness to gain power plotted with some soldiers to stage a coup. Some were said to have been privy to what occurred on December 31, 1981. Earlier in June 1981, the PFP, UNC, ACP, and the Third Force came together to form the All Peoples' Party (APP), a greatly increased threat to the ruling party.

Paradoxically enough, however, one of the most serious and persistent conflicts that Limann faced was with his own party, the PNP. Within four months of assumption of office, a serious division occurred in the leadership of the PNP between Imoru Egala, the "father of the party," and its chairman, Nana Okutwer Bekoe. Indeed, Egala asked for an investigation into the issue of import licenses to a company owned by Bekoe. Not only did this polarization get worse, but it became even more complex as time rolled on. By April 1981, three more camps had emerged. The first was the Nkrumaist old guard led by people such as Kojo Botsio, Ayeh Kumi, Kwesi Armah, Kofi Batsa, and Kofi Badu. Though mouthing Nkrumaist and socialist rhetoric and slogans, they were at heart right wing and big businessmen.

The second camp was the leftist wing of the Nkrumaist old guard. It consisted of people such as Kojo Addison, Johnny Hansen, Kwesi Gyan-Apenteng, and Kwesi Ghapson, all of the Kwame Nkrumah Revolutionary Guards (KNRG). Because they were associates of the Winneba Ideological Institute established by Nkrumah, they were opposed to any dealings with the International Monetary Fund and the World Bank and disapproved of the pro-Western and capitalist tendencies of Limann. They advocated a return to Kwame Nkrumah's scientific socialism. The last group consisted of the new guard Nkrumaists who were younger PNP members of Parliament led by people such as George Benneh and Amon Nikoi, the minister of finance, who favored cooperation with the World Bank and the IMF over devaluation and advocated a pragmatic and democratic approach.

Limann did not originally belong to the Nkrumaist tradition but was imposed on the PNP by the "father of the party" and his clansman,

Egala, when he was disqualified from becoming the leader of the party by a commission of inquiry. Limann's hold on the party was therefore weak and grew weaker still when Egala died suddenly of a heart attack in March 1981. He could therefore not impose any measures that were considered radical or neocolonialist. In October 1981, he tried to assert his leadership and strengthen his hold on the party by reshuffling his cabinet, removing three cabinet ministers, four regional ministers, and two deputy ministers, and introducing a new party constitution, which would have enabled him to make appointments to all key party committees.

To thwart this last move, the "old guard" instituted an action in the high court in December 1981. These people also asked for details on all monies received in the name of the party.[46] Though this case was later settled out of court, in the opinion of the public it confirmed the widespread allegations of corruption in the top hierarchy of the party. It also led to the resignation of Okutwer Bekoe, the dissolution of the national executive, and the seizure of the control of the party once more by the old guards who were generally believed to be corrupt. In the light of all these circumstances, it is not surprising that Limann and his government failed to deal with the pressing economic problems and were overthrown at the end of the year.

However, the most interesting and significant development that took place in the politics of the country during the second half of the 1970s was the emergence of a number of left-wing radical organizations and pressure groups. The main ones were the June Fourth Movement (JFM), the Movement on National Affairs (MONAS), the New Democratic Movement (NDM), the Movement for Peace and Democracy (MOPAD), the Kwame Nkrumah Revolutionary Guards (KNRG), and the People's Revolutionary League of Ghana (PRLG). The founders and leaders of all these movements were university lecturers and students and some ex-soldiers such as Flight Lieutenant Rawlings, Captain Kojo Tsikata, Captain Boakye Gyan, and Sergeant Allolga Akata-Pore.[47] All these movements were Nkrumaist and Marxist in orientation and favored the socialist reconstruction of the society. They were also against neocolonialism and therefore opposed to any deals with the World Bank and the IMF, against devaluation and the privatization of state enterprises; only the NDM was ready to strike a deal with the IMF as a temporary measure. These radical groups mobilized the students and workers. They constituted the main support to Rawlings and were his principal advisers during the first two years of the PNDC's regime. Indeed, without their initial support, the "second coming" of Rawlings would have failed.

However, the greatest challenge that the Limann regime faced was from Rawlings, the former members of the AFRC, and the army. Rawlings had handed over power in September 1979 and returned to the air force with one strong determination, which was to see that what he called the "gains of the June 4 Revolution" were not destroyed or tampered with.[48] To him, these gains included the punishment by imprisonment of corrupt people, the confiscation of the assets of others, and the heavy fines paid to the state. This meant keeping an eagle eye on Limann and his PNP government, which Rawlings and the radical groups did with demagogic enthusiasm.

To end this policing and populism of Rawlings, Limann offered him and other members of the AFRC scholarships for further studies abroad. However, while all the other members accepted this offer and left the country, Rawlings rejected it and stayed behind to concentrate on his self-imposed policing responsibilities. Still bent on silencing him, Limann offered him a place on the Council of State, which Rawlings again turned down. Limann's last move was to take advantage of the jailbreak of four soldiers and a civilian from the Ussher Fort in November 1979, in which Rawlings was suspected to have been implicated, to retire him rather unceremoniously from the army.[49]

After his retirement in November 1979, Rawlings teamed up with three main groups to plan and execute the coup of December 31, 1981. These were the radical left-wing organizations, especially the JFM, Pan-African Youth Movement (PANYMO), and PRLG, a right-wing, civilian, mainly Ewe group; and finally the more radical soldiers in the armed forces. The civilian group, whose existence was not known to the radical groups, consisted of "Lebanese businessmen, right wing Ewes—mainly politicians and academics, a few Akans, retired as well as serving army officers."[50] This group became the financial backbone of the coup and was to play a decisive role in the PNDC administration. The predominantly Ewe nature of this group highlights the old ethnic factor in the 1981 coup.

The third group in the making of the 1981 coup was the Ghana armed forces. Relations between the armed forces and the Limann regime were never cordial and grew worse by month until the final confrontation in December 1981. The experiences of the 1970s had made the army not only politicized but also radicalized. The failure of the regime to detect this situation and completely depoliticize and deradicalize the army precipitated the regime's downfall.

This radicalization of sections of the Ghana Army began in the late 1970s, probably in 1978 with the formation of a clandestine group of junior officers, Africa 70s, under the leadership of Captain Boakye Djan, a Legon graduate who was later to become the spokesman of the AFRC. According to Zaya Yeebo, Rawlings was later recruited into that group, "a Nkrumaist politico-military organization of radical soldiers."[51] After the June 4 revolution, which was not the work of the radical wing of the army but rather that of the lower ranks, the radicalization of the army continued and was intensified by the spread of the JFM into the army and the recruitment of radical soldiers.

Some of the key radical soldiers were from the northern part of the country, Limann's area. They had important links with military intelligence and the Special Branch of the Police Force, and, because of their origins, were entrusted with the use of vital information on troop movements that these northern radical soldiers exploited for the success of the December 31, 1981, coup. In a way, then, this coup was comparable to Acheampong's coup of 1972; just as Acheampong betrayed his Akan head of state, Busia, these northerners also betrayed their northern head of state, Limann. However, since the term "northern" here is geographical rather than ethnic, and the northern soldiers did not belong to a single ethnic group, the ethnic factor in the December 31, 1981, coup should not be exaggerated. Rather, as Zaya Yeebo has sought to explain, what bound all these northern radical soldiers together was the fact that most of them were products of the Boys Company training school based in Kumasi and had therefore developed certain professional loyalties that enabled them to support one another.[52]

Indeed, Limann had to confront numerous problems, and relations were tense between him and the various demand-bearing groups. Unfortunately, Limann failed dismally to solve any of the problems or conflicts. He could not deal with the serious socioeconomic problems facing the country, nor could he satisfy the demands of the workers, the students, or the opposition for a fairer allocation of the economy. He could not even control his party members and restore discipline in his own party. Still, he would have survived if he had only been able to contain the threat from the army. However, even though everybody knew that coups were being plotted by both politicians and the radical soldiers, and especially by Rawlings and Kojo Tsikata, Limann simply refused to believe them. It was therefore no surprise to anyone but Limann when with the help of the radical soldiers drawn mainly from the Fifth Battalion of the Army, the air force, sections of the One Reconnaissance Unit, and some members of the JFM, Rawlings staged his coup in the early hours of December 31, 1981, to the joy of virtually all the demand-bearing groups.

## Rawlings and His PNDC Regime, since 1981

Rawlings envisaged his second intervention in the political affairs of the country or his "second coming," as nothing short of a revolution. In his first broadcast to the nation on December 31, 1981, he made it clear that his intervention was not a coup but a revolution that would transform the social and economic order of the country. To understand the nature of the revolution, governance, and conflict management, the PNDC rule should be divided into three phases. These are the populist and ideological phase from December 3, 1981, to March 1983; the adjustment and "culture of silence" phase from March 1983 to July 1987; and the consolidation and peaceful confrontationist phase since February 1988.

### The Populist and Ideological Phase

Under the first phase, Rawlings envisaged the revolution politically as the transfer of power to workers and the participation of the masses in the decisionmaking process. Socially, the revolution was seen as the continuation of the housecleaning exercise of June 4, the bridging of the yawning gap between the rich and the poor, and a move to ensure accountability, probity, and social justice in public life. Economically, the revolution was to see the end of neocolonialism and capitalist exploitation, the abolition of the reliance on foreign aid and agreements with the IMF, the World Bank, and other international capitalist and Western agencies, and the acquisition of the ownership of the means of production and exchange by the state. Most of these ideas were borrowed from the program of the JFM.

For the attainment of these objectives, Rawlings and his revolutionaries established a number of institutions and structures. The Provisional National Defense Council (PNDC), established on January 2, 1982, was to serve as the central government. Its membership consisted of four soldiers and three civilians, with Rawlings as chairman. The defense committees were to serve as "instruments of popular participation, political education, channels of communication to and from the leadership, and political control."[53] There were two types of defense committees: Workers' Defense Committees (WDC) formed by workers at their workplaces and in institutions, and the People's Defense Committees (PDC) organized by communities in the urban and rural areas. To oversee and coordinate their activities, an Interim National Coordinating Committee (INCC) was established in February 1982. The defense communities and the INCC were dominated by members of JFM.

Other institutions were the Citizens' Vetting Committee (CVC), public tribunals, the National Investigation Committee (NIC), the National Youth Organizing Commission (NYOC), the Students' Task Force and the December 31 Women's Movement. Public tribunals were established in all the regions to try cases of crime against the state and to introduce a new system of social justice, probity, and accountability. The CVC based in Accra was to investigate persons "whose lifestyles and expenditures substantially exceeded their own or declared incomes."[54] The NIC was also based in Accra to investigate persons reported to them by the public or referred to them by the PNDC. The December 31 Women's Movement was inaugurated at the Burma Camp on May 17, 1982, on the prompting of the JFM and later taken over by Konadu Agjeman Rawlings (Rawlings's wife) to organize and mobilize women in support of the revolution.

During this first phase, these bodies pursued the socialist and neo-Marxist objectives of the revolution with fanatical zeal, using harsh, unorthodox, and radical methods in the absence of any fixed program. Hundreds of businessmen and affluent citizens were hauled before the NIC, the CVC, and the tribunals, and savage sentences ranging from ten to sixty years of imprisonment and confiscation of assets to death by firing squad were imposed on them; price controls were reintroduced and rigidly enforced; and traders and market women were subjected to molestation, humiliation, harassment, and indecent and cruel treatment. To reduce the huge amount in circulation the PNDC withdrew the 50.00 cedi note, the highest note then available. Bank accounts of individuals and companies were frozen to facilitate the various investigations in progress.

The PDCs and WDCs, which soon sprang up throughout the country, took the law into their own hands and arbitrarily reduced rents, seized unoccupied houses and rooms, took over the administration of some factories and departments, and insisted on being or becoming part of the decisionmaking process. They took over the distribution and sale of goods through the peoples' shops which they set up, and they mobilized the people to undertake communal labor. The task force made up of students from the three universities evacuated cocoa locked up in the rural areas, repaired roads, cleared choked gutters in the cities, assisted in enforcing price controls, and launched self-help projects. Finally, in conformity with its radical and populist principles, the PNDC turned its attention to Libya and the eastern countries for assistance for reviving the country's economy, emphasized nationalization, preached self-reliance, and vehemently opposed any deals with the World Bank, IMF, and multinational corporations. In the short run, conflicting demands were met by a burst of popular revolutionary energy.

This populist phase also witnessed the kidnapping, brutal murder, and the burning of the bodies of three high court judges and a retired army major and group personnel manager of the Ghana Industrial Holding Corporation (GIHOC) on June 30, 1982. The main reason for the gruesome murder, which was planned by some members of the PNDC, was to punish the three judges for trying and acquitting some of the victims of the June 4 revolution.

The overall effects of all these radical and revolutionary measures and the failure of the PNDC to obtain any assistance from Libya and the communist countries were disastrous. Shops were empty, the infrastructure collapsed, and industries closed down or operated far below capacity. Although inflation was galloping, gasoline and petroleum products were rationed and queues were formed to buy basic foodstuffs such as kenkey and bread. Socially, infant mortality, hunger, physical deterioration of the human body, disease, poverty, moral degeneration, corruption, and nepotism became the order of the day. In short, Ghana was on the verge of economic collapse and social disintegration by the end of the populist phase while the fate of the PNDC itself was hanging on a very thin thread. However, to the surprise of all, including the PNDC itself, it did survive and has remained in the saddle ever since. How and why this feat of survival was accomplished will be discussed later. Of immediate concern are the interest groups that emerged during the first phase and the nature of the conflicts that were provoked by these populist measures.

During this period the interest groups remained virtually the same as in the immediate preceding period, namely, the radical and left-wing groups, the TUC, NUGS, ARPB, the Ghana Bar Association (GBA), religious groups such as the Christian Council, the Catholic Secretariat, and the Muslim Association, and the former political parties. Although all the radical and left-wing groups, the NUGS, and the TUC supported the PNDC, the other interest groups reacted negatively. The conflicts took the usual form of a combination of peaceful confrontation and violent military interventions. There were five countercoups d'etat during the period—March, July, October, November 1982, and February 1983. The first two attempts were organized and financed by some of the Ghanaian businessmen and politicians who had fled the country following the December 31 coup. The other three attempts were "basically military affairs arising out of the ideological conflicts within the PNDC and their supporters among the rank and file of the Army."[55]

Rawlings and his PNDC government resolved these conflicts through a mixture of peaceful negotiation, compromise, ruthlessness, and violence characterized by gross abuse of human rights, detention without trial, secret murders, and firing squads. Although the demands of the students, lawyers, and the other professionals were by and large ignored during the period, the public outcry evoked by the murder of the judges was such that the PNDC reluctantly agreed to institute a five-member special investigation board (SIB) under the chairmanship of a retired chief justice of Ghana to investigate these murders. In its report, the SIB concluded that the murders were planned by Kojo Tsikata, Sergeant Allolga Akata-Pore, and Amartey Kwei, all members of the PNDC, and executed by five soldiers selected by Tsikata.[56] Though the trial and execution of Kwei and the soldiers involved went some way to defuse the tension created by the murders, the government's refusal to accept the earlier finding and punish Tsikata enraged and has continued to enrage Ghanaians to this day. However, the most widespread methods resorted to in solving the conflicts of the day were secret and open murders, arbitrary arrests, detentions, and dismissals from the army. During the investigation by the SIB, some of the soldiers involved intimated that they had carried out three similar operations between March and June 1982 on the orders of their superior officers. Following the attempted coup of October 28 and 29, 1982, several members of the NDC and the Accra and Tema PDCs and WDCs were detained.

Taking advantage of the November 1982 coup, Rawlings moved to get rid of the radicals in both the army and the leftist organizations even though they were not implicated in the coup. Thus, Akata-Pore, five of his fellow officers, and all the soldiers known to be his supporters or belonging to the radical faction were arrested. Rawlings similarly arrested many of the cadres and coordinators of the United Front, an amalgamation of June 4 and KNRG in Accra and Tema, and dissolved the Upper, Greater Accra, and Volta regional secretariats of the NDC seen as the strongholds of the United Front. In protest against these atrocities, Chris Atim, Nyeya Yen (of the NDC), Kwesi Adu (of NYOC), Emmanuel Hansen (secretary to the PNDC), and Zaya Yeebo, secretary for youth and sports, resigned between December 1982 and January 1983. Most of them later fled the country, leaving only two of the original members of the PNDC, Rawlings and W. O. Adjei Boadi. Thus, by the end of the populist period, the radical challenge to Rawlings had been contained, the revolution had been betrayed, and the way was cleared for the launching of the adjustment and culture of silence phase of the PNDC regime.

## The Adjustment and Culture of Silence Phase

The adjustment phase of the PNDC regime began on March 6, 1983, with a dawn broadcast by the chairman of the PNDC. This speech was characterized by a series of policy initiatives that were diametrically opposed to those of the former phase but were calculated to solve the crises of economic decline and political survival facing the regime. They involved the introduction of the Economic Recovery or Structural Adjustment Program (ERP/SAP), the institution of new governmental machinery, and the designing and institution of a new political structure or in PNDC parlance, the "establishment of a new democratic order."

The ERP/SAP was drawn up as a result of consultations and negotiations conducted secretly, starting in April 1982, and publicly between September 1982 and the beginning of 1983. Parties included the PNDC, the IMF, and the World Bank, after a series of bitter conflicts between the PNDC and the NDM on the one hand and the JFM and the other very radical groups on the other. The objectives of the ERP were to restore incentives for production of food, industrial raw materials, and export commodities; to increase the availability of consumer goods and improve the distribution system; to increase the overall availability of foreign exchange; to lower the rate of inflation; to rehabilitate the physical infrastructure of the country in support of directly productive activities; and to restructure economic institutions, in a word, to manage the conflicts that had destroyed previous governments by providing enough economic growth to meet the demands of society.[57]

The strategies adopted to achieve these objectives, most of which the IMF had previously insisted upon, were devaluation of the cedi, removal of many subsidies on social services, abolition of price controls, liberalization of trade or the introduction of a free market economy, denationalization or disinvestiture of state enterprises, and retrenchment or retirement of workers from the public service. These harsh strategies imposed on the people in the budget of April 1983 were anathema to the radical populist forces and neo-Marxist intellectuals.

The implementation of the ERP greatly improved productivity, foreign exchange earnings, international trade, and the infrastructure in the country. However, its social impact has been disastrous. The removal of subsidies on social services raised hospital and education fees above the capability of most families and workers; though, as a result of trade liberalization, all kinds of goods became available, only the upper class and the affluent could afford them. The importation of goods of all kinds killed many local industries while unemployment, including even among graduates from the universities, worsened over the years. The abolition of price controls and devaluation of the cedi led to the escalation of the prices of locally produced and imported goods, while wages and salaries remained virtually the same. Indeed, under the ERP, the lot of the average Ghanaian became worse rather than better. Finally, the country became saddled with a huge foreign debt, which rose from $1.81 billion in 1983 to $2.4 billion in 1985, and $2. 88 billion in 1988.[58] As a result, the PNDC lost the support of the workers, students, the radical intellectuals, junior army officers, and populist forces while it antagonized or alienated the middle and upper classes—business people, large traders, bureaucrats, professionals, and managers— because of the strategies adopted and the undemocratic, arbitrary, and authoritarian mode of their implementation.

At the same time, during the adjustment phase, the PNDC was concerned with its political survival, stability, and legitimacy. These were achieved through several institutional changes and the broadening of the social base of the PNDC. First, the PNDC was restructured to include two middle-class women, three senior military officers, a former justice of the Supreme Court, and a civilian as the coordinating secretary of the Committee of Secretaries. This restructuring signified the shift of the PNDC from the left to the right in its conflict management strategies, from popular mobilization and people's power to pragmatism and conservative policies and from class struggle to class cooperation.

Second, in conformity with one of the conditionalities of the IMF, the PDCs and WDCs were abolished in 1984 and were replaced by Committees for the Defense of the Revolution (CDRs) whose membership was open to all classes of the society. The interim management committees were also replaced by joint consultative committees, which were to advise and not to dictate to management nor were they to be part of the decisionmaking process. These changes confirmed the feelings of betrayal of the workers, the radical and progressive forces, and an end to the slogan "power to the people."

The third preoccupation of the PNDC during this phase was the evolution, starting in 1984, of a new political structure or a new form of government for the country, beginning with the creation of district political authorities in the form of elected district assemblies. As Chazan has pointed out, "The decision to launch a program of political reform was in all probability prompted by a growing awareness that the government's stability could not be guaranteed unless some changes were made on the political front."[59]

This task of political reform was assigned to the National Commission for Democracy (NCD), which was established by the PNDC in 1981. Beginning in 1984 the NCD collected and collated the views of the public on the future form of government for the country either through memoranda submitted by the public or through seminars, symposia, and durbars organized by the NCD.[60] In 1987 the NCD published its book, *Creation of District Political Authority and Modalities for District Level Elections*, which became known as the *Blue Book*.[61] In this book, the NCD recommended the establishment of district assemblies, which were to be partly elected on a no-party basis. "The elections were held in zone one (Asante, Western, Eastern, and Central Regions) in December 1988 and in zones two and three (the remaining six regions) in February 1989. According to official sources, participation was higher in the rural areas than in the urban areas and among the illiterate than the educated, especially the highly educated folk. Thus, Kumasi saw only a

45 percent turn-out and Legon only 11 percent while rural Upper-East [participation was] as high as 62 percent."[62] One hundred and ten district assemblies have since been operating.

Besides the usual demand-bearing groups—the TUC, GBA, NUGS, ARPB, GNAT, the Ghana Chamber of Commerce, and the radical groups—a whole host of new societies and associations emerged during this phase. The law setting up the Consultative Assembly (PNDCL 253 of May 1991) listed as many as sixty-two "electoral bodies." Many had never been heard of before. However, most of these new associations were formed by the PNDC itself and were therefore pro-PNDC. Serious and effective reactions therefore came from a few of them, including the old professional and political groups, for example, the GBA, NUGS, TUC, and the Catholic Secretariat.

The Ghana Bar Association, pursuing peaceful and legalistic rather than confrontational strategies, never relented in its conflict with the PNDC over the Adjustment Program. It passed resolutions on issues such as the trade liberalization policy; the reduction of the cost of living to ease the hardships, particularly of the low-income earner; revitalization of the economy, especially agriculture; abuse of human rights; official control of the press and other news media; and the political system. As in earlier periods of military rule, the association expressed its deep concern "at the absence of a permanent and popularly accepted political framework within which the economic and social development of Ghana can take place in an atmosphere of peace." It therefore called upon the PNDC to take urgent measures to secure for the country "a democratic constitution which enshrines the principle of one man one vote, secret voting in freely and fairly conducted elections, the change of government only through the ballot box, protect[ion of] the fundamental human rights of citizens, and the absolute illegality and illegitimacy of coups d'etat and other violent means of changing governments."[63] The GBA also confirmed its decision not to appear before the public tribunals. Other PNDC measures that provoked the dire anger of the GBA during the period under review were the withdrawal of the registration of the *Catholic Standard*, the deprivation of eight natural-born Ghanaians of their citizenship and their subsequent deportation to the United States, and the dismissal of nineteen judges and magistrates.[64]

The nature of the conflict between the TUC and the PNDC took a decidedly different turn with the introduction of the draconic IMF-inspired budget of April 1983. A rally called by the TUC on May 1, 1983, in Accra to explain the budget was virtually boycotted by workers. The few workers who did attend booed and jeered at the TUC and PNDC representatives. Similar meetings at Kumasi and Tema were disrupted by workers. Nothing illustrates the disgust and anger of the workers and the unions better than the defeat of the PNDC nominees and supporters at the TUC Congress between December 13 and 17, 1983.[65] From then on the conflict ceased to be inter-TUC conflict and became a direct one between the TUC and a majority of the workers supported by the radical groups such as the JFM, on the one hand, and the PNDC and its principal ally the NDM, on the other.

At first the new TUC leadership did not embark on confrontationist strategies but confined itself to criticisms, protests, and demands. It protested against the huge increases in food prices and hinted at a possible strike action, which the government averted by lowering food prices. In January 1984 it demanded that the minimum daily wage be raised from 35.00 to 300.00 cedis, which Rawlings rejected as "rubbish and unwarranted." But the TUC insisted on its demand for wage increases and strongly denounced the PNDC for submitting to the dictates of the IMF and the World Bank, which had created "unbearable conditions of life," inflation, rising unemployment, and crime.[66] In April 1984, the workers in the Tema area staged a mass demonstration in support of dismissed workers of the Pioneer Food Company (PFC) and demanded their reinstatement. The PNDC ordered the reinstatement of the dismissed workers to reduce tension. But the dissolution of the PDCs and WDCs and their replacement by CDRs and the replacement of the INCC by JCC worsened the tense relations between the workers and the PNDC.[67] To defuse this tension, the government announced an across-the-board increase of wages for all employees by 50 percent for December 1984 and a flat 17.5 cedi increase (which doubled the minimum wage) in January 1985.[68]

However, these increases were considered inadequate, and since then relations between the TUC and the PNDC have been characterized by increasing hostile conflict rather than accommodation and cooperation. This is evident from the strongly worded statement issued by the TUC in February 1985.[69] It bitterly criticized, among other things, the PNDC's failure to consult labor on policies and implement the measures of mobilization and relief that it had promised, the massive retrenchment, the loss of union power, the change in the name and roles of the WDCs and PDCs and their subordination to the state, the rising costs of hitherto free health and education services and the sale of state enterprises. It called for the reversal of the IMF austerity measures and advocated increased state intervention in the economy.

Relations between workers and the government worsened in 1986 particularly over two events: the budget in January and the abolition of leave allowance in April. Following the announcement of the budget, more than 20,000 workers staged a demonstration on January 20 to reject the budget in general and in particular the increase of the minimum daily wage from 70.00 to 90.00 cedis. The TUC backed the workers and insisted that the daily wage should have been raised to 105.00 in view of the devaluation of the cedi by about 50 percent. The government, however, expressed its inability to pay such an increase and persuaded the TUC to accept the original figure of 90.00. Then, following the unilateral decision of the PNDC to cancel leave allowances on April 4, the workers in Accra-Tema and Sekondi-Takoradi staged demonstrations. The TUC followed this step with an ultimatum to the government to reverse its decision before April 11 or face strike action. To avoid this head-on collision, the government capitulated and announced the restoration of the leave allowance on the morning of April 11.

In another memo, entitled "Views on Economic, Social and Political Affairs," the TUC reiterated its objections to IMF and World Bank policies being pursued by the government and also called for a popularly and democratically constituted people's assembly at all levels, district, regional, and national, to be composed of representative factions from the different sectors of the society. The government readily welcomed this memo and opened a dialogue with the labor movement, which resulted in the setting up of a standing committee to discuss future issues and an economic review committee to review the government's economic policies.

TUC political demands rose from 1987 onward. In February, a paper to the NCD, "Trade Unions and Democracy in Ghana," called for the establishment of institutions that would guarantee the interest of the majority and the free and unfettered expression of views on all national issues. It also insisted on the right of workers to undertake mass demonstrations and go on strike without police restrictions and harassment. Tension escalated during the year with the introduction of a new tax law on allowances in May and the detention of the head of the political department of the TUC. Thus, by the end of the adjustment phase, tension and conflicts increased between the labor movement and the PNDC, and both seemed destined for a head-on collision.

The initial warm relationship between the NUGS and the PNDC had cooled off by mid-1982 and collapsed completely by April 1983 following the budget. The reasons for the collapse of this relationship are found in the statement issued by NUGS at its Cape Coast congress in July 1982 and at its meeting in Kumasi in April 1983. In the 1982 statement NUGS condemned the killing of the judges and the ex-army officer and called for the probing of the assets of all PNDC members, secretaries, and all other high officials. In the 1983 April statement, NUGS vehemently condemned the draconic budget and for the first time asked the PNDC to hand over power to the chief justice of Ghana. The PNDC replied to the attack by the students with the invasion of the campus of UST in Kumasi by the workers of the Obuasi gold mines in May 1983, and the raiding of the offices of NUGS in Accra, the closing down of the two universities for ten months, and the arrest of student leaders. In this encounter, one student died, another was detained, while two others went into exile.

The government's new educational program precipitated renewed student opposition. The program involved the abolition of subsidies on food, the replacement of scholarships with loans, the privatization of campus facilities such as kitchens, and finally a five-year compulsory service after graduation. The students reacted in March 1987 with protests and demonstrations leading to the closing down of Legon and UST and the arrest and dismissal of eight student leaders. Tension rose again in June when the students demanded a threefold increase in their allowances, and the demand was rejected.[70] From then until elections, NUGS seems to have lost its militancy and interest in national affairs and confined itself to protests over purely campus issues such as bonding of students, accommodation, and other facilities. The ARPB and the churches also protested against most of the measures of the PNDC, but, like the students and the Bar Association, they confined themselves to issuing statements and calling press conferences and had little impact. Not much was heard of political groups, parties, or ethnic groups during the adjustment period.

The general populace had their own strategies of reducing conflict, by reducing demands in the face of reduced supplies. These were the reaction of "voting with the feet" or "exit and attempt to escape the state's reach," as Stephen John Stedman has termed it, and "the culture of silence" or "obey without complying" as Rawlings and Stedman have respectively categorized it.[71] The strategy of exit first used during Acheampong's regime involved the reduction by emigration of two groups: highly trained and skilled professionals such as engineers, architects, university lecturers, technocrats, bureaucrats, and teachers; and unemployed primary and secondary school leavers, workers, and illiterates. By the late 1970s, most secondary schools and universities in the country had lost more than half their staff. This situation grew worse during the PNDC regime as thousands of these professionals migrated to the neighboring West African countries especially Nigeria, and even to South Africa, while the highly skilled bureaucrats and technocrats increasingly took up jobs in various international and UN agencies and organizations abroad. All these migrants moved out in protest against the deteriorating economic conditions, the oppression and tyranny of the regime, the lack of job satisfaction, and inadequate wages and salaries.

During 1983 to 1987 the "culture of silence" became the principal and most widespread strategy.[72] This strategy had two forms: the first aspect was the refusal of people and groups to comment on or react in any way to whatever the government was doing for fear of being arrested, detained, brutalized, or dragged before a vetting committee or a public tribunal. The second aspect was the refusal of highly qualified persons to accept appointments or participate in communal activities and official functions and celebrations, and their attempt to seek premature retirements from the public service or refusal to register or vote in elections. By April 1987 the culture of silence had become so pervasive that Rawlings felt compelled to draw the attention of the nation to this phenomenon in a public speech while the NCD launched a program of public education "to break the culture of silence which has trapped Ghanaians."[73]

Thus the PNDC's attempt to handle conflicts and demands during the adjustment period took the form of a mixture of brutal repression with gross violation of human rights, capitulation to demands, and downright indifference and contemptuous neglect. Other measures of the period included the passage and use of such draconian decrees as the Preventive Custody Law, the Newspaper Licensing Law, which suppressed freedom of the press, and the Habeas Corpus Amendment Law, which guaranteed the loss of the liberty of Ghanaians. By the end of the period though some economic recovery had occurred, Ghana was politically and psychologically in a state of paralysis and disillusionment under the unchallenged and unchallengeable military dictatorship of Jerry Rawlings and his PNDC.

## The Return to Democracy and Political Pluralism, 1988 and after

The primary preoccupation of the PNDC during this third and final phase has been political: to transform, strengthen, and consolidate its political base and win real legitimacy in response to procedural demands that began mounting in 1988.

Far from leading to the establishment of his peculiar and unique nonpartisan political system based on the district assemblies, the process that Rawlings launched in July 1990 culminated in the return of the country to a fully fledged civilian constitutional and multiparty democratic system of government embodied in a new constitution of the Fourth Republic of Ghana, which was inaugurated on January 7, 1993. This extremely unanticipated turn of events can be attributed to external pressures exerted by the donor countries and internal pressures exerted by the old and new demand-bearing groups. They were attempting to resolve the conflicts emanating from the transition to civilian rule.

After the district assembly elections the PNDC then decided to extend this democratization process to the national level in July 1990. This task was assigned to the NCD, which began its work by conducting regional seminars on the theme "District Assemblies and the Evolving Democratic Process." In March 1991, the NCD submitted a report, "Evolving True Democracy," showing

> —a clear consensus on the district assembly concept;
> —a consensus on a National Assembly and an executive presidency;
> —a division on whether entry into the National Assembly should be through the direct election system; and
> —a divergence of views on whether the new constitutional order should be partisan or nonpartisan but with the majority in favor of the multiparty system.[74]

In its statement on the NCD report on May 10, 1991, the PNDC announced plans for the return of the country to civilian rule on the basis of political pluralism. It also decided to establish a consultative assembly to be composed of "elected representatives of district assemblies, identifiable bodies and appointed persons in accordance with previous practice in 1968 and 1978." This assembly was to prepare a draft constitution, which "will be submitted to the people of Ghana for their approval in a national referendum." The PNDC further decided that "in accordance with such practice the government recognizes that the process of constitutional deliberation should be non-partisan and therefore the ban on political parties will remain for the time being."[75]

To facilitate and expedite the work of the consultative assembly, the government appointed a Committee of Experts in June 1991 "to draw up and submit to the Council proposals for a draft constitution of Ghana."[76] They would "provide for an executive president to be elected on the basis of universal adult suffrage; provide for a prime minister who must command a majority in the National Assembly; provide for a National Assembly to be elected on the basis of universal adult suffrage."[77]

The committee, whose ten members were appointed by the PNDC, started work under the chairmanship of S. K. B. Asante, a Ghanaian UN legal expert, on June 11, 1991, and submitted its report on July 31, 1991.

The constitution of the fourth republic presented to the PNDC on March 31, 1992, provided for a multiparty democratic system of government, guarantees of the basic human rights and the independence of the judiciary, an executive president (instead of a president and prime minister as prescribed by the PNDC), and a single-chamber Parliament. A thirty-six-article transition section imposed on the consultative assembly by the PNDC contained a blanket and perpetual indemnity for the PNDC for any act committed by any member or agent of the PNDC during its tenure of office. In January 1992 the PNDC appointed an interim electoral commission to organize and oversee the entire electoral process. All subsequent steps took place as planned except for the parliamentary election, postponed for three weeks to December 29. The fourth republic was inaugurated as scheduled on January 7, 1993, with Jerry J. Rawlings as its elected president. The entire transition process was unilaterally planned and executed by Rawlings and the PNDC without any consultation whatsoever with the opposition and pro-democracy groups in the country.

The first new group to mount a systematic and sustained attack for the PNDC to change its preprogrammed agenda for the transition was rather strangely though significantly the club of the donor countries led by the United States and Britain. From limited success after nearly six years of the implementation of the Structural Adjustment and Economic Recovery Programs, both the World Bank and the IMF came around to the view that two new prescriptions had to be added to SAP-ERP: political liberalization and good governance. This view was first propounded in 1989 by the World Bank in *Sub-Saharan Africa*, a report stipulating that both prescriptions would henceforth become the conditions for its continued support.[78] These prescriptions were accepted by all the Western powers and imposed on developing countries that had accepted the SAP since 1990.

Rawlings's peculiar brand of democracy fell far short of this new blueprint and had therefore to be abandoned. The first intimation of this change was given in his announcement in July 1990 of the national discussion of the political future. His first formal announcement of his conversion from the nonpartisan democratic option to multiparty politics was made on May 10, 1991, only four days before the beginning of the donors' conference in Paris, in the same speech in which he announced the appointment of a committee and an assembly to draft the new constitution.

Rawlings's decision, an external factor, was crucial and decisive. However, no less crucial was the intensification of the internal pressure for political liberalization since the 1970s and 1980s by the new groups. The number of demand-bearing groups increased tremendously during the period of the PNDC regime. Most of them were created during the consolidation phase for the constitutional and democratization exercise then in progress.[79]

The emergence of these political clubs and societies was inspired and precipitated by the creation of the Movement for Freedom and Justice (MFJ). It was formed by a group of public-spirited Ghanaian men and women representing the whole spectrum of political, ideological, and religious persuasion from different social class, occupational, and ethnic backgrounds, initiated by Kwesi Pratt, Johnny Hansen, Akoto Ampaw, and John Ndebugire, young radical leaders of the Marxist wing of the Nkrumaist tradition. Its aims and objectives included democracy, civilian rule, fundamental human democratic rights, free and fair elections, human rights, and mobilization. Adu Boahen was its chairman, Johnny Hansen its general secretary, and Kwesi Pratt its deputy general secretary. Most of the existing prodemocracy groups such as NUGS, the

Bar Association, and the Catholic Secretariat issued similar statements in support of the demands of the MFJ between August and December 1990. All of the new groups, apart from the MFJ, its offspring, the Coordinating Committee of the Democratic Forces of Ghana (CCDF), the EGLE Club (Every Ghanaian Living Everywhere), and the Alliance of Democratic Forces (ADF), reflected the two main political traditions that have emerged in the country since the late 1940s: the UGCC or UP/PP tradition of J. B. Danquah and Kofi A. Busia, and the CPP tradition of Kwame Nkrumah. These clubs were therefore surrogates for the real political parties to be formed after the lifting of the ban. Although only a single club, the Danquah-Busia Memorial Club (DBMC), has emerged within the UP/PP tradition, all the others, except the EGLE Club, descended from the CPP tradition. Indeed, the Heritage, the National Coordinating Committee of Nkrumaists (NCCN), and the Kwame Nkrumah Youngsters Club (KNYS) were hived off from the Kwame Nkrumah Welfare Society, originally by agents and members of the PNDC such as John Tettegah and Captain Kojo Tsikata. The EGLE Club, however, was a completely new one created by the PNDC itself as its own nucleus of its own political party and the third political tradition that it intended to inaugurate.

One group whose impact on events gradually weakened was the military. The only coup attempt, by Major Courage Quarshigah in September 1989, was quickly overcome. Radical elements in the armed forces who had been responsible for earlier coup efforts appear to have been eliminated or controlled. Procedural demands for a return to civilian rule had overwhelmed the agenda.

Following the lifting of the ban on party activities in May 1992 a host of political parties was formed and seven were recognized: the New Patriotic Party (NPP) of UGCC/UP tradition; the National Democratic Congress (NDC) of the PNDC; the National Convention Party (NCP); People's National Convention (PNC); National Independent Party (NIP); People's Heritage Party (PHP); and the Every Ghanaian Living Everywhere (EGLE), all products of the CPP tradition. In the elections the NDC, NCP, and EGLE formed an alliance. This result clearly illustrates the fragmentation of the Nkrumaist tradition caused by the infiltration and the manipulations by the PNDC, ideological cleavages, and the selfish ambitions, personality conflicts, and graft by some of its leaders.

The conflicts between the PNDC and the existing and new demand-bearing groups centered on the economic program and the human rights record of the PNDC, and on the nature of the new political order and the transition process. The conflicts over socioeconomic policies pitted demands for employment, social services, economic diversification, and debt relief against programs of structural adjustment (SAP) and economic recovery (ERP). An opposition statement issued on January 8, 1992, charged as follows: "The cumulative effect of these policies is that (notwithstanding the 6 percent average rate of growth in GDP that the PNDC and its praise-singers never fail to boast of) the people of Ghana are today faced with severe social and economic hardships and their standard of living has deteriorated drastically."[80] Another conflict was over human rights: imprisonment, detention, murder and the exile of opposition figures, lack of press freedom, the banning of certain newspapers, and above all the Newspaper Licensing Decree.

The most serious areas of conflict centered around procedural demands regarding the transitional process to multiparty democracy and the type of political system. All the opposition and democratic forces led by the MFJ as well as the donor countries insisted on a multiparty system of parliamentary democracy. In making its case for the multiparty system of government, the MFJ contended in its August 1990 statement:

> Supporters of the status quo have said that the multi-party system is being imposed on the country by foreign interests, that it breeds corruption, and that it provokes tribalism, violence, animosity and polarization. They also insist that a sound economic base needs to be established before thought is given to democracy based on the multi-party system. All these arguments are mere red-herring, for the multi-party system is not just concerned with freedom to form parties, it provides the political framework for ensuring that in the art of public life and government, the fundamental human rights of the people including the rights of free expression, association, personal security are guaranteed.[81]

This view gained such overwhelming support during the national debate that the NCD felt compelled to recommend it, and the PNDC therefore had no choice but to accept it in its statement of May 1991.

The other aspect of the procedural demands concerned the transition process. The PNDC had appointed itself as the sole manager of the transition and unilaterally formulated all the laws and institutions without any public consultation. In contrast, the opposition called for a Constitutional Conference, the resignation of the PNDC, the establishment of a neutral interim government to manage the process, an elected constituent assembly to draft and promulgate the new constitution, the replacement of the National Commission for Democracy by an independent electoral commission appointed in consultation with all interested bodies, and a new voter register in place of the highly flawed one prepared in 1987. When the PNDC created the consultative assembly instead, opposition groups bitterly criticized it while the GBA and NUGS boycotted it mainly because its membership of 260 was carefully packed with 190 pro-PNDC members selected from the CDOs, CDRs, December 31 Women's Movement, the armed forces, the police, clubs and associations, and the district assemblies.

The PNDC rejected all these demands but the voter registration and electoral commission. An interim electoral commission was established in January 1992, but its membership was unilaterally appointed by the PNDC. The PNDC also agreed to undertake limited revisions and rectifications of the voters' register, but this plan did not meet the approval of the opposition or of the International Foundation of Electoral Systems (IFES). After studying the electoral process in Ghana from April 22 to May 8, 1992, the IFES concluded that

—deceased voters had not been removed since 1987;
—many voters with registration receipts were not on the register;
—the register was larger than statistically possible;
—names were entered on the register as they were given, resulting in inconsistency in the order of entering surnames, first, middle, and day names; and
—reportedly the register contained non-Ghanaian citizens and nonexistent addresses.[82]

It recommended a "complete re-registration of eligible voters as a matter of urgency to provide a consistent and comprehensive register for the elections of November 3 and December 8, respectively." The PNDC refused.

Other aspects of the electoral playing field were also subject to procedural demands. The Catholic Bishops Conference of Ghana emphasized the "need for creating an appropriate atmosphere and environment for meaningful exchange of views on our constitutional future."[83] An even playing field meant:

(i) the dissolution and replacement of the PNDC by an interim government;

(ii) the dissolution of all the PNDC's para-military organizations, such as the CDOs, CDRs, the Forces Reserve Battalion or Commandos, the 31st December Women's Movement and the militias;

(iii) the repeal of restrictive laws, such as the Preventive Custody Law, the Newspapers Licensing Law, the Religious Bodies Registration Law, the Habeas Corpus (Amendment) Law and sections of the Public Tribunal Law dealing with executions for political offenses;

(iv) lifting the ban on party political activities;

(v) amnesty for all Ghanaian exiles;

(vi) the repeal of the ban of the use of the names, symbols and slogans of former political parties and on financial contributions to political parties by foreigners, and the limit individual Ghanaian may contribute to a political party; and

(vii) the holding of the presidential and parliamentary elections on the same day.[84]

The PNDC rejected these demands or conceded them belatedly—such as the lifting of the ban on party political activities, or partially, such as the amnesty for political exiles and detainees. IFES concluded after its visit to Ghana in April–May 1992 that "the transition to democratic civilian rule in Ghana is a process characterized by control . . . The IFES team was troubled about civil rights and liberties which were not guaranteed at the time of its visit. . . . Moreover the Constitution is not scheduled to go into effect until January 7, 1993. The long delay before its effective date is of special concern because many of its provisions in particular those regarding freedom of speech, association and movement are central to free and fair elections."[85] Consequently, the elections of 1992 were conducted on an uneven playing field, with Rawlings and his PNDC simultaneously acting as players, referees, linesmen, and match commissioners.

The presidential election took place as scheduled on November 3, 1992. Since then Ghana has been plunged into more heated and rancorous controversy than ever before. The five presidential candidates were Adu Boahen (NPP), Lieutenant General E. A. Erskine (PHP), Hilla Limann (PNC), Kwabena Darko (NIP), and Flight Lieutenant Jerry J. Rawlings (NDC–EGLE–NCP alliance). International observer groups from the Commonwealth, the Carter Center, and the OAU were present. According to the official results declared by the Interim National Electoral Commission, Rawlings of NDC won the election with 2.3 million votes (58.4 percent) followed by Adu Boahen of the NPP with 1.2 million votes (30.3 percent), Hilla Limann of PNC with 266,700 votes (6.7 percent), Kwabena Darko with 113,600 votes (2.9 percent) and Lieutenant General Erskine with 69,800 (1.8 percent) votes. These results were accepted by the international observer groups as "free and fair," but they were greeted with incredulity by many Ghanaians, and they provoked spontaneous demonstrations in Kumasi and other towns.

Even before the announcement of the final results on November 4, the opposition parties issued a joint statement expressing their shock and dismay at "the fraudulent manipulation of the presidential election" and declared that "if any final results are published without a thorough and satisfactory investigation of the malpractices complained of we shall be obliged to refuse to accept the final result irrespective of who is declared the winner. In the meantime, we decline to participate in any further electoral process based on a voters' register which is so seriously flawed that it has made this extent of rigging possible."[86] As a result, the opposition parties boycotted the December parliamentary election.

In the hope of enticing some of the opposition parliamentary candidates to defy their leaders and participate in the parliamentary election, the PNDC postponed the parliamentary election from December 8 first to December 22 and then to December 29. However, not a single candidate defected. The government rejected the opposition demands, while INEC challenged the opposition parties to resort to the weapon provided for them under the electoral laws, namely, to challenge the results of the election in the Supreme Court. The opposition forces decided not to go to court because of their belief that no impartial judgment would be given following the abduction and murder of three members.

With no contest from the opposition, the NDC cleared 189 of the 200 seats in the parliamentary election on November 29, 1992. The rest of the seats were won by its former allies or friendly independents—NCP with eight seats, the EGLE Party with one seat, and the two independent candidates won their seats. It was on the basis of flawed presidential and parliamentary elections and a one-party parliament that the fourth republic under the presidency of Flight Lieutenant Jerry J. Rawlings was inaugurated on January 7, 1993. Since July 1990, conflict has centered around the single theme of transition from military to civilian democratic constitutional rule, and the manner of its resolution has hung over the ensuing republic.

## The Nature of Conflict and Conflict Resolution in Ghana

What lessons can be learned from this study of conflict in Ghana since it gained independence? What political and socioeconomic institutions and strategies can be devised to manage and resolve conflict?

In the first place, this study of conflict in Ghana clearly justifies Stephen John Stedman's view that "although conflict may turn violent, violence is not an inherent aspect of conflict, but rather a potential form that conflict may take."[87] Apart from the occasions of military coups and attempted coups, conflict in Ghana has not assumed any violent form. Even military coups have not occurred in the 1990s. Conflict has been characterized by peaceful forms of protests, petitions, and press conferences. Demonstrations or even widespread strikes or hold-ups in the country have been relatively rare. A typical feature of conflict in Ghana, then, is its peaceful and bloodless nature.

Second, conflict in Ghana has not been seriously centered on or caused by issues of identity, race, religion, or ethnicity. The ethnoregional and subnationalist factors as agents of conflict, valid in the period just before and immediately after independence, that is, in the 1950s and 1960s, have lost their salience. The irredentist movements of those days have virtually disappeared and are hardly featured in the 1970s and 1980s. Nor has religion ever become a dominant issue in politics or social relations. In none of the conflicts since independence has religion—Christianity, Islam, or traditional—been an underlying factor. In this respect, Ghana stands in sharp contrast to countries such as Nigeria, Uganda, and Sudan in Africa. Ethnically, there is some animosity and rivalry between the Akan and Ewe, but this antagonism has never resulted in any direct conflict between those two ethnic groups except occasionally within the armed forces. Zaya Yeebo and others have shown that even in the armed forces, what had formerly been categorized as a Northern-Ewe confrontation of the 1980s is less an issue of ethnicity than of ideology. The violent countercoups of the early

1980s led primarily by northern soldiers were not cases of clashes between northern soldiers and Ewe military rulers but rather radical leftist or revolutionary soldiers versus a military dictatorship that was betraying its own revolution with its slogans of "power to the people," "people's participation in the decision-making process," and "no sellout to neocolonialism and Western capitalist institutions." On the whole, then, apart from the latent Akan-Ewe animosity, which contains seeds of a future violent explosion, ethnicity as a source of conflict in Ghana has lost its primacy.

Third, conflict in Ghana has not been along class lines. At no time has it taken the form of the poor versus the rich, the proletariat versus the bourgeoisie, the urban dwellers versus the rural folk, or the literate versus the illiterate. Conflict in Ghana has been mainly between the educated elite and urban groups, on one hand, and the government and military regimes, on the other. That is, a conflict within a horizontal stratum rather than between horizontal strata with haves and have-nots.

Fourth, if conflict in Ghana has not centered so much around the issues of regionalism, religion, ethnicity, race, and class, it has been primarily around the issue of governance. All the conflicts in Ghana have been between the various organized demand-bearing and interest groups and the government. The bones of contention have been primarily political and socioeconomic, namely, the type of government under which people would like to live, and economic development and sharing of the national economic cake. The issues of governance that have precipitated conflicts in Ghana have been dictatorship versus democracy, civilian versus military rule, political pluralism or no-party system, respect or abuse of human rights, socialist or free market systems of economic development, probity and accountability in government or not, and the nature of the transitional process from military dictatorship to civilian multiparty democracy. All the coups in Ghana and the conflicts between the government and demand-bearing groups have centered around these issues.

Of all the demand-bearing groups, the one that has been the principal source of conflict has been the military. Five successful coups in 1966, 1972, 1978, 1979 and 1981—and numerous unsuccessful countercoups—have occurred in Ghana over a quarter century. Some of them have been very bloody indeed. What is more, a great deal of the conflict in Ghana in the 1970s and 1980s has centered around the issue of democratization, that is, the ending of military governments and the transition from military to civilian rule. This was certainly the primary objective of the conflicts in the country between 1972 and 1979 and especially since 1987 with the launching of the search for a new democratic order.

Many scholars have attributed the conflicts between the demand-bearing groups and the government on the issue of democratization especially since the late 1980s to external factors such as the revolutionary events in eastern Europe and the insistence on human rights and political pluralism by the Western industrialized countries and their financial institutions, the World Bank and the IMF.[88] This view is palpably erroneous as far as Ghana is concerned. The demand for an end to one-party rule and military dictatorship and for the establishment of civilian constitutional rule based on the multiparty democracy has been raging in Ghana since the conversion of the country into a one-party state by Nkrumah in 1964, and it became intensified, after the coup of 1966 and especially after Acheampong's coup of 1972 and since Rawlings's second coming. Adu Boahen was detained in 1978 for his role in the formation and campaigns of the People's Movement for Freedom and Justice for the reintroduction of multiparty democracy in Ghana, that is, long before anybody heard of Mikhail Gorbachev or of World Bank and IMF conditionalities. The MFJ of August 1990 was merely a graphic illustration of the doctrine of history repeating itself. What the events of eastern Europe and the conditionalities of the Western countries, the World Bank, and the IMF have done has been merely to compel African civilian and military governments to become more responsive and less repressive in their reactions to the democratic demands that have been raging in Africa since the 1960s. Boahen was not detained in 1988 or 1990 or since, and Rawlings has not violently suppressed the prodemocracy movements since the late 1980s. Rather he has reluctantly agreed to return the country to the multiparty democratic system of government from 1990 onward. This consent is owing to external factors. The thesis of the external origins of the prodemocracy movements and the ensuing conflicts in Africa in general and in Ghana in particular cannot be supported by the evidence, but the catalytic effect and importance of external intervention, especially if it is objective, timely, and transparent in conflict resolution or management, is clearly proven.

Any resolution and avoidance of conflict must primarily and essentially address the factors of governance. The establishment of a political order that would guarantee democracy, respect for the rule of law, respect for human rights, the welfare and happiness of the individual, and freedom of the press, and that would in turn ensure periodic changes of government through the ballot box rather than the barrel of the gun is the first solution. Another is a transitional process that will guarantee free and fair elections. Ghana, as well as other states such as Nigeria and Cameroon, is still in a state of crisis and confrontation between the opposition and the government because of the fraudulent nature of the transitional process between 1990 and 1993, and the only way of ensuring peace, stability, and progress and eliminating or minimizing conflict in the future is the leveling of the electoral playing field along the lines outlined above.

There can be no effective government unless those in charge display probity, accountability, and social justice, which will guarantee an even and fair distribution of the national cake. This can be achieved through such institutions as an Ombudsman, a National Ethics Commission, and a Commission on Human Rights and Administrative Justice. Furthermore, there can be no effective governance unless government is decentralized to ensure grass-roots participation in the decisionmaking process and a bottom-up approach to development. A properly educated, trained, and disciplined bureaucracy is another requirement. Finally, the recognition and promotion of the roles of demand-bearing groups and nongovernmental organizations is also necessary.

The simple solution to the involvement of the armed forces in conflict is their depoliticization. Almost all armed forces in Africa have become politicized, and some of them, such as those of Ghana, have even become radicalized since independence. Unless African armies are purged of their politically ambitious and radical elements and turned into politically uncommitted national institutions dedicated to the preservation of the security, stability, and survival of the state, there can be no end to military coups and conflicts in Africa.

In conclusion, conflicts have become part of the political culture of practically every African state, and some have been characterized by bloody violence and anarchy. Fortunately, Ghana has been saved from such bloody confrontations thanks to the general tolerance and good sense of the people. But conflicts have been destructive nevertheless, a potent source of instability and barrier to progress and development. They therefore should be managed and eliminated through good, effective, and honest governance and the depoliticization of the armed forces.

## Chapter 5

# Nigeria: Conflict Unresolved

*Alex Gboyega*

L IKE ITS NEIGHBORS, Nigeria's political structure too was frozen at a critical juncture. But it was twice frozen, along different dimensions, providing fault lines heading in opposite directions and the basis for seismic blockage and tensions as a result. Colonial decisions at the beginning of the century, and repeated in the post–World War II period, protected the sociopolitical system of the North. When a single Nigeria of several federated pieces was created, however, the stage was set for conflict and competition. The two halves of the country vied for leadership on the basis of conflicting notions of legitimacy—one based on traditional status and the other on the basis of modernity. That the South was subdivided into two parts—East and West—further weakened the politically subordinated side by opening it up to alliance politics practiced by the North. No matter into how many states the original three have been subdivided, the tripartite regionalization effected by the colonizer with its imposed ranking has provided the basis for identity, conflict, and order in independent Nigeria. These units are not ethnic but rather "super-ethno-regional" constructions whose longevity is ensured by the fact that they have become competing teams. Along with cheering fans, they fight for the trophy, both symbolic and tangible, of the right to rule.

Civilian incapacity has allowed the military to take over politics, producing another fault line. Initially, in 1966, the military intervened to escalate the regional confrontation, but that group was set aside by a restorative military junta that took fifteen years to achieve its goal. Again, civilian incapacity invited a new military intervention, but this time restoration was mixed more and more often with personal profiteering, in which successive juntas claimed their time at the trough while still carrying on the regional conflict.

As a result, no consensual normative code governs expectations and behaviors in Nigerian politics. Even electoral victories are only expected to confirm the North's predetermined right to rule, and if they do not, they are treated as illegitimate and subject to reversal. Civilian and military rulers and candidate rulers alike regard their incumbency as a turn at the trough, necessarily limited, assuredly enriching. "If I can become minster for a year," exclaimed a Nigerian politician in a private comment, "I can take care of my family for the next three generations."

Time at the trough has become the ethos that unites military and civilian rulers in a complex timetable that alternates elections and coups to allow different groups and generations to take their turn at personal gain. A political version of Gresham's law not only drives out good politicians by bad but also drains the coffers of the state in repeated fast-feeding frenzies, continuing the habit of corruption instilled in the 1970s under the days of high oil prices.[1] Thus even competitive elections, civilian rule, and democratic governance have continued the debilitating practice and the ethical ambiguities.

Yet throughout the successive republics and coups, Nigeria's conflicts have been at least attenuated by active measures at management through redistributive revenue allocation formulas in the years of the oil boom but also through institutionalization of electoral competition and alternate repression and accommodation of social protest groups, among others. The federal system allows regions to gain additional benefits by being subdivided into increasing numbers of states. In the one ethnoregion, the Southeast (Biafra), that attempted to secede from the country, a healing and reconstruction process, exemplary by global standards, took place in the 1970s at the end of the civil war, even if the issue of regional dominance in federal governance has still not been settled. Moreover, the extraordinary size and vitality of Nigeria produced a burst of groups and associations in civil society in the late 1980s and early 1990s that made the democracy movement a match for the predatory tendencies of those in charge of the state.

Nigeria's three and a half decades of independence have known only ten years of civilian rule in two periods—the first republic from independence in 1960 to 1966, and the second republic from 1979 to its overthrow at the end of 1983, with the third republic waiting to happen. The first republic under Ahmadu Tafawa Balewa was preoccupied with new policy initiatives dealing with postcolonial issues, but even then, the country was beginning its slide down the slope of interregional rivalry, past rigged elections, and into ethnoregional riots and coups. The second republic under Shehu Shagari took office on the basis of more or less fair elections and made major decisions on federal organization, oil revenue allocation, and the implementation of constitutional provisions creating national leadership. But it foundered on the issue of personal corruption rather than regional dominance and was felled when military officers felt that their turn at the trough had come.

Both military periods began with a period of weak and self-serving rule, followed by a longer show of firm leadership and statesmanship. After a half-year of Igbo dominance in 1966, northern predominance was restored and federal power consolidated for a decade during and after the Biafran war under Lieutenant Colonel Yakubu Gowon. Similarly, after a year and a half under General Muhammadu Buhari in 1984–85, a period of reform and federal consolidation under General Ibrahim Babangida occupied the following decade. Gowon was replaced for his slowness in democratization by the liberal reformist regime of Generals Murtala Muhammad and then Obasanjo, who firmly led the country back to civilian rule and then voluntarily retired. Babangida had great difficulties bringing himself to relinquish power to the civilian regime he created. He finally canceled the election of one of his friends and collaborators, Chief Moshood Abiola. But in the end, Babangida too was forced out of power by public pressure, only to have the civilian transition he had appointed overthrown soon afterward by General Abacha. No Nigerian regime has been more devoted to personal gain than his.

Nigeria is the giant of the West—or indeed, all—Africa, and the way it leans and falls has a major impact on its neighbors. The heritages of historic regional conflict, widespread personal and predatory rule, and newly declining resources have provided the basis for an arbitrary and repressive mode of conflict management that is only conflict exacerbation, pushing aside the rising procedural demands for an institutionalized, participatory mode of handling conflicts. Although nothing is ever finally decided, the heavy hand of Nigeria's regional and social divisions and the growing resource shortfall make it more and more difficult to replace the private with the public mode and ethos of governance.

## Roots of Conflict in Colonial Rule

Although in a sense Nigeria is a creature of British colonial enterprise, the three hundred linguistic groups brought together under

British rule between 1850 and 1914 were already interacting in expanding ways before colonial imposition.[2] Integration was promoted by certain factors such as language, religion, commerce, and social interaction.[3] Nevertheless, the incorporation of each group into the Nigerian state was done on British terms ranging from conquest and force to cajolery and treaties. The twists and turns of British colonial policy and the strategies of state formation have had and continue to have a constraining influence on intergroup relations even today.

But whatever the constraints of British colonial policy and strategies, the very act of bringing together such a large number of heterogeneous peoples with their different languages, religions, cultures, and political systems was bound to be inherently conflict prone, no matter the agent of such incorporation. Indeed, the factors responsible for precolonial integration also had a disintegrative effect on Nigeria.

Religion, for instance, as Ade Ajayi has argued, was an important integrative factor in precolonial intergroup relations. Islam, besides being a religion, was also a way of life, a system of education, and a body of ideas that diffused a common culture wherever it predominated. The Sokoto jihad in 1804, which more than anything else was responsible for the rapid spread of Islam from the North, created a huge region of homogenous culture, religion, and ideology in what later became northern Nigeria.[4] At the same time, the areas of the region that successfully resisted the spread of Islam came under severe pressures of slave raids and other discriminatory adversities perpetrated by the dominant Muslims. The cultural minorities of the region had to adopt aggressive mechanisms for protecting their separate identities, which reinforced their alienation from the dominant Muslims. Thus the people of the region were already dichotomized by religion before colonial rule.

In southern Nigeria Christianity was introduced in the 1840s to the southwestern and southeastern areas. With Christianity came a new language, culture, and civilization. Although its spread was gradual, a more or less homogeneous cultural area evolved that could be contrasted with the North where Islam was the religion of the vast majority of communities.

The interpenetration of both religions—Islam and Christianity—into each other's area of dominance created dichotomies in the North generally and in the western and midwestern areas. Traditional religions persisted without any discernible impact on the state-building process, except that within the communities that professed them, they helped to maintain the political regime. Since they were nonevangelistic, their integrative impact was less significant, particularly when the spatial scale is taken into account.

Language also performed a major integrative role in precolonial times. The Hausa language, paradoxically not Fulfude, the language of the conquering jihadists, spread across most of northern Nigeria, thereby providing a medium of communication that facilitated social cohesion and solidarity. Yoruba and Igbo, though to a lesser extent, served much the same purpose in the western and eastern parts respectively. But again language was merely a facilitator, not a guarantor of integration. People speaking the same language were as prone to fighting one another as those lacking a common language when vital interests such as land or water were at stake.

One other historical factor, rooted in the culture of various peoples, that has had profound effect on the management of intergroup relations has been the principle of indigeneity. As indicated by Awa, the practical implication of the principle was that only people who descended from the ancestor or founder of a town, village, or settlement were and remain the only indigenous people or citizens of the locality. This has been a profound source of differentiation and unequal access to rights. Because of the significance of this cultural attitude to the enforcement of citizen rights in the Nigerian state and the management of intergroup conflicts arising from that belief, Eme O. Awa deserves to be quoted on it. In his words, "Only the indigenes could traditionally participate in the government system and in certain other forms of social activities. A stranger had to be indigenized in a formal ceremony before he would be allowed to participate in the normal processes of politics and government."[5]

The intervention of British colonial rule altered the emerging patterns of intergroup relations and indeed the self-definition of the various ethnic groups. The arbitrary external boundaries divided some ethnic groups between British, German, and French jurisdictions and set the spatial parameters of intergroup relations for the future. The process of incorporation was segmental, and for quite some time the component units of the British colony of Nigeria were administered as if they were really separate entities.

Before 1900 there were three basic units, each under a politically separate authority: the Niger territories under the Royal Niger Company chartered by the British Crown in 1886, the Crown Colony and Protectorate of Lagos (Yoruba Protectorate) administered from Lagos, and the Niger Coast Protectorate governed from Calabar. In 1900 these three units fell under the jurisdiction of the British government. In 1906 the two southern protectorates were merged and in 1914 the two units— the Protectorate of Northern Nigeria and the Colony and Protectorate of Southern Nigeria—were amalgamated. The amalgamation was, however, more theoretical than practical. The two units were still administered separately, the only link between them being the governor general, who himself wanted as little contact as possible between the units. The motive behind the amalgamation was economic rather than political. The British government wanted to end the subsidy it provided to balance the budget of northern Nigeria through the transfer of the budget surplus of southern Nigeria,[6] foreshadowing the revenue allocation conflicts of the rest of the century. The main reason why political—as opposed to economic—integration was scarcely pursued was the fact that the governor general, Sir Frederick Lugard, wanted to preserve the integrity of the traditional system of government of the emirates, the reverse of the French policy in Côte d'Ivoire and the British policy in the Gold Coast. There were two basic sources of social changes that were considered threats to the interests of the people and institutions of northern Nigeria. These were the southern immigrants and Christian missionaries.[7] Both were effectively prevented from integrating themselves into northern society. The southerners were kept in isolation through segregated settlement, while the missionaries were discouraged from operating freely and vigorously in northern Nigeria.

Since Christian missionaries were a principal source of Western education, the restrictions placed on them retarded the spread of Western education. As Hugh Clifford was to lament later, after twenty years of British rule not a single trainee from the northern educational system served as a clerk in the colonial administration. In effect, as in Côte d'Ivoire and Ghana, the educational imbalance between the North and the South, originally the result of the South's earlier contact with Europeans, was reinforced through deliberate colonial policy. This imbalance has been the source of some of the most intractable problems in Nigeria until the present day.

On the political plane, as a result of the growth of urbanization, rising unemployment, adverse discrimination against Nigerians in public employment and commerce, and increasing literacy in English which facilitated communication and mobilization, southerners began to agitate for greater and greater participation in governance.[8] In particular, they demanded differential rates of political advancement so that the South might not be held back unduly by the North. The *Lagos Standard* in its opinion of April 15, 1914, captured the prevailing mood when it commented

> For the purpose of administration this vast territory of Nigeria is now divided into three areas, . . . This would be an excellent arrangement if the principle was also laid down that each division shall be autonomous. Each area shall have within it a perfect machine for effective government, subject nevertheless to a central control. This central authority should have the power of dealing with matters peculiar to each. They would thereby become a federated state in which the Governor-General would be as it were a Foreman of works, but not the fountain from which all authority and power should emanate.[9]

Much more than "fortuitously expedient,"[10] federalism was, for the British administrators, an imperative. They could accommodate the federating groups with their different levels of socioeconomic development and different aspirations and administer more effectively the vast territory brought together under British rule. The problem was the asymmetric territorial composition of the federation and the adoption of policies and practices within the component units and the federation that exacerbated, rather than ameliorated, conflicts between the federation and the units, between the units and within them.

Besides the policies already discussed, the constitutional evolution of the country tended to emphasize separateness based on the artificially defined territorial boundaries that the British drew for administrative convenience. In 1939, for example, the South was divided into the western and eastern groups of provinces for administrative purposes. Six years later, Arthur Richards, the colonial governor, observed that "Nigeria falls naturally into three regions, the North, the West and the East, and the people of those regions differ widely in customs, in outlook and in their traditional systems of government."[11] If the accuracy of that tripartite division can be assumed, the great diversity of peoples within each of the regions was overlooked, however. The new constitution, which the governor introduced in 1947, legalized the tripartite division and established a regional council for each region.

The Richards constitution was a significant landmark in the political development of Nigeria because it ended the practice whereby the colonial governor alone legislated for northern Nigeria, while the legislative council at Lagos deliberated on legislation for the rest of the country. In spite of this change, however, the constitution was not entirely satisfactory to the southern nationalists. To protest some of its objectionable clauses and other unpopular legislation on land, minerals, and the status of chiefs enacted about the same time, the leaders of the National Council for Nigeria and the Cameroons (NCNC) campaigned throughout the country to raise funds and send a delegation to the colonial secretary in London to formally make a protest.[12] The protest achieved nothing as the delegation was rebuffed by the British authorities, but it did reveal a wide gap in the attitudes of northern and southern leaders toward British rule.

The NCNC leaders received enthusiastic welcome in most parts of southern Nigeria but met with indifference or hostility in most parts of northern Nigeria.[13] The NCNC campaign appeared to have encouraged southern artisans in the employment of native authorities in the major northern emirates of Sokoto, Kano, and Maiduguri to embark on a strike for higher wages to the discomfiture and anger of their traditional rulers, the emirs. The campaigners made critical comments about northern leaders, which provoked their resentment and opposition.[14] As a result, "The Constitution, which was intended by its author to bring the peoples of Nigeria into closer unity and foster the spirit of co-operation between them, had instead revealed the wide gap which separated the North from the South, a gap already recognized by the British administrators and which they did very little to bridge (if they did not actually help to widen it by their policies in the North)."[15] East-West conflict was not too far behind. The NCNC delegation, originally broadly composed, split along ethnic lines (Yoruba-Igbo) before the end of the campaign.

The net effect of all these developments was the regionalization of politics and intergroup conflicts that manifested themselves starkly at the constitutional conferences that took place before independence. In addition and, perhaps, more important, the conflicting interests embedded in the developments described above structured the demands that were being made on the political system with lasting effect, as follows:

*The Western Region:* improved revenue allocation through consideration of level of social development, greater regional autonomy, access to ministerial positions at the center, favorable basis of representation other than on population, and boundary adjustment to incorporate Yorubas in the North in the Western Region.

*The Eastern Region:* improved revenue allocation through consideration of level of social development, ministerial responsibility at the center, favorable basis of representation through productivity rather than population, and maintenance of existing boundaries.

*The Northern Region:* distribution of revenue and representation on the basis of population, rejection of ministerial responsibility at the center, and maintenance of existing boundaries.[16]

These different demands of the various groups at the constitutional conferences prove Stedman's contention that, in Africa, conflict arises from "the tugs and pulls of different identities, the differential distribution of resources and access to power, and competing definitions of what is right, fair and just."[17] Since then the only changes that have taken place are in the self-definition of the groups making the demands and their strategies, resources, and leadership. The nature of the demands has not changed.

It would be wrong, however, to conclude that only ethnic groups and the instrumentalities they employ in expressing their claims make demands on the political system. Demands also emanate from organized labor and students, both of which were more active in the South. The former became prominent actors on the political scene in the 1940s as a result of the deepening economic hardship workers faced because of wartime austerity. The period witnessed proliferation of trade unions, leading eventually to the formation of a central labor union, the Federated Trade Union of Nigeria. The Nigerian Trades Union Congress, as it later became known, wanted, "among other things, industrialization, nationalization of all natural resources and public utilities, establishment of a labor party, and the unity of all Nigerian trade unions."[18]

After the 1940s, the nationalist movements perceived the unions as instruments of mobilization and sought collaboration with them in common opposition to the colonial administration. The general strike of 1945 involving more than 30,000 workers pointed up this potential. It was not therefore surprising that trade unions were among the founding unions of the first mass political party in Nigeria, the NCNC.[19] The attempts of the colonial government to repress the agitation of trade unions for better wages drove them into the embrace of the politicians whose ultimate goal was the termination of colonial rule. Political independence, therefore, came to be perceived by workers as the means by which they could hope to attain adequate wages.

Students, too, as already mentioned are prominent in making demands on the political system. The Nigerian Union of Students (NUS) was formed in 1940 by students of Abeokuta Grammar School at the instigation of their principal, Reverend I. O. Ransome-Kuti, with the aim of fostering intertribal unity among students. The conference in Glover Memorial Hall, Lagos, at which the NCNC was formed was an initiative of the NUS, to challenge the suspension and conscription of some students of King's College as punishment for leading a demonstration to protest army occupation of their college.

Significantly, the nationalist movement was at this time deeply fragmented. The possibility of working together to fight the colonial government was impaired by interethnic rivalries and personal jealousies. It required the intervention of these students to forge a common nationalist front. That their goals went beyond their narrow interests as students is demonstrated by the agenda of the Glover Hall Conference: "(1) the King's College strike (2) the possibility of raising funds for a national school, and (3) the immediate formation of a representative national committee."[20] However, it was not until after independence that student agitation had a direct impact on government policy.

## Political Conflict in the First Republic

The road to independence was marked by constitutional changes that emphasized separate development and revenue allocation based on derivation. The compromises (in revenue allocation formula and political representation) that sustained the amalgamation of the North and the South now gave way to pursuit of narrow regional interests. As a result of increasing unwillingness to compromise, no methods were too bad to employ in the quest for political power, especially of the center.

The 1959 election, the last before independence, was the beginning of a new era when the basic rules of conflict management changed dramatically. A constitutional conference ceased to be an adequate mechanism for reaching a consensus on basic demands. An election became threatening, rather than enabling, to the three ethnic giants, and its rules were no longer respected as procedures for determining legitimacy. As Ken W. J. Post observed, "There were no such rules which were generally accepted by the politicians in 1959," nor since, it may be added.[21] The new strategy for the regional participants was, in the long run, to achieve unilateral hegemony.

After the election, the Northern People's Congress (NPC) had 134 seats, the NCNC 89, the Action Group (AG) of the West 73, while 16 seats went to independent candidates. The NPC and the NCNC formed the coalition government that led Nigeria into independence. According to Dudley, the NPC entered a coalition with the NCNC rather than the AG because the AG's tactics had been offensive to the religious sensibilities of the northern leaders. The NCNC joined the coalition with the NPC rather than the AG because the North had fewer educated people than the West to compete for federal jobs.[22] But above all, the basis of the coalition was the fear that the western region, with its higher educational advancement and the higher revenues gained from the adoption of the derivative principle and regionalization of the agricultural products' marketing boards since 1954, would develop much faster than the other two regions if the AG was a coalition partner.

As table 5-1 shows, the changes in recurrent revenues of the federal and regional governments in the period 1953–60 favored the latter.

Between 1953 and 1960 federal revenue increased 74.4 percent while regional revenues increased 181.5 percent. Thus, while in 1953 regional revenue of £19 million was little more than a quarter (27 percent) of total public revenue, federal revenue was £51 million (73 percent); by 1960 federal revenue of £89 million was five-eighths of the total and regional revenue of £53 million was three-eighths. The Western Region accounted for most of the gains. In 1953 the proportionate shares of the regions were 45 percent for the Northern Region, 25 percent for the Eastern Region, and 30 percent for the Western Region; by 1960 these had changed to 31 percent, 28.0 percent, and 37 percent respectively.

Consequently, the AG and by implication the Western Region, became an out-group. This adversely affected the solidarity of the Yoruba, its dominant ethnic group, as the leadership of the AG split over the strategy to be adopted in dealing with the setback: should the party seek rapprochement with the NPC, or should it attempt to radicalize itself by adopting "democratic socialism" to challenge the coalition more

TABLE 5-1. *Recurrent Revenue, Federal and Regional Government,*
*1953–60*

*In £ thousands*

| Year | Federal government | Regional governments, total[a] | North | East | West |
|---|---|---|---|---|---|
| 1953 | 50,906 | 18,938 | 8,540 | 4,730 | 5,668 |
| 1954 | 59,256 | 18,993 | 6,338 | 5,348 | 7,307 |
| 1955 | 62,481 | 36,238 | 13,123 | 9,397 | 13,718 |
| 1956 | 59,950 | 38,150 | 13,748 | 9,008 | 14,381 |
| 1957 | 70,567 | 43,276 | 14,549 | 12,184 | 15,522 |
| 1958 | 70,945 | 44,475 | 14,319 | 13,380 | 15,709 |
| 1959 | 77,316 | 47,335 | 15,059 | 14,216 | 16,649 |
| 1960 | 88,824 | 53,323 | 16,608 | 14,875 | 19,681 |
| Percent change 1953–60 | 74.4 | 181.5 | 94.4 | 214.4 | 247.2 |

Source: B. J. Dudley, *Parties and Politics in Northern Nigeria* (London: Frank Cass, 1968), p. 269.

a. Total may not be exact owing to discrepancies in the original data.

effectively for federal power as a mass party? The former option meant respect for the regional boundaries as they were and tacit agreement that each of the dominant ethnic groups could keep its domain; the latter option, which was chosen, meant throwing down the gauntlet to the coalition partners, who lost no time in picking it up.

The conflict over strategies tore the party apart, the radical majority became one faction following the national leader, Obafemi Awolowo, and the losing faction backed the first option, the deputy national leader, Samuel L. Akintola. The federal government then supported the deputy national leader, who was the premier of the Western Region. When the party tried to remove him through a vote of no confidence in Parliament, his supporters created a disturbance, Parliament was sacked by the police using tear gas, and a "state of emergency" was declared for six months during which time a federal administrator ruled the region. Under his rule, Awolowo and his lieutenants were confined. The administrator instituted probes into some statutory corporations in the region through which the leader and his lieutenants were indicted while the deputy national leader was exonerated.[23] The systematic political assault on the AG leadership provoked widespread violence throughout the region as both factions fought for control of the major cities. The violence that was unleashed then was, indeed, one of the causes of the military coup of 1966.

At the same time, the coalition partners were also falling out over the allocation of federal resources. Control over them was the basic motivation for their alliance, and the allocation of political control to fill the political vacuum created in the Western Region by the split of the AG leadership. The NCNC had become thoroughly disillusioned with the payoffs from the coalition partnership. Most capital expenditures were going to the Northern Region. The eastern (NCNC) regional government declared in 1964:

Take a look at what they have done with the little power we surrendered to them to preserve a unity which does not exist: Kainji Dam Project—about £150 million of *our money* when completed—all in the North. . . . Bornu Railway Extension—about £75 million of *our money* when completed—all in the North. . . . spending over £50 million on the Northern Nigerian Army in the name of the Federal Republic. . . . Military training and ammunition factories and installations are based in the North, thereby using *your money* to train Northerners to fight Southerners. . . . Building of a road to link the dam site and the Sokoto cement works—£7 million when completed—all in the North . . . . Total on all these four projects about £262 million. Now they have refused to allow the building of an iron and steel industry in the East and paid experts to produce a distorted report.[24]

The break-up of the AG presented an opportunity for the NCNC to strengthen itself in comparison with the NPC. It had always been a strong party in the West, benefiting from subethnic conflicts among the Yoruba and the alienation of the non-Yoruba Benin and Delta provinces. In 1963 the coalition partners took advantage of the political crisis in western Nigeria and the paralysis of Yoruba political leadership to create the Midwest Region (while blocking demands of their own minorities for the creation of new regions in the North and the East). The federal government saw the fragmentation of the Western Region as a way of weakening the Western Region and the AG. The Midwestern Region promptly fell under the control of the NCNC. If the West were also to fall under the control of the NCNC, the political system would become bipolar, and the bargaining power of the NCNC would greatly increase by its support to the minorities agitating for the fragmentation of the Northern Region.[25]

The NPC forestalled this event by supporting and strengthening the new United People's Party (UPP) of Samuel Ladoke Akintola. Together with the western parliamentary NCNC, the UPP formed a new political party, the Nigerian National Democratic Party (NNDP). Since the Western Region was engulfed in violent protests against the restoration of Akintola to power, the NNDP was totally dependent on federal coercive machinery for survival. Failure to control the Western Region, which thus fell under the rule of an ally of the NPC, meant the Eastern Region had been completely outmaneuvered.

To all these problems were added the 1962–63 census crises. Since the dominance of the NPC derived from the North's population advantage, the census was the ultimate source of power and the place where its domination could be broken. The 1952–53 census on the basis of which representation was distributed for the 1959 elections calculated 55.4 percent of the population to be in the North, 20.9 percent in the West, and 23.7 percent in the East.[26] The provisional results of the 1962 census had the North with 53.5 percent of the 55.7 million population; the East, 22.3 percent; the West, 18.5 percent; the Midwest, 4.5 percent; and Lagos Federal Capital Territory, 1.2 percent.[27] The Eastern Region demanded a recount, which did not change much from the 1962 figures. With that avenue of contesting for political power closed, attention shifted to the 1964 federal elections and the Western Regional elections of 1965.

As indicated already, elections had ceased to be a mechanism for recruiting political leaders and legitimating authority. The pending elections were in fact a battle for collective survival for southerners rather than just a political contest. It was "a last chance" to break the North's stranglehold on political power. However, with the western regional government replacing the Eastern Region as the ally of the northern leadership, the battle was between unequally equipped adversaries. The two grand alliances that were formed for the elections were the Nigerian National Alliance (NNA), composed of the NPC, the NNDP, and the Mid-West Democratic Front; and the United Progressive Grand Alliance (UPGA), which grouped together the NCNC, AG, Northern Elements Progressive Union, and the United Middle Belt Congress.

Absolute northern domination of the political system could only be averted if the southern-led UPGA could make substantial electoral gains in the North. If such gains had been made, it would have moderated the increasingly insensitive disposition of the NPC leaders. Unfortunately, this did not happen, given the blatant violations of the electoral rules all over the country.[28]

The UPGA sought postponement of the elections and when that failed called a boycott of the elections that was only partially observed. The NPC "won" 162 of the 167 seats in the Northern Region while its ally, the NNDP, "won" 36 in the Western Region. The NCNC and AG "won" 33 and 15 seats respectively. The elections were repeated where the boycott was effective, after which the NCNC had 84 seats, AG 21, Nigerian Progressive Front 4 seats, and Independents 5. The significant outcome was that the NPC, after this election, could govern alone, having more than half of the 312 seats.[29]

As Leo Dare has noted, "The formation of the two grand alliances only consolidated the North/South political division, and since the NPC was able to win an absolute majority of the federal seats by concentrating on the North, the southern parties were rendered irrelevant and frustrated."[30] The frustration found expression in violence in which political assassinations and arson were the order of the day. The approach of the western regional elections in October 1965 provided opportunity for further manifestation of the frustrations of political impotence. Violence escalated to the point of anarchy as the urban unemployed found in the political violence an outlet for avenging their economic marginalization.[31]

The students turned against the government soon after independence over an issue of national sovereignty. During the 1958 constitutional conference, an agreement on defense, the Anglo-Nigerian Defense Pact, was reached to enable Britain to assist in the defense of Nigeria in case of external aggression and to ensure British support for the government in case of internal subversion and violent overthrow.[32] Ratified in November 1960 against much opposition spearheaded by the AG, the pact met student protest in a 150-kilometer march in 1961 from the University of Ibadan to the federal Parliament at Lagos when it was presented for its extension. The students' protest march aroused considerable public interest in foreign policy. Since the AG had frequently alleged that the government was subservient to foreign interests, it was politically inexpedient to maintain the pact after the students' intervention.

Workers aligned themselves with politicians before independence in the expectation that they would receive a better deal from the Nigerian government after independence. Unfortunately, it did not take too long after independence for them to become disillusioned. The politicians were so incompetent, corrupt, and insensitive to their demands that the trade unions temporarily sank their differences to organize a general strike in 1964. The main issues were the deterioration in the real income of workers and the rejection of the report of the Morgan Commission set up to deal with the problem, but these events were only specific instances of the general indifference of the political class to the suffering of the masses. More than 70,000 workers participated in the two-week strike. Government first responded by detaining the strike leaders but then had to relent because of its success and massive public support. The 30,000 people at Ibadan race course chanted, "No AG, No NCNC," despite the AG and NCNC leaders' support for the strike. In Gavin Williams's view, the strike "focused popular grievances against all politicians and their practices."[33]

The manner in which the demands made by the workers and students were handled had ominous implications for the stability of the political system. First, it portrayed the absence of regular institutional mechanisms for such conflict resolution or the unwillingness of the actors to utilize them. Second, the success of extralegal methods before which the government appeared impotent increased the propensity to resort to them. These showed the politicians' lack of faith in the constitutional and legal processes of governance. The collapse of the political system so totally incapable of formulating consensual rules for conflict management was only a matter of time.

## Management by Violence and the Military Regime

Military intervention in 1966 was the ultimate move in the gradually escalating use of physical violence to settle political conflicts. The military forces had unfortunately been frequently called on or put on the alert to intervene in political conflict since they were first used to quell the Tiv ethnic riots in 1960. Adekanye lists eight such cases.[34] Thus when they intervened to seize political power in 1966, the difference lay in the object of their violence, the political class, rather than its followers, ordinary citizens, who had been the cannon fodder in previous forays.

The military coup resulted in the death of the federal prime minister, Tafawa Balewa, and the premiers of the Northern and Western Regions, as well as other prominent politicians. Since most of the coup plotters were Igbo, and the victims were all (except one) northern officers and politicians of the Nigerian National Alliance, the obvious inference was that it was a sectional coup intended to serve Igbo political interests. That the coup was not fully successful and that the general officer commanding the Nigerian Army, Major General Johnson Aguiyi Ironsi, who foiled the coup was also Igbo did nothing to assuage the grief of the northerners.

The indecision of General Ironsi over what to do with the coup plotters worsened matters. They were held in detention when many expected that they should have faced immediate court martial. More seriously, a decree promulgated in May 1966 (decree no. 34) introduced a unitary system of government, abolishing all regions and renaming them groups of provinces. A national military government was proclaimed, military prefects appointed, and the regional public services unified. These centralization measures were strongly opposed by the northerners.

Northern leaders now seethed with anger and frustration. On May 29–30, 1966, Ahmadu Bello University students, apparently acting with the consent of northern leaders, started a protest that turned into a riot. The erosion of governmental authority had been obvious for months previously. The head of state and commander in chief of the armed forces seemed to rely on the advice of Igbo technocrats, his kinsmen.[35] Northern soldiers would only take orders from officers of northern origin.[36] It was in this situation that on July 29, 1966, Major General Ironsi was toppled by northern army officers who killed him and several army officers, most of them Igbo. This action led to de facto regionalization of the army.

In September and October 1966 Igbos were wantonly massacred all over the Northern Region without intervention from the security agents. The march toward civil war was thereafter swift. The ad hoc constitutional conference composed of members of the "old political class," such as Chief Awolowo, Chief Anthony Enahoro, Professor Eni Njoku, and Sir Kashim Ibrahim, which had been sitting since September 12, 1966, was suspended. Real dialogue between the Eastern Region under Lieutenant Colonel Ojukwu and other Nigerian military rulers (Lieutenant Colonel Yakubu Gowon as head of state and other military governors) resumed in January 1967 on neutral grounds at Aburi (Ghana) since Ojukwu had refused to acknowledge that Gowon, now next in line of seniority to the assassinated head of state and general officer commanding the Nigerian Armed Forces, could succeed him.

At Aburi it became clear that the old order could not be easily restored. Ojukwu would not settle for anything less than a consociational arrangement in which the military headquarters had equal representation from the regions and the army in the region would be exclusively composed of men from the region; the Supreme Military Council would take decisions only with the concurrence of all members and thus give each region the power of veto over national issues; and all centralization decrees would be repealed.[37]

The terms of the agreement would, if implemented, have turned Nigeria into a confederal state and permanently weakened central authority. Consequently, senior federal civil servants encouraged Gowon to back out of the concessions that he had apparently agreed to at Aburi. Ojukwu, for his part, threatened to implement them unilaterally if the federal government did not do so by March. In the meantime, at the end of February he seized key federal statutory corporations in the Eastern Region and set up a regional court of appeal.

On May 27, 1967, the federal government promulgated a decree that divided the country into twelve states—six in the North and six in the South. The Middle Belt people had two states, Benue-Plateau and Kwara, while the southeastern minorities also had two, Cross River and Rivers. The twelve-state structure dealt decisively with one of the vexatious issues of the Nigerian federal system, its imbalanced structure.[38] Yet it was the last straw as far the Eastern Region was concerned. On May 30, 1967, the Eastern Region declared secession and proclaimed itself Biafra, taking along the Rivers and Cross River states newly created by the federal government a few days earlier but effectively under its control.

A large body of literature exists on the Nigerian Civil War that soon ensued.[39] For purpose of this analysis, it is not the civil war itself that is important but the strategies by which national unity was maintained in a period of great national distress. The coming into power of Gowon in July 1967 marked the beginning of attempts to associate the sacked politicians more formally with governance. Even the young military officers who initiated the coup, but had not succeeded in retaining power, had planned to pacify the political class by releasing Awolowo and his lieutenants from a jail sentence for treason during the Action Group crises of 1962–65. They had also planned to subdivide the regions as a means of satisfying the demands of minority ethnic groups.[40] Awolowo became commissioner (minister) for finance and vice chairman of the federal executive council.

The federal system was so much restructured between 1967 and 1969 that the states were no longer able to resist federal dictation. Fragmentation of the states and adverse changes in the revenue allocation formula had made them politically weaker. The process was enhanced by the nature of military rule and military organization with its hierarchical command structure.[41] No civilian administration could have restructured the federation so much, creating new states simultaneously all over the country when it was considered punitive by the dominant group in each region.

Changes in the revenue allocation formula in 1970 deemphasized derivation as one of the criteria of allocation. These have been succinctly analyzed by Egite Oyovbaire.[42] The portion of excise duties shared to states and mining rents and royalties distributed on the basis of derivation were reduced and added to the distributable pool account (DPA). This account was, henceforth, shared half on the basis of population and half on the basis of equality. Thus greater revenues became available to be shared by the states. But at the same time, the federal government took over control of the marketing boards and thereby denied the states another independent source of revenue.

In 1975 the revenue allocation formula was further amended. Henceforth no portion of customs and excise duties was paid to the states on the basis of derivation; instead that portion was diverted into the DPA. By the new arrangements most of the revenue that previously went to the states on the basis of derivation/consumption became centralized and all the states became dependent on federally collected revenues.

Gowon's administration was toppled in 1975 after nearly nine years in office. During this period Nigeria had survived a civil war, thereby allaying fears of disintegration, and created new states, thereby allaying fears of domination by centralized political authority. And yet the nation was not exactly at peace with itself. There was high-level corruption, incompetence, insensitivity, and drift in the management of the nation's conflicts. In spite of steady growth in petroleum revenues, the performance of the economy and the use of its revenues were not reassuring.

The new administration headed by Brigadier Murtala Mohammed and then, after a failed coup by his colleague Lieutenant General Olusegun Obasanjo, introduced a program of transition to civil democratic rule. Careful attempts were made to consolidate federal authority while making access to it competitive. The emphasis was on the evolution of a federal system in which federal dominance was accepted by the states, which in turn would have adequate scope to cater to the needs of their people in the assigned sphere.

The new administration increased the number of states from twelve to nineteen, ten in the North and nine in the South. Given the formula of allocation of revenue to the states—half on equality and half by population—the states that were newly subdivided gained from the equality factor. Thus the areas that benefited from the exercise were the western state (subdivided into Ogun, Ondo, and Oyo); the Northeast (subdivided into Borno, Bauchi, and Gongola); the Northwest (subdivided into Niger and Sokoto); Benue-Plateau (split into Benue and Plateau); and East-Central (split into Imo and Anambra).[43] The impact of this change was to leave the oil-producing states of Cross River, Rivers, and Bendel disappointed and disgruntled.

The military administration set up a constitution drafting committee, which was told that the Supreme Military Council had decided that Nigeria needed, among other things, a limited number of genuine and truly national political parties, an executive presidential system of government with a cabinet chosen to reflect the federal character of Nigeria, and constitutional limitation on the number of states to be further created. All of these issues were reflected in the constitution of 1979, which had broad national goals devoid of sectional appeals and empowered the Federal Electoral Commission to register only those parties that reflected the federal character in the composition of their leadership. It also introduced the presidential system and provided a complicated procedure for creating new states.[44]

## Conflicts under the Second Republic

The second republic (1979–83) witnessed more or less a replay of the politics of the first republic with new rules and new men carrying the old ethnic banners. The only significant change was in the definition and scope of the concept of ethnic group. The frequent fragmentation of states had created new identities where previously the elite had forged pan-tribal identities and boundaries. As Eghosa Osaghae has pointed out, "The ethnic groups in Nigeria today . . . and the boundaries claimed for them, are actually the parcels of influence carved out by the men of power."[45] With the creation of new states, new leaders emerged whose status depended on the new identity forged by the boundaries of the new states.

Thus new alliances had to be forged for the 1979 elections. As usual, the three major ethnic groups were the main coalition building blocs. The National Party of Nigeria (NPN), which was dominated by the northern establishment, forged a successful alliance with the elites of Cross River and Rivers states. The NPN was successful because it adopted a zoning system for sharing offices, which indicated before-hand the payoff to the participating groups. The Nigerian People's Party (NPP), controlled by the Igbo, was able to win control of the pre-dominantly Christian Plateau state in the Middle Belt. The Yoruba-led Unity Party of Nigeria (UPN) was confined to the Western Region be-cause the Yoruba leaders could not forge any significant alliance out-side the Yoruba culture area. In Bendel the UPN won the elections more because of memories of the performance of the party's leader, Chief Awolowo, as western regional premier than anything else. The party leaders tried once more to portray themselves as socialists, with de-mands for free education, free health, integrated rural development, and full employment, the so-called four cardinal programs.

The Igbos suffered a split in leadership affiliation, similar to the one the Yorubas experienced in 1962–63. There was a powerful group, ini-tially made up of new-breed politicians like Sam Mbakwe and Jim Nwobodo, who did not want a repeat of the alliance of 1959 that led to the formation of the NPC-NCNC coalition government. The main ar-gument of this group was that nothing much was achieved by the al-liance and that the northern elites had not only betrayed the Igbos but had used their grip on power to restrict the Igbos to only two states out of nineteen.

The other group felt that the real rival of the Igbos was the Yoruba, not the Hausa-Fulani North. The Yoruba had aligned with the North to ensure the defeat of the Igbos in the civil war and had taken most of the public service positions vacated by Igbos who fled the federation for Biafra, and the Igbos could do the same. The Young Turks seeking fresh alignment succeeded in recruiting Nnamdi Azikiwe into the NPP as its flagbearer and thus won the two Igbo states of Anambra and Imo as well as Plateau in the Middle Belt.

The 1979 elections ended in favor of the NPN. The party won the presidential election and won 36 Senate seats against 28 for the UPN, 16 for the NPP, 8 for the GNPP, and 7 for PRP.[46] In the House of Representatives it won 168 seats against 112 for the UPN, 77 for NPP, 43 for GNPP, and 49 for PRP. Thus although the NPN was the single largest political party, it needed to build a coalition in the Legislative House to be able to govern effectively. The NPP negotiated with both the NPN and the UPN before deciding which party to align with.

The UPN, whose national leader had a petition pending challenging the declaration of Alhaji Shehu Shagari as winner of the presidential elections, tried to build a coalition. It was styled the Nigerian Progressive Front and was composed of the UPN, NPP, and GNPP. It was not yet certain whether the PRP would join. According to the Suggested Blueprint for Action agreed to by the three parties, the long-term objective was to "fuse into one political party in the nearest future," but the immediate goal was to share legislative power and, in the event of the UPN leader's winning his legal tussle to elect him at the electoral college to share the patronage positions of the executive.[47]

The NPP also simultaneously negotiated with the NPN in August 1979. It is obvious from the wide-ranging issues covered by the meeting with the NPN that the NPP never seriously intended to align with the UPN. Besides agreeing to vote for Shagari should the presidential election be referred to the electoral college by the tribunal, the two parties agreed to reexamine the creation of more states and review the issue of property deemed to have been "abandoned" by Igbos, mainly in non-Igbo areas of the Eastern Region during the civil war. In addition, a special development agency would be established to "ensure the rapid economic development of those states in the country whose social and economic development are lagging behind the older states or have suffered serious set-backs arising from natural disasters, war or the difficult nature of their terrain." Finally, the formula for sharing offices was more favorable than what the Nigerian Progressive Front offered.[48] The terms of the agreement offered the Igbos greater opportunities to advance ethnic interests, and the NPP went into alliance with the NPN. As a result the party provided the speaker of the House of Representatives, the deputy senate leader, and ten ministers.

By June 1981 the accord had broken down completely. There were many points of disagreement. All the other political parties opposed the appointment of presidential liaison officers, who conducted themselves as alternate governors in the states under their control. In addi-

tion, a vice presidential assistant was also appointed for Imo and Anambra states to cultivate political support for the vice president in his
political base. This was resented by the NPP as a deliberate design to
undermine their governors in both states. The NPP too did not fully
back the revenue allocation bill submitted by the president to the legislature.[49] The final blow was the impeachment of Balarabe Musa as Kaduna state governor.

The other very controversial issue was the application of the federal
character principle. This was enshrined in the constitution as follows:
"The composition of the Government of the Federation or any of its
agencies and the conduct of its affairs shall be carried out in such manner as to reflect the federal character of Nigeria and the need to promote
national unity, and also to command national loyalty thereby ensuring
that there shall be no predominance of persons from a few States or
from a few ethnic or other sectional groups in that government or in
any of its agencies."[50]

This clause of the constitution has been referred to as emphasizing
"the need for the accommodation of the ethnic groups that constitute
Nigeria."[51] In higher educational institutions, it led to the imposition of
admission quotas as a means of reducing the educational gap between
the North and South.[52] In the bureaucracy, the attempt to create a representative bureaucracy was similarly favorable to the North. As a result of the lack of proper and acceptable modalities for its implementation, it caused resentment and panic among southern civil servants.[53]

The fact that states were the units of distribution in effecting the federal character principle promoted statism and agitation for more states.[54]
In many respects, the politics of the second republic defied most of the
prophylactics administered to sanitize the system. The collapse of the
NPN-NPP accord showed the government as being narrowly based socially and the Hausa-Fulani as being, once again, in hegemonic control
of political power. The agitation for the creation of more states snow-
balled. At a point demands were made for a staggering fifty-three new
states before the national assembly. In the meantime existing states
were all financially dependent on the federation account, and the cost
of administration was getting higher and higher. These negative consequences of the solutions have been described as the "boomerang effect"
of Nigerian federalism.[55]

Attempts by all the other four political parties to combine in an alliance named the Progressive Parties' Alliance (PPA) to dislodge the

NPN from power failed because they could not sink their ethnic differences to agree on a common leader.[56] These contradictions led to the overthrow of the second republic by the military in 1983.

## Conflict Management under the Military after 1984

The new military leaders led by General Muhammadu Buhari were "predominantly northern in composition and conservative in outlook. . . . They were part of the generation of northerner officers encouraged by northern civilian ministers in the 1960s to join the army straight from school, in order to make up the northern quota in the officer corps of the armed forces."[57] The ethnic composition of the new military administration was a source of much adverse comment by the southerners. Schism within the group led to its overthrow in August 1985 by General Ibrahim Babangida, the chief of army staff, who broadened the composition of the supreme ruling body, the Armed Forces Ruling Council.

More significantly, the new military administration empaneled a political bureau in January 1986 to

(a) Review Nigeria's political history and identify the basic problems which have led to our failure in the past and suggest ways of resolving and coping with these problems;

(b) Identify a basic philosophy of government which will determine goals and serve as a guide to the activities of Government;

(c) Collect relevant information and data for the Government as well as identify other political problems that may arise from the debate;

(d) Gather, collate and evaluate the contribution of Nigerians to the search for a viable political future and provide guidelines for the attainment of the consensus objectives;

(e) Deliberate on the political problems as may be referred to it from time to time.[58]

### Creation of States

The issue of creation of states has become a primary problem of governance and perennial source of conflict since it became obvious that fragmentation is rewarding to the affected regions. They gain not only financially but also in public appointments and other forms of political patronage. Thus the Igbos have for long complained of being disadvantaged by being confined into two states in the nineteen-state structure. Other areas where the demands for creation of new governmental units were persistent were Bendel, old Kaduna state, old Cross River state, and Gongola state.

In 1987 the government created two new states, Katsina and Akwa Ibom, and said the matter was closed. But if it was closed for others, it was not for the Igbos who had consistently agitated for subdivision of their states since the 1970s. In August 1991 the Igbos, as if on cue, began a public campaign for creation of more states out of Imo and Anambra. The first salvo was fired by Igbo elites of eminent credentials. In a memorandum to the AFRC they pointed out the disadvantages to Igbos in the federal structure. They compared the populations of the so-called majority ethnic groups from the 1953 census, which were roughly equal, and referred to the fact that there was now disparity in the number of states that each of them had.[59]

Many Igbo groups followed with an avalanche of advertising campaigns and letters to the editors of newspapers. As Chief Ojukwu pointed out, the so-called minorities of the former Eastern Region had been grouped into three states while the more populous Igbos were confined in two.[60] The Yoruba Obas also began agitation for new states as did the elites and traditional rulers of the Delta area of Bendel and the minorities of Gongola and Kwara. In September 1991 nine additional states were created. The Igbos had two new state. Bendel, Oyo, Gongola, Sokoto, Borno, Kano were split into two each while Kogi was created through merger of a part of Kwara with a part of Benue. Kwara also lost a slice of territory to Niger state. With thirty states (sixteen in the North and fourteen in the South) the government must have been surprised at the persistence of protests against the decisions.

Yet demands continued, for example, to split Rivers state and to accord Oke-Ogun a separate state, and against location of Delta's capital the locations and the capitals of Kebbi and Jigawa states and the boundaries of many of the states. Three years after, agitations persisted and advertisements were still being placed in major newspapers calling for redress of these grievances.[61] Even more shocking to the government but indicative of the futility of state-creation exercises as a way of managing conflict is the rancor and bitterness that have come to characterize relations between the new states over asset sharing and public employment in nearly all parts of the country.

The matter is compounded by the fact that the new census figures show that the distribution of House of Representative seats based on the number of local governments has nothing to do with size of population. For example, Lagos with the largest population (5,685,781) has fifteen seats while Kogi with less than half of that population (2,099,046) has sixteen seats.[62]

Nor does revenue allocation have to do with population size alone. Allocation is torn between demand criteria of size and supply criteria of revenue production. In 1982 the civilian administration passed the Allocation of Revenue Act of 1981, assigning 55 percent of the federation account to the federal government, 35 percent to the state government, and 10 percent to the local governments. Of the 35 percent to the states, 30.5 percent went to all the states allocated as follows: equality, 40 percent; population, 40 percent; primary school enrollment, 15 percent; internal revenue effort, 5 percent. The remaining 4.5 percent of the states' share was allocated as follows: 1.0 percent to the federal government for the amelioration of ecological problems in any part of Nigeria; 2 percent on the basis of derivation to mineral-producing areas in direct proportion to the value of mineral extracted; and 1.5 percent to the federal government for the development of oil-producing areas at the discretion of the president.[63]

The allocation formula was not satisfactory to the oil-producing areas because it underemphasized derivation, and even the small portion assigned on the basis of derivation was to be used at the discretion of the president. This meant he could use it discriminately for partisan political purposes. But there was nothing much that oil-producing areas could do politically. As a former federal permanent secretary in the Ministry of Mines and Power observed at a public lecture in 1980, "[As] in many other areas of the world, the regions where oil is found in this country are very inhospitable. They are mainly in swamps and creeks. They require massive injection of money if their conditions and standards of living are to compare with what attains elsewhere in the country where possibilities of agriculture and diversified industry are much greater. There is a nudging acceptance of the special needs of oil areas in the latest proposals being discussed by the government but I believe there is a long way to go to meet the claims of oil-producing areas. . . Given, however, the small size and population of oil-producing areas, it is not cynical to observe that even if the resentments of oil-producing states continue, they cannot threaten the stability of the country nor affect its continued economic development."[64]

The views above permeated not only federal bureaucracy but also the political class. But this did not stop agitation in the oil-producing areas for a fairer deal. Instead of improvement in the situation, it rather worsened in 1984 when the military passed the Allocation of Revenue Federation Account (Amendment) Decree of 1984 (that is, Decree no. 36 of 1984). Whereas the earlier formula allocated 1.5 percent of the entire federation account to the federal government for the development of mineral-producing areas, in 1984 it was reduced to 1.5 percent of revenue derived from minerals. In 1985 total federally collected revenue was N15,041.8 million. On the old formula, the fund for mineral-producing areas would have been N225.63 million, but with the new one it was N163.7 million, a loss of N61.93 million for the oil-producing areas.[65]

The military regime's newly created political bureau noted the deplorable conditions in the oil-producing areas and therefore recommended improvement in the accruals to them from the federation account. Specifically, it asked that the dichotomy between on-shore and off-shore oil in the allocation of revenue due to the oil-producing states be abolished.[66] It also recommended an increase from 1.5 percent to 2.0 percent of the revenue appropriated to the federal government for the development of the mineral-producing areas, to be sent directly to the local governments concerned.

In 1990 the federal government changed the revenue allocation formula again. Federal government's revenue was fixed at 50 percent: states, 30 percent; local governments, 15 percent; and special funds, 5 percent. The breakdown of the special funds was federal capital territory, 1.0 percent; stabilization fund, 0.5 percent; derivation, 1.0 percent; development of oil-mineral-producing areas, 1.5 percent; and development of non-oil-mineral-producing areas, 1.0 percent. The revenues to be allocated on the basis of derivation and to oil-mineral-producing and non-oil-mineral-producing areas were direct proportions of actual contribution from these sources.[67]

In April 1990 many officers from the oil-producing areas participated in an abortive military coup. The plotters made a provocative broadcast alluding to exploitation of minorities, in response to which, perhaps, the federal government began to send the fund for the development of mineral-producing areas under its control directly to them and to pay greater attention to their infrastructural needs. Presidential tours of the areas resulted in huge federal extrabudgetary capital expenditures in Rivers, Cross River, and Akwa-Ibom states.

But these responses were like personal favors from the head of state instead of legal and regular appropriations, and so they had only temporary palliative effects. The oil-producing communities began to sabotage oil production infrastructures, not only of the foreign, multinational corporations but also of the Nigerian National Petroleum Corporation (NNPC). Whole communities rose up in rebellion against increasing immiseration. For example, in October 1990 the Umuechem community in Rivers state began a demonstration in protest against neglect by the Shell Petroleum Development Company. The company invited the police, who dispersed the demonstrators with tear gas, thereby creating pandemonium. The community rioted, killing three policemen. In the police reprisal which followed, at least twenty villagers were killed.[68]

Such uprisings and repressions were repeated in several oil-producing communities fueled by increasing awareness of their relative deprivation in a federal system of which they were the financial backbone. The undeclared war between the oil-producing communities, on the one hand, and the multinational oil companies (principally Shell, Mobil, Chevron, Agip) and government, on the other, was promoted by the very articulate, tenacious, and popular demands of the Ogoni people for redress of the historical neglect and degradation of the environment of Nigeria's first oil-producing community.

In August 1990 Ogoni chiefs and community leaders met and signed the Ogoni Bill of Rights in which they demanded political autonomy, meaning political control of Ogoni affairs by Ogoni people; control and use of a fair proportion of Ogoni economic resources for Ogoni development; adequate and direct representation in all Nigerian national institutions; use and development of Ogoni languages in Ogoni territory; full development of Ogoni culture; religious freedom; and protection of the Ogoni environment and ecology from further degradation.[69]

The Ogonis began a massive local and international media campaign, interspersed with sporadic acts of violence against oil installations and personnel as well as local elites who disagreed with such methods, to draw attention to their plight and to pressure both the Shell Petroleum Development Company and the government to meet their demands.

The radical appeal of their message to other minority, oil-producing communities should be evident from the articulation of their grievances. According to the first president of the Movement for the Survival of the Ogoni People (MOSOP), "The Ogoni case is of genocide being committed in the dying years of the twentieth century by multinational oil companies under the supervision of the Government of the Federal Republic of Nigeria . . . an estimated US 100 billion dollars worth of oil has been carted away from Ogoniland. In return for this, the Ogoni have no pipe-borne water, no electricity, very few roads, ill-equipped schools and hospitals and no industry whatsoever."[70]

Since the Ogoni have been in the forefront of the agitation to create awareness of deprivation among oil-producing communities, government selected the area for intense security attention. The army has occupied Ogoniland since the signing of the Ogoni Bill of Rights. The army's massive use of force and human rights abuses in Ogoniland and government's insensitivity to allegations of genocide indicate that repression rather than negotiation and accommodation is government's preferred solution.

The increasing tendency toward violence as a result of perceived deprivation has been a source of worry and concern to the government. When the oil-producing areas formed associations such as the Committee of Oil Producing Areas (COPA) and Association of Minority Oil States (AMOS), the government began to search frantically for a means of weakening the growth of sectional organizations based on the most vital resource of the country. The clear danger was that if the elites united with the communities whose anger had so far found expression only in blind violence, the politics of the country would be dramatically restructured with different bargaining options as well as unfathomable hazards.

The situation was not helped much, ironically, by the government's attempt to indigenize oil production. Among those given concessions to prospect for oil were Alhaji Wahab Folawiyo (Yinka Folawiyo Holdings); the Ooni of Ife, Oba Okunade Sijuade (Alfred James); Alhaji O. Abija Ramos; Dan Obuekwe; Chief Gabriel Igbinedion (Moncroief Oil); Chief M. K. O. Abiola (Summit Oil); A. K. Belgore (PACLANTIC); Alhaji Dantata (Dantata Investment and Securities); Chief Michael Ibru (Queens Oil); Alhaji Mai Deribe (Cavendish Oil); Alhaji Inko Muhammed Ndimi (Indimi Oil); IPEC; DEMINEX; Alhaji Ado Ibrahim (Nigus Petroleum); and Otunba Michael Adenuga (Consolidated Oil).[71] The fact that senior appointments were also manipulated in favor of

northerners on the excuse of "lopsidedness" in the composition of top
management staff of the Nigerian National Petroleum Corporation
spread alarm among technocratic staff of the oil industry. A typical example was the appointment of a university registrar to the position of
top management staff of the corporation mainly because he had served
under Jibril Aminu, the petroleum minister, when the latter was the
vice chancellor at the University of Maiduguri. The influx of such political patronage appointees into the vital oil industry proved to many
that the northern oligarchy would consider no move too blatant to
make to ensure complete domination of the commanding heights of the
polity and economy.

The publicity given these moves strongly affected public perceptions
of uses of power to serve political ends.[72] In particular it promoted the
feeling abroad in the oil-producing areas that the natural resources of
their areas were being parceled out for exploitation to the benefit of out-
siders but to their detriment. To respond to the foregoing misgivings, in
January 1992 government changed the revenue allocation formula once
more. The new formula gave to local governments 20 percent of the
revenue, slashing the states' share to 25 percent. Again in June 1992
government announced another formula as follows: federal government, 48.5 percent; state governments, 24.0 percent; local governments,
20 percent; federal capital territory, 1.0 percent; general ecology, 2.0 percent; stabilization, 0.5 percent; derivation, 1.0 percent (of mineral revenue); and development of mineral-producing areas, 3.0 percent (of
mineral revenue).[73]

The government also established an agency, Oil-Mineral Producing
Areas Development Corporation (OMPADEC), located at Port Harcourt in one of the oil-producing states to administer the fund for the
development of mineral-producing areas while the derivation fund still
goes directly to the local governments of origin. The OMPADEC has
been able to provide impressive levels of social infrastructures but not
nearly enough to pacify oil-producing areas completely. Indeed, it has
generated much controversy of its own concerning its allocation of resources, citing of projects, and choice of contractors. As a result, the
sense of exploitation felt by the oil-producing areas did not diminish.

The states also complained of declining revenue and mounted a
lobby on the federal government for a change. Since the National Revenue Mobilization, Allocation and Fiscal Commission recommended 47
percent of the federation account to the federal government, the agita-

tion by the states had a persuasive ring to it.[74] However, given the federal government's fiscal indiscipline as manifested in huge budget deficits arising from extrabudget expenses, it was unlikely that they would receive a favorable response until the military hands over power to a democratically elected government at the center. From historical evidence, the revenue allocation formula would have to be dynamic to respond to new exigencies if it is to diminish as a source of instability to the next republic.

## Political Restructuring

The political bureau's report, in effect, became the government's manifesto for political restructuring Its main recommendation for achieving a more cohesive political class concerned how to make political parties more integrative. In this connection, the bureau came "to the conclusion that a two party system is best for Nigeria at this time." Such a two-party system had to be made to function under the following conditions:

(a) that both political parties accept the national philosophy of government;

(b) that the differences between the two political parties are the priorities and strategies of implementation of the national objectives;

(c) that membership of the political parties be open to every citizen of Nigeria irrespective of place of origin, sex, religion or ethnic grouping;

(d) that the national executive organ and the principal officers of each political party reflect the federal character of Nigeria;

(e) that each of the political parties be firmly established in at least two-thirds of the local government areas in each of the states including the Federal Capital Territory (Abuja); and

(f) that the law establishing a two-party system should be decreed and confirmed by the constitution. [75]

The only really new decision was to limit the number of political parties to two. The other recommendations on the political parties were mere echoes of conditions that had been instituted in the 1979 constitution. The government accepted these recommendations. In his inaugural speech to the constitutional Review Committee on September 7, 1987, the president, in justification of the decision to limit the political parties to two, observed, "No political system survives through the multiplication of areas and units of conflict and discord. Moreover, those who claim that our decision violates the principles of freedom of association need to think again . . . . The freedom to choose is satisfied so long as an alternative avenue exists . . . Our decision, therefore, is meant to put an end to inter-ethnic and inter-personal feuds which dominated the pattern of politics in the past. People must learn to fit into two political parties."[76]

The decision was fundamental, and all that the Review Committee was required to do was to recommend measures to avert the realization of the fear that the two-party system would promote North-South or Muslim-Christian dichotomy. Thus the two-party system was entrenched in the 1989 constitution.[77] The decision was, of course, easier taken than implemented. In May 1989 when the constitution was ratified by the Armed Forces Ruling Council and the ban on party politics lifted, the government asked politicians to form political associations on the basis of guidelines to be provided by the National Electoral Commission (NEC).[78]

The NEC's assessment of the extent to which its guidelines were complied with was negative. The associations had only two months to fulfill NEC's guidelines, and yet they were criticized for poor organization, rigging and falsification of claims, factionalism, and the dominance of the associations by rich and powerful men. The government declined to approve the registration of any two of the six short-listed political associations. Instead it decided to form its own political parties—the Social Democratic Party (SDP) and the National Republican Convention (NRC).[79]

The two parties were fostered by government-appointed administrative officers who registered the initial members and supervised the elections of officers at ward, local government, state, and national levels. The government also wrote their constitutions and manifestos, designed their symbols, and built offices for them at each local government headquarters, each state capital, and the federal capital. It also gave them hefty, annual grants of several millions of naira to provide office infrastructure, buy campaign vehicles, conduct primaries, and generally to administer their affairs. This state of affairs has led to the two political parties' being widely regarded as little different from public corporations of the government.

Nevertheless, the two-party system appeared to have served the main purpose for which it was established but, like many Nigerian political solutions, created one or two problems of its own. It seemed to have fulfilled the role of encouraging "cohesion in a land of pluralistic interests" as the president had hoped.[80] Judged by their performance in the state houses of assembly and gubernatorial elections of December 1991, the two political parties had gained broad national spread and acceptance across religious and geographical boundaries. The SDP won control of fourteen state governorships, seven of them in the North and seven in the South. The NRC won nine states in the North and seven states in the South. In the national assembly elections held on July 4, 1992, the SDP won 53 out of 91 Senate seats to the NRC's 37. The SDP had half of its senatorial seats in the North and half in the south. The NRC similarly had sixteen of its 37 senatorial seats from the South and 21 from the North. The spread of House of Representative seats follows the same pattern.

On surface appearances, therefore, the attempts to portray the parties as distinct ethnoregional entities and an elite ploy to influence electoral choices of voters through emotive appeal did not succeed. The SDP was tagged the Southern Democratic Party and the NRC the Northern Republican Convention. However, there were reasons still for caution in reaching conclusions. These political parties as the only legitimate vehicles for pursuing political ambitions were conglomerations, not of individuals as government had hoped, but of ethnic groups with different agenda and strategies. The groups were kept within the folds of their parties because they had no other options.

Meanwhile ethnic associations proliferated within the political parties, or rather, straddled both political parties. The main objective of each of them was to try to determine who became the next president, and the major consideration appears to be the ethnic origin of the candidate. In this context, Yorubas were the most clamorous, arguing that they had been excluded from sharing in the exercise of power at the federal level for too long, save the period of Obasanjo's leadership. Their elites formed the *Egbe Ilosiwaju Yoruba* (Club for the Advancement of Yorubas) with a view to presenting a common political front to the rest of the country, subordinating substantive to procedural demands.[81]

The other ethnic groups similarly formed groups outside the framework of the political parties also singing the same refrain. "It's our time to lead the country." Arthur Nzeribe formed CARIA, grouping elites/

political aspirants from the states of the former Eastern Region (Cross River, Akwa Ibom, Rivers, Imo, and Anambra from which the acronym is derived). The purpose was to bridge the gap of mutual misunderstanding and dislike that had existed between Igbos and non-Igbos of the former Eastern Region since the agitation for the creation of new states in the 1950s and the civil war particularly.[82] The Middle Belt Forum was also formed to press the claims of the region for a candidate of its choice.

Meanwhile, the Hausa-Fulani North also formed the Association of Northern Elders to scheme how to elect a northern candidate. Their fear as expressed by Hassan Sani Kontagora is quite candid. He said of southerners: "You are advanced educationally, because when the Europeans came, you were the people that they first made contact with . . . We recognize the fact. You're more educated. Especially the Yorubas. They're all over. The civil service, they're all over. The Igbos had their setback during the civil war and which also helped them because they tried to learn a lot of technologies which is now paying off. Up here, [north] we have nothing, apart from the population. And therefore you find that the Igbos have the economy and the technology, and the Yorubas have the education and also the economy because of the virtue of the port in Lagos . . . Therefore what are we left with? My people . . . Today when I say *north*, I mean those parts of the country that don't have the education you're talking about. We only rely on the population we have . . . sitting under the trees, having nothing to do."[83]

When the *Egbe Ilosiwaju Yoruba* extended its activities to the eastern states and later the Middle Belt states, the federal government became alarmed at the trend of coalition building. The *Egbe* promoted the formation of the Council for Unity and Understanding (CUU), grouping together retired army generals and top civilian politicians from the West, East, and the Middle Belt, deliberately, perhaps, excluding the far North.[84] Igbo-Yoruba rapprochement portended a deepening of the North-South dichotomy since no serious, effective effort seemed to have been made to integrate the Hausas and Fulanis of the North in the coalition-building exercise. The inclusion of the Middle Belt raised unpleasant memories of the April 1990 abortive coup during which the plotters announced the excision of some far northern states from the federation until they purged themselves of the propensity to seek hegemonic control of the political system. Besides, the formation of groups exclusive to the oil-producing areas such as the Association of Mineral-

Oil Areas and Association of Minority States raised other security problems; as a result a decree was passed proscribing them in May 1992.[85]

The proscription could, of course, only achieve what such instruments do, namely, drive the movements underground. Rather than ethnosectional groupings diminishing in number and activities, they proliferated and blossomed openly.

The problem of sectionalism within the political parties was compounded by the fact that there was a strong lobby for a national conference to debate afresh key demands that are collectively referred to in Nigerian public discourse as the "national question." Such issues include interethnic relations revenue allocation, state-federal relations, the federal character principle, citizenship, and the like. The persistent and increasing appeal of the demand for a national conference spoke quite a lot about the legitimacy of the transition to civil rule program and, thus, the potential stability of the third republic. The problem, ironically, can be partly traced to the bureau's report.

It had recommended that in order to offer the country a fresh beginning, all those who had held certain political offices between August 1975 and August 1985 should be banned from participating in politics for ten years. This was done through the Participation in Politics and Elections (Prohibition) Decree (no. 25 of 1987). It also proscribed from participating in politics for life certain public officers who had been found guilty of any misdeed between 1960 and 1966 and between 1979 and 1983. Another category of public servants were proscribed only during the transition period.

The prohibitions were widely and roundly condemned. At any rate they were freely flouted. As Nzeribe publicly confessed, although he and General Shehu Musa Yar'Adua were both prohibited, they had collaborated to ensure that their candidates were elected to the National Executive Committee of the Social Democratic Party.[86] Some of the affected politicians even ridiculed the prohibition stating, like Abubakar Rimi (ex-governor of Kano), that they were still in politics or, like Bola Ige (ex-governor of Oyo), that he was "waiting for midnight, October 1, 1992," when it was assumed that the military would hand over power on the symbolic day of independence anniversary.[87]

The politicians' challenge to the ban on participation in politics was reinforced by that of radical critics who are fundamentally opposed to military rule and key government policies such as the Structural Adjustment Program (SAP), establishment of two political parties by government and the various attempts by government to prohibit the free discussion of sensitive issues. Among this group were radical university lecturers, the several civil liberties associations that have sprouted since 1987 such as the Committee for the Defense of Human Rights, the Civil Liberties Organization, National Association of Democratic Lawyers, and the Campaign for Democracy. They demanded a national conference to seek national consensus on key issues rather than the spurious consensus that was being propagated by government.

It was not only radical critics of the government who promoted the idea of a national conference. A group of technocrats had in March 1990 proposed a national conference to review the Constitution already approved and promulgated nearly a year before. The group, which included establishment figures like Ade Martins, P. C. Asiodu, Olu Apara, Ibrahim Damcida, Ahmed Joda, Tayo Akpata, Walter Ollor, Oladapo Fafowora, and S. O. Fadahunsi, proposed the admixture of the presidential executive and parliamentary system as in the French model of government. They were opposed to a blanket ban on old politicians and also wanted the forum to discuss other burning national issues. In effect, they were voicing their dissatisfaction with the ongoing processes of transition.[88]

The government discouraged the technocrats from co-organizing a national conference with the radicals, which was scheduled for July 15, 1990. The government was apprehensive that the sentiments expressed by the plotters on sectional domination of government since independence would resurface at such a forum, coming so soon after an abortive military coup in April 1990. Such sentiments might be detrimental to the fresh attempts that were being made to pacify aggrieved segments of the country. The government also feared that radical proponents of the national conference had a hidden agenda that, if followed, might disrupt the transition program.

Nonetheless, the idea of a national conference was supported by a formidable group of people. This included former heads of state, Generals Gowon and Obasanjo, and former chief of army staff, General Yakubu Danjuma. It certainly spoke volumes for the legitimacy of the transition program if a motley group of old, banned, or disqualified politicians, technocrats (some of whom once were federal permanent secretaries), radical intelligentsia, and retired, top military officers could find common ground to demand the convening of a national conference.

Since that time the idea of a national conference has been a permanent demand of radical opponents of the government, the human rights and civil liberties associations, minority groups, ethnic associations representing oil-producing areas, and intellectuals concerned about the need to reform the political system. Whenever the transition to democratic, civil rule program suffered a hiccup, these groups rose in unison to demand that a national conference be convened.

In December 1991 thirteen prominent politicians were arrested and detained, allegedly for sponsoring candidates for elections and thus infringing the law prohibiting them from participating in politics.[89]

After eighteen days in detention, long enough for the elections to be concluded, they were released by the government, and the blanket prohibition against participation in politics by old politicians was lifted. They replied to the government's gesture promptly by calling for a government of "national consensus." The government, as usual, condemned the suggestion. The minister of information, Sam Oyovbaire, described the idea as "stale, outworn, meaningless and dubious."[90] Bolaji Akinyemi (ex-minister of foreign affairs) replied that it was the only way of ensuring stability, while General Obasanjo also said, "We need all hands on deck. This is no time for vertical or horizontal divisions or polarization of the society and exclusion; it is time for collective positive action by all. The only division tolerable is division of labor for the same objective and purpose."[91]

The nomination process of the presidential candidates of the two political parties showed clearly that the main competition was not going to be about contending ideologies or policies but transfer of power from one coalition of regional and ethnic groups to another. To a great extent, the government itself had ensured that groups and personalities, rather than policies, would dominate the campaign by the similarities in the manifestos it had written out for the parties. The North-South dichotomy was evident from the outset. When at the Abuja Convention the SDP and NRC selected their party chairman from the North and South respectively, given the norm of zoning offices, it was presumed that the SDP's presidential candidate would be a southerner and the NRC's a northerner.[92]

In the South, the odds favored the Yoruba to produce the SDP's presidential candidate for many reasons. The SDP was the dominant party in the five Yoruba states of Lagos, Ogun, Oyo, Osun, and Ondo.[93] In the

East, only one state was under the SDP. Besides, the coalition-building effort started by the *Egbe Ilosiwaju Yoruba* had built a consensus around the subject of a Yoruba candidate. Consequently, before the nominations, tacitly the presidential ticket of the party had been zoned to the North, East, and the West.[94] But these advantages were still subject to the formal processes of endorsement through the party primaries.

In the NRC, the East appeared to have formidable claims that did not receive deserved attention. All but one of the seven states voted NRC. Three of the six NRC-controlled states (Enugu, Abia, and Imo) were Igbo states, and thus they constituted the single largest ethnic unit in the NRC in the East. Furthermore, the Igbo had played second fiddle to the northern ruling class twice before (in the coalition that ruled from 1959–66 and 1979–83) and, therefore, demanded that their candidate be given priority for a change. The North of course could not countenance giving up power to a group they regarded as a useful ally but a potentially difficult senior partner.

Although the northern political oligarchy is as ethnically diverse as its southern counterpart, a common religion and the spiritual and political leadership of the Sokoto Caliphate provide a rallying point. Since northern ethnic minorities, predominantly Christian, had in recent years distanced themselves from its influence, a development underscored by their prominence in the SDP, the political clout of this group nationally had become diminished. Northern and southern minorities could not themselves bid for power because none of them had the numbers to make an impact in the din of claims and counterclaims in both parties, and several attempts to forge a coalition of minorities failed as a result of rivalries and lack of mutual trust.

The presidential primaries of 1992 were therefore expected to return a southern candidate on the SDP ticket and a northern candidate on the NRC ticket. The presidential primaries scheduled for August 1 to September 5, 1992, were marred by partisanship of the party executives saddled with the responsibility of running them, massive rigging, a hung result in the NRC, and boycott of the last segment by ten of the twelve candidates in the SDP.[95] As a result of the massive protests from candidates and partisans of the parties and the demand for government's intervention, the National Electoral Commission was directed by government to investigate the allegation. The commission confirmed the alleged malpractices, thereby paving the way for government to annul the primaries and order the NEC to restart the nomination process.

At the time that the primaries were aborted, General Shehu Musa Yar'Adua, a northerner, had a commanding lead in the SDP while the run-off elections in the NRC would have been between Melam Adamu Ciroma and Alhaji Umaru Shinkafi, both northerners. This fact was to become significant in the campaign to rationalize the annulment of the presidential elections in 1993. The new round of presidential primaries was controversial in a different sense. The Abuja Convention of the SDP at which Chief M. K. O. Abiola was nominated was characterized by intense horse-trading facilitated by heavy financial inducements.

In the presidential elections of June 12, 1993, the SDP's Chief Moshood Kashimawo Olawale Abiola won a comprehensive victory over the NRC's Alhaji Bashir Othman Tofa. Voter turnout was 14,137,795 of which Chief Abiola won 8,187,023 (57.9 percent). He took nineteen of the thirty states (nine of them in the North, three in the East, and seven in the West) and the Federal Capital Territory of Abuja.[96] His opponent, Tofa, won in nine states (seven in the North and four in the East). Before these results were fully announced officially by the National Electoral Commission, General Babangida stepped in and suspended the process. However, the results were common knowledge because official certificates of results had been issued at each ward and at local government and state levels. Collation of the results at the national level was thus a mere formality. A national election monitoring group and international observers had also pronounced the elections free and fair.

It was therefore exceedingly stupid for General Babangida to have annulled the elections as he did on June 23, 1993, a stupidity exceeded only by the subsequent behavior of the political class. Since the electoral mandate had been won so broadly and comprehensively, the annulment was greeted with violent, popular protests from several areas. The politicians, rather than defending democracy by resisting such a treasonable act, accepted bribes from the embattled military dictator and compromised their mandate from the electorate.[97] In any event, the military was able to broker an interim national government headed by Chief Ernest Shonekan, another Yoruba like Abiola.

But the annulment did not go down well with the masses and prodemocracy civil organizations. Operating under the umbrella organization, Campaign for Democracy (CD), they were able to mount civil resistance to the interim government and the military even when it was apparent that the political class had given up. As a result of the intensity of their pressure, the military toppled the interim government in

November 1993. The annulment has generated Nigeria's most dangerous conflict since the civil war of 1967–70. Just as the events leading up
to the civil war showed, the military, three decades and a half after, remain totally inept in conflict resolution on the basis of equity and justice.

The military administration had its back against the wall again following resurgence of pro-democracy demonstrations and strikes. A
pro-democracy strike by the National Union of Petroleum and Natural
Gas Workers (NUPENG) and the Petroleum and Natural Gas Senior
Staff Association of Nigeria (PENGASSAN) threatened the country
with economic paralysis. A new coalition of pro-democracy forces, the
National Democratic Coalition (NADECO), has provided the Campaign for Democracy and its affiliates with greater geographical spread
and influence. But the military rulers remain impervious to the dictates
of honor, national interests, and democracy. The repressive Nigerian
system of government was restored over democratic demands in November 1993 by the coup of General Sani Abacha. It seems violence is
the only language of conflict resolution capable of settling Nigeria's latest conflict.

## Social Demand and Conflicts

Beneath demands and conflicts over federal organization and allocation lay deeper grievances over social demands that challenge the
capacities for governance of the regimes. Leading demand-bearing
groups are students, labor, and communal groups. The government has
been inept in dealing with demands from university students and faculty. Generally, student demands are ignored until they are spectacu-
larly advertised through violent demonstrations. As a result, student
demands are more likely to be made through violent demonstrations
than dialogue because that seems to be a more powerful way of getting
the authorities to sit up and respond. Student demands were concerned
with the deterioration in the educational sector, declining support for
indigent students, specific policies considered detrimental to the national interest, such as the adoption of the Structural Adjustment Program (SAP), and the government's generally poor management of the
economy. Since there are a few detailed studies of the causes and management of earlier student protests, this analysis will concentrate on the
more recent ones,[98] focusing on the protests or demands that challenged the government to adopt or repeal a policy. There have, of

course, been other university-specific protests, but these are usually the result of the management failures of the university authorities.

In April and May 1988, two years into the implementation of the SAP students took to the streets in violent protest against the partial withdrawal of oil subsidies announced by government. The protest was popularly received by the urban proletariat and the unemployed who joined the demonstrations and unleashed violence on all those perceived to be part of the establishment. The government responded by calling in the riot police, who shot and killed many students and civilians.

In May 1989 there was another round of anti-SAP riots, once more led by students who, following the success of government's attempt to weaken the Nigerian Labor Congress, became the only group apparently capable of protesting against the harshness of government's economic policies. The riots, which were started by students of the Universities of Benin and Lagos, rapidly spread to other major cities, even more violently than the previous year's. This time the government responded with even more massive repression, causing considerable civilian casualties. The government obviously wanted to deter future violent students' demonstrations by the enormous brutality employed in repressing the conflict.

Although the government blamed the riots on disgruntled, banned politicians, the political implications could not be treated lightly. The anti-SAP riots struck a popular chord. Thus the government combined the carrot with the stick in dealing with the substantive issues raised by the protesters. It announced an SAP relief package of increases in wages and allowances for workers, particularly junior staff, while at the same time some universities were closed for about five months.[99] However, those palliatives and deterrents had worn thin by May 1992 when there was another round of anti-SAP riots. The cycle of riots and pattern of responses would seem to suggest that government was so insensitive that it required the periodic shocks of violent demonstration to activate its machinery for conflict management. This fire-brigade approach was also employed in dealing with the demands of academic staff of universities.

The economic deterioration of the 1980s and 1990s hit the universities harder than most other public institutions. Salaries declined in real terms, library holdings became obsolete and pilfered, laboratory equipment was antiquated and broken down, and staff members were voting with their feet for greener pastures in a massive brain drain. To arrest the decline and save the university system from collapse the Academic Staff Union of Universities (ASUU) called a strike in July 1988 to press demands for improved salaries and upgrading of facilities in the universities. Government responded by proscribing the union and detaining its leaders without trial. The passports of ASUU's national executive council members were impounded, and the Immigration Department was instructed to prevent them from traveling abroad.

In the light of the government's sledge hammer response and the union's poor preparedness for the strike, the strike was short-lived. When the ban was lifted after two years, the union reorganized and resumed negotiations for higher salaries and improvement in the learning environment within the universities to stem the exodus of academic staff to places abroad, which had meanwhile assumed an alarming proportion. When negotiations failed, the union once more called a strike that lasted seven weeks, and a shocked nation learned that its professors, no matter how eminent, earned less than $150 monthly.

The government, as usual, displayed extreme insensitivity and total lack of negotiating skills when it declared the academic staff of all Nigerian universities sacked and ordered them to be ejected from their government-provided residences within a month. But the government had to swallow its pride and back down to negotiate with them when public sympathy shifted to the university staff. The agreement that was reached with the academic staff raised basic salaries about 80 percent and introduced several new allowances such as a journal allowance and a supervision allowance.

The success of the academic staff in wresting improved conditions of service from government seemed to have revived the fighting spirit of other labor unions. Some of the lessons learned from the ASUU strike were that with tight organization, discipline, and commitment of both leaders and their followers, even a military government could not withstand just claims. Prior to this time the government had emasculated the labor movement through its interference in the elections of the Executive National Council of the National Labor Congress in 1988.[100] As a result of its intervention, the reelection of a leftist National Executive was aborted. The controversy surrounding the election of the National Executive Council of the Nigerian Labor Congress was evidently contrived to create an opportunity for government to get a grip on the trade unions.

An intra-Congress dispute over electoral procedures provided the government with the opportunity to intervene by appointing a sole administrator to run the affairs of the central and state executive committees of the National Labor Congress for ten (initially only six) months. At the end of the tenure of the sole administrator, a new executive council was elected, headed by Pascal Bafyau, a pro-government trade unionist and personal friend of General Babangida. Although there is no evidence to support allegations that the government aided his well-funded campaign, it clearly was in favor of his election.[101] Subsequent events and the directions in which he led labor during the protracted negotiations to resolve the crisis generated by the annulment of the presidential elections leave no doubt that he was a reliable ally of the military.

Because of the close ties of the new national president of the NLC to the government, the central labor organization found it increasingly difficult thereafter to call a strike to back wage demands. As a matter of fact, it could be said that the leadership had become comatose. After the ASUU strike, however, pressure mounted on the NLC to demand its own wage increases. The government itself made matters worse when after the anti-SAP protests of 1992, it granted 45 percent salary increases to federal workers, while the states were to determine what they could afford. This was the final issue that made a strike inevitable, even to labor leaders widely believed to be in the pocket of government. The lessons of the ASUU strike were fully applied as striking workers in all the states heeded only their leaders and stood firm for the five weeks it took for the states to begin to capitulate.

### Sectarian/Communal Violence

Sectarian and communal violence has grown in frequency in recent years. Religion has been volatile in northern Nigeria since the 1950s when the late Sardauna of Sokoto and Regional Premier Alhaji Ahmadu Bello tried to Islamize the entire region. But the genesis of recent conflicts can be traced to more immediate issues: increasing economic deterioration of the country, the search for answers in fundamentalism (both Muslim and Christian), and the exploitation of religion by the elites. Of these, the last two deserve attention.

Since the debate in the constituent assembly in 1979 on the establishment of a federal Sharia Court of Appeal, which was voted down, Muslim ulama have vowed to ensure that the injury is redressed. Muslim youths have become progressively better organized and radicalized with respect to sectarian interests, particularly in higher institutions of learning but even more dangerously so in Quranic schools. More or less the same thing has happened to Christian youths in higher institutions, but militancy is less intense, since the jihadist doctrine is nonexistent in Christianity.

Attempts to satisfy religious demands led to violent conflict after the admission of Nigeria into full membership in the Organization of the Islamic Conference in early 1986. The resulting massive outcry from the Christian community demanded Nigeria's return to its prior status as observer in the conference, while Muslims rationalized the action by comparing it with the diplomatic relations with the Holy See. To find a way round the controversy, the government set up a Presidential Committee under the Minister of Internal Affairs Lieutenant Colonel John Shagaya to advise it on "the implications of Nigeria's full membership" in the OIC.[102] The recommendations of the committee led to the establishment of the Advisory Commission on Religious Affairs, but it was not able to function because of the disagreement of Muslim and Christian leaders on the committee.

The tension among the leaders has radiated to their followers. In 1987 Kaduna state erupted in sectarian violence as a result of a clash initially between Christian and Muslim students at Kafanchan College of Education. It spread to Kankia, Funtua, Katsina, Zaria, and Kaduna City. Since then there have been similar clashes in Bauchi state, Plateau state, and Kano state.[103] These clashes were conducted with atrocious ferocity and resulted in massive losses in lives and property.

Some of these clashes take on a communal character as occurred in October 1991 when violence erupted in Kano as Muslim youths took to the streets to protest the arrival of a German evangelist to preach in the city. Southerners, especially Igbos, were the targets of attack perhaps because of their commercial successes in the North. Sometimes, as in February and April 1992 in the clashes at Zangon-Kataf, the conflict was communal (over land in this case) but found expression in a religious differentiation. The violent clashes in Wukari (Taraba state) between the Jukuns and Tivs were basically communal.

These sectarian-communal clashes pose a great threat to national stability. The army had to be deployed to stop the riots in Kano in October

1991, and then in Bauchi, and Kaduna, and it was permanently deployed at Wukari. If these things happened under a civilian administration, they would be more difficult to handle. The government perceived the danger of employing the army on civil riot operations and therefore formed a national guard that was better armed than the police for dealing with civil riots. But for the national guard to be useful, it has to be very well armed, perhaps as much as the military, which could provoke interforce rivalry and intervention in the political process. The national guard was embroiled in controversy from its inception because of this reason and had to be disbanded after Babangida vacated office.

## Managing the Politics of the Economy

The social forces making the various types of demands indicated above, their strategies and tactics, and state responses to them were motivated and shaped by only one consideration: the desire to control the economy and, by implication, oil revenues. Since the state dominated the economy completely, individual and corporate fortunes depended on the ability to control the state or be on its right side. Since the 1970s it was possible for the state, using the huge earnings from oil, to accommodate the desires of ethnic elites to occupy governmental and parastatal positions by creating additional states and local governments. In addition, the indigenization of businesses program of the 1970s similarly responded to elite demands to Nigerianize the economy and thereby create greater opportunities for them to prosper.[104]

In more recent years, the cost of creating more states and local governments has become so staggering that it has ceased to be the easy option it once was for managing the conflicts among ethnic elites for state-office-based resources. The states and the local governments are all so dependent on the federal government for revenues that control of the government of the country (which receives half of the federation account) is by far the biggest prize of the competition. Yet, as a result of mismanagement and corruption, the value of that prize has become greatly diminished.

The period of the oil boom was rather short-lived. Although oil revenues increased fivefold between 1972 and 1974, they were not wisely invested, and the demand for crude oil collapsed sooner than the authorities expected. A substantial part of the revenues went to finance post–civil war reconstruction and white elephant projects such as inviable airports at most state capitals and motor vehicle assembly plants. By the late 1970s the economy was already in decline. In 1978 the federal government took its first major external loan of $1 billion.

Throughout the second republic (1979–83) the federal government played the ostrich with the economy, first claiming that it was buoyant and later introducing a half-hearted regime of austerity.[105] For political reasons the government could not bring about the necessary restructuring of the economy nor reduce public expenditures to match reduced earning capacity. Therefore, budget deficits began to rise and debts to accumulate. In 1983 the deficit had risen to 12 percent of GDP.[106] The military intervened in December 1983 following controversial elections marred by blatant rigging and violence. The new military government introduced a harsher economic regime that fell short of what was required by the World Bank and the IMF in order to attract their support.[107]

With deteriorating economic performance and consequential dwindling middle-class incomes, the adoption of more drastic measures became imperative to salvage the economy and bolster the regime's diminishing legitimacy. This seemed assured when in August 1985 General Ibrahim Babangida toppled the Buhari administration and declared that "austerity without structural adjustment is not the solution" to the country's economic problems and that his administration would "break the deadlock that frustrated the negotiations" with the IMF.[108] In 1986, therefore, the government introduced the Structural Adjustment Program (SAP) after a national debate that seemed to have engendered political support for it. Key elements of the program included the adoption of tight fiscal and monetary policies to reduce inflationary pressures and to rationalize public expenditures, including public investment programs; the dismantling of exchange controls and the adoption of a market-determined exchange rate policy; the liberalization of the trade regime, the rationalization of customs tariffs and excise duties, and the abolition of price controls; financial sector reforms; and the privatization and commercialization of public enterprises and the abolition of marketing boards.[109]

The Structural Adjustment Program was effectively implemented only partially. Marketing boards were dismantled, the currency devaluated, and attempts made to reduce budget deficits. However, as a result of violent protests against the harshness of the SAP regime, in 1988, 1989, and 1990 in the abortive coup, the government lost the political will to effectively implement measures aimed at reducing budget deficits. Indeed, budget deficits grew phenomenally between 1990 and 1993 partly as a result of extrabudgetary expenditures on projects not included in the budget and huge salary increases meant to buy political support for the government. In addition, privatization stalled because the government's desire to create a large population of small share-holders evenly distributed nationally could not be fulfilled.

But perhaps the most telling of all the shortcomings of the imple-mentation of SAP was the massive corruption characteristic of the Nigerian government. The pervasive and growing fraud in the Niger-ian National Petroleum Corporation sensitized the elite of the oil-producing communities to a new consciousness that they were giving up a natural resource. They realized that their environment was being degraded not for the national interest but for the advantage of a few members of the ruling class.[110] As a Yoruba proverb says, "Fish rots from the head." The unchecked corruption at the highest levels of gov-ernment made people cynical and turned them against those whom they held directly responsible for it, that is, the military, and its benefi-ciaries, perceived to be predominantly members of the northern politi-cal oligarchy and a few southern allies. As the political transition pro-gram drew toward a close, this perception and attitude translated into a demand for the total disengagement of the military from politics and the termination of the stranglehold of the conservative, northern oli-garchy on political power.

As General Theophilus Yakubu Danjuma said in 1990, the persis-tence of old cleavages and the emergence of new sources of conflict could only be resolved through a national conference, although he thought the appropriate time was after the military had vacated office. In his words, "I cannot think of any time in this country's history that people were so divided against each other as now. The most obvious is the religious division and it is the most potent. Then there is the politi-cal divide between the ancient and the modern, the old and the new breed. There is also the economic divide which is equally dangerous . . . We must address the decay in the armed forces."[111]

From the foregoing it was certain that when General Babanigida did vacate office, he would leave behind a country more divided than the one he inherited. There was no elite consensus on goals or strategies, much less talk of who should lead the government to implement them. In any event, political energies were focused on gaining control over political power at the center. The maneuvers to achieve this goal were basically conducted by ethnic associations within and outside the political parties. This became evident in the conduct of the presidential race, the annulment of the June 12, 1993, presidential elections, and the struggle to restore democracy thereafter.

Chapter 6

# Conclusion: Management of Conflict in West Africa

*Donald Rothchild*

"CONFLICT IS AN INEVITABLE aspect of human interaction, an unavoidable concomitant of choices and decisions. . . The problem, then, is not to court the frustrations of seeking to remove an inevitability but rather of trying to keep conflict in bounds."[1]

As analyzed in the three West African examples of Ghana, Nigeria, and Côte d'Ivoire governance concerns interplay on several levels: among local groups of society, between state and groups in the national arena, and between these and other state and nonstate actors on the regional and global level. State and society are intertwined in complex ways as societal interests penetrate and sometimes achieve control of the state, and as state institutions exercise a direct influence over societal activities. To appreciate the interplay of the forces at work, one must consider several factors: in particular, the nature and intensity of the demands made by societal, state, and international groups; the strategies for establishing conflict management that regimes used in structuring reciprocities and political exchanges; and the institutions for policymaking and policy implementation. Such regimes are organized (and reorganized) to reduce state-societal tensions to moderate levels of intensity, thereby freeing the public and its leaders to deal with the demands and interests associated with economic and political development.

The effectiveness of governance depends not simply on individual measures for managing demands but also on well-understood and

I wish to express my appreciation to I. William Zartman, Stephen Stedman, James Scarritt, Alex Gboyega, Adu Boahen, Tessy D. Bakary, Letitia Lawson, and Caroline Hartzell for helpful comments on the first draft of this chapter.

widely accepted rules of interaction among societal, state, and extrastate representatives. Critical to achieving these cooperative relationships is the emergence of accepted ties of reciprocity among elites and between these elites and their constituents. Also important to social coherence is the existence of recognized rules of political exchange, based on formal laws or regulations or revealed by less formal conventions, customs, and understandings. As the processes for articulating and reconciling conflicting demands become recurrent over time, the rules regulating state-society relations gain acceptance, and stable and restrained interactions may take place.[2] The emergence of regularized and persistent interactions is central to strengthening the weak state (Thomas Callaghy's "lame leviathan"),[3] enabling it to cope more meaningfully with an articulate civil society and with the tasks of social and economic development.

Effective governance depends on the establishment of regimes—patterns of behavior accepted by the dominant state coalition and the general public as the legitimate formula for the exercise of political power. State regimes organize and validate procedures for the articulation of demands and for the determination of appropriate state responses to manage the conflicts among them.[4] Governance, Goran Hyden asserts, "is concerned with how rules (or structures) affect political action."[5] He adds a problem-solving component to the normally rather detached comparative analysis of authority systems in different societies; in Hyden's view, the task of a creative political leadership is to engage in regime maintenance, the conscious tendency of regime structures to generate legitimacy and therefore to increase public participation and manage societal conflicts.[6] The normative and analytical dimensions are now joined for governance links regime maintenance to the search for constructive state leadership in conflict management.

This connection provides a basis for evaluating African regimes' performance at governance and conflict management; nevertheless, the effectiveness of a particular regime must take local social institutions and practices into account.[7] The transition to democracy, for example, may have to occur in stages, taking account of the reality of strong patron-client ties in the interim periods. Therefore, what legitimates authority structures and promotes ongoing cooperative routines in one country may not avail in another. This relativity represents a challenge for students as well as practitioners of conflict management, requiring them to examine carefully the costs and benefits of various combinations of regime rules and routines, both in the short and long term, in order to draw conclusions about the comparative efficiency of different political alternatives.[8]

Difficulties arise when analysts (and bearers of procedural demands) become too narrowly specific about the type of regime required. For example, Claude Ake asserts that "the type of governance needed in circumstances of social pluralism is democracy."[9] Richard Joseph, the former director of the African Governance Program at the Carter Center, contends that Africa's downward economic slide can only be countered by a transition to democratic politics.[10] Despite the importance of such a normative vision for the mobilizing of political and social groups and developing enduring and legitimate links between a strong state and a strong civil society, there needs to be a broader look at three other modes of governance as well—elite power sharing, radical populism, and state corporatism. Not only have these been present on the Western African scene, but they represent important alternatives that may contribute to sustained development (by sequencing political and economic reform) and conflict management (by establishing structures that promote a balance between political participation and stability).

Although majoritarian democracy stands out as a preferred option, largely because of its unique capacity to develop legitimate state-society relations, the other regime structures of elite power sharing, populism, and state corporatism can also facilitate some measures of state-society reciprocity and political exchange. Such regime types are mutually exclusive as concepts, even though concrete regimes in Western Africa have characteristics of more than one regime type (for example, state corporatism and radical populism can contain strong elements of participatory democracy). Because these rules and routines of state-society interaction involve dynamic relationships among various powerful (or potentially powerful) actors, changes within regime structures can be anticipated over time. As shifts occur between these structures, enormous strains are unleashed, causing sharp conflicts to surface between those wielding power (groups in charge of the state and their allies), those aspiring to power (counterelites and their followers), and those subject to power (the governed as groups of civil society or society generally). Africa's move in the 1990s from hegemonic (high state control and low participation) toward polyarchical and various alternative systems involves dramatic shifts in structural relations and power as well as the interests championing this transformation (figure 6-1).[11]

FIGURE 6-1. *Regime Options for Managing Societal Demands*

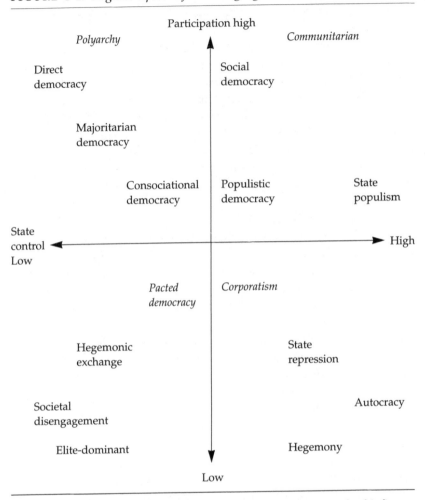

Letitia Lawson and Tessy D. Bakary contributed valuable suggestions for this figure.

## The Tenuous Balance between Group Demands and State Responses

In Western Africa, demands are linked above all to the prevailing scarcity of resources. Not only are goods in short supply, but inequalities in their distribution prevail along class, ethnic, religious, and sub-

regional lines. As a consequence, some reasonable demands for publicly controlled goods and services are likely to go unsatisfied. Differential rates of growth have proved perplexing for the postcolonial
regimes to overcome, leading to the development of a wide gulf between the relatively advantaged and relatively disadvantaged peoples
and subregions in these countries.[12] Where the elite spokespersons of
the various groups and subregions perceive the share of their group's
allocations to be unfair, intense conflicts materialize over the formulas
used in determining these distributions.[13] To a large extent, the demands made by domestic and international interest groups upon the
West African state can be considered reasonable and negotiable. They
consist largely of claims for distributable goods and therefore can be accommodated within the political system if adequate resources are available. Elastic and realistic in their expectations, the groups that bear
these negotiable demands generally accept the legitimacy of the political order in which they operate. The result is to enhance the possibilities
for constructive social interaction—and for effective governance over
time. Certainly, where the state elite spurns these reasonable demands
and adopts a defensive (or worse, hostile) demeanor toward them, a
switch in demand patterns from negotiable to nonnegotiable is indicated. This is shown, for example, in chapter 4, in Adu Boahen's discussion of the abortive 1975 coup led by Ewe officers dissatisfied over
promotion policies in Ghana's army. Such a change in the direction of
nonnegotiability represents a failure in the governance process. Nevertheless, in the West African context, group demands remain open to the
political exchange process for the most part.

Unless presented to state authorities by the spokespersons of the
group, however, demands are likely to remain latent and unfulfilled.[14]
What catches the attention of the state and evokes a response is the
spokesperson's ability to marshal symbolic and substantive resources
in such a way as to raise the costs on central government inaction.

### Negotiable Demands by Broad Identity Groups

In the West African environment, elite brokers or "political entrepreneurs"[15] are well equipped for the task of channeling collective demands to those controlling state resources. The great southern Nigerian
leaders of the postindependence period, Chief Obafemi Awolowo in
the West and Nnamdi Azikiwe in the East, played critical roles in creat-

ing ethnic group associations, and then in uniting and mobilizing their peoples for political party competition in the struggle for central government power and resources; in the North, Ahmadu Bello, the Sardauna of Sokoto, and other leaders "espoused pan-regionalism rather than pan-tribalism," asserting northern interests against a possible "southern domination."[16] Less dramatically, but equally persistently, ethnic and subregional champions in Côte d'Ivoire asserted the claims of their constituents from within the governmental cartel and the national assembly. Aristide Zolberg described the pattern of patron-client relations and ethnoregional intermediation found in that country after independence as follows:

> Viewing themselves as ambassadors of their region and of the ethnic group to the center, or as the spokesmen for the organization to which they belong, the députés are concerned mainly with gaining access to the ministers in order to secure tangible benefits for their constituents. Regardless of his specific duties as a member of the executive, each minister is also a kind of superrepresentative who keeps in touch with the country through his clientele of deputies.[17]

Given the weakness of the state and the relatively low level of economic development and specialization, it is not surprising that ethnic and subregional elites remain powerful in the current West African setting. "Ethnic groups persist," Robert Bates observes, "largely because of their capacity to extract goods and services from the modern sector and thereby satisfy the demands of their members. Insofar as they provide these benefits to their members, they are able to gain their support and achieve their loyalty."[18] The ethnic group continues to act as a significant pole around which people mobilize to make claims upon the state. It retains its resiliency in the face of new, crosscutting ties of party, socioeconomic class, and religious loyalty.[19]

Hence, the role of the ethnic and subregional patron in shaping public grievances into demands and presenting these demands to decision-making elites in the central government remains critical. The patron, as Naomi Chazan observes with respect to Ghanaian politics, "furnishe[s] an effective link to goods and services." Such a mechanism of resource allocation is not without its obstacles, she notes, for the patronage system can be abused, leading to inefficiency, self-aggrandizement, and injustice.[20] For all the possible shortcomings of the system, however, the communal patron nonetheless does champion the demands of his or her constituents at the political center and acts as a key communication link between the center and the periphery. As a member of the dominant political elite, the ethnoregional representative is well equipped to perform a linking role, speaking simultaneously for both state and societal interests. Useful to both sides, the communal buffer's position is inevitably precarious. Because of the need to bargain on two fronts—with diverse ethnoregional groups in society and with the central leadership in the bureaucracy, legislature, cabinet, or party national council—the intermediary faces the ever-present possibility of being unable to deliver on bargains or of offending key groups in one of the arenas of contention.[21]

Contrary to conventional wisdom on the subject, ethnicity can contribute to negotiable politics in the West African context. In all three West African countries, there is extensive evidence of demands by ethnic and subregional groups for recruitment into cabinet, civil service, and party positions on a proportional basis. Given the state's central role in allocating public values in these societies, the competition to ensure a place for each group within the decisionmaking coalition at the political center is inevitably intense.[22] Pointing out that ethnic groups are central to contemporary politics in Côte d'Ivoire, Tessy Bakary notes in chapter 3 that Ivorian ethnic group relations do not display the bitterness of other countries. Furthermore, the management of political conflicts has proved relatively stable over the years. Ethnicity is an important fact of life, which politicians prudently take into account as they organize their political parties, form their ruling coalitions, and engage in exchanges with ethnic and subregional patrons. Where politicians build inclusive coalitions or practice proportionality in their resource allocation policies, they are likely to be responding to the claims of ethnic representatives. They thereby seek to "invest" in processes aimed at keeping ethnic politics manageable—even at a possible cost in economic efficiency.[23] Especially in the 1960s and early 1970s, when the rules of the game involved an "acknowledge[ment]," but not a public display, of ethnic politics, Houphouët-Boigny nonetheless structured the Democratic Party of Côte d'Ivoire (PDCI) at the branch and sub-branch levels along ethnic lines.[24] At the national level, moreover, he sought to promote an ethnic balance in his cabinets, in part at least "to mollify the resentment of Baule dominance."[25] Clearly, such ethnic groups as the Bété, the Dioula, and the Senufo were anxious over the prospect of inadequate representation at the seat of power. Rather than challenge the validity of these ethnic-based fears, Houphouët-Boigny accepted them as reality. He sought to demobilize major ethnic challengers by carefully distributing tangible benefits to key components in the ruling coalition and coopting important patrons on a generally proportional basis into the one-party government at the political center.[26] The resulting cabinet was inclusive of all major ethnic interests, and on a basis roughly in line with their position in the National Assembly. Informal practices shifted in the 1980s with a greater emphasis on regional identity, educational achievement and, above all, "fidelity, loyalty, and attachment to PDCI ideals and to its principal and prestigious leader, Houphouët-Boigny."[27] Ethnic identity factors remained important for recruitment into high government or party position. And although interethnic tensions remain latent, and, according to J. F. Medard, could be stirred up by members of the ruling class, subregional cleavages based upon unequal rates of growth have emerged as a more significant source of conflicting demands.[28]

In contrast to Côte d'Ivoire's ability to manage ethnic and subregional demands through cooptation, control, and depoliticization, Nigeria has been more destabilized by ethnic-related conflicts and demands. Expressing the sentiments of many Nigerian intellectuals on such issues, Victor Olorunsola warned that "the problems posed by cultural sub-nationalism are not those which will disappear with time if left unattended."[29] Hence, instead of glossing over these matters, Nigerian constitution framers have been more inclined to take such practices as broad-ranging coalitions, a rough equity in the allocative patterns, and the decentralization of administrative power fully into their calculations. In response to intense demands by various ethnic and state groups to be involved in the decisionmaking process, Nigerians stipulated in the 1979 and 1992 federal constitutions that the country's "federal character" must be taken into account when making federal (and, in the latter case, lower-level) appointments.[30]

In Nigeria, the idea of incorporating the main ethnoregional groups in key federal institutions in a balanced manner has a long history. As early as 1958, the federal government applied quotas when recruiting enlisted personnel into the military services, a practice that was extended to the officer corps three years later. Although the principle of proportionality in recruiting military personnel was largely set aside at the time of the Nigerian civil war and immediately afterward, practices of balanced recruitment were applied again during the 1979 transition to civilian rule.[31] With the adoption of the 1979 constitution the federal character rule in making federal appointments became a "cardinal principle"of Nigerian political life.[32] Article 135(3) of the 1979 constitution stated that the appointment of federal ministers should be in conformity with the guideline on ethnic balancing set out in Article 14(3); it declared, "In giving effect to the provisions aforesaid the President shall appoint at least one Minister from each State, who shall be an indigene of such State."[33] The framers of the 1979 basic law sought to promote national unity. Thus article 14(3) spoke of taking steps to "ensur[e] that there shall be no predominance of persons from a few States or from a few ethnic or other sectional groups in that government or in any of its agencies." The principle of including major ethnic and state groups in the decisionmaking process at the political center, described by Peter P. Ekeh as "the supreme principle of state and government business in the 1979 Constitution," has been carried over and expanded by the new constitution framers.[34]

If this conscious commitment by the constituent assembly to balanced appointments and opportunities did manage to prod the administration of Alhaji Shehu Shagari (1979–83) to close some gaps in the areas of higher education and in the recruitment of minorities into the cabinet and public service, some Nigerian analysts nonetheless describe its implementation of corrective equity guidelines as creating a host of new problems: heightened politicization, hardening of transient ethnic identities into more fixed and permanent ones, exacerbation of interethnic and interregional tensions, use of noneconomic criteria (for example, in determining the location of plants for manufacturing steel), weakening of civil service professionalism and morale, and overloading the bureaucracy. Consequently, fear became widespread that precise application of the proportionality principle could lead to an undermining of the merit principle.[35]

Despite such evident misgivings, proportional recruitment practices survived several changes of government. Following his assumption of power in 1983, Major General Muhammed Buhari displayed a "northern character" in his most critical cabinet appointments.[36] Even so, he included Yoruba and Igbo members on his Supreme Military Council and appointed a member from every state except Bendel to his Federal Executive Council. That state was compensated by having an indigene selected as head of the civil service.

In August 1985 Major General Ibrahim Babangida took power in a bloodless coup d'état. Babangida, seeking to adopt a more liberal political style than his predecessor, moved quickly on various fronts. For one thing, he took a more open approach to recruiting southerners into high administrative positions. Although the 1989 cabinet shifts, which saw several Christian members discharged from their positions, raised questions about Babangida's continuing commitment to liberalism, the constitution framers working on the return to civilian government remained committed to the principle of balanced state representation. Using the 1979 constitution as their guide, the members of the 1987 Political Bureau recommended that the principle of "federal character" be taken into consideration in the selection of government ministers.[37] In light of this recommendation, the 1992 constitution provided that "the composition of the Government of the Federation or any of its agencies and the conduct of its affairs shall be carried out in such a manner as to reflect the federal character of Nigeria."[38] Ethnic and subregional participation has also been ensured through the creation of additional states and the decentralization of significant powers to the states and local authorities.

Ghanaian reactions to the calls for ethnic inclusion were somewhat ambivalent, falling between Côte d'Ivoire's corporatist tendencies and Nigeria's formal recognition of the legitimacy of reasonable ethnoregional demands. Concerned over the demands of subregional and ethnic spokespersons for a greater share of state power, leaders as different as Kwame Nkrumah, Joseph Ankrah, and Ignatius Acheampong were alike in attempting to depoliticize ethnicity.[39] Nkrumah, after assuming power, quickly banned the formation of ethnic parties and placed limits on the uses of ethnic symbolism; the military administrations of Ankrah and Acheampong, both evincing a disdain for politics and politicians, sought at different times to mute effective group politics through the establishment of no-party systems. Although he was also seeking mechanisms of conflict avoidance, Acheampong, as Adu Boahen shows, nonetheless took ethnic sensitivities into account when making cabinet and administrative appointments. In selecting his cabinets, he was careful to maintain a rough equivalence between Akans and non-Akans; as of November 1975, moreover, five of nine regional commissioners hailed from their own areas.[40] This was the highest proportion of indigenes in such posts in many years.

With the 1981 Rawlings coup, an abrupt shift occurred in the ethnic composition of the ruling coalition—from the disproportional representation of northern interests in the Limann period to an extensive Ewe influence under the Provisional National Defense Council (PNDC). Whether consciously or unconsciously, Adu Boahen described Rawlings as "fanning ethnicity" through his appointment of Ewes to high-level positions in the banks and security services.[41] Yet, despite a widespread perception of the PNDC as Ewe-dominated, it is important to note that Rawlings was not inattentive to ethnic and subregional feelings when he made his cabinet appointments. Besides Rawlings (an Ewe himself), the PNDC, as of July 1984, included two Akans, two Gas, and two northerners; moreover, the twenty-nine-member cabinet was composed of seven northerners, seven Fante, three Gas, and twelve Akan members. Some inclination toward subregional and ethnic power sharing is also evident in the proposals of the 1991 Committee of Experts, for this body spoke of the need in certain circumstances to appoint ministers from outside of Parliament to preserve a subregional balance.[42]

Ethnic demands, largely of a negotiable nature, were also evident in all three countries regarding the allocation of public resources. In light of the prevailing scarcity of goods and services in the region, it is not surprising to see a broad array of ethnic and subregional claims upon publicly controlled resources. In response to northern demands for increased investments and job opportunities in Côte d'Ivoire, the Houphouët-Boigny government constructed six sugar complexes in the area. Not only were resources transferred from the relatively advantaged South to build industrial plants in the North, but these complexes involved an accompanying infrastructure of roads, schools, and clinics.[43]

Similarly in Ghana, various administrations have responded over the years to continuing demands by leaders in the relatively disadvantaged North for improved allocations, though in a cautious and somewhat restrained manner. Although beset by competing claims and tight budgets, these governments recognized the fairness of the northern claim to some redistribution; in addition, they viewed the North as an important ally, strengthening the ruling coalition in its struggle to maintain power against its adversaries. For a variety of reasons, then, the administration of Kofi Busia set up a National Development Levy in 1971 to channel resources to the neglected rural parts of the country. Acheampong's regime suspended this levy; at the same time, however, he was careful to give special attention to northern claims for favorable allocations. While on tour of northern and upper regions, Acheampong reacted favorably to the appeals of local notables for the provision of electricity, dams and feeder roads, livestock, processing plants—even a university and a brewery. Moreover, his administration favored the North in certain budgetary allocations, as in the per capita capital fund expenditures for secondary schools in 1975–76.[44] Subsequently, the short-lived civilian regime of Hilla Limann raised the prices of cash crops such as cocoa in an effort to improve rural-urban terms of trade, and his successor, Rawlings, limited urban expenditures in order to channel scarce resources to the less advantaged areas.[45] The PNDC's adoption of a Structural Adjustment Program had a significant impact on the rural-urban terms of trade in Ghana. Jeffrey Herbst describes Ghana's Economic Recovery Program as "biased toward the rural areas," resulting in an important shift in the terms of trade between the agricultural areas and the urban center.[46] Increasing disparities among subregions, warns the World Bank, may increase as a consequence of these policies, "thereby exacerbating ethnic tensions."[47] Paradoxically, however, the ethnic split between what was perceived as an Ewe-backed PNDC and the largely cocoa-producing Ashanti subregions distances the regime from the ethnoregional grouping that has benefited most from its economic reforms, aggravating state-societal tensions.[48]

In Nigeria, with its complex mosaic of ethnic peoples and political units, state intermediaries have made unremitting demands upon the political elite at the country's center for public resources. As one Nigerian lecturer comments on this dynamic interplay at work:

> The nature of political competition in Nigeria imposes severe strains on the Federation's stability. In spite of remarkable institutional and constitutional reforms designed to reduce their impact on political life, 'Ethnicity and region still provide the basis on which political values are defined, articulated, contested or challenged.'[49]

In general, a cleavage in the geographical distribution in educational opportunities has long been apparent between the relatively disadvantaged states of the North and those in the South. The northern cluster of states, with 54 percent of the country's total population and 79 percent of the total area, had only 21 percent of primary school enrollments and 15 percent of secondary school places in 1973.[50] These disparities, regarded by northerners as an intolerable situation, contributed to the student unrest in 1979 that led to the temporary closure of two universities. In time, the government sought to reduce Nigeria's educational disparities, shifting budgetary allocations among the subregions in a more balanced direction (see below). Thus, for Nigeria's subregional per capita capital expenditures as a proportion of national per capita expenditures on education, the index of variation in the period between 1975–76 and 1979–80 decreased from .70 to .51.[51]

## Negotiable Demands by Societal Interest Groups

Over time, the character of postcolonial demands has become more complex with the change in West African social and economic processes. As new professional organizations and trade unions, student bodies, women's, business, religious, and rural and urban interest groups have emerged or expanded in the three West African countries, it becomes possible to speak of an "increasing pluralism of *associational life*."[52] Thus a variety of political and economic claims of a negotiable nature are made by the leaders of assorted societal groups upon the state. At the outset at least, such demands tend to be elastic and modest in resource cost and to be accepting of the legitimacy of the political order in which they are asserted. However, if the state elite fails to act in a responsive manner to these moderate appeals, what begins as something negotiable gains a symbolic significance, emerging over time as an intense grievance with grave, possibly zero-sum, implications, and compromise becomes difficult.

A variety of societal organizations have all made demands on the states of West Africa. For example, the National Union of Secondary Teachers of Côte d'Ivoire (SYNESCI) has been important in politics as well as in the economy, and a group for farmers' demands, the Farm Syndicate of Côte d'Ivoire (SYNACI)), normally the most difficult of all interests to bring together into an effective organization, gained formal governmental recognition in 1991. Despite the authoritarian nature of the systems in which they frequently operate, such groups in West African civil society have for the most part made appeals and followed behavioral patterns not very different from those found in other parts of the world. Thus business and commercial interests, which seek preferential treatment on such matters as import licensing, access to currency, infrastructural support, and the availability of labor, have carefully built up effective lines of communication for their demands with governmental elites.

In Nigeria, the links between northern business and the Buhari administration have been described as unusually strong, and in the Babangida period that followed, business interests such as the Nigerian Chamber of Commerce and the Manufacturers Association of Nigeria were in the forefront of those resisting calls by the Nigerian Labour Congress and others for socialism and, on occasion, for the nationalization of the banks and oil industry.[53] Another influential demand-bearing group with strong ties to the Nigerian business community is the military officer corps. As a consequence of the Nigerian civil war, there was a dramatic increase not only in the size of the military forces but in the costs of provisioning and purchasing military equipment for these contingents in the period that followed. The results could be seen in the significant leap that took place in military expenditures, including lucrative contracts signed with various companies for the supply of military-related items. Arguing that military and ex-military officers have been prominent among those profiting greatly from these contracts, Pita Ogaba Agbese observes:

> Retired and serving military officers now dominate critical sectors of the Nigerian economy. Gens. Olusegun Obasanjo, Shehu Musa Yar'Adua, Alani Akinrinade, Joseph Garba, Yakubu Danjuma, and a host of other senior military off[ic]ers now own some of the largest farms in Nigeria. In addition, military officers such as Gen. Yar'Adua and Gen. Emmanuel Ejiga own or serve as chairmen of banks and other financial establishments. Military officers also run huge parastatals such as the Nigerian Airways, Nigerian Railways, and the Directorate of Foods, Roads, and Rural Infrastructure.[54]

A challenge to the management skills of any new government in Nigeria is to handle the conflict between the demands of the ex-military and the elected civilians for leadership of public enterprises.[55]

In Ghana, pro-government civil associations such as the Ghana Private Road Transport Union, the National Council on Women and Development, and the December 31 Women's Movement have been encouraged and backed by the Rawlings regime, while such independent-minded and sometimes critical associations as the Christian Council of Ghana, the Catholic Bishops' Conference, the Ghana Bar Association, and the Association of Recognized Professional Bodies have been discouraged, even repressed.[56] Trade unionists, who were prominent among the early supporters of the Rawlings revolution, protested bitterly over the austerity budget of 1983 and the decline in purchasing power that occurred around that time.[57] Farmers, who are potentially the largest and most potent group with their own demands, have proved difficult to organize. Yet even here coalescing groups within the farming community have been highly effective at times in pressing their interests upon the state; in 1975–76, for example, protests by Ghana's rice farmers over prices paid by the mills brought government concession on prices, government subsidies, commercial loans, and infrastructural support. In all countries, powerful university student strikes and demonstrations, determined claims by professional bodies and other middle-class interests, and persistent multinational corporation and International Monetary Fund and World Bank pressures round out a picture of diverse, and sometimes overwhelming, groups at work in a weak state environment. As Joel Migdal observes, "The state leaders' drive for predominance . . . has stalled in many countries because of tenacious and resilient organizations scattered throughout their societies."[58]

Rural dwellers, who are difficult to organize into demand-bearing groups, nonetheless sometimes inform central leaderships of their demands through patron-client networks of traditional authorities, local administrators, or party officials. Yet they lack voice and, on the whole, feel neglected. Not surprisingly, therefore, the state is viewed by the peasants as alien and beyond their reach. In the authoritarian regimes that have been prevalent in West Africa in postcolonial times, many societal demands have been unrecognized or suppressed, finding no ready intermediary or channel to decisionmakers. Such isolation on the part of state elites from the public's wishes and dissatisfactions is an obstacle to effective governance.

A clear expression of such diverse demands is found in several surveys conducted by the Department of Political Science at the University of Ghana, Legon, in 1973. For all the problems of incompleteness and lack of precision plaguing such surveys when administered under current West African conditions, they are nonetheless useful in pointing up latent public grievances and variations in demands and expectations among the relatively advantaged and relatively disadvantaged subregions.[59] In all, roughly 77 percent of respondents in the University of Ghana surveys called for the establishment of new local council services not being provided at that time, with people in the relatively advantaged Ghanaian subregions in the South being considerably more

assertive about this need than their northern counterparts. Whereas respondents in relatively disadvantaged Northern and Upper Regions
expressed dissatisfaction over a limited number of issues such as lack of
sanitation, market stalls, and piped water, those in the relatively advantaged areas of Western, Ashanti, and Accra included a wider array
of grievances of a more costly nature: sanitation, roads, schools, hospitals, and clinics.[60] The survey showed people in the relatively better off
subregions to have a greater sense of deprivation and to be the most in-
sistent that government act to improve the conditions in their area.[61]

But which agency of government was the preferred one for acting
upon these demands? Significantly, respondents in the relatively disadvantaged parts of the country expressed a stronger predilection for central government engagement in development activities in their area. By
contrast, the relatively advantaged subregions were more likely to look
to the local council as the primary agency for problem solving. The
North, with lower overall expectations of improvement than the South,
emphasized a strong role for the central government in local self-im-
provement; southerners, meanwhile, stressed the closeness of the local
council to their constituents' needs and expressed a greater desire for a
decentralization of governmental responsibilities.

Religion is currently emerging as another primary political pole
around which many West Africans are mobilizing to make demands on
the state for valued resources. As discussed below, these demands are
not necessarily reasonable and modest. There is ample evidence of rising religious tensions in contemporary Nigeria, with fundamentalist
Muslims and Christians tending increasingly to shape and present their
demands in nonnegotiable terms. Similar pressures are felt in Senegal,
Niger, and Cameroon, among others.

Yet even with respect to religion, some groups on the West African
scene continue to operate within the political system and to advance
claims for distributable benefits. In Ghana, for example, members of the
Muslim Representative Council in Kumasi outlined their efforts in 1986
to present demands through regular channels to advance Muslim religious, welfare, and economic interest.[62] For Alhaji Alhassan Abdulai
and his colleagues, increased government support for Muslim education, particularly in secondary schools, was a primary objective. In addition, they wanted Koranic studies added to religious programs at
schools, increased government support for the *Hajj* (Muslim pilgrimage
to Mecca), screening by Islamic organizations of candidates for the *Hajj*,

Islamic holidays to be made national holidays, and Muslim inheritance laws and Muslim marriage certificates to be recognized for Muslims.[63] As presented, these requests in their present form appear to be negotiable matters that do not seem threatening to the integrity of the state.

Although they are neither domestic nor societal groups, multilateral donor agencies also convey negotiable demands. West Africans often express resentment over the way the IMF and World Bank condition their loans and grants on the African governments' acceptance of certain principles.[64] Certainly, in regard to such principles as increases in the producer prices of specified crops, a tight monetary policy, reduced budgetary deficits, limits on subsidies and social overhead costs, devaluation, the privatization of inefficient parastatal organizations, and a slimmed down state bureaucracy, the standard IMF-World Bank package often appears to be advanced in uncompromising terms. In practice, however, international donor agencies have bargained extensively with African governments over the implementation of policy. Thus Matthew Martin notes that the international agencies showed some pragmatism in the Ghanaian negotiations of the 1980s over the achievement of reforms in the exchange rate by such means as a foreign exchange auction, revisions in monetary and fiscal policies, price increases for fertilizer, the extent of the privatization program, charges to private patients for prescription drugs, and the restructuring of the educational system.[65] "The PNDC," Martin concludes, "showed a remarkable ability to fine-tune measures by flexible implementation and, by sustaining adjustment, to convince the Fund and Bank to react flexibly."[66]

## Non-negotiable Demands by Societal Groups

At the same time as they make demands for distributable goods, civil associations, concerned with their cultural identity, status, participation, political or physical survival or other intangibles, have also made inflexible, nonnegotiable demands for various autonomous "rights" inside or outside the jurisdiction of the state or even for its total transformation into an Islamic state, for example.[67] Thus in Ghana just prior to independence, the Ashanti-based National Liberation Movement and its allies declared their secession from the Colony, bringing on a sharp counterreaction from the unitarist-minded government in Accra; taking such statements quite seriously, F. C. Bourne, Britain's constitutional adviser, described the NLM's attitude as one "of complete negation, on the grounds that they are engaged in a life and death struggle to preserve their Ashanti heritage and culture."[68] In attempting to secede from the Nigerian federation, Biafrans and their supporters contended that they could not get security and justice within the political order and therefore required a recognition of their separate sovereignty.[69] The government of President Houphouët-Boigny in Côte d'Ivoire treated Agni demands for separate statehood and the Bété demands for control over their cultivable lands in the southwest as matters over which there could be no negotiations.[70] Nigeria's Muslim fundamentalists, who call for the institutionalization of a federal sharia court, are perceived by some as seeking a full-going implementation of Islamic law throughout the country.[71] Refusing to recognize either Nigerian federal or local government laws on the right to stage public demonstrations, Mallam Yakubu Yahaya, the leader of the Shiite Muslim sect in Katsina State, declared, "If there is any grievance between Muslims and the government, we can only settle these grievances on the battle field and not on a round table."[72] Certainly, not all of these demands can be taken at face value. Some represent rhetorical statements; others are a prelude to intense bargaining. Yet to the extent that religious fundamentalists and separatist leaders have pressed demands for autonomous rights and jurisdictions, in absolute, nonnegotiable terms, they pose fundamental problems for conflict management.

When nonnegotiable claims for autonomy and state transformation are presented in an inflexible and intransigent manner, the groups making such demands often adopt an "essentialist" perception of their adversaries, leading them to view any compromises on their part as representing a weakening of their position. Such perceptions, and the demands they bring with them, may in turn be threatening to the integrity of the state and its survival. Posing a challenge to the legitimacy of the political order, the nonnegotiable demand often precludes a conciliatory response on the part of the state and causes the routines of political exchange to dissolve. Where this leads to state repression or conflict escalation, which may give rise to violence and armed encounter, a marked change in the relationship between the state and certain of the groups in civil society has occurred.[73]

In the 1990s, Nigeria's religious groups bearing extreme demands probably represent the greatest challenge to the state's ability to manage conflict. Combining class as well as religious grievances, Islamic fundamentalism (and, at times, Christian fundamentalism in reaction) has emerged as a threat to Nigeria's political stability and national unity. "Not since the Civil War (1967-1970)," writes Jacob K. Olupona, "has Nigeria been so close to disintegration as the events of the last few years would indicate."[74] The religious violence that occurred in Kano in December 1980 continued throughout the 1980s and early 1990s and spread to include the South. Generally attributed to the Maitatsine sect, which rejects materialism and privilege as well as orthodox Islam and the secular state, the 1980 riots had something of a "contagion effect" among the Muslim poor.[75] Disaffection became evident in much of the Muslim North, extending southward to Oyo in the years that followed.[76] Local observers equated anti-establishment demands with religious group revival, a combination that seemed particularly threatening to the dominant political class when widespread hunger held the area in its grip in the mid-1980s. Conflict then escalated between religious groups, a fallout from the deep grievances held by the Muslim poor and the resulting anxieties of the various Christian sects in the country.[77] As Alex Gboyega notes, the announcement in 1986 that Nigeria planned to become a member of the Organization of the Islamic Conference (OIC) touched a raw nerve among Christian leaders, and the Christian Students' Movement of Nigeria warned of a possible religious war.[78] In fact, serious religious and class-based riots broke out after 1987, triggered first by the banning of religious organizations in postsecondary educational institutions.

Religious conflict broadened into regional conflict by the end of the 1980s. The succession to the sultanate of Sokoto split the Muslim community into supporters of the late Sultan's son from the North and those, including Babangida, favoring Ibrahim Dasuki from the Middle Belt, setting off riots in Sokoto among those supporting the northern traditional hierarchy.[79] At the same time, as two leading southerners were dismissed from their cabinet posts, southerners charged that the ruling coalition had become heavily weighted in favor of northern, Muslim interests.[80] These issues figured prominently in the coup attempted by Christian army officers from the Middle Belt in April 1990. The coup leaders, who claimed to represent "the patriotic and well-meaning people of the middle belt and the southern parts of Nigeria," justified their intervention as a corrective to the "distasteful intrigues" of Nigeria's ruling coalition,[81] notably the "inexplicable removal" of southern and Middle Belt officials from office during the recent cabinet reshuffles. In addition, they announced the temporary exclusion of the northern states of Sokoto, Bornu, Katsina, Kano, and Bauchi from the country, to be readmitted only when "the rightful heir to the Sultanate, Alhaji Maccido" (the late sultan's son) was installed, and a delegation sent by the new sultan vouched that the "aristocratic quest for domination and oppression will be a thing of the past."[82] After heavy fighting, the conflict was settled by the military victory of the Babangida government, but its underlying tensions remained.

In sum, then, West African regimes are encountering an increasingly complex mix of demands, as civil society becomes more differentiated and new interest groups coalesce to articulate claims on the state. In addition, with the declining efficacy of the exit option in such corporatist-inclined countries as Côte d'Ivoire, more traditional interest groups are increasingly disposed toward the exercise of voice.[83] For the most part, these growing demands involve distributable benefits and are negotiable; they tend to allow for regularized rules of relationships to develop between state, civil society, and external donors. However, when issues of identity and participation or of basic personal privilege are at stake, and when the actions of one group infringe on the privacy or identity of others (as occurred during the religious rioting in Bauchi in May 1991),[84] these demands may come to involve nonnegotiable claims on the part of both state and state-linked civil associations. In these circumstances, the appeals are not easily reduced to demands of moderate intensity. The result is a threat to political stability and sustained development—especially where religious commitment leads to harassment and attacks on others.

## The Structuring of Cooperation

How have the West African regimes responded to these challenges? Assuming good governance to involve the effective management of demands among competing groups in society, the strategies that West African governments have adopted are evaluated. In an analysis of the processes of conflict management, the roles of both structure and choice are important. With respect to structure, state elites create regimes in order to establish guides to action—both by establishing principles on the allocation of scarce values and by setting the rules for internal state and state-society relationships. Political regimes exist to organize legitimate procedures for the articulation of demands and the determination of appropriate responses. To the extent these regimes provide constructive principles for reducing the area of incompatibility between society and state-linked interests on the issues and values in contention, they can be said to be effective in the tasks of conflict management. Although regimes play an important role in organizing the rules of encounter and determining policy outcomes, in the end key choices affecting the interlinked relations between civil associations and the state must be made by political elites. Operating within domestic and international limits, governmental authorities must also be able to impose their preferences on society or to reflect society's preferences where a consensus exists. Thus alongside the demands of societal and international interests on the state, there are significant demands that state institutions and officeholders can make upon demand-bearing groups beyond the restraints and orientations imposed by domestic (and international) regimes. The state's policies and regulations (its "within-puts") therefore add another critical dimension to the dynamic interplay of partially autonomous actors, considering supports as groups' responses to state demands.

In an effort to manage conflict, state leaders have not pulled back from attempting to impose broad rules of the game contained in regimes upon civil society. The single-party system (and its various strategies of control and cooptation), I. William Zartman correctly points out, has been a primary mechanism of conflict management—at least in the short term. The leaders in the countries of the region have in various ways mixed the politics of compromise with the threat or use of coercion to gain acceptance for their policies.[85] In contemporary Côte d'Ivoire, Ghana, and Nigeria, personal leadership has been critical in the decisionmaking process. Côte d'Ivoire's Houphouët-Boigny, described as the "active center" of an institutionalized state structure, has played a critically important role in ruling on such key issues as the initiation of formal Dialogues with interest groups and party cadres, the holding of multiparty elections, and the processes of succession.[86] In Ghana, Rawlings, seeking to defuse opposition pressure on the PNDC, suddenly announced plans that would lead to a return of civilian rule.[87] In Nigeria, Babangida took decisive measures to put his own stamp on the transition to democratic institutions, limiting the number of political parties in the third republic to two (an effort to build truly national political parties that crosscut the country's pattern of ethnic, subregional, and religious loyalties), restructuring Nigeria's federal system (strengthening the federal center, ensuring the role of local governments and their direct access to federal funding, and creating additional states), and finally rejecting the electoral victor and imposing his own (once again) interim president (who was ejected by a more arbitrary autocrat, General Sani Abacha).

In reality, then, an understanding of the way regimes structure state-society relations must be complemented by an insight into the key role of political leaders in taking initiatives that may prove to have a long-term impact.[88] How do governments in Côte d'Ivoire, Ghana, and Nigeria attempt to organize civil society to promote the rules and routines buttressing reciprocity and exchange relations? Will the recent trend toward more open, responsive polyarchical structures prevail, or will the countertrend toward maintaining unaccountable personal rule persist? Will the governments manage to reduce the incompatibilities between demands on issues and values? And what are the anticipated costs and benefits of these regimes over the long term with respect to reducing intense conflict and promoting constructive conflict relations?

As figure 6-1 shows, these regimes differ significantly in terms of societal participation and government control in the political process, creating different state options for finding a point of reconciliation between these two dimensions. Although experience with some of these regime patterns has been very limited in the period since independence, there would seem to be sufficient clues to come to some tentative hypotheses about their implications for managing conflict in West Africa in the decade ahead. The experience in West Africa in independent times shows that regime change occurred frequently in the past. In light of economic scarcity and the interplay of political forces, there is little reason not to anticipate further shifts in the future. Ghana, for example, witnessed several moves in the direction of increased state control, including periodic shifts from polyarchy to hegemonic control during the administration of Kwame Nkrumah, a decisive movement from majoritarian democracy to military autocracy in 1972, and a change from democracy to military-led populism in 1981; the latter case of state populism gave way to a more classical form of hegemony by 1983. Shifts toward reduced state control and a more open form of participation are also evident in Ghana as military autocracies organized the transition to polyarchy in 1969 and 1979; elections, although somewhat controlled, were held in 1992 and another is planned for December 1996. Nigeria has also experienced dramatic fluctuations of regime since independence, including the change from polyarchy to military autocracy in 1966 and 1983, and the switch back to open party contestation in 1979 and then to stalemate and autocracy in 1994. The relative peace and stability of Côte d'Ivoire is apparent; nevertheless, grievances can be discerned just beneath the surface, particularly among ex-prime minister Alassane Dramane Ouattara's northern Muslim supporters, who resented President Henri Konan Bédié's passage of restrictive legislation that prevented their candidate from competing in the 1995 presidential election.

## Majoritarian Democracy

In the best of circumstances, fully democratic regimes are uniquely well suited to manage conflict through institutionalization for they combine vibrant and active civil associations with dynamic and secure states (see figure 6-1). As Vivienne Shue has written, "Under certain conditions at least strong and robust civil associations can 'go together' with powerful and resilient states."[89] The effect is to link these forceful actors in a constructive manner, establishing a foundation for legitimate governance. This point on the potential legitimacy of democracy, especially where buttressed by a broad consensus on values and procedures, is emphasized by Richard Rose: "A fully legitimate government," he writes, "is foolproof, whereas a government that lacks full legitimacy can be destabilized by the shortcomings of its governors as well as by the actions of its opponents."[90] Vigorous group demands and vigorous conflict management go together.

Majoritarian democracies create both significant opportunities for mobilizing and articulating group demands and inescapable requirements for state accountability and responsiveness to legitimate demand-bearing groups. In Zartman's terms, they allow normal demand politics to come to the fore. When a communitywide consensus emerges on the desirability of a free and dynamic interplay of competing group interests, it becomes possible to reduce the incompatibilities over issues and values among political actors. The interplay among rival organizations and actors must take place within a well-understood normative order, one which ensures that demands remain reasonable and that contestation proceeds according to the rules of the game. Where this overriding agreement on democratic rules of encounter gains acceptance over an extended period of time, the foundations are in place for stable competition between interests and demands aggregated by political parties.

In the way that it structures state-society relations, majoritarian democracy places boundaries on the permissible actions of leaders and constituents. To the extent that it is able to avoid the worst excesses of adversarial politics, it facilitates moderation and self-restraint. When political leaders are prepared to keep the stakes of politics under control, majoritarian democracy builds empathy among rivals.[91] The effect is to provide an incentive for the development of regularized flows of political exchanges among the representatives of the state and the various group representatives in the national arena. By allowing for a reasonable and open articulation of demands and by supplying electoral means for accountability and monitoring, democracies can, under favorable circumstances, extend legitimacy to the process of political interaction. The result is to keep competition and conflict at manageable levels, making majoritarian democracy a potentially preferred option.

Up to the 1990s, sub-Saharan Africa had a decidedly limited experience with majoritarian democracy. In the West African countries of Gambia and Senegal (since 1976), plus Botswana, Mauritius, and Morocco elsewhere in Africa, politics was structured in such a way as to promote two- or multiparty competition. Elections occurred on a regular basis, and governments remained more or less responsive to the demands of civil society. Yet each has been governed from the beginning by a single party or coalition. In each case these countries are relatively small in size or population, and their local social configurations have been supportive of a democratic experiment; in Morocco, the monarchical system also creates special conditions. Thus Senegal's ruling *Parti Socialiste*, largely backed by the country's powerful religious leaders, has won substantial majorities in the 1983 and 1988 elections but had to resort to vote rigging in 1993 to ensure that it would prevail. The stability of Gambia's and Botswana's electoral processes is secured by the presence of a preponderant ethnic core group—the Mandinka in Gambia and the Tswana in Botswana—backing a predominant party (until the military took over in Gambia in 1994). The beneficial experience of multiethnic Mauritius with constitutional democracy and open, competitive elections has been largely ensured by the existence of an overriding agreement on democratic norms and practices, including its own locally devised procedures for representation of the most successful losing candidates from communities deemed to be underrepresented in the legislature. In Morocco, the *makhzen* (palace) coalition has consistently been dominant over the nationalist parties' opposition, no matter how large and vigorous. In all of these countries, then, democratic forms of governance are in evidence, but the system "legitimates the rule of the powerholders without endangering their continued supremacy."[92]

In the first half of the 1990s, more than three-fourths of the countries in sub-Saharan Africa, caught up in the wave of political liberalization sweeping the continent, were scheduled to adopt or had already committed themselves to some form of democratic governance.[93] Côte d'Ivoire and Ghana, and, abortively, Nigeria, have moved along roughly parallel lines to the common objective of multiparty elections, even though the incumbents remain in power in one form or another. All are experimenting with efforts to shape the nature of the new political orders through a process of change from above. Whether or not such top-down initiatives can gain legitimacy, encompass procedural demands for participation from below, and be sustained in the years ahead will be a difficult test for the new regimes. President Houphouët-Boigny, described as exercising a virtual monopoly over the decisionmaking process in Côte d'Ivoire over the years, held resolutely on to political power while guiding his country through a series of multiparty elections in 1990.[94] On various occasions in the past Houphouët-Boigny indicated a strong preference for one-party rule, declaring that thirty years of the single party was not sufficient to realize national unity in a society "marked by tribalism." In his words, "Between injustice and disorder, I would not hesitate to choose injustice."[95] Even so, in the face of the rising conflict and demands for economic and political reforms within Côte d'Ivoire as well as pressures by various foreign donors for democratization, "the old man" shifted his position and announced his support for multiparty elections. In adjusting swiftly to the newly ascendant aspirations around him, Houphouët-Boigny moved before the opposition could join forces effectively against him. Unlike Daniel arap Moi in Kenya and Mobutu Sese Seko in Zaire, he showed a pragmatism that deflected the rising dissent away from his own person and enabled him to rally the ruling PDCI, just as he had done three decades earlier over the demand for independence. As Jennifer Widner observes,

because the PDCI retained control of critical political resources and because elections would take place quickly, limiting the time available for opposition groups to form alliances with one another and build organizations in the countryside, it was reasonably certain that the incumbent party and its candidate for president would win the contest.[96]

In elections among several candidates for the presidency in October 1990, for the legislature in November, and for offices in the municipalities in December, the PDCI won an overwhelming victory. Although multiparty elections had indeed returned to Côte d'Ivoire, the achievement seemed incomplete. On the one hand, there was low voter turnout (an estimated abstention rate of more than 60 percent in the legislative elections) and widespread charges of electoral rigging, raising doubts about the decisiveness (but not the fact) of the PDCI victory; on the other hand, the irregularities in the electoral process are not sufficient to explain the relatively poor showing of the opposition parties.[97] The presence of democracy cannot be determined by one set of multiparty elections; rather it must be viewed as a developmental process over time. The 1990 elections introduced democracy in a loaded contest that managed no real conflict. The 1995 elections continued this pattern; even though President Bédié probably could have won in a fair election, he prevented his main rival from competing in 1995 and consequently secured more than 90 percent of the vote in all the subregions. This manipulated election process led to unprecedented outbreaks of violence in the country.[98]

In the other two cases under review, Nigeria and Ghana, military-led administrations orchestrated more formal and controlled moves toward democracy. Although the transitions ran parallel to each other, they diverged markedly in styles, objectives, and outcomes. Whereas the Babangida administration imposed and then deposed a handpicked two-party system of governance in Nigeria to eliminate what it perceived as the wrongdoings of the past, and then was itself deposed by an unabashed authoritarian military coup, the PNDC allowed multiple parties to contest the 1992 parliamentary and presidential elections and lose to a well-orchestrated effort by candidate Rawlings himself. Moreover, the Rawlings government, described as "consistently populist in outlook," stressed the links it perceived between the new constitutional era and the 1981 populist revolution.[99] "No one can fail to appreciate," declared Rawlings in his inaugural address as Ghana's fourth president, "the significance of the 31st December Revolution in bringing us

to the threshold of the Fourth Republic, and in establishing firm principles of social justice which will make the constitution a living reality."[100]
Ghana's experiences are only the beginning of a transition and it seems
premature to comment on the structure of relations that will gain acceptance in the years ahead.

Nigeria's constitution makers, determined to put an end to the
abuses of the Shagari period, shunned a dramatic overhaul and concentrated instead on reforming the country's basic laws. Looking largely
to the United States for inspiration, these constitutional engineers em-
braced representative democracy as an institutionalized system for
managing conflict. At the same time, they included a variety of safe-
guards to limit the effects of adversarial politics. The 1987 Political Bureau recommended a directly elected federal president and vice president, and a unicameral federal legislature composed of 302 members
(one from each local government area, selected according to a single-
member district, plurality system of elections with seats reserved for
women and trade unions). The ultimate check on an expansive executive,
they asserted, was "an active and politically conscious electorate."[101]

More novel were the Political Bureau's proposals aimed at creating
"truly integrative national institutions."[102] Thus the bureau recommended a broadly inclusive two-party system, provisions to ensure
widespread support for the president in elections, the enshrinement of
the "federal character" principle (discussed above), the modification of
the federal arrangement by creating new states, and a slightly altered
revenue allocation procedure. Despite fears that a two-party scheme
would exacerbate North-South or religious tensions, the bureau saw a
better potential in it for conflict management than in a no-party, one-
party, or multiparty option. In order to guard against exacerbating intergroup conflict, it recommended that the parties articulate national
philosophies and purposes, open their party memberships to all groups,
make appointments to high party offices reflecting the country's federal
character, and establish branches in at least two-thirds of the local government areas.[103] The 1991 state and gubernatorial elections showed the
two new parties—the Social Democratic Party and the National Republican Convention—to be successful in securing a broad base of support in the country. But, as Alex Gboyega astutely cautions in chapter 5,
the two parties were conglomerations "of ethnic groups with different
agenda and strategies."

To ensure that the president has the support of an overarching, national constituency and to overcome the confusion of the past, the Political Bureau proposed that, in order to win an election, the president must secure a simple majority of the total vote in the country as a whole as well as 25 percent of the total votes cast in at least 230 of the local government areas. If no candidate meets those requirements, an electoral college consisting of the national and state assemblies would meet and elect a president on the basis of a simple majority of those present and voting.[104]

If there was substantial agreement among Nigerian leaders as to the substance of the new constitutional order, there was less harmony regarding the transition process. Retired General Obasanjo and others publicly chastised the Babangida government for prolonging the transition period.[105] Frustrations were evident not only over the length of the transition process, which continued after it was to have ended in June 1993, but also over what some Nigerians perceived as Babangida's heavy-handed management style. He supervised and controlled every item on the agenda down to the very procedures of the election. Describing the transition program in its entirety as the work and responsibility of the military government, Wole Soyinka remarked that "the duration, the parties, the constitution, the manifestoes, the changes upon changes upon changes and reverses of gear to various starting points, the decision on open balloting, the erstwhile pariah moneybags translated into cash-tankers, every detail and consequence, including even [the design of the parties' headquarters], all was the handiwork of this military regime."[106]

Indeed, in August 1992 the government canceled the first round of presidential primaries held under the transition program on the grounds of widespread malpractices and electoral fraud. After further postponements and the disqualification of twenty-three presidential aspirants who had participated in the earlier primaries, a number of revised procedures were put into effect, including a modified open ballot system, the creation of party caretaker committees to watch over possible financial malpractices, a complicated primary process leading up to national conventions, guidelines to ensure a well-financed and well-trained press, and so forth. In November, a new timetable was published, extending the date for a new presidential election to June 12, 1993. When the Social Democratic candidate from the South, Muslim millionaire Moshood Abiola, won, Babangida annulled the election. As the process dragged on, a chorus of criticisms of Babangida's prolonged, stage-by-stage handling of the changeover was expressed.[107] Rising protest from sources ranging from the younger officers to progressive intellectuals forced him to appoint a civilian interim president and to withdraw to a place behind the scenes. His system came to an end when General Abacha overthrew the briefly serving interim president, arrested Abiola for treason, and ended the democratization experiment in November 1993. Abacha broke the back of the labor unions, which were striking for procedural and substantive demands and arrested many of his critics and subjected them to secret trials and heavy sentencing in 1995.

In Ghana, Rawlings also took great pains to manage the process of political liberalization, attempting to strengthen his claim to domestic and international legitimacy while organizing the presidential and parliamentary elections in such a way as to ensure continued PNDC leadership. The government charged a Committee of Experts with the task of making proposals for such representative democratic institutions as an executive president, a national assembly elected by universal adult suffrage, and a prime minister commanding a legislative majority. The proposal for a split executive, modeled in part on the experiences of France and a number of French-speaking African countries, was viewed as a restraint on the abuse of executive power and a means of securing political accountability.[108] Ultimately, the consultative assembly scrapped the proposal for a mixed political system and, concerned over the "immobilism" that such divided authority might entail, favored instead a strong presidential form of governance, which suited Rawlings fine.

The new Ghanaian constitution framers took pains to reassure ethnic and subregional minority groups that they would be involved in the decisionmaking process. They proposed a number of mechanisms toward this end: a requirement that the president secure a minimum of 50 percent of the votes cast to be elected; a provision for a council of state with one elected representative from each subregion to advise on balanced appointments to the civil service; and stipulations that political parties maintain branches in all the subregions and that their national executive committees include members from every subregion of the country.

For all this progress toward a return of constitutional government in Ghana, many questions remained "about the PNDC's management of and fairness in the transition process."[109] The ban on political parties was not lifted until May 18, 1992, several weeks after the national referendum on the constitution, and the transitional process was left in the hands of the PNDC. The transitional provisions of the constitution provide that no future court or tribunal could take any member of the PNDC or its officials to account for anything they did or failed to do during their stay in office.[110] Finally, doubts were expressed by the Committee of Experts and others on the adequacy of the new constitutional mechanism to deter future military interventions.

Rawlings's firm hand was quite evident throughout the transition to the fourth republic. In the district assembly elections, those elected to office ran without party affiliation, and the remaining representatives were appointed by the PNDC (and included a variety of traditional authorities, retired civil servants, and activists drawn from the ranks of local political movements and populist organizations). Not only did the PNDC appoint the members of the Committee of Experts and heavily influence the selection of people to participate in the consultative assembly deliberations, but it controlled the agenda and timetable of the transition program.

As Ghana prepared for national elections in 1992, Rawlings was shown to have a clear advantage over his opponents in the way that his government organized the terms of competition. According to respondents on the scene, Rawlings's ability to create employment opportunities in rural areas and boost civil service salaries gave him a distinct edge. His ability, moreover, to utilize state resources (permits for rallies, government vehicles, and the mass media) and to campaign for months before the ban on party politics was lifted, created an uneven field on which to play out the competition among parties. To make matters worse, Rawlings's refusal to open up the voting lists to those who had not registered for the referendum on district assemblies or the partially updated register in 1991 meant, in effect, that hundreds of thousands of opponents were left without a chance to participate. The combined effect of these factors was to leave the opposition convinced that the process was "rigged" from the outset, creating doubts about the credibility of the electoral outcome even before the voting had occurred.[111]

In the short time allowed for party politics before the 1992 presidential election, several parties and leaders came forward to campaign for the high office. Rawlings's intentions remained unclear until late in the preparatory period. Then, with the public becoming impatient as to his plans, he resigned his Ghana Air Force position and began an active solicitation for votes. His position was strengthened by an alliance he forged between his own National Democratic Congress (NDC) and the Egle Party and National Convention Party (NCP), both Nkrumaist-inclined organizations. Opposed to this grouping were four main parties and presidential candidates: A. Adu Boahen's New Patriotic Party (NPP), the inheritor of the liberal Danquah-Busia tradition, and three parties with an Nkrumaist thrust to their program—former president Hilla Limann's People's National Convention (PNC); businessman Kwabena Darko's New Independence Party (NIP); and Lieutenant General (retired) Emmanuel Erskine's People's Heritage Party (PHP). The inability of people in the opposition to forge a common front until after the elections placed limits on their ability to compete effectively with the Rawlings-led alliance.

Although Rawlings drew large crowds, especially in the rural areas, many analysts assumed that in the end the presidential contest would prove a close one between Rawlings and Boahen, with some giving Boahen the edge. The results, therefore, came as a surprise to these observers. The final tallies showed that Rawlings had won a clear majority of 58.3 percent of the votes cast in the country, negating the need for a run-off election. Rawlings ran especially well in the rural areas as well as in most parts of the country (93.3 percent in Volta Region, 60.7 percent and 66.5 percent in the Western and Central Regions respectively, 61.9 percent in Brong-Ahafo Region, and 63.2 percent in the Northern Region). The great exception here was Ashanti Region, where Boahen won 60.5 percent of the votes cast.[112] Clearly the election outcome represented a tremendous victory for Rawlings, who overcame the hard times brought on by structural adjustment to become the first leader of an African coup regime to win a competitive, multiparty election. Even so, the controlled nature of the transition process combined with the disunity among opposition leaders was important in the equation. In addition, peasants appeared extremely wary of any shift of regimes that might cause reduced employment, a fall in cocoa prices, or a slowdown in rural electrification.

Despite the magnitude of the Rawlings victory in the presidential election, the main opposition leaders questioned the accuracy of the final tallies, charging widespread malpractices. In some instances, opposition supporters went beyond expressing their dissatisfaction to demonstrate their disapproval, and in Kumasi, demonstrations led to the imposition of a dusk-to-dawn curfew for several days. People interviewed on the scene by this author expressed anger over alleged incidents of intimidation, ballot stuffing, and impersonation and went on to speak darkly of the possibilities of violent resistance. Boahen issued a joint statement on behalf of his NPP and the PNC, PHP, and NIP, expressing shock and dismay over various alleged abuses during the presidential elections. These charges received some external validation from the interim report of the Carter Center Election Mission, which concluded that "serious irregularities" had occurred in the election process. The Carter team did not doubt the validity of the Rawlings victory as such but did raise questions about the dated nature of the voter register, the absence of a reliable and consistent procedure for identifying eligible voters, the determination of spoiled ballots, and the undue influence of polling agents.[113]

As a result of the opposition parties' decision to boycott the parliamentary elections, Rawlings's NDC won 95 percent of 200 parliamentary seats, and its two allies won most of the rest. By choosing to deny themselves and their supporters representation in the legislature, the opposition parties further limited the process of democratization. Rawlings and his Progressive Alliance in parliament (the NDC, NCP, and Egle Party) had emerged as a *"de facto* one-party state."[114] In a case of mutual damage, the Rawlings government was again isolated, and the opposition powerless, unable to play a parliamentary role on a variety of pressing issues. In an attempt to strengthen their position prior to the 1996 election, many of the Nkrumaist leaders have declared their willingness to back the leading NPP candidate, John Kuffour, in a bid to oust Rawlings; however with the opposition united on little else except their hostility to Rawlings, any victory on their part could well prove the prelude to a difficult transition period.[115]

In a word, in West Africa none of the three major states' experiments with democratization has unambiguously made its first step, let alone arrived at its goal. For all of majoritarian democracy's apparent strengths, then, it is unwise to underestimate the difficulties of introducing it to societies that lack a consensus on political values and rules of the game, are rent by class and ethnic inequalities, have developed a tradition of conflict between state and society, mistrust the state as a manager of conflict, and suffer from limited resources. In all the West African countries under review, the return to multiparty elections in the early 1990s was a guided process, one that reflected internal pressures and the determination of those in power to establish rules of the game that would protect their interests in future times. Unable to agree on a pact that would emphasize shared concerns and keep conflict at manageable levels, government and opposition viewed elections as adversarial encounters that enabled the winners to benefit at the expense of their opponents. "Democracy, unless handled properly," warns Adebayo Adedeji, the head of Nigeria's African Centre for Development and Strategic Studies, "can be divisive and can lead to polarization."[116] Where polarization is already in place, democracy can amplify the conflict among groups. In such a political environment, there is an ever-present possibility that distribution and recruitment will become overpoliticized and that groups will mobilize around inflexible principles, greatly increasing existing class, religious, and ethnoregional tensions. The adversarial tendencies inherent in Anglo-Saxon practices of rule by the majority party exacerbate inclinations toward intense rivalries and the pursuit of political power, particularly when an ethos of exclusive power contest already exists. Hence despite the popularity of democracy at this time, it seems likely, as Larry Diamond warns, to remain "insecure and embattled" throughout the 1990s.[117]

Clearly, where the conditions are favorable, majoritarian democracy remains a preferred option for the effective management of conflict. Majoritarian democracies may be the most effective way of encouraging strong states and strong societies and building linkages across organizations and elites over time, but they do not necessarily resolve such interactional problems as overpoliticization or such normative problems as patronage and corruption. Moreover, democratic systems may exacerbate latent social conflict, particularly where outbidding (appeals to extremist elements) occurs in societies that are deeply divided along religious and ethnic lines. In part, the risks of full democracy can be mitigated by grafting various consociational features (proportional representation, balanced recruitment and fiscal allocation policies, grand coalition, mutual veto, segmental autonomy) onto the majoritarian model.[118] This might promote consensus decisionmaking and perhaps even a further move away from participation toward pacted democratic regimes, thereby reducing the probabilities of open, adversarial encounters.

### Pacted Democracy

In contemporary Africa, where the state is often weak and public demands and expectations highly burdensome, state elites seem likely to resort to alternative forms of governance to majoritarian democracy, which allow them to include representatives of the main groups in the decisionmaking process and to be less responsive to the demands of the public. Some elites have resisted a complete transition to democratic forms, building upon the existing configurations of group power to achieve a consensus among themselves at the top of the political system while excluding the general public from a significant role in the decisionmaking process. Such elite pacts represent negotiated agreements among party leaders "in which parties forswear the use of violence to achieve their aims in exchange for protection under agreed-upon rules of the political game."[119] Although these elite pacts fall short of pure democracy, they hold out the possibility of an easing of the burdens of governance and, through measures of depoliticization, of encouraging moderate behavior on the part of leaders and their constituents.

Such regimes can be moderately authoritarian (the old African hegemonic exchange system of the 1960s and 1970s and their recent expressions in Gabon and the Congo) or moderately democratic (pacted democratic systems such as South Africa and the interim constitution that provide, among their features, for regular, contested elections). Either way, these elite power-sharing regimes unite the competing thrusts of political control and political exchange among genuine group representatives. Relying upon an elite acceptance of informal codes of procedure, these state or interest group leaders (often ethnoregional patrons or spokespersons) engage in an ongoing process of tacit or formal exchanges in the cabinet, the legislature, or high party organs. For a limited time, such elite power-sharing arrangements may promote conciliatory behavior and bring about stable and effective conflict management, even in deeply divided societies. Because hegemonic exchange regimes tend to lack legitimacy in the eyes of the general public, restrict full and meaningful participation, limit information, and do little to reduce the conflicts of value and interest in society, their continuance seems dependent upon the survival of the pact and the ability of the group intermediaries to renegotiate the terms of the original bargain from time to time.[120] Pacted democratic regimes share many of these tendencies; however, because they allow for more participation, they are likely to gain a greater validity—and staying power—in the eyes of the general public.

In West Africa, the initial postindependence experience with elite power sharing leaned heavily toward hegemonic exchange. Political exchange and compromise occurred within perimeters of state control.

Houphouët-Boigny in Côte d'Ivoire and Presidents Ahmadou Ahidjo and, after 1982, Paul Biya of Cameroon, skillfully used ministerial appointments as a means of balancing ethnoregional, religious, linguistic, and economic interests in their societies. They consciously sought to include key demand-bearing group representatives in the decision-making process in an effort to encourage cooperation with government purposes under conditions of weak institutionalization and resource scarcity. In Côte d'Ivoire, Houphouët-Boigny took care to incorporate the representatives of all major ethnic groups in his cabinet on a roughly proportional basis. He sought to defuse conflict through a process of coopting ethnic notables into what Aristide Zolberg aptly called "a one-party coalition, a heterogeneous monolith."[121] Such practices of ethnic balancing within a one-party framework held sway beyond the 1970s, when they were joined in importance by educational attainment, party loyalty at the regional level, and personal commitment to the head of state.

One of the most salient cases of pacted democracy in the region is Senegal, where a limited multiparty system existed for a decade and a half before the 1993 elections.[122] Opposition parties exist as political safety valves, and when the major opposition party—the Senegalese Democratic Party (PDS)—gathered its own strength, its secretary general, Abdoulaye Wade, was coopted into the government as a minister of state without portfolio. The main organizations of society collaborate with the ruling Democratic Socialist Party, since they know that is the one that makes the decisions. Thus these organizations make sure their interests are considered and demands met.

In the current period of political liberalization and given the frailty of majoritarian democracy, pacted democracy seems likely to remain relevant to West Africa. Experience elsewhere indicates that where the state remains weak, resources scarce, clientelism entrenched, and demand-bearing groups overshadowed by politicoeconomic, ethnoregional, or other broad aggregatory dimensions as in Colombia, Brazil, Venezuela, or Lebanon, some form of pacted democracy is likely to gain support as a conflict-regulating mechanism. To the extent that West African leaders view majoritarian democracy as divisive, conflict producing rather than conflict managing, or a hindrance to governmental effectiveness, they will opt for models of governance that utilize the outward forms of democracy while relying on pacts among civilian and military elites to stabilize the regime. In Nigeria, proposals for a sharing of significant powers between the military and publicly elected civilians—referred to locally as "diarchy"—have received support from various political analysts intent upon moderating conflict and protecting the new constitution from future military interventions.[123] In Ghana, these same ideas were hooted down in the mid-1970s as a barely disguised vehicle for Acheampong to remain in power. Those negotiating such interelite pacts hope that bringing the military within the ruling coalition will reduce its uncertainties about the transition and lower its incentives to intervene again. Clearly such civilian-military pacts run the risk of strengthening undemocratic forces at the political center; nevertheless, there is a real possibility that such temporary arrangements may set the stage for future transitions toward full democracy.[124] At times, then, political logic may require some accommodation with military, bureaucratic, economic group, and communal elites who remain powerful during the transition from the old authoritarian order. The state's weakness and absence of a vigorous, differentiated society in many countries leave little room for maneuver; hence new coordinated adjustments aimed at finding a balance between participation and control can be anticipated in Africa.

*Populism*

Another alternative to majoritarian democracy—radical state populism—set out deliberately to transform the conflictual relations that marked the postcolonial political order, creating in its place a new and legitimate community of the previously disadvantaged. In Ghana, Burkina Faso, and initially in Liberia in the early 1980s, a populist ruling coalition displayed considerable sensitivity to the demands of the citizenry for public participation and equal distribution of benefits. The Ghanaian regime had adopted a line of vision that was generally compatible with the wishes of the populace at large; however, its general unresponsiveness to the concerns of professional and business demand-bearing groups during its initial populist phase created distance between the new ruling coalition and these still influential groups. This inhibiting of middle-class participation in the political process led to a series of counterdemands, creating an unstable and only partially informed environment in which to implement the populist program.[125] Thus the radical populist regime, with its support base among the disadvantaged and disaffected, lacked a communitywide consensus. It attempted to compensate by repression and accommodations with domestic and international capitalist interests—adjustments that left the regime with an even more limited number of supporters as well as a blurred sense of purpose.[126]

Radical populist regimes, such as those of Jerry Rawlings in Ghana and Thomas Sankara in Burkina Faso in the 1980s, sought to combine extensive state leadership and control with active public participation in the political process. Indignant over the conditions of poverty, indebtedness, and external dependence that were prevalent, Rawlings and Sankara opted for a full reorganization of their societies to promote national unity, social equality, and broad citizen participation in the decisionmaking processes. They sought the elimination of neocolonial linkages and a reduced role for such groups as lawyers, church leaders, and civil servants deemed to be opposed to the populist transformation.[127] Rejecting such values as individualism and acquisitiveness, these regimes emphasized instead authentic African solutions such as communalism and decentralized and participatory democracy. In this vein, Sankara declared himself determined "to reform Voltaic society, to clean it up, and to purify it."[128]

A hallmark of the Western African populist regime was its stress on the importance of public political participation. Both Ghana and Burkina Faso experimented with Committees for the Defense of the Revolution in villages and urban areas, established public tribunals to administer popular justice, and purged their bureaucracies and armies of people they regarded as unsympathetic to their populist vision.[129] These regimes also sought to promote local participation through the decentralization of certain public activities and the institutionalization of demand-bearing groups in the conflict-management structure. Although the initial program outlined by Rawlings to achieve decentralization in 1982 was slow to be implemented, by the late 1980s, the central service ministries had allowed the local authorities some autonomy to deal with their own affairs. Moreover, the decision to set up district assemblies with responsibilities to supervise and control political and administrative authorities in their districts represented a cautious step in the direction of decentralization. Paradoxically, such efforts to spur the public's involvement in governmental activities had the aim of strengthening the state, enabling it to tap into additional resources, mobilize a solid base of supporters, and channel societal pressures into constructive and conciliatory paths. The effect of heightened public participation, however, was to undercut the state's autonomy, for the leadership accommodated the inflated demands of the public at some cost in achieving their productionist objectives.

Radical state populism, then, was an expression of widespread dissatisfaction in Ghana and Burkina Faso over the structure of inequalities inherited from the past and the despair that many group spokespersons (and constituents) felt over their inability to change this pattern of relations. In Ghana, populist measures did provide something of a short-term uplift, broadening general involvement on the part of the citizenry. Various elements normally left on the sidelines—trade unionists, students, market traders, farmers, the lower ranks of the bureaucracy and military—coalesced as groups and were brought to the center of politics and power. In the initial fifteen-month period, it proved an exhilarating experience. Then, as disappointment increased over the inability to attract assistance from other radical countries and as the need to accommodate the rather muted counterpressures of the middle class became apparent to those in power, a shift toward more pragmatic policies took place. The Rawlings regime continued to make extensive use of populist rhetoric while changing its policy priorities and practices on fiscal and economic matters in a more orthodox direction. This so-called U-turn reestablished local confidence on the part of middle-class groups and elicited a relatively generous response from bilateral and multilateral donors, but at an evident cost in terms of disaffection from the regime's initial base of urban supporters. As the regime reduced state subsidies, increased taxes and surcharges, cut back on the number of state employees, encouraged privatization, and generally invoked painful deflationary monetary policies, its legitimacy declined and many of its rank-and-file supporters drifted away.

Radical populism had a relatively short life in West Africa in the 1980s, with the high expectations of the Ghanaian and Burkinabé (and, even more rapidly, Liberian) revolutions quickly giving way to a more cautious appraisal. Populist principles seemed to be sacrificed on the altar of political and economic realism. However, if this realism fails to ensure a minimally satisfactory existence for the broad masses of the population, a new skepticism ensues. In that case, either the state may collapse or radical populism—linking a relatively strong government with effective popular mobilization and broad public participation in political institutions—may reappear in one guise or another. It is a formidable outlet for a despairing public, intent upon achieving its consummatory (that is, moral) values, even if at a possible cost in terms of its instrumental (that is, efficiency) values.[130]

## Corporatism

Still another alternative, state corporatism, involves a heavily state-regulated and supervised political process; not only does the ruling coalition exercise extensive influence over the legitimation of demand-bearing groups, but it organizes the way that these officially sanctioned, functionally based interests are allowed to present their claims to central authorities. State-societal conflicts are intensely managed by a strong state with substantial political and economic resources at its disposal. State elites attempt to define and limit political participation to designated, functionally based groups, regulating conflict by sanctioning the participation of legitimate interests and controlling the way that these state-linked groups mobilize to make demands upon decision-makers. Philippe Schmitter's definition of corporatism is a classic one: corporatism, he states, is

> a system of interest representation in which the constituent units are organized into a limited number of singular, compulsory, non-competitive, hierarchically ordered and functionally differentiated categories, recognized or licensed (if not created) by the state and granted a deliberate representational monopoly within their respective categories in exchange for observing certain controls on their selection of leaders and articulation of demands and supports.[131]

Corporatism, then, is an elite-regulated system that seeks to establish a form of controlled political pluralism. It incorporates (and first creates where necessary) officially recognized organizations for the representation of group interests; civil and political associations that attempt to maintain an autonomous existence may be undermined or excluded by state authorities. Following an outbreak of antigovernment demonstrations in Côte d'Ivoire in February 1992, state authorities moved swiftly to outlaw the student movement, the Student and School Federation of the Côte d'Ivoire (FESCI) and to sentence its leader to three years in prison.[132] Côte d'Ivoire's corporatist ruling class responded to a perceived threat by shoring up its dominant position in the face of potential challengers, using its extensive powers to determine which interest groups were to be viewed as politically legitimate and which illegitimate and therefore excluded.

Although few African countries have the robust institutional capacity required by a full corporatist model, corporatist tendencies have been in evidence in Côte d'Ivoire since the 1970s. Many varied civil associations and commercial firms were integrated into the state and the ruling PDCI. State and party control was first extended to ethnic associations in the urban areas, then to large business and trading enterprises, trade unions, and tenant organizations.[133] Where desired, demand-bearing groups (such as ethnic associations) did not exist, they were sponsored by the state. And where it did not prove possible to co-opt groups (for example, an incipient organization of the urban unemployed), the state acted to undermine them.

In the rural areas, the state and party pursued a similar strategy of integrating the various organized social groups into their structures. By comparison with experiences elsewhere, the efforts of party and state to "capture" the peasantry were relatively successful. In part, this success is explained by the ability and willingness of the state to maintain reasonable producer prices over the years and to keep rates of taxation at moderate levels. The farmers, large and small, generally responded in a positive manner to these price and tax incentives, resulting in substantial outputs of such export crops as cocoa, coffee, and palm oil. Subsistence agriculture no longer seemed an attractive option, as many members of the rural population became engaged in producing cash crops to pay for education, medicine, and other benefits.[134] Thus in contrast with the flourishing informal economy of neighboring Ghana, Côte d'Ivoire's state and PDCI organizations had proved relatively effective in incorporating both urban and rural interests into their fold.

In the process of incorporating interest groups into the state and party structures, Côte d'Ivoire's nascent corporatism inevitably encountered resistance from societal organizations, something the ruling elite attempted to deal with through a system of state-initiated Dialogues. The use of such Dialogues became particularly evident during the educational crises of 1982–83. Initially, state authorities reacted to a strike by students, secondary school teachers, and university students over worsening conditions in a heavy-handed manner: the university was closed, student scholarships were suspended, striking lecturers were denied their salaries and evicted from their state-owned housing, and the trade unions for university lecturers and secondary school teachers were banned. Then, as such harsh tactics failed to produce their desired results, the government reconsidered its strategy and called on the strike leaders to meet and submit their recommendations to the president. In a process described as "intensified competition among corporatist groups," representatives of the government, PDCI, and the striking unions assembled to engage one another on the issues.[135] The result was an easing of tensions, as Houphouët-Boigny accepted the need to work with striking interests through legitimate channels, ultimately pardoning the strikers and reopening the university. In 1989, as a more serious clash of interests emerged over political reforms and economic relief, the system of state-guided Dialogues again managed to ease the strains arising between state and civil society. Houphouët-Boigny, startled by the extent of dissatisfaction over political and economic conditions in the country, arranged a meeting with some 2,000 government and interest group representatives to discuss the issues. Realizing the need to act in a conciliatory manner, he agreed to multiparty elections and subsequently guided the country through a closely controlled electoral process. In another gesture of conciliation, the president also appointed Alassane Ouattara, a well-known economist, as prime minister. When, prior to the implementation of these measures, new street demonstrations broke out over various economic grievances, Houphouët-Boigny again managed to contain the conflict, granting wage increases and job security to designated demand-bearing groups.

## Implications for Conflict Management

In the encounter between state and civil society in West Africa, recurrent interactions are possible as long as demands are generally reasonable and elastic and focus largely on the distribution of resources, tempered by an awareness of the limitations imposed by their scarcity. The result is to open up the possibility of a balance between conflict and stability. In such circumstances, conflict can be creative in the way that it promotes a dynamic relationship between political demands and state responses—so long as it takes place within the boundaries of understood and tacitly accepted rules. Stability can be nurturant to the relationship if it provides a context in which constructive conflict (that is, growth-producing interactions) is feasible. The problem facing those concerned with conflict management is to determine appropriate guidelines for counterbalancing demand loads and system capabilities and, when this does not prove attainable, to encourage more realistic and negotiable demands and a return to regularized modes of relationships.

As discussed earlier in this chapter, regimes play a critical role in structuring the routines of encounter between the state and civil society. They can organize intergroup interactions to facilitate the channeling of demands along conventional lines or, alternatively, block access and thwart interelite and intergroup reciprocity and political exchange. Regime organization makes a critical difference in the nature of outcomes: that is, whether norms for constructive relationships can develop over time or whether the connections among groups will be weakened or broken, leading to destructive, polarizing conflict. State regimes structure intergroup encounters in quite different ways: they can allow varying scope for the aggregation of collective demands, facilitate or obstruct the channeling of these demands to decisionmakers, respond or fail to respond to legitimate claims on state elites, or implement or refuse to implement public policies as intended.

In part, the fully authoritarian regimes represent the ambitions of powerful political actors as well as their responses to uncompromising and inelastic demands advanced by various groups—in particular, subregional, religious, ethnic, and ideological interests. Authoritarian systems, which rely to some extent on the threat or actual use of coercion, combine various but generally low degrees of societal participation with the repression of dissent. Not only do their repressive tendencies cause them to be low in securing information and responding to legitimate demands, but their heavyhandedness is destabilizing over the long term, provoking a bitter, even violent, response on the part of civil associations. The effect is to discourage the emergence of stable and persistent interactions over time, and worse yet, to train society to expect such treatment from the state, no matter in whose hands it operates. For some years, authoritarian regimes may not allow antagonism to come out in the open, but deterring conflict is not tantamount to providing internal incentives for cooperation. Often incapable of building networks of reciprocities and contexts of consensus over norms and values, the hegemonic pattern of governance proves brittle; fissures occur within the ruling coalition and, in some cases at least, society overwhelms the ruling state elite. Such authoritarian regimes fail to suppress destructive conflict and succumb to the turbulence in their midst.

By limiting and guiding public participation along desired lines, various partially authoritarian regimes (that is, radical state populist, state corporatist, and pacted democratic regime-types) are sometimes advantageously placed to impose creative policies on society. Because of the way the partially authoritarian regime consolidates power, it insulates its elites from certain members of the public—state populism excludes many of its middle-class and professional members as well a significant number of traditional leaders; corporatism places spontaneous groups and associations outside its sphere of concerns and leaves state-linked groups with insufficient autonomy; and pacted democracies tend to be elitist in their orientation. Such regimes may enable rulers to live with a certain amount of incoherence. They may preserve the appearance of normality while denying oppositional elements a legitimate arena in which to fight out their differences. In brief, the partially authoritarian regimes represent something of a middle point between the poles of autocracy and majoritarian democracy. They offer a limited scope for bargaining and compromise among various pluralistic interests; yet such political exchanges take place within firm parameters determined in each case by the ruling state coalition. These regimes may prove to be transitionary forms on the way to greater political liberalization—but movement in the direction of full democracy remains anything but a certainty.

Democratic regimes, by contrast, provide their own internal incentives for cooperation. Although democratic regimes have been difficult to construct and maintain, they nonetheless hold out the greatest hope for developing constructive rules for the management of state-society relations over time. Such regimes contribute to the development of strong states and vibrant and active civil societies, thereby providing the basis for legitimate and well-informed governance. To the extent that West African polyarchies emphasize such organizing processes as federalism, balanced recruitment, inclusive coalitions, proportional distributions, and so forth, they promote a sense of "fairness" that encourages empathy toward rival groups and factions and so provide incentives for stability, moderation, and compromise. Clearly, in the absence of an overriding agreement on norms and values, democratic regimes inevitably exacerbate inherent risks. Particularly under conditions of economic scarcity and regime uncertainty, uncompromising demands advanced by subregional, ethnic, religious, and ideological interests can prove highly threatening to basic system norms. In a political environment lacking an overriding consensus on values and issues, adversarial politics, as practiced by many West African leaders, can go beyond healthy competition and contribute to intense and highly destructive conflicts. Given the volatility of the times, effective conflict management depends on a retreat from nonnegotiable positions—or the political coalition necessary to democratic or semiauthoritarian regime survival may well unravel.

For all the difficulties in the way of democratic reform, the first half of the 1990s has marked an important transition toward new political choices. Crucial steps forward and backward were taken, with the resulting (but never final) position still uncertain. As a wave of demonstrations calling for multiparty democracy and greater openness and accountability swept across the African continent in that period, West African governments under review found themselves under increasing pressure to reconsider the rules shaping societal participation. In Côte d'Ivoire, President Houphouët-Boigny responded quickly, increasing the tempo of the government's Dialogues with interest groups and allowing competitive—though rather controlled—elections to take place; his successor, President Konan Bédié, allowed multiparty elections to take place but restricted his field of competition in such a way as to achieve an easy (but false) victory. The Rawlings regime in Ghana entered into discussions within a limited political circle on the nature of the new constitution-organized elections from district assemblies to the presidency, which it organized to its advantage; new elections are scheduled for 1996. In Nigeria, an elaborate process leading to a renewal of constitutional government was invigorated, resulting in a revised consociational-type constitution and transfer of power to civilians, and then brutally back to the military, breaking the legs—but probably not the back—of the democracy movement.[136] For all its frailties, political democracy was the preferred option in early 1990s in all three countries, received some setbacks in the mid-1990s, and is the hope of many for the rest of the decade.

Can the momentum of change be sustained and the next steps be taken forward? Can the reform effort be a catalyst for the establishment of new rules and understandings on state accountability and openness and new routines of regularized management of conflicting demands? Can change prevail over the recalcitrance of incumbents who, by clinging to power, promote rather than manage conflict? In times of chronically scarce resources, can demands be kept reasonable and self-limiting with groups contributing to the management of their own conflicts, or will demands increasingly focused against government become the entrenched ethos of state-security relationships? Certainly, democracy is distinguishable from its partially authoritarian counterparts in its increased capacity for developing norms of encounter acceptable to the main societal groups over time. Building upon political reciprocity and exchange, political leaders become engaged in an extended learning process. Seen in these terms, the initial act of constitution making is not an end in itself but part of a larger process leading to repeated interactions. To the extent that leaders of the state and groups in society succeed in establishing political routines of reciprocity and exchange for the handling of demands and the management of conflict, relations among groups are likely to become more predictable. Networks of relations may emerge that promote intergroup cooperation. The result may be to clarify and normalize the channels for advancing collective demands and to facilitate state responsiveness, leading to a more effective management of social conflict. In brief, the thrust of the democratic regimes toward a recognition of convergent interests, even a consensus on norms, acts as a general incentive for intergroup cooperation. When the principles of inclusiveness, proportionality, and electoral competition gain increasing acceptance, and as a consensus on goals and values emerges, regularized relationships may become an accepted feature of the society. Where conciliatory behavior and political stability result, political leaders will be in a more advantageous position to meet demands for economic and social development.

# Notes

## Chapter One

1. Thomas Ohlson and Stephen John Stedman with Robert Davies, *The New Is Not Yet Born: Conflict Resolution in Southern Africa* (Brookings, 1994); Francis Deng, *War of Visions* (Brookings, 1995); Marina Ottaway, *South Africa: The Struggle for a New Order* (Brookings, 1993); Terrence Lyons and Ahmed Samatar, *Somalia: State Collapse, Multilateral Intervention, and Strategies for Political Reconstruction* (Brookings, 1995); and I. William Zartman, ed., *Collapsed States: The Disintegration and Restoration of Legitimate Authority* (Lynne Rienner, 1995).

2. Including central Africa also brings in a third major civil war, the endemic conflict between 1965 and 1982 in Chad.

3. Resolution here means removing the causes of the conflict as well as its manifestations; management means dealing with alternative outcomes on a political level so as to preclude violence, leaving time and politics to deal with causes.

4. Seymore Martin Lipset and Stein Rokkan, eds., *Party Systems and Voter Alignments* (Free Press, 1967), p. 47; Ruth Berins Collier and David Collier, *Shaping the Political Arena: Critical Juncture, the Labor Movement, and Regional Dynamics in Latin America* (Princeton University Press, 1991); and Arthur Stinchcombe, *Constructing Social Theories* (Harcourt, Brace and World, 1968), esp. pp. 102-03.

5. Barrington Moore, *The Social Origins of Dictatorship and Democracy: Lord and Peasant in the Making of the Modern World* (Beacon, 1967).

6. Ruth Collier, *Regimes in Tropical Africa* (University of California Press, 1982).

7. Zartman, *Collapsed States*.

8. See Robert Boyer, *The Regulation School: A Critical Introduction* (Columbia University Press, 1990); Samuel Bowles, David M. Gordon and Thomas E. Weisskopf, *After the Wasteland: A Democratic Economics for the Year 2000* (M. E. Sharpe, 1990); and Alain Lipietz, *Mirages and Miracles: The Crisis of Global Fordism* (London: Verso, 1987).

9. Dirk Vandewalle and Karen Pfeiffer, "North Africa as a Peripheral Economic Region," in Dirk Vandewalle, ed., *North Africa: Development and Reform in a Changing Global Economy* (St. Martin's Press, 1996), p. 14.

10. Wole Soyinka, quoted in Debra Liang, *Nigeria's Political Crisis: Which Way Forward?* (Washington: National Endowment for Democracy, International Forum for Democratic Studies, 1995).

## Chapter Two

1. David Easton, *The Political System, An Inquiry into the State of Political Science* (Knopf, 1953); and Gabriel A. Almond and James S. Coleman, eds., *The Politics of Developing Areas* (Princeton University Press, 1960).

2. I. William Zartman, ed., *Elites in the Middle East* (Praeger, 1980).

3. "John F. Kennedy Inaugural Address, January 20, 1961," *The Inaugural Addresses of the Presidents of the United States, 1789–1985* (Atlantic City, N.J.: American Inheritance Press, 1985)

4. Morton Halpern, "Four Contrasting Repertories of Human Relations in Islam," in L. Carl Brown and Norman Itzkowitz, eds., *Psychological Dimensions of Near Eastern Studies* (Darwin, 1977); Jeffrey Z. Rubin, Dean G. Pruitt, and Sung Hee Kim, *Social Conflicts: Escalation, Stalemate, and Settlement* (McGraw-Hill, 1994); and Joseph S. Himes, *Conflict and Conflict Management* (University of Georgia Press, 1980).

5. Muzafer Sherif and Carolyn W. Sherif, *Groups in Harmony and Transition: An Integration of Studies on Intergroup Relations* (Harper, 1953).

6. Ernest Barker, ed., *Social Contract: Essays by Locke, Hume, and Rousseau* (Oxford University Press, 1962); Maurice Cranston and Richard S. Peters, eds., *Hobbes and Rousseau: A Collection of Critical Essays* (Garden City, N.Y.: Anchor Books, 1972); and David Boucher and Paul Kelly, eds., *The Social Contract from Hobbes to Rawls* (Routledge, 1994).

7. Celestin Mongo, "Did National Conferences Take Place ?" paper presented at Democratization: Phase Two conference at the Johns Hopkins University School of Advanced International Studies; and Timothy D. Sisk, *Democratization in South Africa: The Elusive Social Contract* (Princeton University Press, 1995).

8. I. William Zartman, "Revolution and Development," *Civilizations*, vol. 20, no. 2 (1970), pp. 181–99.

9. Antonio Gramsci, *The Modern Prince and Other Writings* (New York: International Publishers, 1967)

10. Jacob Bercovitz and Jeffrey Z. Rubin, eds., *Mediation in International Relations: Multiple Approaches to Conflict Management* (St. Martin's Press, 1992); Kenneth Kressel and others, *Mediation Research: The Process and Effectiveness of Third-Party Intervention* (Jossey-Bass, 1989); C. R. Mitchell and K. Webb, eds., *New Approaches to International Mediation* (Greenwood Press, 1988); Jacob Bercovitz, *Resolving International Conflicts: The Theory and Practice of Mediation* (Lynne Rienner,1996); and Saadia Touval and I. William Zartman, eds., *The Man in the Middle: International Mediation in Theory and Practice* (Westview, 1984).

11. Thomas Ohlson and Stephen John Stedman with Robert Davies, *The New Is Not Yet Born: Conflict Resolution in Southern Africa* (Brookings, 1994);

Francis Deng, *War of Visions* (Brookings, 1995); Marina Ottaway, *South Africa: The Struggle for a New Order* (Brookings, 1993); and Terrence Lyons and Ahmed Samatar, *Somalia: State Collapse, Multilateral Intervention, and Strategies for Political Reconstruction* (Brookings, 1995).

12. Thomas Lionel Hodgkin, *African Political Parties, An Introductory Guide* (Penguin, 1962); Charles A. Micaud with Leon Carl Brown and Clement Henry Moore, *Tunisia: The Politics of Modernization* (Praeger, 1964); and Zartman, *Elites in the Middle East*.

13. Joyce Cary, *Mister Johnson, A Novel* (Harper,1951); Chinua Achebe, *Things Fall Apart* (New York: Astor-Honor, 1959); Margaret Laurence, *This Side Jordan* (St. Martin's Press, 1960); Albert Memmi, trans. Howard Greenfeld, *The Colonizer and the Colonized* (Orion Press, 1965); and J. Barry Riddell, "Let There Be Light: The Voices of West African Novels," *Journal of Modern African Studies,* vol. 28 (September 1990), pp. 473–86.

14. Dennis Austin, *Politics in Ghana, 1946–1960* (London: Oxford University Press, 1964) p. 154; Thomas Hodgkin, *Nationalism in Colonial Africa* (London: Muller, 1956); Immanuel Wallerstein, "Voluntary Associations," in James S. Coleman and Carl G. Rosberg, Jr., eds., *Political Parties and National Integration in Tropical Africa* (University of California Press, 1964), pp. 318–19; Kenneth Little, *West African Urbanization: A Study of Voluntary Associations in Social Change* (New York: Cambridge University Press, 1965); and Claude Meillassoux, *Urbanization of an African Community: Voluntary Associations in Bamako* (University of Washington Press, 1968).

15. Kwame Appiah, "Altered States," *Wilson Quarterly,* vol. 25 (Winter 1991), pp. 20–32. Aristide R. Zolberg, *Creating Political Order: The Party-States of West Africa* (Rand McNally, 1966), p.15n; and Olajide Aluko, "Politics of Decolonisation in British West Africa 1945–1960," in J. F. A. Ajayi and Michael Crowder, *History of West Africa,* vol. 2 (London: Longman, 1974), pp. 633f., 640.

16. Some groups saw their interests served in more rapid accession to self-rule while others were more cautious—Convention People's Party (CPP) versus United Gold Coast Convention (UGCC) in Gold Coast, Progressives versus Conservatives in Sierra Leone, African Socialist Movement (MSA)/Sawaba versus Nigerien People's Party (PPN) in Niger and MSA versus the Democratic Union for the Defense of the Interests (UDDI) in Congo, Democratic Party of Guinea (PDG) versus Democratic Party of Ivory Coast (PDCI) within the African Democratic Rally (RDA) in French West Africa, the Cameroonian People's Union (UPC) versus the Cameroonian Union (UC) in Cameroon, and the National Liberation Movement of Equatorial Guinea (MoNaLiGE) versus the National Union Movement of Equatorial Guinea (MUNGE). See Zolberg, *Creating Political Order,* p. 35.

17. Ibid., p. 17.

18. Few writers at the time mentioned a social contract. Zolberg, ibid., pp. 27, 35, 75.

19. On other parts of Africa, see "Decolonization and Intergroup Bargaining," in Donald Rothchild, *Racial Bargaining in Independent Kenya: A Study of Minorities and Colonialization* (London: Oxford University Press, 1973), pp. 104–155;

and I. William Zartman, "Les relations entre la France et l'Algerie," *Revue Française de Science Politique*, vol. 6 (December 1964), pp. 1087–13.

20. Michael Schatzberg, *Mobutu or Chaos: The United States and Zaire, 1960–1990* (University Press of America; Foreign Policy Research Institute, 1991).

21. John Esseks, ed., *L'Afrique de l'indépendance politique à l'indépendance économique* (Maspero, 1975); and Robert H. Bates, *Markets and States in Tropical Africa: The Political Basis of Agricultural Policies* (University of California Press, 1981).

22. Zolberg, *Creating Political Order*; Aristide Zolberg, *One-Party Government in the Ivory Coast* (Princeton University Press, 1964); Ruth Schachter Morgenthau, *Political Parties in French-Speaking West Africa* (Oxford: Clarendon Press, 1964); Hodgkin, *African Political Parties*; David Apter, *Ghana in Transition* (New York: Atheneum, 1963); and Ruth Berins Collier, *Regimes in Tropical Africa: Changing Forms of Supremacy, 1945–75* (University of California Press, 1982).

23. Victor T. Le Vine, *Political Leadership in Africa: Post-Independence Generational Conflict in Upper Volta, Senegal, Niger, Dahomey, and the Central African Republic* (Stanford, Calif.: Hoover Institution on War, Revolution, and Peace, 1967).

24. It is significant of the structure of politics that no such cases occurred in Guinea and Mali, where party unity was consolidated earlier, and that the same issue, taking the form of the tripartite rivalry, was never resolved at all in Dahomey, laying the ground for the military coup. See Coleman and Rosberg, eds., *Political Parties and National Integration in Tropical Africa*; and Samuel Decalo, *Coups and Army Rule in Africa: Studies in Military Style* (Yale University Press, 1990).

25. As well as Berbers in North Africa—Riffis in Morocco (1958), Kabyles in Algeria (1963), and southerners in Tunisia (1956–57)—Ndebele in Zimbabwe, Nilotes in Sudan, Hutus in Burundi, and Tutsis in Rwanda.

26. Ajayi and Crowder, *History of West Africa*, p. 633; Donal B. Cruise O'Brien and others, eds., *Contemporary West African States* (New York: Cambridge University Press, 1989), p. 16; David Brown, "Sieges and Scapegoats: The Politics of Pluralism in Ghana and Togo," *Journal of Modern African Studies*, vol. 21 (September 1983), pp. 431–60; and Rene Lamarchand, "Chad: The Misadventures of the North-South Dialect," *African Studies Review*, vol. 29 ( September 1983), pp. 27–41.

27. Zolberg, *Creating Political Order*, pp. 68–70.

28. Chibo Ofong, "Nigerian Trade Union Politics," Ph. D dissertation, The Johns Hopkins University, 1983.

29. Fred Hayward, "Political Leadership, Power, and the State," *African Studies Review*, vol. 27 (September 1984), pp. 19–39, especially pp. 23–24, 32..

30. Robert Nelson, "Nigerian Politics and the General Strike of 1964," in Robert Rotberg and Ali Mazrui, eds., *Protest and Power in Black Africa* (Oxford University Press, 1970); Robert Buijtenhuijs, *Le frolinat et les guerres civiles du Tchad (1977–1984)* (Paris: Karthala, 1987); and Victor Le Vine, "The Coups in Upper Volta, Dahomey, and Central African Republic," in Rotberg and Mazrui, *Protest and Power in Black Africa*.

31. That was the motivation, for example, in Egypt in the Nasserite type of secondary coup against a Naguib government. Similar motives inspired Major

Kouandete's Military Vigilance Committee against the regime of General Christophe Soglo in Dahomey in 1967; the series of coups by Generals Joseph Ankrah, A. A. Afrifa, Ignatius Acheampong, and Frederick Akuffo in 1966, 1969, 1972, and 1972 (the latter three were executed by Flight Lieutenant Jerry Rawlings in Ghana in 1979), and the almost textbook succession of coups from General Sanyoule Lamizana in 1966 to Colonel Saye Zerbo in 1980 to Major Ouedraogo in 1980 to Captain Thomas Sankara in 1983 in Upper Volta. Note also the series of junior officers' coups (Lieutenant Pierre Kikanga and Captain Miaouma in 1970, Lieutenant Ange Diawara in 1972, Captain Kikadidi in 1977) against Captain Marien Ngouabi and Colonel Denis Sasso Nguesso against General Joachim Yhomby-Opango in 1979 in Congo; and the reverse sequence of Majors Nzeogwu, Ifeajuna, and Okafor ousted by General Aguiyi-Ironsi in 1966 in Nigeria. Later General Yakubu Gowon was replaced by younger Generals Murtala Mohammed and then Olusegun Obasanjo in Nigeria in 1975. On military coups and rule, see Decalo, *Coups and Army Rule in Africa*; Aristide R. Zolberg, "The Military Decade in Africa," *World Politics*, vol. 25 (January 1973), pp. 309–31; A.A. Afrifa, *The Ghana Coup, 24th February 1966* (London: Cass, 1966); J. M. Lee, *African Armies and Civil Order* (London: Chatto and Windus, 1969); Claude Emerson Welch, eds., *Soldier and State in Africa: A Comparative Analysis of Military Intervention and Political Change* (Northwestern University Press, 1970); Le Vine, "*The Coups in Upper Volta, Dahomey, and Central African Republic*"; Theophilus Olatunde Odetola, *Military Regimes and Development: A Comparative Analysis of African States* (Allen and Unwin, 1982); Jean-Pierre Pabanel, *Les coup d'etats militaires en Afrique Noire* (Paris: L'Harmattan, 1984); and John Harbeson, ed., *The African Military in Politics* (Praeger, 1987).

32. For example, the coups in Liberia by Sergeant Samuel Doe in 1980 and further attempts by Major General Thomas Weh Syen, Brigadier General Thomas Quiwonkpa and Gabriel Kpollah in 1981, 1985, and 1988, respectively, and possibly those by Charles Taylor and Prince Johnson in 1990 and 1991, the attempted coup in Ghana by Lieutenants Arthur and Yeboah in 1967 and in Benin by Colonel Maurice Kouandete in 1969 and 1972, among others.

33. Pierre Francois, "Class Struggles in Mali 1982," *Review of African Political Economy*, vol. 24 (May 1992), pp. 22–38; and Max Liniger-Goumaz, "La Republique de Guiness équitoriale: une indépendance à refaire," *Afrique Contemporaire*, vol. 28, no. 105 (1979), pp. 8–21.

34. Samuel P. Huntington, *Political Order in Changing Societies* (Yale University Press, 1969).

35. Francois, "Class Struggles in Mali 1982," pp. 22–38.

36. O'Brien and others, eds., *Contemporary West African States*, p. 17; Hayward, "Political Leadership, Power, and the State," pp. 19–39 ; Brown, "Seiges and Scapegoats: The Politics of Pluralism in Ghana and Togo," and Pita Ogaba Agbese, "The Impending Demise of Nigeria's Forthcoming Third Republic," *Africa Today*, vol. 38, no. 3 (1990), pp. 23–44.

37. World Bank, *World Development Report 1990* (Washington, 1990).

38. C. O. Lerche, "Social Strife in Nigeria, 1971–78," *Journal of Modern African Studies*, vol. 9 (Spring 1982), p. 7.

39. Le Vine, *Political Leadership in Africa*.

40. John Wiseman, "Urban Riots in West Africa 1977–85," *Journal of Modern African Studies*, vol. 24 (September 1986), p. 513.

41. Richard Sandbrook and Robin Cohen, eds., *The Development of an African Working Class: Studies in Class Formation and Action* (University of Toronto Press, 1995); and Jon Kraus, "Strikes and Labor Power in Ghana," *Development and Social Change*, vol. 10 (1979), pp. 252–86.

42. Henry Bienen, "Populist Military Regimes in Africa," *Armed Forces and Society*, vol. 11 (Spring 1985), pp. 357–77; and Jeffrey Haynes, "Railway Workers and the PNDC Government in Ghana," *Journal of Modern African Studies*, vol. 29 (March 1991), pp. 137–54.

43. Walter Dean Burnham, *Critical Elections and the Mainsprings of American Politics* (Norton, 1970); and Peter F. Nardulli, "The Concept of a Critical Realignment, Electoral Behavior, and Political Change," *American Political Science Review*, vol. 89 (March 1995), pp. 10–22.

44. Jeanne Favret, "Traditionalism through Ultra-Modernism," in Ernest Gellner and Charles Micaud, eds., *Arabs and Berbers: From Tribe to Nation in North Africa* (Lexington Books, 1972).

45. Martin Lowenkopf, "Liberia: Putting the State Back Together," and William J. Foltz, "Reconstructing the State of Chad," in I. William Zartman, ed., *Collapsed States: The Disintegration and Restoration of Legitimate Authority* (Lynne Rienner, 1995), pp. 91– 108 and 15–32.

46. *Human Rights Internet Reporter*, vol. 12, no. 4 (1988); *The Status of Human Rights Organizations in Sub-Saharan Africa* (Washington: International Human Rights Internship Program and the Swedish NCO Foundation for Human Rights, 1994).

47. Jeff Haynes, "The State, Governance, and Democracy in Sub-Saharan Africa," *Journal of Modern African Studies*, vol. 31 (September 1993), pp. 535–39.

48. John R. Heilbrunn, "Social Origins of National Conferences in Benin and Togo," *Journal of Modern African Studies*, vol. 31 (June 1993), pp. 277–99.

49. "Nigeria: Austerity Reaches Its Limits," *Africa Confidential*, vol. 29 (January 8, 1988), pp. 1–2; and "The IMF and the World Bank: Arguing about Africa," *Africa Confidential*, vol. 34 (October 8, 1993), pp. 1–4.

50. Joan Nelson, "Poverty, Equity, and the Politics of Adjustment," in Stephan Haggard and Robert R. Kaufman, eds., *The Politics of Economic Adjustment: International Constraints, Distributive Conflicts, and the State* (Princeton University Press, 1992).

51. Speech to the House of Commons, November 1947; and Lewis D. Eigen and Johnathan P. Siegal, *The Macmillian Dictionary of Political Quotations* (Macmillian, 1993), p. 109.

52. I. William Zartman, "The Conduct of Political Reform: The Path toward Democracy," in Zartman, ed., *Tunisia: The Political Economy of Reform* (Lynne Rienner, 1991).

53. The national conference also draws on French history in the *états généraux* of 1788, but the African experience is closer at hand. The culminating national conference in the series was outside the Western African region, the Conference for a Democratic South Africa (CoDeSA) and its variant forms, be-

tween 1991 and 1994. See William Miles, "Tragic Tradeoffs: Democracy and Security in Chad," *Journal of Modern African Studies*, vol. 33 (March 1995), pp. 277–300; Heilbrunn, "Social Origins of National Conferences in Benin and Togo," *Journal of Modern African Studies*; and F. Eboussi Boulaga, *Les conférences nationales en Afrique Noire* (Paris: Karthala, 1993); Nicolas van de Walle, "Economic Reform and the Consolidation of Democratic Rule," in Marina Ottaway, ed., *Democratization in Africa* (Lynne Rienner, 1976).

54. Barrington Moore, *Social Origins of Dicatatorship and Democracy: Lord and Peasant in the Making of the Modern World* (Beacon, 1996); and Samuel P. Huntington, *Political Order in Changing Societies* (Yale University Press, 1968).

55. A Nigerian politician in the 1990s was heard to remark, "Just give me a year as Transport Minister, and I and my children will be set up for the rest of our lives."

56. Joan Nelson, ed., *Economic Crisis and Policy Choice: The Politics of Adjustment in Developing Countries* (Princeton University Press, 1990).

57. Saadia Touval and I. William Zartman, eds., *International Mediation in Theory and Practice* (Westview Press, 1985).

58. Mohammed Beshir, "The African Debate: Democratization and Conditionality" (Washington: Woodrow Wilson International Center 1993); and Adebayo Adedeji, ed., *Africa within the World: Beyond Dispossession and Dependence* (London: Zed, 1993).

## Chapter Three

1. See Hermann Baumann and D. Westermann, *Les Peuples et les civilisations de l'Afrique* (Paris: Payot, 1957); Maurice Delafosse, *Vocabulaires comparatifs de plus de soixante langues et dialectes parlés en Côte d'Ivoire et dans les régions limitrophes* (Paris: Editions Leroux, 1904); J. N. Loucou, "Histoire de la Côte d'Ivoire," *Le Peuplement*, vol. 1 (Abidjan: CEDA, 1979); Gabriel Rougerie, *La Côte d'Ivoire, Que-sais-je?* no. 1137 (Paris: Presses Universitaires de France, 1967); Michael A. Cohen, "Urban Policy and the Decline of the Machine: Cross-Ethnic Politics in the Ivory Coast," *Journal of Developing Area*, vol. 8 (January 1974), pp. 227– 234; Aristide R. Zolberg, *One-Party Government in the Ivory Coast* (Princeton University Press, 1964); and Albert Sarraut, *La mise en valeur des colonies françaises* (Paris: Payot, 1923).

2. Daniel Gaxie, "Economie des partis et rétributions du militantisme," *Revue française de science politique*, vol. 27, no. 1 (1977), pp. 123–54.

3. C. Legum, "The Coming of Africa's Second Independence," *Third World Quarterly*, vol. 13 (Winter 1990).

4. Zolberg, *One-Party Government*; and Samir Amin, *Le développement du capitalisme en Côte d'Ivoire* (Paris: Les Editions de Minuit, 1967).

5. Jean-Pierre Chauveau and Jean Pierre Dozon, "Au Coeur des ethnies ivoiriennes . . . L'Etat," in Emmanuel Terrey, ed., *L'Etat contemporain en Afrique* (Paris: L'Harmattan, 1987), pp. 221–96; and Jean-Pierre Chauveau and Jean Pierre Dozon, "Ethnies et Etat en Côte d'Ivoire," *Revue française de science politique*, vol. 38, no. 5 (1988), pp. 732–47.

6. Seymour Martin Lipset and Stein Rokkan, eds., *Party Systems and Voter Alignments: Cross-National Perspectives* (Free Press, 1967), pp. 1–64, especially pp. 47, 50; and Gabriel A. Almond, Scott C. Flanagan, and Robert J. Mundt, eds., *Crises, Choice and Change: Historical Studies of Political Development* (Little, Brown and Company, 1973), pp. 1–102.

7. Jean Elleinstein, "Les Années ethniques," *Cosmopolitiques*, no. 19 (June 1991), p. 17.

8. Ekkart Zimmerman, "Crises and Crises Outcomes: Towards a new Synthetic Approach," *European Journal of Political Research*, vol. 7, no. 1 (1979), pp. 67–115.

9. Delafosse, *Vocabulaires comparatifs*.

10. Chauveau and Dozon, "Ethnies et Etat en Côte d'Ivoire"; Jean-Pierre Dozon, "Les Bété: une création coloniale," in Jean-Loup Amselle and Elikia M'Bokolo, eds., *Au Coeur de l'ethnie: ethnies, tribalisme et Etat en Afrique* (Paris: Editions La Decouverte, 1985); and Jean-Pierre Dozon, *La Société Bété: Histoires d'une "ethnie" de Côte d'Ivoire* (Paris: Editions de l'OSTROM, 1985).

11. F. J. Amon d'Aby, *La Côte d'Ivoire dans la cité africaine* (Paris: Larose, 1951); Jean Pierre Chauveau, "Economie de plantation et nouveaux milieux sociaux: Essai d'analyse comparative et historique à partir d'observations en pays Gban et Baoulé," *Cahiers de l'OSTROM*, série Sciences Humaines, vol. 16, nos. 1–2 (1979) pp. 59–82; Zolberg, *One-Pary Government*; and Chauveau and Dozon, "Colonisation, économie de plantation et société civile," *Cahiers de l'OSTROM*, série Sciences Humaines, vol. 21, no. 1 (1985), pp. 63–80; Jean Pierre Dozon, "Economie marchande et structures sociales: Le cas des Bété de Côte d'Ivoire," *Cahiers d'Etudes Africaines*, vol. 68, no. 17 (1977), pp. 463–84; and Jean Pierre Chauveau, "Agricultural Production and Social Formation: The Baule Region of Toumodikokumbo in Historical Perspective," in Martin A. Klein, ed., *Peasants in Africa* (Sage Publications, 1980), pp. 143–76.

12. Maddox J. Toungara, "The Apotheosis of Côte d'Ivoire's Nana Houphouët-Boigny," *Journal of Modern African Studies*, vol. 28, no. 1 (1990), pp. 23–54.

13. Amon d'Aby, *La Côte d'Ivoire*; Marcel Amondji, *Félix Houphouët et la Côte d'Ivoire: L'Envers d'une legende* (Paris: Karthala, 1984); Mercel Amondji, *Côte d'Ivoire, Le PDCI et la vie politique de 1944 à 1985* (Paris: L'Hartmattan, 1986); Philip J. Foster and Aristide Zolberg, eds., *Ghana and the Ivory Coast: Perspectives on Modernization* (University of Chicagao Press, 1971); Immanual Maurice Wallerstein, *The Road to Independence: Ghana and the Ivory Coast* (The Hague: Mouton, 1964); Zolberg, *One-Party Government*; J. N. Loucou, "Les premières élections de 1945 en Côte d'Ivoire," *Annales de l'Université d'Abidjan*, vol. 5, no. 1, série Histoire (1976), pp. 5–33.

14. Rougerie, *La Côte d'Ivoire*, p. 63.

15. Essy N'Gatta, "Le phénomène ethnique dans la vie politque en Côte d'Ivoire Mémoire," DES de Science Politique (Strasbourg, 1970), p. 4.

16. Zolberg, *One-Party Government*, p. 74.

17. R. L. Heilbronner, "Societies and Change," *New Republic*, July 13, 1968, pp. 27–28.

18. E. Dunglas, "Coutumes et moeurs des Bété," *Coutumiers juridiques de l'Afrique Occidentale Française*, no. 3 (1939), pp. 7–237; and Denise Paulme, *Une Société de Côte d'Ivoire hier et aujourd'hui: Les Bété* (Paris: Mouton, 1962).

19. Dozon, "Au Coeur de l'ethnie."

20. Barrington Moore, *The Social Origins of Dictatorship and Democracy: Lord and Peasant in the Making of the Modern World* (Beacon Press, 1966), pp. 413–14.

21. Jean Pierre Chauveau, *Bodiba en Côte d'Ivoire: du Terroir à l'Etat, petite production paysanne et salariat agricole dans un village Gban* (Abidjan: OSTROM, 1977); Chauveau, "Economie de plantation et nouveaux milieux sociaux"; Chauvaeu, "La part Baule, effectif de population et domination ethnique: Une perspective historique," *Cahiers d'études africaines*, vol. 27, no. 1–2 (1987), pp. 122–59; Chauveau, "Agricultural Production and Social Formation"; Jean-Marc Gastellu, *Une économie du trésor: Les grands planteurs du Moronou, I et II* (Abidjan: Centre OSTROM de Petit-Bassam, 1980); Chauveau and Dozon, "Colonisation, économie de plantation et société civile"; Marguerite Dupire, "Planteurs autochtones et étrangers en Basse-Côte d'Ivoire orientale," *Etudes Eburnéennes*, vol. 8 (1960), pp. 7–237; Herbert Fréchou, "Les Plantations européennes en Côte d'Ivoire," *Cahiers d'Outre-Mer*, no. 29 (January–March, 1955); A. J. F. Köbben, "Le Planteur noir: Essai d'une ethnographie d'aspect," *Etudes Eburnéennes*, vol. 5 (1956), pp. 7–190; Henri Raulin, *Mission d'étude des groupements immigrés en Côte d'Ivoire* (Paris: Office de la Recherche Scientifique et Technique Outre-Mer, 1957); Rougerie, *La Côte d'Ivoire*; Timothy C. Weiskel, "Labor in the Emergent Periphery: From Slavery to Migrant Labor among the Baule Peoples," in Walter L. Goldfrank, ed., *The World-System of Capitalism: Past and Present* (Sage Publications, 1979), and Yapi S. Affou, *Le grand planteur villageois dans le procès de valorisation du capital social: Une introduction à l'organisation socio-économique Akyé* (Abidjan: OSTROM, Centre de Petit-Bassam, 1979).

22. Ruth Berins Collier and David Collier, *Shaping the Political Arena: Critical Junctures, the Labor Movement and Regime Dynamics in Latin America* (Princeton University Press, 1991), p. 29.

23. Wallerstein, *The Road to Independence*; Zolberg, *One-Party Government*; and Marie-Therese Aissata Bocoum, "La naissance d'une élite nouvelle en Côte d'Ivoire: Premier quart du xxe siècle," Mémoire maîtrise d'histoire (Aix-en-Provence, 1973).

24. Ruth Schachter Morgenthau, *Political Parties in French-Speaking Africa* (Oxford University Press, 1964) pp. 166–218; Zolberg, *One-Party Government*; and Loucou, "Les premières élections de 1945."

25. Samir Amin, *Le développement du capitalisme en Côte d'Ivoire* (Paris: Editions de Minuit, 1967).

26. Sarraut, *La mise en valeur*, 1923.

27. Gastellu, *Une économie du trésor*; Chauveau, "Economie de plantation"; Chauveau and Dozon, "Colonisation, économie de plantation"; Chauveau and Dozon, "Ethnies et Etat en Côte d'Ivoire"; Dozon, "Les Bété une création coloniale"; Dozon, "La Société Bété"; and Dozon, "Economie marchande et structures sociales."

28. Amin, *Le développement du capitalisme*.

29. P. Boiral, J. F. Laterni, and J. P. Olivier de Sardan, eds., *Paysans, experts et chercheurs en Afrique Noire* (Paris: CIFACE, Karthala, 1985), p. 27.

30. Marie Francois Joseph Clozel and Roger Villamur, *Les Coutumes indigènes de la Côte d'Ivoire* (Paris: Challamel, 1902); Marie Francois Joseph Clozel, "The Agni Race of the Ivory Coast and Land Tenure," *Journal of the African Society*, vol. 1 (1902), pp. 299–415; Gastellu, *Une Economie du trésor*; Rougerie, *La Côte d'Ivoire*, Roger Villamur and Maurice Delafosse, *Les Coutumes Agni rédigées et codifiées d'après les documents officiels les plus récents* (Paris: Challamel, 1904); and d'Aby, *La Côte d'Ivoire dans la cité africaine*.

31. Dozon, "Au Coeur de l'ethnie"; Dozon, *La Société Bété*; Dunglas, "Coutumes et moeurs des Bété"; and Paulme, *Une Société de Côte d'Ivoire*.

32. Jean-Pierre Chauveau, "La part Baule, Effectif de population et domination ethnique: une perspective historique," *Cahiers d'études africaines*, vol. 27, no. 1–2 (1987).

33. Gastellu, *Une Economie du trésor*; N. N'Zi, "L'évolution des revenus engendrés par les exportations de café en Côte d'Ivoire," Mémoire (D.E.A., Economie du développement, Université de Paris, 1978); and Bocoum, "La naissance d'une élite."

34. Jean Pierre Dozon, "L'anthropologie politique aujourd'hui: De deux ou trois choses dont est fait l'Etat ivorien," *Communication présentée au colloque de l'Association française de science politique*, May 29–30, 1986, p. 10.

35. Dozon, *La société Bété*, pp. 276–305.

36. Dozon, "L'anthropologie politique aujourd'hui," p. 11.

37. P. Etienne and M. Etienne, "L'émigration Baoulé actuelle," *Cahiers d'Outre-mer*, vol. 21, no. 82 (1968), pp. 155–95.

38. Dozon, "L'anthropologie politique aujourd'hui," p. 12.

39. See Zolberg, *One-Party Government*, p. 25; and Morgenthau, *Political Parties in French-Speaking Africa*, p. 169.

40. C. H. Pérrot, *Les Ani-Ndenye et le pouvoir aux xviiie et xixe siècles en Côte d'Ivoire* (Paris: Editions de la Sorbonne, 1982), pp. 187–210.

41. Zolberg, *One-Party Government*, p. 151.

42. Amondji, *Félix Houphouët et la Côte d'Ivoire*; Amondji, *Côte d'Ivoire, Le PDCI et la vie politique*; Amondji, *Côte d'Ivoire, La dépendence et l'épreuve des faits* (Paris: L'Harmattan, 1988); Jaques Baulin, *La politique intérieure d'Houphouët-Boigny* (Paris: Eurafor Press, 1982); Jaques Baulin, *La succession d'Houphouët-Boigny* (Paris: Eurafor Press, 1989); Laurent Gbagbo, *Côte d'Ivoire: Economie et société à la veille de l'indépendance, 1940–1960* (Paris, L'Harmattan, 1982); and Laurent Gbagbo, *Pour une alternative démocratique* (Paris: L'Harmattan, 1983). See also Tessy D. Bakary, "L'ouverture pluraliste sans effet," *Journal des Elections*, no. 16 (January–February 1991), pp. 51–53; Tessy D. Bakary, "Le retour au pluralisme politique en Côte d'Ivoire," *Année Africaine* (1990–91), pp. 161–89; Richard C. Crook, "Les changements politiques en Côte d'Ivoire: une approche institutionelle," *Année Africaine*, (1990–91), pp. 87–114; Yves A. Flauré, "Sur la démocratisation en Côte d'Ivoire: Passé et présent," *Année Africaine* (1990–91), pp. 115–160; Jennifer Anne Widner, "The 1990 Elections in Côte d'Ivoire," *Issue: A Journal of Opinion*, vol. 20, no. 1 (1991–92), pp. 31–40; and K. A. Cissé, "Le

Comportement électoral en Côte d'Ivoire," thèse 3e cycle sociologie (Abidjan: Institut d'Ethno-sociologie, 1984).

43. A good example can be found in Mali where it seems like the US-RDA could not exist without its old rival of the 1940s, the PSP. Moreover, it is striking that the US-RDA was "exhumed" with its old steering committee of the 1960s and the surviving members still split in the two former factions, the radicals around Madeira Keita, former ideologue and interior minister, and the conservatives with Seydou Badian Kouyate. The fact that US-RDA supported two different candidates during the presidential elections (Tiéoulé Mamadou Konate, son of Mamadou Konate, for the "conservatives" and Baba Akhib Haidara for the "radicals") is a good indication of the pervasiveness of the former political cleavages.

44. Gabriel Louis Angoulvant, *La Pacification de la Côte d'Ivoire, 1908–1915: Méthodes et résultats* (Paris: Editions Larousse, 1916).

45. Chauveau and Dozon, "Au Coeur des ethnies ivoirennes," p. 152.

46. R. Joseph, "Class, State and Prebendal Politics in Nigeria," *Journal of Commonwealth and Comparative Studies*, vol. 21, no. 3 (1983), pp. 21–38; and R. Joseph, "Nigeria, the Unfinished State" (London: SOAS, June 1987).

47. Michael Lipsky, "Protest as a Political Resource," *American Political Science Review*, vol. 62 (1968), pp. 1144–58; and Peter K. Eisenger, "The Conditions of Protest Behavior in American Cities," *American Political Science Review*, vol. 67 (1973), pp. 11–28.

48. Cohen, *Urban Policy*, pp. 67–182, 57–66.

49. Ibid.

50. Tessy D. Bakary, "Elite Transformation and Political Succession," in I. William Zartman and Christopher Delgado., eds, *The Political Economy of the Ivory Coast* (Praeger, 1984), pp. 21–55; and Tessy D. Bakary, "Les élites politiques en Côte d'Ivoire: Modernisation du système politique ou formation d'une classe dirigeante," thèse de doctorat d'Etat en science politique (Université Paris Nanterre, 1983); and Bocoum, *La naissance d'une élite.*

51. Baulin, *La politique intérieure d'Houphouët-Boigny*; and Gbagbo, *Côte d'Ivoire.*

52. Basil Davidson, *Black Star: A View of the Life and Times of Kwame Nkrumah* (Praeger, 1973).

53. Ayi Kwei Armah, *The Beautiful Ones Are Not Yet Born* (London: Heinemann Educational Books, 1968); and Bernard Benin Dadie, *Monsieur Thogo-Gnini* (Paris: Présence Africaine, 1970).

54. Naomi Chazan, "African Voters at the Polls: A Re-examination of the Role of Elections in African Politics," *Journal of Commonwealth and Comparative Politics*, vol 17, no. 2 (1979), pp. 136–58; R. Rathbone, "Businessmen in Politics: Party Struggle in Ghana, 1947–1957," *Journal of Development Studies*, vol. 9, no. 3 (1973), pp. 391–402.

55. D'Aby, *La Côte d'Ivoire*, pp. 55–57; Morgenthau, *Political Parties in French-Speaking Africa*; and T. Hodgkin, *Nationalism in Colonial Africa* (New York University Press, 1957).

56. D'Aby, *La Côte d'Ivoire*, p. 56.

57. D'Aby, *La Côte d'Ivoire*, pp. 31–56; Zolberg, *One-Party Government*, pp. 62– 68; Wallerstein, *The Road to Independence*, pp. 85–134; and T. Hodgkin, *African Political Parties* (Middlesex, England: Penguin Books, 1961), pp. 84–92.

58. Jean Noël Loucou, *Le Multipartisme en Côte d'Ivoire* (Abidjan: Editions Neter, 1992), pp. 27–78.

59. Zolberg, *One-Party Government*, p. 49.

60. Reinhard Bendix, *Nation-building and Citizenships: Studies of Our Changing Social Order* (Wiley, 1964); Leonard Binder and others, *Crises and Sequences in Political Development* (Princeton University Press, 1971); Cyril Edwin Black, *The Dynamics of Modernization: A Study in Comparative History* (Harper and Row, 1967); Kitson George Sidney Roberts Clark, *The Making of Victorian England* (Atheneum, 1976); Samuel Noah Eisenstadt, "Modernization and Conditions of Sustained Growth," *World Politics*, vol. 16 (July 1964), pp. 576–94; Samuel P. Huntington and Joan M. Nelson, *No Easy Choice: Political Participation in Developing Countries* (London: Harvard University Press, 1976); Samuel Huntington, *Political Order in Changing Societies* (Yale University Press, 1968); Thomas Humphrey Marshall, *Class, Citizenship, and Social Development: Essays* (Anchor Books, 1965); Stein Rokkan and others, *Citizens, Elections, Parties: Approaches to the Comparative Study of the Processes of Development* (McKay, 1970); Elmer Eric Schattschneider, *Party Government* (Holt, Rinehart and Winston, 1942).

61. Ruth Berins Collier, *Regimes in Tropical Africa: Changing Forms of Supremacy, 1945–1975* (University of California Press, 1982).

62. Ibid., p. 67.

63. D'Aby, *La Côte d'Ivoire*; see also Zolberg, *One-Party Government*, pp. 106–215; Zolberg, "Politics in the Ivory Coast," part 1: "The Heterogeneous Monolith," part 2: "The 1959 Election and After," part 3; "The Machine at Work," *West Africa* (July 30, August 6, August 20, 1960), pp. 847, 883, 939.

64. T. Weiskel, "Independence and the Longue Duree," in P. Gifford and W. M. Roger Louis, eds., *Decolonization and African Independence* (Yale University Press, 1988), p. 365.

65. Foster and Zolberg, *Ghana and the Ivory Coast.*

66. Loucou, *Le Multipartisme en Côte d'Ivoire*; Zolberg, *One-Party Government*, pp. 106–215; and Zolberg, "Politics in the Ivory Coast," parts 1, 2, 3.

67. Lipset and Rokkan, *Party Systems and Voter Alignments*, p. 1.

68. Amondji, *Félix Houphouët et la Côte d'Ivoire*; Morgenthau, *Political Parties in French-Speaking Africa*; and Zolberg, *One-Party Government.*

69. Dozon, "Les Bété."

70. Zolberg, *One-Party Government*, pp. 121–46.

71. Ibid., pp. 184–98.

72. Morgenthau, *Political Parties in French-Speaking Africa*, pp. 188–202.

73. Zolberg, *One-Party Government*, pp. 149–82.

74. Ibid., pp. 183–215.

75. Moussa Cherif, "Le Rassemblement Démocratique Africain et les questions fondamentales de l'apparentement et du désapparentement," Mémoire, DEA, Études politiques (Université de Paris 10, 1978).

76. Collier, *Regimes in Tropical Africa*; Amondji, *Félix Houphouët et la Côte*

*d'Ivoire*; Morgenthau, *Political Parties in French-Speaking Africa*; Zolberg, *One-Party Government*, pp. 81–146 and 188–218; and Zolberg, "Politics in the Ivory Coast," parts 1, 2, 3; and Francis Wodié, "La vie politique en Côte d'Ivoire de 1945 à 1969," *Revue Algérienne de Sciences Juridiques, Politiques et Economiques*, vol. 6, no. 3 (1969), pp. 822–42.

77. L. Pye, "The Non-Western Political Process," in Harry Eckstein and David E. Apter, eds., *Comparative Politics* (Free Press of Glencoe, 1963).

78. Baulin, *La politique intérieure d'Houphouët-Boigny*, pp. 99–110; and Gbagbo, *Pour une alternative démocratique*, pp. 26–28.

79. Gbagbo, *Côte d'Ivoire*, pp. 169–72.

80. Jacques Baulin, *La politique africaine d'Houphouët-Boigny* (Paris: Editions Eurafor-Presses, 1980), pp. 19–46; Gbagbo, *Pour une alternative démocratique*, pp. 69–82; Zolberg, *One-Party Government*, pp. 289–94; and William Zartman, *International Relations in the New Africa* (University Press of America, 1987), pp. 24, 53, 96, 98, 113.

81. Amondji, *Félix Houphouët et la Côte d'Ivoire*, pp. 181–217; and Baulin, *La politique intérieure d'Houphouët-Boigny*, pp. 115–46.

82. Flanagan, "Models and Methods of Analysis," p. 48.

83. Loucou, *Le multipartisme en Côte d'Ivoire*, pp. 119–22.

84. Ibid. pp. 117–18.

85. Foster and Zolberg, 1971, *Ghana and the Ivory Coast*, p. 13.

86. Aristide Zolberg, "The Structure of Political Conflict in the New States of Tropical Africa," *American Political Science Review*, vol. 62, no. 1 (1968), p. 76.

87. Zolberg, *One-Party Government*, pp. 285–320.

88. J. Lacam, "Le politicien investisseur," *Revue Française de Science Politique*, vol. 38, no. 1 (1988). See also a review, published in Paris, discussed by Jacques Baulin, *Peuples Noirs, Peuples Africains*.

89. Claude Isaac Salem, "Pluralism in the Ivory Coast: The Persistence of Ethnic Identities in a One-Party State," Ph.D. dissertation (Los Angeles: University of California, 1975); R. D. Tice, "Administrative Structure, Ethnicity and Nation-Building in the Ivory Coast, *Journal of Modern African Studies*, vol. 12, no. 2 (1974), pp. 211–29.

90. Catherine Aubertin, *Histoire et création d'une région sous-développée: le nord ivoirien*, vol. 19 (Paris: OSTROM, 1983), pp. 23–57; and Catherine Aubertin, *Le programme sucrier ivoirien: Une industrialisation régionale volontariste* (Paris: OSTROM, 1983).

91. Baulin, *La politique intérieure d'Houphouët-Boigny*, pp. 116–34.

92. Howard W. Wriggins, *The Ruler's Imperative: Strategies for Political Survival in Asia and Africa* (Columbia University Press, 1969); Baulin, *La politique intérieure d'Houphouët-Boigny*; Bakary, "L'ouverture pluraliste"; Bakary, "Le retour au pluralisme politique." The following publications are all by Tessy D. Bakary: "Les élites politiques en Côte d'Ivoire: Modernisation du système politique ou formation d'une classe dirigeante," thèse de doctorat d'Etat en science politique (Nanterre: Université de Paris, 1983); "Elite Transformation and Political Succession"; "Les élections législatives ivoiriennes de novembre 1980 et le système politique: essai d'analyse des comportements électoraux," *Travaux et documents*,

no. 8 (Bordeaux: Centre d'Etudes d'Afrique noire, 1985); "Côte d'Ivoire: logiques du recrutement politique et éventuels changements à la tête de l'Etat, *Le Mois en Afrique*, nos. 237–238 (October–November 1985), pp. 3–32; "Le rôle du statut social des candidats dans les élections législatives ivoirennes de novembre 1980," *Le Mois en Afrique*, nos. 245–246 (June–July 1986), pp. 142–571; "La démocratie par le haut en Côte d'Ivoire," *Géopolitique Africaine*, Ière partie (June 1986), pp. 205–30; IIe partie (October 1986), pp. 71–103; and N. Leconte, "L'après Houphouët-Boigny (Paris: Nord-Sud Export Consultants, 1989).

93. Bakary, "L'ouverture pluraliste"; Bakary, "Le retour au pluralisme politique."

94. Baulin, *La politique intérieure d'Houphouët-Boigny*, pp. 116–34.

95. J. Kolela, "Les difficultés de l'ivoirisation," *L'Economiste du Tiers-Monde* (June 1979), pp. 14–16; M. Penouil, "Le Miracle ivoirien ou l'application réaliste de théories irréalistes," *Année Africaine* (1971), pp. 321–48; A. Valette, "Résultats et réflexions sur une étude empirique d'industrialisation de la Côte d'Ivoire," *Cahiers de l'OSTROM*, série Sciences Humaines, nos. 1–2 (1980), pp. 45–66.

96. Amin, *Le développement du capitalisme*; B. A. Tuinder, *Ivory Coast: The Challenge of Success: A World Book Country Report* (Johns Hopkins University Press, 1978); and Bonnie K. Campbell, "Social Change and Class Formation in a French West African State," *Canadian Journal of African Studies*, no. 2 (1976), pp. 285–306.

97. Bakary, "L'ouverture pluraliste."

98. Moustapha Diabaté, "Le Modèle ivoirien du développement," *Annales de l'Université d'Abidjan* (Abidjan: Institut d'ethno-sociologie de l'Université d'Abidjan, 1973).

99. Diabaté, "Le Modèle ivoirien du développement"; E. J. Berg, "Structural Transformation versus Gradualism: Recent Economic Development in Ghana and the Ivory Coast," in Foster and Zolberg, *Ghana and the Ivory Coast*.

100. A. Rouze, "L'avenir de la Côte d'Ivoire n'est pas menacé," *Africa* (April 1980), pp. 23–25.

101. Rouze, "Le prix d'un étudiant ivoirien," *Africa* (April 1981), pp. 25–28.

102. Benin, Burkina Faso, Guinea, Mali, Togo, and others.

103. Paul N'Da, *Les intellectuels et le pouvoir en Afrique noire* (Paris: L'Harmattan, 1987), pp. 110–22.

104. D. Woods, "State Action and Class Interests in the Ivory Coast," *African Studies Review*, vol. 31, no. 1 (1988), pp. 93–116.

105. Amin, *Le développement du capitalisme*; Amondji, *Félix Houphouët et la Côte d'Ivoire*; Amondji, *Côte d'Ivoire, La dépendance et l'épreuve des faits*; Yves A. Fauré and J. F. Ménard, *Etat et bourgeoisie en Côte d'Ivoire* (Paris: Karthala, 1982); N'Da, *Les Intellectuels et le pouvoir en Afrique Noire*; Gbagbo, *Pour une alternative démocratique*; Abdou Touré, "Paysans et fonctionnaires devant la culture et l'Etat," in Yves A. Fauré and J. F. Ménard, *Etat et bourgeoisie en Côte d'Ivoire* (Paris: Karthala, 1982); Claudine Vidal, *Sociologie des passions: Côte d'Ivoire, Rwanda* (Paris: Karthala, 1991); I. William Zartman and Christopher Delgado, *The Political Economy of the Ivory Coast* (Praeger, 1984); Bonnie K. Campbell, "The Social, Political, and Economic Consequences of French Private Investment in

the Ivory Coast, 1960–1970," Ph. D. thesis (University of Sussex, 1974); Bonnie K. Campbell, "Neo-Colonialism, Economic Dependence and Political Change: A Case Study of Cotton and Textile Production in the Ivory Coast, 1960–1979," *Review of African Political Economy*, no. 2 (1975), pp. 36–53; Bonnie K. Campbell, "Ivory Coast," in T. Dunn, ed., *West African States: Failure and Promise* (Cambridge: Cambridge University Press, 1978), pp. 66–116.

106. Cohen, *Urban Policy*.

107. Amin, *Le développement du capitalisme*. The literature does not reveal fundamental long-term and short-term domestic changes affecting the political system and thus the structure and composition of political demands and the distribution of political resources. After Samir Amin's seminal work, the contrasting views in the literature over the Ivorian economic achievements—"miracle" or "mirage"—point out the permanence of Ivorian social formation.

108. Bakary, *Les élites politiques en Côte d'Ivoire*; Bakary, "Les élections législatives ivoiriennes"; Bocoum, "La naissance d'une élite"; and Campbell, "Ivory Coast."

109. Cohen, *Urban Policy*; Fauré and J. F. Ménard, *Etat et bourgeoisie en Côte d'Ivoire*; Yves Fauré, "La Côte d'Ivoire à la Côte d'alerte," *Politique Africaine*, vol. 9 (March 1983), pp. 140–43; and Aristide R. Zolberg, "La Redécouverte de la Côte d'Ivoire," *Politique Africaine*, vol. 9 (March 1983), pp. 118–31; Campbell, "Ivory Coast"; Bonnie K. Campbell, "Le débat sur la dépendance: À quand un renouveau?" *Politique Africaine*, no. 9 (March 1983), pp. 131–39; Baulin, *La politique intérieure d'Houphouët-Boigny*; and Woods, "State Action and Class Interests."

110. Bakary, "Elite Transformation and Political Succession"; and Bakary, "Les élites politiques en Côte d' Ivoire."

111. Vidal, *Sociologie des passions*.

112. Touré, "Paysans et fonctionnaires devant la culture et l'Etat"; J. M. Gibbal, *Citadins et Villageois dans la ville Africaine* (Paris: Maspéro, 1974).

113. Ronald Inglehart, "Value, Priorities, and Socio-economic Change," in Samuel H. Barnes, Max Kaase, and Klause R. Allerback and others, eds., *Political Action: Mass Participation in Five Western Democracies* (Sage Publications, 1979), pp. 305–42; and Ronald Inglehart, "Value Change in Industrial Societies," *American Political Science Review*, no. 81 (1987), pp. 1290–1303; and Ronald Inglehart, *Culture Shift in Advanced Industrial Society* (Princeton University Press, 1990).

114. "Attiéké poisson" is a local and cheap meal known throughout the country and in many neighbor states.

115. Fred Hirsch, *Social Limits to Growth* (London: Harvard University Press, 1976); and Mancur Olson, *The Rise and Decline of Nations: Economic Growth, Stagnation, and Social Rigidities* (Yale University Press, 1982).

116. Flanagan, "Models and Methods of Analysis," p. 48.

117. Eisenger, *The Conditions of Protest Behavior*; Doug McAdam, *Political Process and the Development of Black Insurgency, 1930–1970* (University of Chicago Press, 1982); Lipsky, "Protest as a Political Resource"; Francis Fox Piven and Richard A. Coward *Poor People's Movements: Why They Succeed, How They Fail*

(Vintage Books, 1977); Sidney G. Tarrow, *Struggle, Politics, and Reform: Collective Action, Social Movements and Cycles of Protest,* Western Societies Program Occasional Paper 21 (Cornell University, 1989); Charles Tilly, *From Mobilization to Revolution* (McGraw-Hill, 1978); H. P. Kitschelt, "Political Opportunity Structures and Political Protest: Anti-Nuclear Movements in Four Democracies," *British Journal of Political Science,* vol. 16, no.1–34 (1986), pp. 58–85; and J. Jenkins and M. Perrow, "Insurgencies of the Powerless: Farm Worker Movements, 1946–1972," *American Sociological Review,* no. 42 (1977), pp. 249–68.

118. Abdou Touré, "Paysans et fonctionnaires devant la culture et l'Etat," in Fauré and Médard, *Etat et bourgeoise,* pp. 231–51.

119. J. C. Davies, "Toward a Theory of Revolution," *American Sociological Review,* no. 27 (1962), pp. 5–19.

120. George Blankensten, "Transference of Social and Political Loyalties," in B. Hoselitz and W. Morre, *Industrialization and Society* (UNESCO, 1963), p. 184, quoted in Anthony R. Oberschall, "Rising Expectations and Political Turmoil, *Journal of Development Studies,* vol. 6 (October 1969), p. 5.

121. Flanagan, "Models and Methods of Analysis," p. 55.

122. Cohen, *Urban Policy.*

123. Flanagan, "Models and Methods of Analysis," p. 55.

124. Olson, *The Rise and Decline of Nations,* p. 44.

125. Christopher Clapham, ed., *Private Patronage and Public Power: Political Clientelism in the Modern State* (St. Martin's Press, 1982); Jean François Médard, "L' Etat sous-développé en Afrique noire: clientélisme politique ou néo-patrimonialisme?" *Travaux et documents,* no. 1 (Bordeaux: Centre d'études d'Afrique noire, Institut d'études politiques de Bordeaux, 1982).

126. Olson, *The Rise and Decline of Nations.*

127. Hirsch, *Social Limits to Growth.*

128. Foster and Zolberg, eds., *Ghana and the Ivory Coast,* pp. 12–15.

129. M. Crozier, *On ne change pas la société par décret* (Paris: Grasset, 1979).

130. Bakary, "Le rôle du statut social"; Bakary, "La démocratique différée"; Bakary, "Côte d'Ivoire"; and Cissé, *Le comportement électoral.*

131. Amondji, *Felix Houphouët et la Côte d'Ivoire*; Gbagbo, *Pour une alternative démocratique* (Paris: L'Harmattan, 1983); Lionel Cliffe, ed., *One-Party Democracy: The 1965 Tanzanian General Elections* (Nairobi: East African Publishing House, 1967); John S. Saul, "The Nature of Tanzania's Political System: Issues Raised by the 1965 and 1970 Elections," part 1, *Journal of Commonwealth Political Studies,* vol. 10 (July 1972), pp. 113–29, and part 2 (November 1972), pp. 198–242; Joel Barkan, "Legislators, Elections, and Political Linkages," in Joel Barkan and John J. Okumu, eds., *Politics and Public Policy in Kenya and Tanzania* (Praeger, 1979), pp. 64–92; and Joel Barkan and John J. Okumu, "Patrons, machines et élections au Kénya," in Centre d'études d'Afrique Noire/CERI, *Aux Urnes l'Afrique! Elections et pouvoirs en Afrique noire* (Paris: Pedone, 1978), pp. 119–47.

132. Barkan, "Legislators, Elections, and Political Linkages"; R. H. Jackson and C. G. Rosberg, "Popular Legitimacy in African Multi-ethnic States," *Journal of Modern African Studies,* vol. 22, no. 2 (1984), pp. 177–98.

133. C. Offe, "Challenging the Boundaries of Institutional Politics: Social

Movements since the 1960s," in Charles S. Maier, ed., *Changing Boundaries of the Political: Essays on the Evolving Balance between the State and Society, Public and Private in Europe* (N.Y.: Cambridge University Press, 1987).

134. Flanagan, "Models and Methods of Analysis," p. 48.

135. A. Przeworski, "Democracy as a Contingent Outcome of Conflicts," in J. Elster and R. Slagstad, eds., *Constitutionalism and Democracy* (Cambridge: Cambridge University Press, 1988).

136. Amin, *Le développement du capitalisme*.

137. Hughes and May, "The Politics of Succession in Black Africa," *Third World Quarterly*, vol. 10, no. 1 (1988), p. 122.

138. One opposition leader has said that the president blocked many political processes, especially democratization, and suggested that the passing of the president will have an important impact on subregional politics.

139. One of the first Kru leaders (Southwest) to join Houphouët-Boigny in the 1940s at the creation of the PDCI.

140. He resigned in 1993, after being involved in a financial scandal revealed by an opposition newspaper.

141. Chauveau, "La part Baule."

142. It could be interesting at this point to put forward similarities and differences with Kenya, for instance, the political sources of social mobility within the Kikuyu, and to know to what extent Daniel arap Moi has succeeded in eroding Kikuyu's social and economic positions acquired during Jomo Kenyatta's presidency.

143. Collier and Collier, *Shaping the Political Arena*, p. 31.

## Chapter Four

1. Naomi Chazan, *An Anatomy of Ghanaian Politics: Managing Political Recession, 1969–1982* (Westview, 1983), p. 15.

2. Donald Rothchild, "Ghana and Structural Adjustment: An Overview," in Rothchild, ed., *Ghana: The Political Economy of Recovery* (Lynne Rienner, 1991), p. 15.

3. Chazan, *An Anatomy of Ghanaian Politics*, p. 4.

4. For details of the independence struggle and its aftermath see A. A. Boahen, *Ghana: Evolution and Change in the Nineteenth and Twentieth Centuries* (London: Longman, 1975).

5. Dennis Austin, *Politics in Ghana 1946–1960* (London, Oxford University Press, 1964), pp. 372–84.

6. For details, see Austin, *Politics in Ghana*; Boahen, *Ghana*, p. 194; and Jon Kraus, "Arms and Politics in Ghana," in Claude E. Welch, Jr., ed., *Soldier and State in Africa: A Comparative Analysis of Military Intervention and Political Change* (Northeastern University Press, 1970), pp. 168–69.

7. Boahen, *Ghana*, p. 207.

8. Kraus, "Arms and Politics," p. 178.

9. B. W. Hodder, "The Ewe Problem: A Reassessment," in Charles A. Fisher,

*Essays in Political Geography* (London, 1968), pp. 271–83; David Brown, "The Political Response to Immiseration: A Case Study of Rural Ghana," *Genève-Afrique*, vol. 18, no. 1 (1980), pp. 55–74.

10. Robert Pinkney, *Ghana under Military Rule 1966–1969* (London: Methuen, 1972), p. 21.

11. David J. Finlay, Roberta E. Koplin, and Charles A. Ballard, Jr., "Ghana," in Donald K. Emmerson, ed., *Students and Politics in Developing Nations* (London: Pall Mall Press, 1968), p. 67.

12. S. A. Amoa, *University Students' Political Action in Ghana* (Tema: Ghana Publishing Corporation, 1979), pp. 34–39; and Finlay, Koplin, and Ballard, "Ghana," pp. 73–76.

13. Kraus, "Arms and Politics," pp. 180–81.

14. A. A. Afrifa, *The Ghana Coup* (London: Frank Cass, 1966).

15. Pinkney, *Ghana under Military Rule*, pp. 18–19.

16. Finlay, Koplin, and Ballard, "Ghana," p. 91.

17. "Justice Delayed Is Justice Denied," *Legon Observer*, December 8–21, 1967; and J. L. F. Abbey, "The 1969 Election, A Preliminary Analysis," *Legon Observer*, September 12–25, 1969.

18. Dan Tetteh and E. A. Boateng, "Attempted Coup Is Crushed," *Daily Graphic*, April 18, 1967, pp. 1–3; and "Ghana Heads for Civilian Rule," *Daily Graphic*, October 5, 1967, pp. 1, 8–9.

19. *Legon Observer*, September 12–25, 1969; and Boahen, *Ghana*, pp. 233–37.

20. Joseph G. Amamoo, *The Ghanaian Revolution* (London: Jafint Co., 1988), pp. 102–03.

21. S. A. Amoa, *University Students' Political Action*, p. 42.

22. Jon Kraus, "The Political Economy of Trade Union–State Relations in Radical and Populist Regimes in Africa," in Roger Southall, ed., *Labor Unions in Asia and Africa* (St. Martin's Press, 1988), pp. 186–87.

23. Kraus, "The Political Economy of Trade Union–State Relations," pp. 186–87.

24. Personal communication.

25. "Ghana: Another New Boom," *Africa Confidential*, vol. 13 (January 21, 1972), pp. 1–2.

26. Kraus, "The Political Economy of Trade Union," p. 190.

27. *NUGS NEWS*, June 1974.

28. "Ghana," in Colin Legum, ed., *Africa Contemporary Record, Annual Survey and Documents, 1977–78*, vol. 10 (Holmes and Meier, 1979), pp. B646.

29. "Ghana," in Colin Legum, ed., *Africa Contemporary Record, 1974–75*, vol. 7, pp. B643–4, and *1976–77*, vol. 9, p. B583.

30. A. A. Boahen, *The Ghanaian Sphinx : Reflections on the Contemporary History of Ghana. 1972–1987* (Accra: Sankofa Educational Publishers, 1989).

31. "Ghana: After the Subversion Trial," *Africa Confidential*, vol. 13 (November 19, 1972), pp. 4–5.

32. Mike Oquaye, *Politics in Ghana (1972–1979)* (Accra: Toronado Publications, 1980), pp. 117–18.

33. John S. Pobee, *Kwame Nkrumah and the Church in Ghana 1949–1966* (Accra: Asempa Publishers, 1988), pp. 45–60.

34. Association of Recognized Professional Bodies, *News Bulletin*, July 19, 1977.

35. NRCD 236; and *Africa Contemporary Record, 1976–1977*, vol. 9, p. B576.

36. Oquaye, *Politics in Ghana*, p. 57.

37. Association of Recognized Professional Bodies, *News Bulletin*, July 28, 1979.

38. For more on this period see A. A. Boahen, *The Ghanaian Sphinx*, pp. 16–18.

39. Kofi Awoonor. *The Ghana Revolution: Background Account from a Personal Perspective* (Oases Publishers, 1984), p. 58.

40. Boahen, *The Ghanaian Sphinx*, pp. 19–22.

41. For details of this election and its outcome, see Boahen, *The Ghanaian Sphinx*, pp. 24–2 8.

42. Institute of Statistical Social and Economic Research, *The State of the Ghanaian Economy in 1994* (Legon, 1995), p. 171.

43. Naomi Chazan, *An Anatomy of Ghanaian Politics* (Westview, 1983), pp. 315–16; and Boahen, *The Ghanaian Sphinx*, p. 38.

44. Ghana Bar Association (GBA), "Delay in Administration of Justice: A Reply by the Ghana Bar Association," Accra, October 1, 1981.

45. Ghana Bar Association, "Resolution of the Ghana Bar Association on the Silver Jubilee Celebrations," Accra, October 1, 1981.

46. "Ghana: The Inevitable Coup," *Africa Confidential*, vol. 23 (January 6, 1982), p. 5.

47. Boahen, *The Ghanaian Sphinx*, pp. 40–42; and Z. Yeebo, *Ghana: The Struggle for Popular Power* (London: New Beacon Books, 1991), pp. 35–46.

48. Yeebo, *Ghana*, p. 36.

49. Kojo Yankah, *The Trial of J. J. Rawlings: Echoes of the 31st December Revolution* (Tema: Ghana Publishing Corporation, 1986), pp. 54–55.

50. Yeebo, *Ghana*, p. 51.

51. Ibid., pp. 51–53.

52. Ibid., p. 52.

53. Donald I. Ray, *Ghana: Politics, Economics and Society* (Lynne Rienner, 1986), p. 68.

54. PNDC Law 1.

55. Boahen, *The Ghanaian Sphinx*, p. 47.

56. Yeebo, *Ghana*, p. 145.

57. *Ghana: Two Years of Transformation, 1982–1983* (Accra: Information Services Department, n.d.).

58. ISSER, *The State of the Ghanaian Economy*, p. 26.

59. Naomi Chazan, "The Political Transformation of Ghana under the PNDC," in Donald Rothchild, ed., *Ghana: The Political Economy of Recovery* (Lynne Rienner, 1991), p. 35.

60. National Commission for Democracy, "Effective Realization of True Democracy in Ghana," Accra, 1984.

61. National Commission for Democracy, "Evolving True Democracy," March 1991, p. ix.

62. Chazan, "The Political Transformation of Ghana," p. 37.

63. Ghana Bar Association, "Resolutions Passed at the 1984–85 Annual General Conference Held in Accra, 25th–27th September 1985," December 6, 1985, p. 1.

64. Ghana Bar Association, "Statement by the Ghana Bar Association on the Recent Dismissal and Retirement of Certain Judges and Magistrates," Accra, March 17, 1986.

65. Yeebo, *Ghana*, pp. 236–37.

66. Jon Kraus, "The Political Economy of Food in Ghana," in Naomi Chazan and Timothy M. Shaw, eds., *Coping with Africa's Food Crisis* (Lynne Rienner, 1988), p. 104.

67. Jeff Haynes, "Inching Towards Democracy: The Ghanaian 'Revolution,' the International Monetary Fund, and the Politics of the Possible," in Robin Cohen and Harry Goulbourne, eds., *Democracy and Socialism in Africa* (Westview Press, 1991), pp. 142–64.

68. Kraus, "The Political Economy of Food," p. 104.

69. Cited in Kraus, "The Political Economy of Trade Union–State Relations," pp. 198–99.

70. Yeebo, *Ghana*, pp. 236–37.

71. Stephen John Stedman, "Conflict and Conflict Resolution in Africa: A Conceptual Framework," in Francis M. Deng and I. William Zartman, eds., *Conflict Resolution in Africa* (Brookings, 1991), pp. 374–75; and Boahen, *The Ghanaian Sphinx*, pp. 17–18, 52, 54–56.

72. Boahen, *The Ghanaian Sphinx*, pp. 54–56.

73. *Daily Graphic*, April 23, 1987, p. 1.

74. National Commission for Democracy, "Evolving a True Democracy," p. 2.

75. Government statement issued on May 10, 1991, Accra, on the National Commission on Democracy, "Evolving a True Democracy," para. 21.

76. *Report of the Committee of Experts on Proposals for a Draft Constitution for Ghana*, Accra, July 1991.

77. PNDC, *Report of Committee of Experts*, July 1991.

78. World Bank, *Sub-Saharan Africa: From Crisis to Sustainable Growth* (Washington, 1989).

79. They included the Movement for Freedom and Justice (MFJ) formed in August 1990; the Danquah–Busia Memorial Club (DBMC), the Kwame Nkrumah Welfare Society (KNWS), Our Heritage, the Coordinating Committee of the Democratic Forces of Ghana (CCDF), the EGLE (Every Ghanaian Living Everywhere) Club, the Kwame Nkrumah Youngsters Club (KNYS), and the National Coordinating Committee of Nkrumaists (NCCN), all formed between September 1990 and December 1991; the Interim National Coordinating Committee of the Danquah–Busia Club (INCC) formed in February 1992; and the Alliance of Democratic Forces (ADF) formed in August 1992. For a full list of these groups, see PNDC Law 253.

80. "Joint statement issued by the Kwame Nkrumah Revolutionary Front, and the New Democratic Movement at a Press Conference to Commemorate Positive Action Day," Accra, January 8, 1992.

81. Movement for Freedom and Justice, "Announcement of the Formation of a Broad-Based National Movement—the Movement for Freedom and Justice (MFJ) at a Press Conference on Wednesday, August 1, 1990," Accra, 1990.

82. International Federation of Electoral Systems (IFES), "Ghana: A Free Election Assessment Report," Accra, June 1, 1992.

83. Communiqué issued by the Catholic Bishops' Conference of Ghana, Wa, Ghana, July 5, 1991, pp. 3–4.

84. IFES, "Ghana."

85. Ibid.

86. New Patriotic Party, *The Stolen Verdict: Ghana November 1992 Presidential Election* (Accra, 1992), apps. 16 (a), 16 (b).

87. Stedman, "Conflict and Conflict Resolution," p. 370.

88. See, in particular, "Africa: Winds of Change," *Africa Confidential*, vol. 35 (March 9, 1990), pp. 1–2.

## Chapter Five

1. For example, General Sani Abacha thwarted the return to civilian rulership in November 1993 when he dismissed the interim national government and set up the secret military tribunal in 1995 that convicted General Olusegun Obasanjo (ret.). Obasanjo was the only Nigerian head of state to give up power to an elected civilian, in 1979, and thereafter became Africa's leading peacemaking elder statesman.

2. Obaro Ikime, *In Search of Nigerians: Changing Patterns of Intergroup Relations in an Evolving Nation State* (Ibadan: Impact Publishers, 1985).

3. Jacob F. Ade Ajayi, *The Problems of National Integration in Nigeria: A Historical Perspective*, Distinguished Lecture Series 11 (Ibadan: Nigerian Institute of Social and Economic Research, 1984).

4. Ade Ajayi, *Problems of National Integration in Nigeria*, p.3.

5. Eme O. Awa, *National Integration in Nigeria: Problems and Prospects*, Distinguished Lecture Series 5 (Ibadan: Nigerian Institute of Social and Economic Research, 1983), p.4.

6. Samuel O. Okafor, *Indirect Rule: The Development of Central Legislature in Nigeria* (Lagos: Thomas Nelson & Sons, 1981), p. 43.

7. Isaac M. Okonjo, *British Administration in Nigeria 1900–1950: A Nigerian View* (New York: NOK Publishers, 1974), p. 88.

8. James S. Coleman, *Nigeria: Background to Nationalism* (Berkeley and Los Angeles, California University Press, 1960), pp. 70–78.

9. Cited in Okafor, *Indirect Rule*, p. 52.

10. John A. A. Ayoade, *Federalism in Nigeria: The Problem with the Solution*, Faculty of the Social Sciences, faculty lecture delivered on July 13, 1988 (University of Ibadan, 1988), p. 20.

11. Cited in Eme O. Awa, *Federal Government in Nigeria* (University of California Press, 1964), p. 17.

12. Richard L. Sklar, *Nigerian Political Parties* (New York: NOK Publishers, 1983), pp. 59–64.

13. Billy J. Dudley, *Parties and Politics in Northern Nigeria* (London: Frank Cass, 1968), p. 22; and James S. Coleman, "Nationalism in Tropical Africa," *American Political Science Review*, vol. 48 (June 1954), pp. 404–26.

14. Dudley, *Parties and Politics in Northern Nigeria*, p.22.

15. Ibid.

16. See, for example, Nigeria, *Proceedings of the General Conference on Review of the Constitution, January 1950* (Lagos: Government Printer, 1950).

17. Stephen J. Stedman, "Conflict and Conflict-Resolution in Africa: A Conceptual Framework," in Francis M. Deng and I. William Zartman, eds., *Conflict Resolution in Africa* (Brookings, 1991), pp. 367–99.

18. Coleman, *Nigeria*, pp. 256–57.

19. Sklar, *Nigerian Political Parties*, p. 57.

20. Ibid.

21. Ken W. J. Post, *The Nigerian Federal Elections of 1959: Politics and Administration in a Developing Political System* (London: Oxford University Press, for the Nigerian Institute of Social and Economic Research, 1963), p. 437.

22. Billy J. Dudley, *Instability and Political Order* (Ibadan University Press, 1973), pp. 62–63.

23. Oyeleye Oyediran, "Background to Military Rule," in Oyediran, *Nigerian Government and Politics under Military Rule 1966–1979* (St. Martin's Press, 1979), p. 15.

24. From John P. Mackintosh, *Nigerian Government and Politics* (London: George Allen and Unwin, 1966), pp. 557–58. Emphasis added.

25. Dudley, *Instability and Political Order*, pp. 74–75.

26. Sam O. Adamu, "Population and Planning in Nigeria," in Tekena N. Tamuno and J. A. Atanda, eds., *Nigeria since Independence: The First 25 Years: vol. 4, Government and Public Policy* (Ibadan: Heinemann Educational Books, 1989), p. 215.

27. Dudley, *Instability and Political Order*, p. 77.

28. The party leaders had in fact reached an agreement to permit unfettered election campaigns in all places and to eschew hooliganism and thuggery. See "Nigeria's Population Explosion," *West Africa*, February 29, 1964, p. 225–26.

29. Leo Dare, "The 1964 Elections and the Collapse of the First Republic," in Peter P. Ekeh, Patrick Dele Cole, and Gabriel O. Olusanya, eds., *Nigeria since Independence: The First Twenty-Five Years: Politics and Constitution*, vol. 5, *Politics and Constitution* (Ibadan: Heinemann Educational Books), p. 118.

30. Ibid., p. 119.

31. Dudley, *Instability and Political Order*, p. 82

32. Tunde Adeniran, "Nigeria and Great Britain," in A. Bolaji Akinyemi, S. O. Agbi, and A. O. Otubanjo, eds., *Nigeria since Independence: The First 25 Years: vol. 10, International Relations* (Ibadan: Heinemann Educational Books, 1989), pp. 29–46.

33. Gavin Williams, *State and Society in Nigeria* (Idanre, Nigeria: Afrografika Publishers, 1980), p. 86.

34. Joel 'Bayo Adekanye, "Politics in a Military Context," in Ekeh, Dele Cole, and Olusanya, *Nigeria since Independence*, vol. 5, pp. 191–92.

35. Dudley, *Instability and Political Order*, pp. 122–25, 129.

36. Alexander A. Madiebo, *The Nigerian Revolution and the Biafran War* (Enugu, Nigeria: Fourth Dimension Publishers, 1980), pp. 31–51.

37. Dudley, *Instability and Political Order*, pp. 174–76.

38. This has been the subject of complaints by various Nigerian leaders, and

yet, besides the Western Region, from which the Mid-West was excised in 1963 as a punitive measure, nothing was done. See, for example, Nnamdi Azikiwe, "Essentials for Nigerian Survival," in *Foreign Affairs*, vol. 43 (April 1965), pp. 447–61; and Obafemi Awolowo, *Thoughts on the Nigerian Constitution* (Ibadan: Oxford University Press, 1966), p. 61.

39. For a review of this literature, see Akinjide Osuntokun, "Review of Literature on the Civil War," in Tekena N. Tamuno and Samson Ukpabi, eds., *Nigeria since Independence, The First 25 Years*: vol. 6, *The Civil War Years* (Ibadan: Heinemann Educational Books, 1989), pp. 85–105.

40. Adewale Ademoyega, *Why We Struck: The Story of the First Nigerian Coup* (Ibadan: Evans Brothers, 1981), p. 33.

41. Jonas Isawa Elaigwu, "The Military and State Building: Federal-State Relations in Nigeria's 'Military Federalism 1966–76,'" in A. Bolaji Akinyemi, Patrick Dele Cole, and Walter Ofonagoro, eds., *Readings on Federalism* (Lagos: Nigerian Institute of International Affairs, 1979), pp. 155–81.

42. S. Egite Oyovbaire, "The Politics of Revenue Allocation," in Keith Panter-Brick, ed., *Soldiers and Oil: The Political Transformation of Nigeria* (London: Frank Cass, 1978), pp. 224–49.

43. Ali D. Yahaya, "The Creation of States," in Panter-Brick, *Soldiers and Oil*, pp. 201–23.

44. Alex E. Gboyega, "The Making of the Nigerian Constitution," in Oyediran, *Nigerian Government under Military Rule 1966–1969*, pp. 235–57.

45. Eghosa Osaghae, "On the Concept of Ethnic Group in Africa: A Nigerian Case," *Plural Societies*, vol. 16 (1986), pp. 161–73.

46. Patrick E. Ollawa, "The 1979 Elections," in Ekeh, Dele Cole, and Olusanya, *Nigeria since Independence*, pp. 123–64.

47. Nigerian Progressive Front, "Suggested Blueprint for Action," undated mimeo; see also "Minutes of Meeting on Terms of Alliance Held at Badagry Room, Eko Hotel, on Saturday 25th August, 1979, at 3 pm," Lagos.

48. Text of the NPN-NPP Accord cited in James O. Ojiako, *1st Four Years of Nigeria's Executive Presidency: Success or Failure* (Lagos: Daily Times, 1983), pp. 47, 51; see also "Conclusions on Working Arrangements between the Representatives of the National Party of Nigeria and the Nigerian Peoples Party at Eko Hotel, Lagos, From the 20th to 23rd of August, 1979," mimeo.

49. Ojiako, *1st Four Years of Nigeria Executive Presidency*, pp. 47–51

50. 1979 Constitution of the Federal Republic of Nigeria, Section 14(3), in Federal Republic of Nigeria, *Official Gazette*, September 30, 1978, p. A142.

51. John A.A. Ayoade, "Ethnic Management in the 1979 Nigerian Constitution," *Publius*, vol. 16 (Spring 1985), p. 82.

52. L. Adele Jinadu, "Federalism, the Consociational State, and Ethnic Conflict in Nigeria," *Publius*, vol. 15 (Spring 1985), pp. 71–100.

53. Alex Gboyega, "The 'Federal Character' or the Attempt to Create Representative Bureaucracies in Nigeria," *International Review of Administrative Sciences*, vol. 50, no. 1 (1984), pp. 17–24.

54. Rotimi Timothy Suberu, "Federalism and Nigeria's Political Future: A Comment," *African Affairs*, vol. 87 (July 1988), pp. 431–39.

55. Daniel C. Bach, "Managing a Plural Society: The Boomerang Effects of Nigerian Federalism," *Journal of Commonwealth and Comparative Politics*, vol. 27 (July 1985), pp. 218–245.

56. Femi Otubanjo, "Ethnic Interests and Political Alignments in Nigeria's Second Republic," *Plural Societies*, vol. 16 (1986), pp. 174–85.

57. Shehu Othman, "Nigeria: Power for Profit—Class, Corporatism, and Factionalism in the Military," in Donald B. Cruise O'Brien, John Dunn, and Richard Rathbone, eds., *Contemporary West African States* (Cambridge: Cambridge University Press, 1989), p. 135.

58. Federal Republic of Nigeria, *Report of the Political Bureau* (Lagos: Government Printer, 1987), p. 7.

59. See "Igbos Are Angry," *Citizen* (Kaduna), August 5–12, 1991, pp. 12–21.

60. See interview in *Newbreed* (Lagos), August 26, 1991, p. 8.

61. See, for example, *Guardian*, Lagos, March 20, 1992, p. 10, and reports of the proceedings of the National Constitutional Conference in the daily newspapers and weekly magazines for the period July 15–29, 1994.

62. Alex Gboyega, "Protecting Local Governments from Arbitrary State and Federal Interference: What Prospects for the 1990s?" *Publius*, vol. 21 (Fall 1991), pp. 45–59.

63. Federal Republic of Nigeria, *Official Gazette*, annex 1, December 31, 1984.

64. Cited in Ken Saro-Wiwa, *On a Darkling Plain: An Account of the Nigerian Civil War* (Port-Harcourt: Saros International Publishers, 1989), pp. 11–12.

65. Central Bank of Nigeria, Annual Report and Statement of Accounts for the Year Ended 31st December 1985.

66. Off-shore oil rent and royalties were treated as federal revenue.

67. National Revenue Allocation, Mobilization, and Fiscal Commission, "Revenue Allocation," paper presented at Seminar for Governors-Elect, Abjua, Nigeria, 1991, p. 16.

68. "Massacre: Deaths, Destruction in Oil Community," *African Concord*, Lagos, December 30, 1990, pp. 23–27.

69. Movement for the Survival of the Ogoni People (MOSOP), *Ogoni Bill of Rights* (Port Harcourt: Saros International Publishers, 1992), p. 11.

70. MOSOP, *Ogoni Bill of Rights*, p. 6.

71. See "Oil: Old Game, New Barons," *Citizen* (Kaduna), September 23–30, 1991; and "Nigeria's Oil Men," *Newswatch*, Lagos, February 17, 1992.

72. See, for example, *African Guardian*, May 14, 1990, p. 40, and May 28, 1990, pp. 36–38.

73. Federal Republic of Nigeria, *Official Gazette*, December 31, 1992, p. A12.

74. National Revenue Mobilisation Allocation and Fiscal Commission, *National Revenue Mobilisation Allocation and Fiscal Commission Report 1989*, main report, vol. 1 (Lagos, May 1989), p. 7.

75. Federal Republic of Nigeria, *Report of the Political Bureau* (Lagos: Government Printer, 1987), p. 126.

76. Text of "Speech Delivered at the Inauguration of the Constitution Review Committee in Abuja on Monday, 7th September1987," in General Ibrahim

Babangida, *Portrait of a New Nigeria: Selected Speeches of IBB* (Marlow, Bucks: Precision Press, 1989), pp. 38–39.

77. Section 220.

78. "Address to the Nation on the Occasion of the Promulgation of the New Constitution in Lagos on 3rd May, 1989," in Babangida, *Portrait of a New Nigeria*, pp. 65–83.

79. "The Grass-Roots Democratic Party System and the Dawn of a New Socio-Political Order," in General Ibrahim Babangida, *For Their Tomorrow We Gave Our Today: Selected Speeches of IBB*, vol. 2 (Jersey, C.I. [U.K]: Safari Books, 1991), pp. 2–25.

80. Babangida, *Portrait of a New Nigeria*, p. 81.

81. The politics of the *Egbe Ilosiwaju Yoruba* has been the subject of many news magazine reports. See, for instance, "What the Yorubas Want," *Newbreed*, Lagos, March 2, 1992.

82. For a good idea of the motivation of the CARIA group, see interviews granted by Arthur Nzeribe, "My Game Plan," *African Concord*, Lagos, June 29, 1992, pp. 17–23; and *African Guardian*, Lagos, July 13, 1992, pp. 10–14.

83. Interview granted to *TSM* (Sunday magazine), Lagos, July 13, 1990, pp. 5–9.

84. See "The Big 'Mafia': Schemes to Elect Next President," *Tell*, Lagos, May 11, 1992, pp. 10–17.

85. See *Daily Times*, Lagos, May 20, 1992, pp. 1, 4.

86. *African Guardian*, Lagos, July 13, 1992, p. 13.

87. See the cover story "2nd Republic Governors Vow: We'll Be Back," *Nigerian Economist*, Lagos, April 19, 1991, pp. 30–39.

88. See "National Conference: Debating Nigeria's Future," *Newswatch*, Lagos, July 9, 1990, pp. 15–19; and "National Conference: Patriots in Disarray," *African Guardian*, Lagos, July 16, 1990, pp. 22–27.

89. Alhaji Lateef Jakande, former Governor of Lagos State; Chief Bola Ige, former Governor of Oyo State; Alhaji Abubakar Rimi, former Governor of Kano state; Chief Jim Nwobodo, former Governor of Anambra state; Chief C. C. Ono, former Governor of Anambra too; Alhaji Lawal Kaita, former Governor of Kaduna state; Mr. Solomon Lar, former Governor of Plateau State; Major-General Musa Yar'Adua, former Chief of Staff, Supreme Headquarters; Dr. Olusola Saraki, former Senate Leader; Chief Arthur Nzeribe, former Senator; Alhaji Bello Maitama Yusuff, former Minister of Commerce; Mr. Paul Unongo, former Minister for Steel, and Alhaji Lamidi Adedibu, a prominent politician in Oyo State.

90. "The Debate on a Government of National Consensus," *Guardian*, January 30, 1992, p. 5.

91. Olusegun Obasanjo, "A Government of Consensus," *Guardian*, Lagos, January 8, 1992, p. 15; "National Government Is the Answer," *Guardian*, January 24, 1992, p. 8; and "The Debate on Government," January 30, 1992, p. 5.

92. "Abuja Convention: What to Expect in 1992," *African Guardian*, August 6, 1990, pp. 20–28.

93. The governor of Lagos State belonged to the NRC, but the House of Assembly was predominantly SDP. The gubernatorial election was lost because of a split in the party over the selection of the candidate.

94. See Alhaji Abubakar Rimi, "Time for Southern President," special interview, *Tell*, June 14, 1993, pp. 10–15.

95. "North vs. North: Why the South Lost Out in the Primaries," *Tell*, October 5, 1992.

96. "States' Presidential Election Results," *African Concord*, June 28, 1993, p. 22.

97. Recent interviews granted by some of the major actors admit improper behavior of the politicians. See, for examples, interview of Senator Chuba Okadigbo, "Our Dirty Senate," *TSM* (Sunday magazine), February 13, 1994, and of Senator Patrick Ani, "Confession: How We Conspired Against June 12," *African Guardian*, May 16, 1994.

98. See, for example, Tekena N. Tamuno, *Nigerian Universities: Their Students and Their Society, Lagos* (Lagos: Government Printer), 1989.

99. For an account of the 1989 anti-SAP riots see "Orgy of Violence," *Newswatch*, Lagos, June 12, 1989, pp. 10–19.

100. Dafe Otobo, "State and Labor: The 1988 Ban of the NLC," in Dafe Otobo, ed., *Labor Relations in Nigeria*, vol. 1 (Lagos: Malthouse Press, 1992), pp. 93–123.

101. Pascal Bafyau was secretary of the Railway Workers Union. As an employee of the union, rather than a dues-paying member, he was not qualified to contest for office in the NLC.

102. "Government Now Calls for Advice on OIC Row," *Guardian*, Lagos, January 29, 1986, p. 1.

103. For an account of some of these clashes see "Massacre in Bauchi: Religious Strife Is Back," *African Concord*, May 6, 1991, and "Funtua, Izombe: How Religious Fanatics Unleashed Terror," February 8, 1993.

104. Thomas J. Biersteker, "Indigenization in Nigeria: Renationalization or Denationalization," in I. William Zartman, ed., *The Political Economy of Nigeria* (Praeger, 1983), pp. 185–206.

105. The Economic Stabilization (Temporary Provisions) Act of 1982 did not have the expected impact because it did not address the issues appropriately.

106. Rashid Faruqee, "Nigeria: Ownership Abandoned," in Ishrat Husain and Rashid Faruqee, eds., *Adjustment in Africa: Lessons from Country Case Studies* (Washington: World Bank, 1994), pp. 238–83.

107. Faruqee, "Nigeria," p. 243.

108. "Maiden Address to the Nation on Assumption of Office on 27th August, 1985," in Babangida, *Portrait of a New Nigeria*, p. 24.

109. Faruqee, "Nigeria," p. 247.

110. The corruption in the oil industry was frequently exposed in the press and debated. See, for example, "Nigeria's Dirty Oil Deals," *African Guardian*, March 5, 1990; "Massive Fraud at NNPC," *Newswatch*, October 25, 1993; and "Government to Overhaul Oil Industry, Pledges Relief," *Guardian* July 20, 1994, p. 1.

111. "Patriots in Disarray," *African Guardian*, July 16, 1990, p. 30.

## Chapter Six

1. I. William Zartman, "Conflict Reduction: Prevention, Management, and Resolution," in Francis M. Deng and I. William Zartman, eds., *Conflict Resolution in Africa* (Brookings, 1991), p. 299.

2. Donald Rothchild and Michael Foley, "The Implications of Scarcity for Governance in Africa," *International Political Science Review*, vol. 4 (July 1983), p. 315.

3. Thomas M. Callaghy, "The State as Lame Leviathan: The Patrimonial Administrative State in Africa," in Zaki Ergas, ed., *The African State in Transition* (St. Martin's Press, 1987), pp. 87–116.

4. Ruth Berins Collier, *Regimes in Tropical Africa: Changing Forms of Supremacy, 1945–1975* (University of California Press, 1982), p. 10.

5. Goran Hyden, "Governance and the Study of Politics," in Goran Hyden and Michael Bratton, eds., *Governance and Politics in Africa* (Lynne Rienner, 1992), p. 14.

6. Ibid., p. 12.

7. On governance as a "highly permissive concept," see Michael F. Lofchie, "Perestroika without Glasnost: Reflections on Structural Adjustment," in Richard Joseph, ed., *Beyond Autocracy in Africa* (Atlanta: Carter Center, 1989), p. 120.

8. Warren F. Ilchman and Norman Thomas Uphoff, *The Political Economy of Change* (University of California Press, 1969), p. 32.

9. Claude Ake, "The Case for Democracy," in Richard Joseph, ed., *African Governance in the 1990s: Objectives, Resources, and Constraints* (Atlanta: Carter Center, 1990), p. 4.

10. Richard Joseph, "The Challenge of Democratization in Africa," in Joseph, *African Governance in the 1990s*, p. 21.

11. On conflict as regime change, see I. William Zartman, "Regional Conflict Resolution," in Victor A. Kremenyuk, ed., *International Negotiation: Analysis, Approaches, Issues* (Jossey-Bass, 1991), pp. 309–10.

12. On the frustrations encountered by the Zambian government in this respect, see Donald Rothchild, "Rural-Urban Inequities and Resource Allocation in Zambia," *Journal of Commonwealth Political Studies*, vol. 10 (November 1972), pp. 222–42.

13. Kenneth Post and Michael Vickers, *Structure and Conflict in Nigeria: 1960–1966* (University of Wisconsin Press, 1973), p. 32; and I. William Zartman, "Toward a Theory of Elite Circulation," in Zartman, ed., *Elites in the Middle East* (Praeger 1980), p. 88.

14. Wayne A. Cornelius, *Politics and the Migrant Poor in Mexico City* (Stanford University Press, 1975), p. 170.

15. Ilchman and Uphoff, *The Political Economy of Change*, p. 22.

16. On this, see Richard L. Sklar, *Nigerian Political Parties: Power in an Emergent African Nation* (Princeton University Press, 1963), pp. 101–12, 205, 326; and Alhaji Sir Ahmadu Bello, *My Life* (Cambridge University Press, 1962), p. 118. See also John N. Paden, *Ahmadu Bello, Sardauna of Sokoto: Values and Leadership in Nigeria* (London: Hodder and Stoughton, 1986), p. 313.

17. Aristide R. Zolberg, *One-Party Government in the Ivory Coast* (Princeton University Press, 1964), p. 283.

18. Robert H. Bates, "Modernization, Ethnic Competition, and the Rationality of Politics in Contemporary Africa," in Donald Rothchild and Victor A. Olorunsola, eds., *State Versus Ethnic Claims: African Policy Dilemmas* (Westview, 1983), p. 161.

19. In 1990 Houphouët-Boigny, when fending off demands for democratic reforms, argued that tribalism remained the main obstacle to national unity. Gerald Bourke, "Côte d'Ivoire: Houphouët's Heavy Hand," *Africa Report*, vol. 35 (May–June 1990), p. 16. On the class dimension in Africa's ethnic politics, see Okwudiba Nnoli, *Ethnic Politics in Nigeria* (Enugu: Fourth Dimension Publishers, 1978), p. 30.

20. Naomi Chazan, *An Anatomy of Ghanaian Politics* (Westview, 1983), p. 103.

21. For a more extended discussion of the political exchange process within a centrally coordinated system, see Donald Rothchild, "Hegemonial Exchange: An Alternative Model for Managing Conflict in Middle Africa," in Dennis L. Thompson and Dov Ronen, eds., *Ethnicity, Politics, and Development* (Lynne Rienner, 1986), pp. 65–104.

22. On the ethnic group as the "primary group" in the present Nigerian political environment, see Claude Ake, "The Nigerian State: Antinomies of a Periphery Formation," in Claude Ake, ed., *Political Economy of Nigeria* (London: Longman, 1985), p. 26.

23. For an example of this in Côte d'Ivoire, see Dwayne Woods, "Ethno-Regional Demands, Symbolic and Redistributive Politics: Sugar Complexes in the North of the Ivory Coast," *Ethnic and Racial Studies*, vol. 12 (October 1989), pp. 470, 486.

24. Robert A. Mortimer, "Ivory Coast: Succession and Recession," *Africa Report*, vol. 28 (January–February, 1983), pp. 5–7; and Jennifer A. Widner, "The Rise of Civic Associations among Farmers in Côte d'Ivoire," in John Harbeson, Donald Rothchild, and Naomi Chazan, eds., *Civil Society and the State in Africa* (Lynne Rienner, 1994), pp. 191–211.

25. Mortimer, "Ivory Coast," pp. 5–7. On subsequent speculation that Houphouët did in fact prefer a Baule successor, see Jean-Baptiste Placca, "Côte d'Ivoire: En attendant les décisions du 'Vieux,'" *Jeune Afrique*, no. 1522 (March 5, 1990), p. 23.

26. See the data in Tessilimi Bakary, "Elite Transformation and Political Succession," in I. William Zartman and Christopher Delgado, eds., *The Political Economy of Ivory Coast* (Praeger, 1984), p. 36; see also J. F. Medard, "La regulation socio-politique," in Y. A. Faure and J. F. Medard, *Etat et Bourgeoisie en Côte-d'Ivoire: Etudes* (Paris: Karthala, 1982), p. 75.

27. Bakary, "Elite Transformation," p. 48.

28. Other important points of tension in Côte d'Ivoire according to Medard are generational, class based, and those between Ivorians and non-Ivorians, both African and European. See Medard, "La regulation socio-politique," p. 87. On the failure of the one-party system to suppress ethnic politics, see Gerald Bourke, "Day of Truth," *West Africa*, October 9–15, 1989, p. 1684.

29. Victor A. Olorunsola, *The Politics of Cultural Sub-Nationalism in Africa* (Doubleday, 1972), p. xv.

30. Federal Republic of Nigeria, *The Constitution of the Federal Republic of Nigeria 1979* (Lagos: Federal Ministry of Information, 1979), articles 14(3), 135(3).

31. Ladipo Adamolekun, John Erero, and Basil Oshionebo, "'Federal Character' and Management of the Federal Civil Service and the Military," *Publius*, vol. 21 (Fall 1991), pp. 83–85.

32. Eghosa E. Osaghae, "The Federal Cabinet, 1951–1984," in Peter P. Ekeh and Eghosa E. Osaghae, eds., *Federal Character and Federalism in Nigeria* (Ibadan: Heinemann, 1989), p. 131.

33. Federal Republic of Nigeria, *The Constitution of the Federal Republic of Nigeria 1979*, article 135(3).

34. Peter P. Ekeh, "The Structure and Meaning of Federal Character in the Nigerian Political System," in Ekeh and Osaghae, *Federal Character and Federalism in Nigeria*, p. 32.

35. A. H. M. Kirk-Greene, "Ethnic Engineering and the 'Federal Character' of Nigeria: Boon of Contentment or Bone of Contention?" *Ethnic and Racial Studies*, vol. 6 (October 1983), p. 467.

36. Nosa Igiebor, "The Tug of Character," *Newswatch* (Ikeja), April 13, 1987, p. 27; and Eghosa E. Osaghae, "The Federal Cabinet, 1951–1984," in Ekeh and Osaghae, *Federal Character*, pp. 150–51.

37. Federal Republic of Nigeria, *Report of the Political Bureau* (Lagos: Government Printer, 1987), p. 93.

38. Federal Republic of Nigeria, *Official Gazette*, May 3, 1989, sect. 15(3), p. A79.

39. Naomi Chazan, "Ethnicity and Politics in Ghana," *Political Science Quarterly*, vol. 97 (Fall 1982), p. 472.

40. David Brown, "Who are the Tribalists? Social Pluralism and Political Ideology in Ghana," *African Affairs*, vol. 81 (January 1982), p. 60.

41. Albert Adu Boahen, *The Ghanaian Sphinx: Reflections on the Temporary History of Ghana 1972–1987* (Accra: Ghana Academy of Arts and Sciences, 1989), p. 53.

42. Republic of Ghana, *Report of the Committee of Experts (Constitution) on Proposals for a Draft Constitution of Ghana* (Accra: Ghana Publishing Corp., 1991), pp. 14–15.

43. Woods, "Ethno-Regional Demands," pp. 482–86.

44. On this, see Donald Rothchild, "Military Regime Performance: An Appraisal of the Ghana Experience, 1972–78," *Comparative Politics*, vol. 12 (July 1980), pp. 474–75; and Donald Rothchild, "Collective Demands for Improved Distributions," in Rothchild and Olorunsola, eds., *State Versus Ethnic Claims*, pp. 187–88.

45. The Rawlings administration limited urban hospitals to 50 percent of the national health budget and, in an attempt to broaden access to the University of Ghana, favored the establishment of campuses in all the subregions. "Focus Is Now on Rural Dwellers," *People's Daily Graphic* (Accra), April 7, 1983, p. 1, and "New Frontiers of Hope," *West Africa*, October 25, 1982, p. 2765.

46. Jeffrey Herbst, *The Politics of Reform in Ghana, 1982–1991* (University of California Press, 1993), p. 83.

47. Western Africa Department, Africa Regional Office, *Ghana 2000 and Beyond* (Washington: World Bank, 1993), p. 89.

48. Herbst, *The Politics of Reform in Ghana, 1982–1991*, p.88. See also Boahen, *The Ghanaian Sphinx*, pp. 53, 64; and Richard Jeffries, "Urban Popular Attitudes towards the Economic Recovery Programme and the PNDC Government in Ghana," *African Affairs*, vol. 91 (April 1992), p. 222.

49. Rotimi Timothy Suberu, "Federalism and Nigeria's Political Future: A Comment," *African Affairs*, vol. 87 (July 1983), p. 437.

50. Federal Republic of Nigeria, *Third National Development Plan, 1975–1980* (Lagos: Central Planning Office, 1975), pp. 238–39.

51. Donald Rothchild, "Middle Africa: Hegemonial Exchange and Resource Allocation," in Alexander J. Groth and Larry L. Wade, eds., *Comparative Resource Allocation: Politics, Performance, and Policy Priorities* (Sage Publications, 1984), p. 174.

52. Larry Diamond, "Nigeria: Pluralism, Statism, and the Struggle for Democracy," in Larry Diamond, Juan J. Linz, and Seymour Martin Lipset, eds., *Democracy in Developing Countries: Africa* (Lynne Rienner, 1988), p. 71. Emphasis in original.

53. "Nigeria: The Generals' Grip," *Africa Confidential*, vol. 26 (January 30, 1985), p. 1; and Lyse Doucet, "Quest for a New Polity," *Africa Report*, vol. 32 (September–October 1987), p. 68.

54. Pita Ogaba Agbese, "Demilitarization and Prospects for Democracy in Nigeria," *Bulletin of Peace Proposals*, vol. 22 (September 1991), pp. 321–22. For additional supporting data, see his "Defense Expenditures and Private Capital Accumulation in Nigeria," *Journal of Asian and African Studies*, vol. 23 (July–October 1988), pp. 270–86.

55. Agbese, "Demilitarization and Prospects for Democracy," p. 316.

56. E. Gyimah-Boadi, "Associational Life, Civil Society, and Democratization in Ghana," in Harbeson, Rothchild, and Chazan, eds., *Civil Society and the State*, pp. 125–48.

57. On this, see Donald Rothchild and E. Gyimah-Boadi, "Ghana's Economic Decline and Development Strategies," in John Ravenhill, ed., *Africa in Economic Crisis* (Columbia University Press, 1986), p. 272.

58. Joel S. Migdal, *Strong Societies and Weak States: State-Society Relations and State Capabilities in the Third World* (Princeton University Press, 1988), p. 32.

59. For a fuller report on the 1973 surveys in Ghana, see Donald Rothchild, "Comparative Public Demand and Expectation Patterns: The Ghana Experience," *African Studies Review*, vol. 22 (April 1979), pp. 127–47.

60. In fact, recent data show that in Upper West, Upper East, and Northern Regions, infant and child mortality rates are more than double those in Greater Accra. World Bank, *Ghana 2000 and Beyond*, p. 23.

61. On the heightened sense of latent public grievances in the relatively advantaged subregions, see also Fred M. Hayward, "Perceptions of Well-Being in Ghana: 1970 and 1975," in *African Studies Review*, vol. 22 (April 1979), p. 114; and Anthony Oberschall, "Communications, Information, and Aspirations in Rural Uganda," *Journal of Asian and African Studies*, vol. 4 (January 1969), p. 48.

62. Donald Rothchild and E. Gyimah-Boadi, "Ethnic and Religious Groups

as Interest Maximizers," paper presented to the African Studies Association, 1986. For an interesting discussion of Muslim divisions and alliances in Ghana, see Deborah Pellow, "Muslim Segmentation: Cohesion and Divisiveness in Accra," *Journal of Modern African Studies*, vol. 23 (1985), pp. 419–44.

63. On demands by Muslims in the north and west of Nigeria for more teachers of Islamic subject matter and more Muslim schools, see Peter B. Clarke, "Religion and Political Attitude since Independence," in Jacob K. Olupona and Toyin Falola, eds., *Religion and Society in Nigeria: Historical and Sociological Perspectives* (Ibadan: Spectrum Books, 1991), p. 225.

64. On urban support for Ghana's structural adjustment program despite declining real incomes, see Jeffries, "Urban Popular Attitudes," pp. 214–16.

65. Matthew Martin, "Negotiating Adjustment and External Finance: Ghana and the International Community, 1982–1989," in Donald Rothchild, ed., *Ghana: The Political Economy of Recovery* (Lynne Reinner, 1990), pp. 237–49. See also Herbst, *The Politics of Reform in Ghana*, chap. 3.

66. Martin, "Negotiating Adjustment," p. 248.

67. Richard Rose and Guy Peters, *Can Government Go Bankrupt?* (Basic Books, 1978), p. 237; and Ted Robert Gurr, *Why Men Rebel* (Princeton University Press, 1970), pp. 25–26.

68. Letter from F. C. Bourne to (Governor) Sir Charles Arden-Clarke, December 19, 1955, Public Records Office (London), CO 554/806, p. 4.

69. Alexander A. Madiebo, for example, explains the Biafran struggle for a separate existence in terms of people protecting themselves "from possible extermination." See his book, *The Nigerian Revolution and the Biafran War* (Enugu: Fourth Dimension Publishing Co., 1980), p. 387; see also Onyeonoro S. Kamanu, "Secession and the Right of Self-Determination: An O.A.U. Dilemma," *Journal of Modern African Studies*, vol. 12 (September 1974), p. 361; and Julius Nyerere, *Case for Recognition of Biafra* (Dar es Salaam: Government Printer, 1986), p. 3.

70. Woods, "Ethno-regional Demands," p. 478.

71. Clarke, "Religion and Political Attitude," p. 225. On the intensity of the debates at the constituent assembly about including a federal Sharia Court of Appeal in the 1979 constitution, see E. Alex Gboyega, "The Making of the Nigerian Constitution," in Oyeleye Oyediran, ed., *Nigerian Government and Politics under Military Rule, 1966–79* (London: Macmillan, 1979), pp. 252–54.

72. *West Africa*, April 15–21, 1991, p. 568.

73. Stephen John Stedman, "Conflict and Conflict Resolution in Africa: A Conceptual Framework," in Deng and Zartman, *Conflict Resolution in Africa*, p. 389.

74. Jacob K. Olupona, "Perspectives on Religion, National Integration, and Intolerance in Contemporary Nigeria," paper presented at the U. S. Institute of Peace Conference, "Intolerance and Conflict: Sudan and Nigeria," Washington, 1991, p. 2.

75. Enukora Joe Okoli, "After the Kano Rioting," *West Africa*, January 12, 1981, p. 53.

76. "Nigeria: Maitatsine Machinations," *Africa Confidential*, vol. 23 (October 20, 1982), p. 1.

77. On the "new fervour shown by Christian sects in fighting what they see

as a Muslim campaign to institutionalise Islam throughout Nigeria," see "Nigeria: The Power Stakes," *Africa Confidential*, vol. 26 (April 10, 1985), p. 3.

78. "Nigeria: Religious Controversy," *West Africa*, February 3, 1986, p. 231. In August 1991, Babangida suspended Nigeria's participation in the OIC. Foreign Broadcast Information Service, *Daily Report: Africa*, August 17, 1991, p. 43. (Hereafter FBIS, *Africa*.)

79. "Nigeria: Turbanning Turbulence," *Africa Confidential*, vol. 31 (April 6, 1990), pp. 3–4.

80. William Keeling and Michael Holman, "Nigerian Coup Attempt Defeated," *Financial Times*, April 23, 1990, p. 1.

81. "A Bloody Attempt," *West Africa*, April 30–May 6, 1990, p. 696.

82. William Keeling and Michael Holman, "Religious Tension behind Challenge to Babangida," *Financial Times*, April 23, 1990, p. 3.

83. Widner, "The Rise of Civic Associations."

84. On the Christian Association of Nigeria's protests over the alleged destruction directed again them, see Bola Olowo, "Nigeria: Prophets and Zealots," *West Africa*, May 20–26, 1991, p. 796.

85. See the discussion in Jonas Isawa Elaigwu, "Federalism and National Leadership in Nigeria," *Publius*, vol. 21 (Fall 1991), pp. 125–26.

86. I. William Zartman and Christopher L. Delgado, "Introduction: Stability, Growth and Challenge," in Zartman and Delgado, *The Political Economy of the Ivory Coast*, p. 3; and Gerald Bourke, "Côte d'Ivoire: Houphouët's Heavy Hand," *Africa Report*, vol. 35 (May–June 1990), p. 16.

87. K. Gyan-Apenteng,"Ghana: To Go or Not to Go?" *West Africa*, July 1–7, 1991, p. 1066.

88. David Collier and Deborah L. Norden, "Strategic Choice Models of Political Change in Latin America," *Comparative Politics*, vol. 24 (January 1992), p. 229.

89. Vivienne Shue, "State Power and Social Organization in China," in Joel S. Migdal, Atul Kahli, and Vivienne Shue, eds., *State Power and Social Forces: Domination and Transformation in the Third World* (Cambridge University Press, 1994), p. 66. On the mutually reinforcing nature of political and civil associations, see Alexis de Tocqueville, *Democracy in America*, vol. 2 (Vintage Books, 1954), p. 123.

90. Richard Rose, "Northern Ireland: The Irreducible Conflict," in Joseph V. Montville, ed., *Conflict and Peacemaking in Multiethnic Societies* (Lexington Books, 1990), p. 142.

91. C. R. Mitchell, "Classifying Conflicts: Asymmetry and Resolution," *Annals of the American Academy of Political and Social Science*, vol. 518 (November 1991), p. 28.

92. Robert Fatton, Jr., *The Making of a Liberal Democracy: Senegal's Passive Revolution, 1975–1985* (Lynne Rienner, 1987), p. 169.

93. On this, see the discussion in Carol Lancaster, "Democracy in Africa," *Foreign Policy*, no. 85 (Winter 1991–92), p. 148. See also Michael Bratton and Nicolas van de Walle, "Popular Demands and State Responses," in Hyden and Bratton, eds., *Governance and Politics in Africa*, p. 51.

94. Bourke, "Houphouët's Heavy Hand," p. 16.

95. Jean-Baptiste Placca, "Le président seul dans l'arène," *Jeune Afrique*, no. 1524 (March 19, 1990), p. 19.

96. Jennifer A. Widner, "The 1990 Elections in Côte d'Ivoire," *Issue*, vol. 20 (Winter 1991), p. 32.

97. Mariam C. Diallo, "Houphouët Maître Du Jeu," *Jeune Afrique*, December 5–11, 1990, pp. 22–23.

98. "Côte d'Ivoire, "*Africa Research Bulletin* (Political, Social, and Cultural Series), November 23, 1995, pp. 12003–05.

99. "A Tale of Two Transitions," *West Africa*, January 13–19, 1992, p. 57; and Jeff Haynes, "Human Rights and Democracy in Ghana: The Record of the Rawlings Regime," *African Affairs*, vol. 90 (July 1991), p. 425.

100. Quoted in Ajoa Yeboah-Afari, "Ghana: Enter the Fourth Republic," *West Africa*, January 18–24, 1993, p. 52.

101. Federal Republic of Nigeria, *Report of the Political Bureau* (Lagos: Government Printer, 1987), p. 92.

102. Ibid., p. 74.

103. Ibid., p. 126.

104. Ibid., p. 137.

105. "Nigeria: The Déjà Vu Agenda," *Africa Confidential*, vol. 33 (December 4, 1992), p. 3; and Olugbenga Ayeni, "Nigeria: Transition Credibility Crisis?" *West Africa*, November 23–29, 1992, p. 2012.

106. Quoted in Baffour Ankomah, "False Servants," *New African*, no. 306 (March 1993), p. 16.

107. "Nigeria," *Africa Confidential*, vol. 33 (December 4, 1992), p. 3.

108. *Report of the Committee of Experts*, p. 12.

109. Gyimah-Boadi, "Notes on Ghana's Current Transition to Constitutional Rule," *Africa Today*, vol. 38 (1991), p. 14.

110. Republic of Ghana, *Constitution of the Republic of Ghana 1992* (Accra: Times Press, 1992), pp. 201–02. See also the comments of Kwame Ninsin in *West Africa*, May 18–24, 1992, p. 849.

111. Kweku Folson, "The Choice of a President: The Issues at Stake," *Ghanaian Chronicle*, Accra, November 2–8, 1992, p.3.

112. Ajoa Yeboah-Afari, "Post-Election Thoughts," *West Africa*, November 16–22, 1992, p. 1963.

113. *Report of the Carter Center Ghana Election Mission*, November 6, 1992, p. 1.

114. "Ghana: Continuity Waives the Rules," *Africa Confidential*, vol. 34 (February 19, 1993), p. 3.

115. "Ghana: Together against Jerry," *Africa Confidential*, June 21, 1996, pp. 4–5.

116. Adebayo Adedeji, "Sustaining Democracy," *Africa Report*, vol. 37 (January–February, 1992), p. 30.

117. Larry Diamond, "The Globalization of Democracy," in Robert O. Slater, Barry M. Schutz, and Steven R. Dorr, eds., *Global Transformation and the Third World* (Lynne Rienner, 1993), pp. 31–69.

118. Arend Lijphart, *Democracy in Plural Societies: A Comparative Exploration* (Yale University Press, 1977), p. 25.

119. Timothy D. Sisk, *Power Sharing and International Mediation in Ethnic Conflicts* (Washington: U. S. Institute of Peace Press, 1996), p. 81.

120. On the process of informal bargaining within elite coalitions, see Rothchild, "Hegemonial Exchange," pp. 70–74.

121. Aristide R. Zolberg, "Politics in the Ivory Coast: 2," *West Africa*, August 6, 1960, p. 883.

122. Robert Fatton, Jr., *The Making of a Liberal Democracy: Senegal's Passive Revolution, 1975–1985* (Lynne Rienner, 1987), pp. 76–79.

123. Larry Diamond, "Issues in the Constitutional Design of a Third Nigerian Republic," *African Affairs*, vol. 86 (April 1987), p. 219; and Pini Jason, "Will Babangida Stay On?" *New African*, no. 296 (May 1992), p. 15.

124. On this, compare Frances Hagopian, "'Democracy by Undemocratic Means'? Elites, Political Pacts, and Regime Transition in Brazil," *Comparative Political Studies*, vol. 23 (July 1990), pp. 147–70; and Terry Lynn Karl and Philippe C. Schmitter, "Modes of Transition in Latin America, Southern and Eastern Europe," *International Social Science Journal*, vol. 128 (May 1991), pp. 269–84.

125. Donald Rothchild, "The Rawlings Revolution in Ghana: Pragmatism with Populist Rhetoric," *CSIS Africa Notes*, no. 42 (May 1985), pp. 1–6.

126. On Sankara's justification for restricting the political liberties of disaffected elites, see Pearl T. Robinson, "Grassroots Legitimation of Military Governance in Burkina Faso and Niger: The Core Contradictions," in Hyden and Bratton, eds., *Governance and Politics in Africa*, p. 152.

127. Jeff Haynes, "Human Rights and Democracy in Ghana," p. 420.

128. Quoted in Elliott P. Skinner, "Sankara and the Burkinabé Revolution: Charisma and Power, Local and External Dimensions," *Journal of Modern African Studies*, vol. 26 (September 1988), p. 441.

129. Donald Rothchild and E. Gyimah-Boadi, "Populism in Ghana and Burkina Faso," *Current History*, vol. 88 (May 1989), pp. 221–24, 241–44; see also Guy Martin, "Ideology and Praxis in Thomas Sankara's Populist Revolution of August 4, 1983, in Burkina Faso," *Issue*, vol. 15 (Waltham, Mass.: African Studies Association, 1987), pp. 70–90.

130. On this distinction, see the discussion in David E. Apter, *The Politics of Modernization* (University of Chicago Press, 1965), pp. 236–37.

131. Philippe C. Schmitter, "Still the Century of Corporatism?" *Review of Politics*, vol. 36 (January 1974), pp. 93–94. See also Ruth Berins Collier and David Collier, "Inducements versus Constraints: Disaggregating 'Corporatism'," *American Political Science Review*, vol. 73 (December 1979), p. 968.

132. "Côte d' Ivoire: Students Sentenced," *West Africa*, March 9–15, 1992, p. 429.

133. Michael A. Cohen, *Urban Policy and Political Conflict in Africa: A Case Study of the Ivory Coast* (University of Chicago Press, 1974), pp. 97–101.

134. Paul Glewwe and Dennis de Tray, *The Poor during Adjustment: A Case Study of Côte d'Ivoire* (Washington: World Bank, 1988), p. 19. See also Jennifer Widner, "The Discovery of 'Politics': Smallholder Reactions to the Cocoa Crisis of 1988–90 in Côte d'Ivoire," in Thomas M. Calleghy and John Ravenhill, eds.,

*Hemmed In: Responses to Africa's Economic Decline* (Columbia University Press, 1993), pp. 279–331.

135. Cyril Kofie Daddiel, "The Management of Educational Crises in Côte d'Ivoire," *Journal of Modern African Studies*, vol. 26 (December 1988), pp. 639–45.

136. For an excellent description of economic mismanagement and predatory rule by President Ibrahim Babangida and his successors, see Peter Lewis, "From Prebendalism to Predation: The Political Economy of Decline in Nigeria," *Journal of Modern African Studies*, vol. 34 (March 1996), pp. 79–103.

# Contributors

**Tessy D. Bakary**  *Department of Political Science, University Laval, Quebec*

**A. Adu Boahen**  *Department of History, University of Ghana, Legon*

**Alex Gboyega**  *Department of Political Science, University of Ibadan, Nigeria*

**Donald Rothchild**  *Department of Political Science, University of California, Davis*

**I. William Zartman**  *The Paul H. Nitze School of Advanced International Studies, Johns Hopkins University*

# Index

Abacha, Sani, 7, 188, 218, 225
Abdulai, Alhaji Alhassan, 212
Abiola, Moshood K.O., 6–7, 151, 187, 224, 225
Academic Staff Union of Universities (ASUU; Nigeria), 190, 191
Acheampong, Ignatius K.: coups d'état, 108, 110, 123; ethnicity, 206, 207–08; as head of state and leader, 97, 111–12, 113–17. *See also* Ghana
Action Group (AG; Nigeria), 159–61, 163, 164, 166
Adamafio, Tawia, 101
Adedeji, Adebayo, 229
Adjei, Ako, 101
Adjudication, 12
Adu, Kwesi, 128
AFJ. *See* Association of Women Jurists
AFRC. *See* Armed Forces Revolutionary Council
Africa: armed forces, 147; conflict, 1, 147, 157, 199; demands, 200–01; democracy in, 220, 229–30; independence movement, 22; foreign and financial pressures, 38–39; politics, 57, 63, 86, 88, 199; socioeconomic change, 69, 86, 199; sub-Saharan, 220–21. *See also* individual countries
African Agricultural Syndicate (SAA; Côte d'Ivoire), 58–61, 62, 64
African Democratic Rally (RDA; Côte d'Ivoire), 57–58, 64, 66, 68
African Independence Party (PAI; Senegal), 37
African Socialist Movement (MSA; Côte d'Ivoire), 59, 64

Africa, West: conflict, 2, 3–4, 9–10, 16, 43; conflict management, 237–41; constituent assemblies, 13; demands, 43, 216; democracy and democratization, 220, 228, 230–32; ethnic issues, 202, 203; foreign aid, 213; governance, 216–37; independence movement, 1, 9–10; military regimes, 16, 36, 40, 43; politics, 71, 90, 201–02; populism, 232–35; regional identity, 15–16; societal interest groups, 209; stability, 47; terms of trade, 28. *See also* individual countries
Afrifa, Akwasi A., 97, 104, 117
AG. *See* Action Group
Agbese, Pita Ogaba, 210
Agi. *See* Côte d'Ivoire
Agip oil company, 176
Agriculture. *See* Economic issues
Ahidjo, Ahmandou, 88, 231
Ajayi, Ade, 152
Akata-Pore, Allolga, 127, 128
Ake, Claude, 199
Akinrinade, Alani, 210
Akintola, Samuel Ladoke, 160, 162
Akinyemi, Bolaji, 185
Akuffo, Frederick W. K., 97, 111, 117
Alexander, H. T., 104
Algeria, 35
Alliali, Camille, 73
Alliances. *See* Coalitions
Allocation: Côte d'Ivoire, 80–81, 207; critical, 47; ethnic issues, 207; Ghana, 207–08; governance, 47; Nigeria, 150, 157, 161, 167, 168, 171, 174–75, 178–79; procedural demands and, 45; strategies of independence, 20, 22

Allocation of Revenue Act of *1981*, 174
All Peoples' Congress (Sierra Leone), 29
All Peoples' Party (APP; Ghana), 120
All People's Representative Party (APRP;
   Ghana), 106, 107, 115, 119
Amin, Samir, 53–54, 85
Amnesty International, 37, 38
Ampaw, Akoto, 138
Ankrah, Joseph A., 97, 206
Anglo-Nigerian Defense Pact, 163
Angola, 32
Angoulvant, Gabriel Louis, 57
Anklo Youth Organization (AYO; Ghana),
   97
Ankrah, Joseph A., 104
APP. *See* All Peoples' Party
APRP. *See* All People's Representative
   Party
Armah, Ayi Kwei, 59
Armed Forces Revolutionary Council
   (AFRC; Ghana), 97, 111, 117
Arthur, S. B., 106
Asante, S. K. B., 137
Association of Women Jurists (AFJ), 89
Associations and interest groups: bar as-
   sociations, 38, 101, 103, 113, 114–15, 119,
   127, 131, 134, 138–39; in corporatism,
   235; Côte d'Ivoire, 62, 77, 89; demands
   by, 209–19, 238; Ghana, 38, 98, 101, 103,
   113–15, 127, 131, 134, 138–39; Nigeria,
   177; professional, 38, 113, 114, 119, 127;
   role of, 40
ASUU. *See* Academic Staff Union of
   Universities
Atim, Chris, 128
Atta, William Ofori, 118
Aubame, Jean-Hilaire, 20
Avoidance of Discrimination Act (Ghana),
   99
Awa, Eme O., 153
Awolowo, Obafemi, 20, 160, 165, 167, 169,
   201–02
Ayarna, Imoru, 106
AYO. *See* Anlo Youth Organization
Azikiwe, Nnamdi, 169, 201–02

Babangida, Ibrahim: coups d'état, 172,
   194, 206; ethnic issues, 215–16; as head
   of state and leader, 151, 191, 195; hy-

pocrisy, 43; national guard under, 193;
   repression by, 40, 43, 187, 224–25; transi-
   tion to democracy, 217. *See also* Nigeria
Bayfau, Pascal, 191
Balewa, Ahmadu Tafawa, 150, 164
Bannerman, H.S., 106
Banny, Jean Konan, 73
Bates, Robert, 202
Baule. *See* Côte d'Ivoire
*Beautiful Ones Are Not Yet Born, The*
   (Armah), 59
Bédié, Henri Konan, 72–73, 86, 87, 88–89,
   90–91, 219, 222, 240
Bekoe, Nana Okutwer, 120, 121
Bello, Alhaji Ahmadu, 191, 202
Benin, 27, 29, 34, 35, 38, 40, 42, 44
Bentum, B. A., 109–10
Beti. *See* Côte d'Ivoire
Biafra, 1, 16, 150, 169, 214. *See also* Nigeria
Big Men, 46. *See also* Nigeria
Biya, Paul, 41, 43, 86, 88, 231
Blanksten, George, 80
*Blue Book. See Creation of District Political
   Authority and*
*Modalities for District Level Elections*
Boadi, W.O. Adjei, 128
Boahen, Adu, 138, 143, 146, 227, 228
Bongo, Omar, 41
Botswana, 220
Bourdieu, Pierre, 92
Bourne, F.C., 213–14
Britain, 15–16, 151–58, 163
Buhari, Muhammadu, 151, 172, 205
Burkina Faso, 21, 27, 33, 38, 42, 232–33
Busia, Kofi A.: exile, 101; as head of state
   and leader, 20, 59, 95, 107–10, 207; polit-
   ical parties of, 99, 106

Cameroon, 23, 35, 43, 44, 46, 88, 147, 212
Cameroonian People's Democratic Rally
   (RDPC), 41
Campaign for Democracy (CD; Nigeria),
   187, 188
Catholic Secretariat (Ghana), 101–02, 113,
   127, 138–39
*Catholic Standard*, 131
Cape Verde, 42
CARIA, 181–82
Carter Center, 143, 199, 228

CD. *See* Campaign for Democracy
Central African Republic, 27, 39, 40, 42,
  43, 44, 88
Chad, 21, 24, 34–35, 40, 42
Chadian Progressive Party (PPT), 27
Chauveau, Jean-Pierre, 54
Chazan, Naomi, 96, 130, 202
Chevron oil company, 176
Christian Council (Ghana), 101–02, 113,
  127
Christianity, 152–53, 154, 191–93, 212, 214,
  215
Christian Students' Movement of
  Nigeria, 215
Churchill, Winston, 40
Ciroma, Melam Adamu, 187
Cities. *See* Urban areas
Citizenship, 12
Citizens' Vetting Committee (CVC;
  Ghana), 125
Clifford, Hugh, 154
Club for the Advancement of Yorubas. See
  *Egbe Ilosiwaju Yoruba*
Coalitions: Côte d'Ivoire, 62, 63–64, 65–66,
  67–68, 72, 73–76; ethnic groups, 46, 98,
  206–07; Ghana, 98, 107, 139, 143, 206–
  07, 227, 228; in independence, 19;
  Morocco, 221; populist, 232
Coalitions, Nigerian: coups d'état, 165,
  215; democratization, 188; discord be-
  tween, 161; ethnic issues, 169, 171–72,
  186; independence and, 159; political
  power, 162–63, 170, 185; trends of, 182
Cocoa, 100
Cohen, Michael, 81
Collier, Ruth Berins, 63
Colonialism, 15, 17. *See also* individual
  countries
Comité de l'Unité Togolaise (CUT),
  100–101
Committees for the Defense of the Revo-
  lution (CDRs; Ghana), 130
Communist Party. *See* French Communist
  Party
Communist Party of Dahomey (PCD), 37
*Conférences des cadres*, 41–42
Conflict, 45–46, 199, 229
Conflict management: African interpre-
  tation, 14–15, 46–47, 231; American in-

terpretation, 14; bilateral conflicts, 15;
  corporatism, 235; definition and analysis, 9, 197; in democracies, 8, 219–20,
  229–32; failure of, 5–7; institutionalization, 48; military, 24–27; nationalist
  movement, 17–18; negotiation and,
  214–16; participatory, 40; political parties, 20, 22, 42–43, 217; typologies,
  12–15, 82; unity and, 21; West Africa,
  3–4. *See also* Demand-bearing groups;
  Governance
Congo, 26, 27, 35, 40, 42, 103, 230
Congolese Labor Party (PCT), 29
Consensus, 2–3
Constituent assembly. *See* Sovereign
  national conference
Constitutions: Côte d'Ivoire, 72, 73, 83;
  Ghana, 98–99, 106, 109, 136,137, 142,
  225, 226; Nigeria, 151, 155–56, 165,
  168, 171, 179, 184, 204, 206, 223; role
  of, 241
Conté, Lansana, 86, 88
Convention People's Party (CPP; Ghana),
  97–98, 99, 100, 101, 102, 103, 107, 110
Corporatism, 235–37
Côte d'Ivoire: 1990s, 5–6, 70, 79–85,
  89–93, 222; colonialism and independence, 52, 53–56, 58, 60–61, 67, 68, 77,
  83; consensus, 57–69; cooptation, 73–76,
  77–78, 82, 236; "critical juncture," 3, 53,
  93; demand structures, 66, 69, 70, 73–74,
  76–79, 80–82, 85–86, 88–89, 91, 92, 236;
  democracy and democratization, 79–80,
  82–83, 84–85, 88–93, 221–22, 240; elections, 82–83, 84; nationalist movement,
  16; political parties, 16, 23, 41, 42, 49–50,
  57–71, 82, 83, 84, 89, 91, 92, 221–22; politics, 50–53, 57–93, 203, 235; regime
  change, 6; social issues, 38, 46, 76–79,
  81, 87, 89–90, 91, 92, 236; student
  groups and youth, 32, 67, 76, 235, 236–
  37; violence, 49–50. *See also* Houphouët-
  Boigny, Félix
Côte d'Ivoire, conflict and crisis: from
  conflict to consensus and, 57–69; from
  consensus to conflict, 69–85; economic
  issues, 70, 89–90, 92, 204; nature of, 45,
  50–51, 56; politics, 49–51, 58, 66, 70, 219;
  students, 76

Côte d'Ivoire, conflict management: allocation of resources, 58, 66, 69, 76, 79, 92; governance and, 81, 82, 231, 236–37; politics, 70; as single-party state, 4; stability and, 16

Côte d'Ivoire, economic issues: allocation, 58; conflict management, 92; ethnic groups, 51; plantation economies, 52–57, 66; political factors, 75, 79–82, 86–88, 90–91; scarcity of resources, 49; state intervention, 70–71

Côte d'Ivoire, ethnic issues: conflict, 64; demands by, 21, 71, 214; economic factors, 54–56; politics and, 34, 51–52, 61, 62, 86– 88, 202, 203–04, 231; social issues, 53; violence, 50

Coulibaly, Lancine Gon, 87

Coulibaly, Lazéni, 87

Coulibaly, Mamadou, 87

Coups d'état: Guinea, 86; resource failures and, 29; role of, 24; Sierra Leone, 88; Togo, 68; West Africa, 16

Coups d'état, Ghana: 1963, 100–101; 1966, 104, 106; 1967, 105; 1969, 105; 1972, 110, 111; 1973, 113; 1978, 115–16, 116–17; 1981, 119, 120, 122–24, 206–07; 1982, 127–28; 1989, 139; conflict management, 16; countercoups, 127, 144–45; economic factors, 29; history, 95

Coups d'état, Nigeria: 1966, 16, 161, 164–65; 1985, 194; 1990, 175–76, 182, 194, 215–16; 1993, 188; history and politics, 29, 150, 222

CNS. See Sovereign national conference

CPP. See Convention People's Party

Crabbe, Coffie, 101

Creation of District Political Authority and Modalities for District Level Elections (Blue Book), 130

Critical junctures. See individual countries

Crown Colony and Protectorate of Lagos (Yoruba Protectorate), 153–54

CVC. See Citizens' Vetting Committee

Dadié, Bernard, 59

Danjuma, Theophilus Yakubu, 184, 195, 210

Danquah, J. B., 20, 59, 101, 102

Dare, Leo, 163

Darko, Kwabena, 143, 227

Dasuki, Ibrahim, 215

December 31 Women's Movement (Ghana), 125

Demand-bearing groups: 1990s, 45–46; conflict between, 1; ethnic, 33–35, 203; government takeovers, 9; grass-roots, 39, 40; independence and, 20; during military regimes, 26, 27; national conferences, 41–42; nationalist movement, 17; role of, 10–11, 211; socioeconomic change and, 86. See also individual countries

Demands: consistency of, 33; in democracies, 219–20, 239–40; economic factors, 200–01; ethnic, 21, 35–36, 46, 202–09; government and, 39; increases in, 35–43, 45; independence and, 23; negotiable and non-negotiable, 201–16; personal rivalries, 20; procedural, 43–45; regimes and, 26–27, 200, 216, 238; role of, 11–12, 45

Democracy and democratization: 1990s, 43, 240–41; colonialism and, 15; conflict management, 8, 239; effects of, 84, 199; failures of, 39, 48, 229, 239–40; majoritarian, 219–29; pacted, 229–32; phases, 43–45, 198–99; role of military regimes, 40; singe-party regimes, 40–41. See also individual countries

Democratic Party of Gabon (PDG), 29, 41

Democratic Party of Côte d'Ivoire (PDCI), 41, 57–58, 59–61, 64, 65, 68, 74, 83, 84, 203, 221–22, 236

Democratic Union of the Malian People (UDPM), 29

Démocratie à la Sénégalaise, 44

Delafosse, Maurice, 51, 55

Denise, Auguste, 72

Deportation Act (Ghana), 99, 101

Dia, Mamadou, 20

Diamond, Larry, 229

Dialogues, 217, 236, 237, 240

Diouf, Abdou, 44, 88

Dioulo, Emmanuel, 73

Djan, Boakye, 123

Doe, Samuel, 35

Doussou, Robert, 41–42

Dozon, Jean-Pierre, 55

Economic issues: 1990s, 47; agriculture, 46, 47–48, 111; drought, 35; effects of development, 31; employment, 38; foreign aid, 29, 44, 48; gross national product, 30; inflation, 29; plantation economies, 51, 53–57; politics and, 45, 80; pressures for accountability, 39; world recession, 36, 47. *See also* individual countries

Economic Recovery/Structural Adjustment Program (ERP/SAP: Ghana), 128–29, 138, 208. *See also* Structural Adjustment Program

Education: Côte d'Ivoire, 76, 154; Ghana, 102, 134, 154, 212; Nigeria, 154, 159, 182, 205, 208–09

Egala, Imoru, 110, 120–21

*Egbe Ilosiwaju Yoruba* (Club for the Advancement of Yorubas), 181, 182

EGLE. *See* Every Ghanaian Living Everywhere Party

Ejiga, Emmanuel, 210

Ekeh, Peter P., 205

Ekra, Mathieu, 86–87

Employment. *See* Economic issues

Enahoro, Anthony, 165

Equatorial Guinea, 27, 29, 88

ERP/SAP. *See* Economic Recovery/ Structural Adjustment Program

Erskine, Emmanuel A., 143, 227

Ethnic issues: demands, 24; dominance in independence, 19; military regimes, 26–27; political stability and, 220; spoils systems, 86. *See also* individual countries

European Community, 38–39

Every Ghanaian Living Everywhere Party (EGLE), 139, 143, 227

Eyadema, Gnassinbe, 43

Farm Syndicate of Côte d'Ivoire (SYNACI), 209

Federated Trade Union of Nigeria, 157

Forced labor, 54, 59–60, 62

Foreign aid. *See* Economic issues

FPI. *See* Ivorian Popular Front

France: colonialism, 15–16; Côte d'Ivoire, 52, 55, 58, 67, 154; Nigeria, 153. *See also* French Communist Party

French Communist Party (PCF), 60, 65, 66, 68

Gabon, 23, 34, 38, 42, 44, 46, 230

Gambia, 23, 38, 220

Ga Party (Ghana), 107

Garba, Joseph, 210

Ga Shifimo Kpee (Ga Standfast Association; Ghana), 99

Gbagbo, Laurent, 73, 87

Gbedemah, Komla A., 101

Gboyega, Alex, 215, 223

GERDDES-Côte d'Ivoire. *See* Group for the Study and Research on Democracy and Economic and Social Development

Germany, 16, 153

Ghana: 1990s, 5–6, 147225–27; army, 103–04, 105, 108, 115–17, 122–23, 139, 145, 147; associations, 38, 98, 101, 103, 113–15, 119, 131, 138–39, 210–11; civilian regimes, 39, 99–105, 107–10, 111, 118–24, 136–44; colonialism and independence, 97, 98, 99–100; "critical juncture," 3, 95; defense committees, 125, 126, 130; demand structures, 96, 97, 104–05, 107, 108, 112, 131, 138, 145, 211–12; economic issues, 96, 100, 104, 108–09, 111–12, 118, 120, 123, 126, 128–29, 213, 236; electoral process, 141–43, 227–28; ethnic issues, 21, 98–100, 106, 107–08, 116, 122, 144–45, 206, 207–08, 211–12, 225; foreign aid, 120, 121, 126, 128, 129, 130, 131–32, 133, 138; human rights leagues, 38; "men on horseback" era, 111–18; nationalist movement, 16, 95; political parties, 16, 42, 97–102, 105, 106–07, 113, 114, 120, 137, 139, 140, 146, 213–14, 225–26, 227; politics, 59, 71, 96, 102, 119–24, 130–32, 136–44, 138, 202–03, 218, 232–34; religious groups, 212–13; republics, 95–96; social issues, 129–30, 134–36, 145, 211–12; student groups and youth, 102–03, 105–06, 109, 111, 112–13, 119, 121, 125, 126, 134. *See also* Nkrumah, Kwame; Provisional National Defense Council; Rawlings, Jerry

Ghana, conflict and crisis: economic factors, 139–40; ethnic factors, 99; history, 95–96; between military and government, 103–05; nature of, 16, 26–27, 29, 45, 127, 144–46; political factors, 98, 131–34, 140–47. *See also* Coups d'état

Ghana, conflict management: 1972–81, 111–36; democratization, 136–44; ethnic factors, 98–99, 107; failure of, 4, 95–97, 110; governance and, 104–05, 146–47; repression, 101

Ghana, democracy and democratization: 1980s, 130–31, 133; 1990s, 136–44, 221, 222–23, 225–28, 240; conflict and, 145–46; political factors, 98, 120, 133, 218; social factors, 74, 114

Ghana, military regimes: conflict management, 16, 95; democracy and civilian rule, 31, 36, 40, 43, 145–46, 222, 232; era of the "men on horseback," 111–18; ethnic factors, 26–27; history, 218; National Liberation Council regime, 105–07; Provisional National Defense Council regime, 124–36

Ghana National Students Organization (GNSO), 102

Ghana Peace and Solidarity Council, 113

Gnoleba, Sery, 87

GNPP. *See* Greater Nigeria People's Party

GNSO. *See* Ghana National Students Organization

Greater Nigeria People's Party (GNPP), 170

Group for the Study and Research on Democracy and Economic and Social Development (GERDDES-Côte d'Ivoire), 89

Gold Coast, 59, 98, 154

Governance: allocation, 47; attitudes, 7; coalition building, 66; conflict management, 1, 9, 10, 21, 22, 47, 95, 216–17, 238–40; effectiveness, 2, 197–98; failures of, 201; institutional policies, 7; internal, 9; social contract and, 13–14; strategies, 7. *See also* States

Gowon, Yakubu, 151, 165–66, 184

Guinea, 23, 29, 38, 40, 42, 43, 86, 88

Guinea Bissau, 29, 38, 40

Hansen, Emmanuel, 128

Hansen, Johnny, 138

Hausa-Fulani. *See* Nigeria

Health care, 75, 119, 126

Herbst, Jeffrey, 208

Houphouët-Boigny, Félix: coalition-building, 63; development of democracy, 83, 88, 91, 221, 231, 237, 240; economic issues, 90; forced labor, 60; head of state and leader, 50, 56, 64, 66, 68, 70, 71, 85, 86, 92, 203–04, 217; in a multiparty system, 41, 73, 83, 221; successor to, 73, 85–86, 87–88, 92; on unity, 51. *See also* Côte d'Ivoire

Human rights leagues, 37–38

Hyden, Goran, 198

Ibrahim, Kashim, 165

IFES. *See* International Foundation of Electoral Systems

Igbos. *See* Nigeria

Ige, Bola, 183

IMF. *See* International Monetary Fund

Incumbents and incumbency, 46, 70–71, 150. *See also* Demand-bearing groups

Independence movement, 16, 17, 18, 22. *See also* Nationalist movement; individual countries

Industrial Relations Act of *1971* (Ghana), 110, 111

Inglehart, Ronald, 78

Institutionalization, 12

Interest groups. *See* Associations and interest groups; Demand-bearing groups

International Foundation of Electoral Systems (IFES), 141

International Monetary Fund (IMF): Benin, 42; Ghana, 120, 121, 126, 129, 130, 131–32, 133; Nigeria, 194; pressures by, 39, 146, 211; resentment of, 213

Ironsi, Aguiyi, 165

Islam, 45, 152–53, 191–93, 212, 214

Ivorian League of Human Rights (LIDHO), 89

Ivorian Movement of Democratic Women (MIFED), 89

Ivorian Popular Front (FPI), 73

Ivory Coast. *See* Côte d'Ivoire

Joseph, Richard, 199

Kalendjin. *See* Côte d'Ivoire

Kanon, Bra, 87

Kenya, 82, 86, 88
Kerekou, Mathieu, 42
Kilingba, André, 88
Kontagora, Hassan Sani, 182
Koran, 45, 212
Kotoka, E.K., 106
Kuffour, John, 228
Kwei, Amertey, 127

Labor groups, 32–33, 38, 163–64. *See also*
    Forced labor; Strikes
*Lagos Standard*, 155
Laubhouet, Marcel, 87
Lebbé, Alexis Thierry, 87
*Legon Observer* (LO), 105, 106, 114
Legon Society on National Affairs (LSNA;
    Ghana), 105, 114
Liberia, 1, 21, 23, 27, 29, 35, 38, 40, 232
Libya, 35, 126
LIDHO. *See* Ivorian League of Human
    Rights
Ligues des Droits de l'Homme, 37
Limann, Hilla, 97, 117, 118–24, 143, 208
LO. See *Legon Observer*
LSNA. *See* Legon Society on National
    Affairs
Lugard, Frederick, 154
Lutterodt, William, 110

Maccido, Alhaji, 216
Mady, Djédjé, 87
Maïnassara, Ibrahim Bare, 43
Mali, 21, 27, 34, 35, 38, 40, 42
MAP. *See* Moslem Association Party
Margai, Albert, 22
Martin, Matthew, 213
Marxism, 11, 100, 121, 125, 129, 138
Mauritania, 29, 35, 38, 40, 42
Mauritius, 220–21
Mbakwe, Sam, 169
Medard, J.F., 204
Media. *See* Press
Mensah, K.A., 109–10
MFJ. *See* Movement for Freedom and
    Justice
Middle Belt Forum, 182
MIFED. *See* Ivorian Movement of
    Democratic Women
Migdal, Joel, 211

Military regimes: conflict management,
    24–31; demands, 24; legitimacy, 27, 36;
    political parties, 27; return of power to
    civilians, 36, 39–40; terms of trade, 29.
    *See also* individual countries
*Mister Johnson* (Cary), 17
MNRCS. *See* National Movement for the
    Cultural and Social Revolution
MNSD. *See* National Movement for Soci-
    ety and Development
Mobil oil company, 176
Mockey, Jean-Baptiste, 20, 67, 71, 72
Mohammed, Murtala, 167
Moi, Daniel arap, 86, 88, 221
MOJA. *See* Movement for Justice in Africa
*Monsieur Thôgô-Gnini* (Dadié), 59
Moore, Barrington, 3
MORENA. *See* National Reform
    Movement
Morgan Commission, 164
Morocco, 220, 221
Moslem Association Party (MAP;
    Ghana), 97
MOSOP. *See* Movement for the Survival
    of the Ogoni People
Movement for Freedom and Justice (MFJ;
    Ghana), 138, 140, 146
Movement for Justice in Africa (MOJA;
    Liberia), 37
Movement for Social Evolution in Black
    Africa (Central African Republic), 27
Movement for the Survival of the Ogoni
    People (MOSOP), 177
MSA. *See* African Socialist Movement
Muhammad, Murtala, 151
Musa, Balarabe, 171
Mwinyi, Ali Hassan, 88

NADECO. *See* National Democratic
    Coalition
NAL. *See* National Alliance of Liberals
National Alliance of Liberals (NAL), 106,
    107
National Cameroonian Union (UNC), 29
National Commission for Democracy
    (NCD; Ghana), 130–31, 140
National conferences, 41–42
National Convention Party (NCP; Ghana),
    139, 143, 227

National Council for Nigeria and the Cameroons (NCNC), 156, 157–58, 161–63, 164, 169

National Democratic Coalition (NADECO; Nigeria), 188

National Democratic Congress (NDC; Ghana), 97, 139, 143, 227, 228

National Investigation Committee (NIC; Ghana), 125

National Party of Nigeria (NPN), 169–70, 171–72

Nationalist movement: colonial period, 15, 17–18; conflict management, 15; definition, 13; elites, 19; ethnic dimensions, 19; as a Great Coalition, 20; power of, 23–24; protest and demands, 34–35, 45; social contract, 13, 18–24. See also individual countries

National Labor Congress (Nigeria), 190–91

National Liberation Council (NCL; Ghana), 97, 104, 105–07

National Liberation Movement (NLM; Ghana), 97, 98, 99, 213–14

National Movement for Society and Development (MNSD; Niger), 29

National Movement for the Cultural and Social Revolution (MNRCS; Chad), 27, 29

National Redemption Council (NRC; Ghana), 111–17

National Reform Movement (MORENA; Gabon), 37

National Republican Convention (NRC; Nigeria), 180, 223

National Union of Ghana Students (NUGS), 102, 106, 113, 127, 134, 138

National Union of Petroleum and Natural Gas Workers (NUPENG; Nigeria), 188

National Union of Secondary Teachers of Côte d'Ivoire (SYNESCI), 209

NCD. See National Commission for Democracy

NCL. See National Liberation Council

NCNC. See National Council for Nigeria and the Cameroons

NCP. See National Convention Party

NDC. See National Democratic Congress

Ndebugire, John, 138

New Independence Party (NIP; Ghana), 227

New Patriotic Party (NPP; Ghana), 227

NIC. See National Investigation Committee

Niger, 21, 29, 35, 38, 40, 42, 43, 44, 212

Niger Coast Protectorate, 153–54

Nigeria: 1990s, 5, 6–7, 196; army, 210; associations, 182–84; census issues, 162, 174; civilian rule, 39, 43–44, 150, 151, 167–672; colonialism, 149, 151–58; conflict, 45, 147, 149, 155, 156, 158–64, 172–74, 187–91, 204, 210; conflict management, 4–5, 16, 150, 158–59, 164–68, 172, 188–89, 190, 193–96, 223; corruption, 150–51, 162–63, 164, 186, 194, 195; "critical juncture," 3; demand structures, 32, 156–58, 184–85, 188–93, 208–10; foreign aid, 44; human rights leagues, 38; military regimes, 5, 16, 26, 31, 36, 40, 43, 149, 151, 164–68, 172–88, 194, 218–19, 222, 224; nationalist movement, 16, 158; political parties, 16, 157–58, 159–64, 169–72, 179–88, 223; politics, 71, 149–50, 154–64, 171, 177–88, 193–96, 204, 214–15; religious groups, 152–53, 154, 159, 191, 195, 212, 214–15; rural society, 46; social issues, 154, 171; states, regions, and provinces, 149, 150, 165, 166–67, 168, 171, 172–79, 185–86, 202, 205–06, 208–09; students and youth groups, 158, 163, 165, 188–90, 208–09; violence, 24, 163, 164, 165, 176, 177, 187, 188–89, 191–93, 194, 215. See also Biafra; Oil production; Strikes, riots, and protests

Nigeria, democracy and democratization: conflict management, 43, 151, 167–68; elections, 223–25; failure of, 240; military participation, 231–32; moment of change, 7, 43, 46, 74, 221, 222; political restructuring, 179–88, 217–18

Nigeria, economic issues: effects on education, 189–90, 208–09; government management, 188; political factors, 193–96; revenue allocation, 150, 154, 157, 158, 159–60, 161, 167, 168, 174–75, 178–79; state administration, 171

Nigeria, ethnic issues: demands and con-

flicts, 21, 144, 151–53, 164–65, 168–69, 201–02, 204–06; federal character of Nigeria, 171, 223; federal states, 34, 172–73; political factors, 156, 159–60, 161, 181–83
Nigerian Civil War, 166
Nigerian Labor Congress, 189, 190, 210
Nigerian National Alliance (NNA), 162, 165
Nigerian National Democratic Party (NNDP), 162, 163
Nigerian National Petroleum Corporation (NNPC), 176, 178, 195
Nigerian People's Party (NPP), 169, 170–71
Nigerian Progressive Front, 170
Nigerian Trades Union Congress, 157
Nigerian Union of Students (NUS), 158
NIP. See New Independence Party
Njoku, Eni, 165
Nkrumah, Kwame: assassination attempts, 101, 104; as chancellor of the universities, 102; followers of, 59; as political leader, 3, 56–57, 96, 103, 206, 218; regime of, 99–105. See also Ghana
NLM. See National Liberation Movement
NNA. See Nigerian National Alliance
NNDP. See Nigerian National Democratic Party
NNPC. See Nigerian National Petroleum Corporation
Nomenklaturists, 84
Northern People's Congress (NPC; Nigeria), 159, 161, 162, 163, 169
Northern People's Party (NPP; Ghana), 97, 98
Northern Republican Convention (NRC), 181, 185, 186–87
NPC. See Northern People's Congress
NPN. See National Party of Nigeria
NPP. See New Patriotic Party
NPP. See Nigerian People's Party
NPP. See Northern People's Party
NRC. See National Redemption Council
NRC. See National Republican Convention
NRC. See Northern Republican Convention

NUGS. See National Union of Ghana Students
NUPENG. See National Union of Petroleum and Natural Gas Workers
NUS. See Nigerian Union of Students
Nwobodo, Jim, 169
Nyobo, Reuben Um, 20
Nzeribe, Arthur, 181, 183

Obasanjo, Olusegun, 151, 181, 185, 210, 224
Obiang, Teodoro, 88
Odartey-Wellington, Neville A., 117
Ogoni. See Nigeria; Oil production
OIC. See Organization of Islamic Conference
Oil-Mineral Producing Areas Development Corporation (OMPADEC), 178
Oil production: Nigeria, 150, 151, 167, 174–75, 176–78, 188, 189, 193–94; producing countries, 29
Ojukwu, 165–66, 173
Olorunsola, Victor, 204
Olupona, Jacob K., 215
Olympio, Sylvanus, 68, 100–01
OMPADEC. See Oil-Mineral Producing Areas Development Corporation
Organization of African Unity (OAU), 143
Organization of Islamic Conference (OIC), 192, 215
Osaghae, Eghosa, 168–69
Otu, M. A., 108
Otu, S. J. A., 104
Ouattara, Alassane, 73, 86, 87, 90, 219, 237
Owusu, Victor, 117–18
Oyovbaire, Egite, 167
Oyovbaire, Sam, 185

PAI. See African Independence Party
PAP. See People's Action Party
Party of the People's Revolution of Benin (PRPB), 29
Pays réel/légal, 15
PCD. See Communist Party of Dahomey
PCF. See French Communist Party
PCT. See Congolese Labor Party
PDA. See Preventive Detention Act

PDCI. *See* Democratic Party of the Côte d'Ivoire
PDCs. *See* People's Defense Committees
PDG. *See* Democratic Party of Gabon
PDS. *See* Senegalese Democratic Party
PENGASSAN. *See* Petroleum and Natural Gas Senior Staff Association of Nigeria
People's Action Party (PAP; Ghana), 106, 107
People's Defense Committees (PDCs; Ghana), 125, 126, 130
People's Heritage Party (PHP; Ghana), 227
People's National Convention (PNC; Ghana), 227
People's National Party (PNP; Ghana), 97, 117, 118, 120
Peoples' Popular Party (Ghana), 110
Petroleum and Natural Gas Senior Staff Association of Nigeria (PENGASSAN), 188
PFP. *See* Popular Front Party
PHP. *See* People's Heritage Party
Pluralism, 15, 42–43
PNC. *See* People's National Convention
PNDC. *See* Provisional National Defense Council
PNP. *See* People's National Party
Political parties: conflict management, 20, 22; leaders, 216–18; nationalist movements and, 16, 31; pluralization, 36–39, 41–42, 73, 97; single-party systems and regimes, 22–24, 25, 27, 28–29, 37, 40–41, 62, 66; socioeconomic groups, 21. *See also* individual countries
Politics: African interpretation, 14–15; consensus and, 2–3; corporatism, 235–37; demands in, 69–70, 198; economic bases, 45, 81; "funnel phase," 13; incumbency, 39–40; military regimes, 24; "normal politics," 14, 21; personal charisma, 19; political competition, 20; political succession, 87; populism, 232–35. *See also* individual countries
Popular Front Party (PFP; Ghana), 117–18
Populism, 124–28, 232–35, 239
Post, Ken W. J., 159
PP. *See* Progressive Party
PPA. *See* Progressive Parties' Alliance
PPCI. *See* Progressive Party

PPP. *See* Progressive People's Party
PPT. *See* Chadian Progressive Party
Pratt, Kwesi, 138
Preventive Detention Act (PDA; Ghana), 99, 101
Professional associations. *See* Associations
Progress Party (PP; Ghana), 97, 106, 107
Progressive Alliance (Ghana), 228
Progressive Parties' Alliance (PPA; Nigeria), 171–72
Progressive Party (PPCI; Côte d'Ivoire), 59, 64
Progressive People's Party (PPP; Liberia), 37
Protests. *See* Strikes, riots, and protests
Provisional National Defense Council (PNDC; Ghana), 97, 122, 124–44, 207, 208, 213, 222, 225–26
PRPB. *See* Party of the People's Revolution of Benin

Quaidoo, P. K. K., 106, 107
Quarshigah, Courage, 139

RAISAR (Reconciling, allocating, institutionalizing, submerging, adjudicating, repressing), 12–15
Ransome-Kuti, I. O., 158
Rawlings, Jerry: coups d'état, 117, 122, 123–24, 206–07; "culture of silence," 135; effectiveness and support, 6, 121–22, 222; head of state and leader, 27, 97, 111, 122, 124–36, 207, 208, 217, 233, 234; Nigeria's failure, 44; transition to democracy, 137, 138, 142, 143–44, 146, 222–23, 225–26. *See also* Ghana; Provisional National Defense Council
RDA. *See* African Democratic Rally
RDPC. *See* Cameroonian People's Democratic Rally
Reconciling, 12
Regimes, 15, 198–200, 216–18, 238–39. *See also* Governance
Religious groups: *Catholic Standard*, 131; Côte d'Ivoire, 77, 78; demands by, 212; Ghana, 101–02, 103, 113, 114, 127, 134, 138–39, 141–42, 144; Nigeria, 152–53, 154, 159. *See also* Islam

Repression: as conflict management, 12–13, 22; Ghana, 99, 101, 104,111, 114, 115, 119, 125, 126, 135, 232–33; Nigeria, 40, 150, 188, 189, 190
Rhodesia, 104
Richards, Arthur, 155–56
Richardson, Kow, 101
Rimi, Abubakar, 183
Rose, Richard, 219
Rothchild, Donald, 96
Royal Niger Company, 153
RPT. *See* Togolese People's Rally
Rural issues, 31, 46, 108, 211, 236

SAA. *See* African Agricultural Syndicate
Sallah, E. K., 109
Sankara, Thomas, 27, 233
SAP. *See* Structural Adjustment Program
Sardauna of Sokoto, 191, 202, 215
Schmitter, Philippe, 235
SDP. *See* Social Democratic Party
SDP. *See* Southern Democratic Party
Seko, Mobutu Sese, 221
Senegal: associations, 38; democracy, 44, 46, 220, 231; ethnic groups, 21, 34, 35; human rights leagues, 38; nationalist movement, 16, 35; political parties, 16, 23, 37, 41, 42, 88; religious groups, 212; rural society, 46
Senegalese Democratic Party (PDS), 231
Senghor, Leopold Sedar, 88
Shagari, Alhaji Shehu, 151, 170, 205
Shagaya, John, 192
Shell Petroleum Development Company, 176
Shinkafi, Alhaji Umaru, 187
Shonekan, Ernest, 187
Shue, Vivienne, 219
Sierra Leone: associations, 38; coups d'état, 16; democracy and democratization, 31, 88; ethnic factors, 34; military regimes, 36, 40, 43; politics, 21–22, 23
SMCs. *See* Supreme Military Councils
Social contract, 13–14, 18–24, 39, 41–42
Social Democratic Party (SDP; Nigeria), 180, 223
Soussou. *See* Côte d'Ivoire
Southern Democratic Party (SDP; Nigeria), 181, 185–87

Sovereign national conference (CNS), 13
Soviet Union, 39
Soyinka, Wole, 224
State-building, 10
States, 14, 15, 35. *See also* Governance
Stedman, Stephen John, 134, 144, 157
Strikes, riots, and protests: Benin, 42; causes, 24, 211; Côte d'Ivoire, 49–50, 67–68, 76, 79, 80, 82, 83–84, 89–90, 235; Ghana, 25, 99, 101, 105, 112, 115, 118–19, 132, 133, 134, 143, 144; Nigeria, 156, 157–58, 160, 162, 164, 176, 187, 188–91, 215. *See also* Coups d'état; Labor groups
Structural Adjustment Program (SAP), 90, 92, 194–95. *See also* Economic Recovery/Structural Adjustment Program
Students, 20, 32, 38. *See also* individual countries
Sudan, 144
Supreme Military Councils (SMCs; Ghana), 97, 111, 112, 114–15, 117
SYNACI. *See* Farm Syndicate of Côte d'Ivoire
SYNESCI. *See* National Union of Secondary Teachers of Côte d'Ivoire

Tanzania, 82, 88
Taylor, Charles
TC. *See* Togoland Congress
*This Side Jordan* (Laurence), 17
Tofa, Alhaji Bashir Othman, 187
Togo: coups d'état, 68; democratization, 42, 43, 44; ethnic factors, 34, 35; Guana and, 98; human rights, 38; military regimes, 29, 40; political factors, 46; protests, 24
Togoland Congress (TC; Ghana), 97, 98, 99, 100
Togolese People's Rally (RPT), 29
Topo, 43
Touré, Abdou, 78
Touré, Sekou, 37
Trade: agricultural, 46; Ghana, 100, 208; military regimes, 29; terms of in West Africa, 28. *See also* Unions
Trade Union Congress (TUC; Ghana), 98, 101, 103, 105, 107, 109–10, 111, 127, 131–34

Tradition and consensus, 2
Tsikata, Kojo, 124, 127
TUC. *See* Trade Union Congress

UDECI. *See* Union for the Economic Development of Côte d'Ivoire
UDPM. *See* Democratic Union of the Malian People
Uganda, 144
UGCC. *See* United Gold Coast Convention
UGFC. *See* United Ghana Farmer's Council
UN. *See* United Nations
UNC. *See* National Cameroonian Union
UNC. *See* United National Convention
UNIGOV. *See* Union Government
Union for the Economic Development of Côte d'Ivoire (UDECI), 65
Union Government (UNIGOV; Ghana), 112, 113, 114–15
Unions: Côte d'Ivoire, 89, 90; Ghana, 110, 210–11; Nigeria, 157–58, 163–64, 188, 189, 225; role of, 21, 32–33. *See also* Labor; Strikes, riots, and protests; Trade Union Congress (Ghana)
United Ghana Farmer's Council (UGFC), 98
United Gold Coast Convention (UGCC; Ghana), 97, 107
United National Convention (UNC; Ghana), 118
United Nationalist Party (UNP; Ghana), 106
United Nations (UN), 100, 103–04
United Party (UP; Ghana), 99, 100–01, 107
United People's Party (UPP; Nigeria), 162
Unity Party of Nigeria (UPN), 169, 170
UNP. *See* United Nationalist Party

UOCOCI, 64, 65
UP. *See* United Party
UPN. *See* Unity Party of Nigeria
UPP. *See* United People's Party
Upper Volta. *See* Volta, Upper
Urban issues, 19, 31–32, 45–46,

Values, 4
Violence, 21, 35. *See also* Coups d'état; Strikes, riots, and protests; individual countries
Volta, Upper, 16, 24, 29, 31, 36

Wade, Abdoulaye, 231
WDCs. *See* Workers' Defense Committees
Weiskel, Timothy, 63–64
West Africa. *See* Africa, West
Widner, Jennifer, 221–22
Williams, Gavin, 164
Women's groups, 21, 32, 76
Workers' Defense Committees (WDCs; Ghana), 125, 126, 130
World Bank: Ghana, 120, 121, 126, 128, 132, 133, 138; Nigeria, 194; pressures by, 39, 146, 208, 211; resentment of, 213

Yacé, Philippe Grégoire, 72, 82, 86
Yahaya, Mallam Yakubu, 214
Yar'Adua, Shehu Musa, 183, 187, 210
Yeboah, Moses, 106
Yeebo, Zaya, 123, 128, 144
Yen, Nyeya, 128
Yorubas. *See* Nigeria
Youth, 27, 72. *See also* individual countries

Zaire, 29, 40, 42, 43, 44, 46
Zolberg, Aristide, 18, 51, 202, 231